ANALYSIS AND DESIGN
OF INFORMATION SYSTEMS

First edition 1986
Sixth edition August 1992

ISBN 0 86277 936 7 (previous edition 0 86277 388 1)

British Library Cataloguing-in-Publication Data

A catalogue record for this book
is available from the British Library

Published by

BPP Publishing Limited
Aldine House, Aldine Place
London W12 8AW

Printed in Great Britain by
Ashford Colour Press, Gosport, Hampshire

We are grateful to the Association of Accounting Technicians, the
Chartered Association of Certified Accountants and the Chartered
Institute of Management Accountants for permission to reproduce past
examination questions. The suggested solutions have been prepared by
BPP Publishing Limited.

©

BPP Publishing Ltd
1992

(ii)

CONTENTS

657 ANA
L
WYC

		Page
PREFACE		(v)
INTRODUCTION		(vii)

Syllabus – format of the paper – analysis of past papers –
flowcharting symbols – study checklist

PART A: ORGANISATION OF SYSTEMS

1	Information: the role of computers	3
2	File and database concepts	23
3	Revision chapter: computer hardware and the operating system	46
4	Distributed processing and networks	78
5	Batch and interactive systems	98
6	The electronic office	109

PART B: APPLICATION OF SYSTEMS

7	The structure of business systems	125
8	Revision chapter: general purpose packages	144

PART C: ANALYSIS OF SYSTEMS

9	Managing systems development	171
10	The stages in a systems development project	190
11	The feasibility study	197
12	Computer bureaux and software houses	214
13	Systems investigation	223
14	Systems analysis	232

PART D: DESIGN AND IMPLEMENTATION OF SYSTEMS

15	Systems design	249
16	Program development	269
17	Systems installation	292
18	Systems documentation and standards	314
19	Security and the control environment	330
20	Application controls	356

GLOSSARY		373
ILLUSTRATIVE QUESTIONS		381
SUGGESTED SOLUTIONS		389
INDEX		423
FURTHER READING		429

(iii)

PREFACE

The examinations of the Association of Accounting Technicians are a demanding test of students' ability to master the wide range of knowledge and skills required of the modern professional. The Association's rapid response to the pace of change is shown both in the content of syllabuses and in the style of examination questions set.

BPP's experience in producing study material for the Association's examinations is unparalleled. Over the years, BPP's Study Texts and Practice and Revision Kits, now supplemented by the Password series of multiple choice (objective test) question books, have helped students to attain the examination success that is a prerequisite of career development.

This Study Text is designed to prepare students for the Paper 11 examination in Analysis and Design of Information Systems. It provides comprehensive and targeted coverage of the syllabus (reproduced on page (vii)) in the light of recent developments and examination questions (analysed on pages (viii) and (ix)).

BPP's Study Texts are noted for their clarity of explanation. They are reviewed and updated each year. BPP's study material, at once comprehensive and up to date, is thus the ideal investment that the aspiring accounting technician can make for examination success.

The August 1992 edition of this Study Text

This Study Text has been improved in the following ways.

(a) Material on computer hardware and software examinable in Paper 6 Elements of Information Systems has been collected in two revision chapters.

(b) New material has been added to reflect developments in the examination and in the subject itself. There are new or expanded sections on the following topics:

- prototyping
- computer aided software engineering (CASE)
- desktop publishing
- operating systems
- the Computer Misuse Act 1990
- ATMs and EFTPOS as applications of IT

(c) Material on security and control, previously contained in one chapter, is now included in two chapters covering administrative controls and application controls. Material on systems analysis and design, previously in a single chapter, has been presented in two chapters. These changes will enable a clearer demonstration and understanding of the subjects and will make study planning easier.

(d) A number of new illustrative questions have been added. Cross references to relevant questions to attempt have been included at the end of each chapter. The number of exercises has been increased.

(e) A glossary of data processing terminology has been added.

BPP Publishing
August 1992

For details of other BPP titles relevant to your studies for this examination, please turn to page 429. If you wish to send in your comments on this text, please turn to page 430.

INTRODUCTION

Syllabus

Aims

To develop further the understanding of the role of information technology gained in studying the Elements of Information Systems and to develop an appreciation of the analysis and design of business systems and their implications to an organisation and its members.

Content	*Chapter(s) in this text*
Organisation of Systems (weighting 25%)	
Organisation of information systems, batch, on line, distributed, centralised, the role of micro-computers and local area networks	1-5
Database concepts	2
Role of the user department, staff training and development	9
The electronic office and information technology	6
Application of Systems (25%)	
The structure of systems commonly found in the major business computer application areas of finance, production, marketing and personnel	7, 8
Analysis of Systems (25%)	
Systems investigation, principles and practice, documenting information flows and procedures, fact finding and interviewing	13
Human aspects of systems analysis	9
Steering committees, project teams, assignment briefs and systems feasibility reports	10, 11, 14
Making decisions on computer acquisition and systems investment	9, 11
Use of computer bureaux and software houses	12
Design of Systems (25%)	
Design philosophies, eg top down and bottom up	14, 15
Principles and practice of design in relation to input media, codes, output media, files and file structures	15, 16
Audit considerations, security and control	19, 20
Systems implementation, file creation and changeover, human aspects	17
Systems standards and documentation	18

When the pilot paper was issued by the Association in 1985 as a guide to what might be expected in the first examinations under the new syllabus, it was accompanied by the introductory comments below.

'This paper aims to test the understanding, which the relevant part of the course of study is assumed to have imparted, of the theory and practice of the analysis and design of computer systems. Particular emphasis will be placed on systems which generate and present information for use within an organisation, and to the problems arising from the management and control of data processing.

Information Technology, and its application to problem solving, is a fast changing field, and it will be necessary for the questions to reflect practices current at the time of the examination, although new topics will not be introduced until they have gained wide acceptance in everyday office use. With that proviso, questions will be designed to give as broad a coverage of the syllabus as possible at each examination.'

INTRODUCTION

Format of the paper

The examination paper consists of six questions, and candidates are required to answer *any five* questions out of the six. All questions are worth 20 marks.

Analysis and Design of Information Systems (ADIS) is Paper 11 at the Final Stage of the AAT examinations. The syllabus requires you to develop the knowledge gained in studying for Paper 6 - Elements of Information Systems. Some topics are common to both syllabuses but Paper 11 of course deals with information systems at a more advanced level. In addition, the parts of the syllabus dealing specifically with systems analysis and design are an advance beyond the Paper 6 syllabus.

Analysis of past papers

A brief analysis of the topics covered in the past six examination papers is given below.

June 1992

1   Factors to consider in software package selection
2   Structured analysis and design; data flow diagrams
3   Systems changeover
4   Information centres and fourth generation languages
5   Output design
6   Decision tables

December 1991

1   Design techniques - decision table and flowchart
2   Data capture in different scenarios
3   Application software - develop or buy
4   Organisational change - dealing with staff problems
5   Security and integrity; controls in batch and on-line systems
6   Desktop publishing - features, advantages and disadvantages

June 1991

1   Costs and benefits of computerised information systems
2   Information and decision-making
3   Purpose and content of a system feasibility report
4   Overcoming the applications backlog
5   Policy guidelines for the acquisition and use of PCs
6   Design of a sales order entry system

December 1990

1   Systems software vs application software
2   Describe the sequence of tasks in a payroll routine
3   Charging the costs of computer services
4   System documentation
5   Fact finding interviews
6   Local area networks

INTRODUCTION

June 1990

1 Office automation: features and benefits
2 Database management system
3 Code design and form design
4 Hardware specification for personal computers for office use
5 Competitive advantage
6 Systems changover; file conversion

December 1989

1 Computerisation of a manual system
2 Distributed processing
3 Staff tasks
4 Systems maintenance and review; network analysis
5 Analysis and design techniques
6 Computer system security

INTRODUCTION

Flowcharting symbols

In the event that you are asked in an examination question to describe the meaning of a flowchart or to use a flowchart, you need to know about the variety of flowcharting symbols used.

The examination paper will probably state that: *'flowcharting templates may be used.'* If the solution to an examination question calls for a flowchart or system diagram, it would be helpful for you to have a template, to make your answer neater and more presentable.

The flowcharting symbols recommended by the National Computing Centre Ltd are deliberately restricted in number, to avoid unnecessary confusion. These symbols are:

Symbol	*Meaning*
	Any type of operation
	Computer backing storage files (magnetic disk, tape, diskette, optical disk etc)
	Input or output
	Connector, to show continuity of the chart's flow where it is not possible to join up symbols with a flowline
	Start or end symbol
	Decision symbol, used in program flowcharts

INTRODUCTION

Study checklist

This checklist is designed to help you chart your progress through this Study Text and thus through the Association's syllabus. You can record the dates on which you complete your study of each chapter, and attempt the corresponding illustrative questions. You will thus ensure that you are on track to complete your study in good time to allow for revision before the exam.

	Text chapters Ch Nos/Date Comp	*Illustrative* questions Ques Nos/Date Comp
Organisation of systems		
Information, files and databases	1,2	1-4
Computer hardware and networks	3,4	5,6
Batch and interactive systems	5	7
The electronic office	6	8
Application of systems		
The structure of business systems	7	9,10
General purpose packages	8	11
Analysis of systems		
Systems development	9,10	12,13
The feasibility study	11	14,15
Computer bureaux and software houses	12	16
Systems investigation and analysis	13,14	17,18
Design and implementation of systems		
Systems design and program development	15,16	19-21
Systems installation	17	22,23
Systems documentation and standards	18	24
Security and controls	19,20	25,26

Study checklist

This checklist is designed to help you chart your progress through this Study Text and into through the Association's syllabus. You can record the dates on which you complete your study of each chapter and attempt the corresponding illustrative questions. You will thus ensure that you are on track to complete your study in good time to allow for revision before the exam.

Organisation of systems

Information, files and databases

Computer hardware and networks

Batch and interactive systems

The electronic office

Application of systems

The structure of business systems

General purpose packages

Analysis of systems

Systems development

The feasibility study

Computer bureaux and software houses

Systems investigation and analysis

Design and implementation of systems

Systems design and program development

Systems installation

Systems documentation and standards

Security and controls

PART A

ORGANISATION OF SYSTEMS

Chapter 1

INFORMATION: THE ROLE OF COMPUTERS

This chapter covers the following topics.

1. Data and information in business
2. Processing business data
3. Data flows
4. Types of information
5. The general characteristics of good information
6. The value of information
7. The sources of information
8. Computers and information processing
9. Transaction processing systems
10. Management information systems (MIS)
11. Information technology and competitive advantage

---

1. DATA AND INFORMATION IN BUSINESS

1.1 Information is sometimes said to be processed data. In normal everyday speech, the terms 'data' and 'information' are often used interchangeably, as meaning the same thing. However, there are stricter definitions of the two terms, which make an important distinction between them.

   (a) *Data* is the 'raw' material for data processing. It is unprocessed information. Data is collected and then processed into information.

   (b) *Information* is data processed in such a way as to be of some meaning to the person who receives it. Information must have a purpose (ie to inform about something) and so it must be sent to someone who can use it. A person might process data into information for his or her own personal use, but the distinction between data and information remains the same as if data is processed by one person to produce information for others.

1.2 Often, when data is processed, the information is communicated immediately to the person who wishes to use it. However, there is no reason why processed information should be used straightaway. It might be kept for later use. If it is, it must be:

   (a) stored, or filed away, and then
   (b) retrieved when it is eventually needed.

1: INFORMATION: THE ROLE OF COMPUTERS

Storage and retrieval

1.3 Storage and retrieval of data are two inter-related aspects of holding data for a later use because data must be stored in such a way that it can be found again when it is eventually wanted. To assist with storage, data (or information) is often stored in a pre-sorted order (eg alphabetical order). Alternatively, it is given a reference number and filed in reference number order. Sometimes, an index helps the storage and retrieval process.

1.4 In business, vast quantities of data are stored and then retrieved when required. In accounting systems, there are many such examples, including the data recorded in the sales ledger, purchase ledger and payroll systems.

Any data processing system might therefore be described as follows.

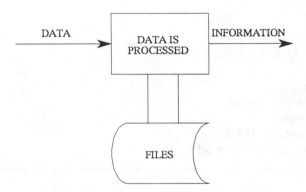

1.5 'Information processing is the organisation, manipulation and distribution of information. As these activities are central to almost every use of the computer, the term is in common use to mean almost the same as 'computing'. (British Computer Society)

2. PROCESSING BUSINESS DATA

2.1 Processing business data can be said to have the following features for both manual as well as electronic DP.

(a) *Collecting data in the first place:* There must be data to process and this may arise in the course of operations. There has to be a system or procedure for ensuring that all the data needed for processing is collected and made available for processing. Collecting data is an important step in DP that must not be overlooked because the quality, accuracy and completeness of the data will affect the quality of information produced.

(b) *Converting the data into information,* perhaps by summarising it or classifying it and/or producing total figures etc. For example, a sales ledger system might be required to process data about goods despatched to satisfy customer orders so as to:

   (i)   produce and send out invoices;
   (ii)   record the invoices sent out in the customers' personal ledgers;
   (iii) produce a report of the total value of invoices sent out in the day/week etc;
   (iv)   record the total value of invoices sent out in the debtors' control account in the nominal ledger.

The output consists of invoices and figures for sales totals (ie management information). Updating the personal ledgers and the debtors control account are file updating activities to keep the sales ledger records up to date.

(c) *Updating files to incorporate the processed data.* The example of sales ledger work has already been mentioned. Updating files means bringing them up to date to record current transactions.

(d) *The dissemination of information to users.* This includes a variety of reports (on-screen, or hard copy), for example:

   (i) *scheduled* reports, routinely prepared on a regular basis (eg payroll report) and reviewed to ensure that any control information it contains is used;

   (ii) *exception reports* which delineate deviations from plan (see paragraph 5.3);

   (iii) reports produced *on demand* (ie only when requested, but not as a matter of course);

   (iv) *planning* reports (eg forecasts).

3. DATA FLOWS

3.1 Data flows are the movement of data or information from one person, group, department or organisation to another. There can be:

(a) *formal and routine* data flows;
(b) *formal but irregular* and non-routine data flows;
(c) *informal* data flows.

In systems analysis and design, we are particularly concerned with the first two of these, the formal information system within an organisation.

3.2 Data flows occur between sub-systems of the same organisation (eg between one department and another, one section and another, or one person and another) and between the organisation and its environment (eg customers, suppliers, government authorities and agencies etc).

3.3 Systems analysts must be able to identify data flows in an existing system and design data flows for any new system they propose to implement. Analysing what data flows occur involves:

(a) what is the content of the data flows;
(b) how the data is transmitted (eg in printed reports, by telephone, via computer screen);
(c) the frequency of transmission.

Example: data flows

3.4 The diagram on the next page shows just a few data flows involving the purchase and receipt of goods from suppliers, and the payment of invoices.

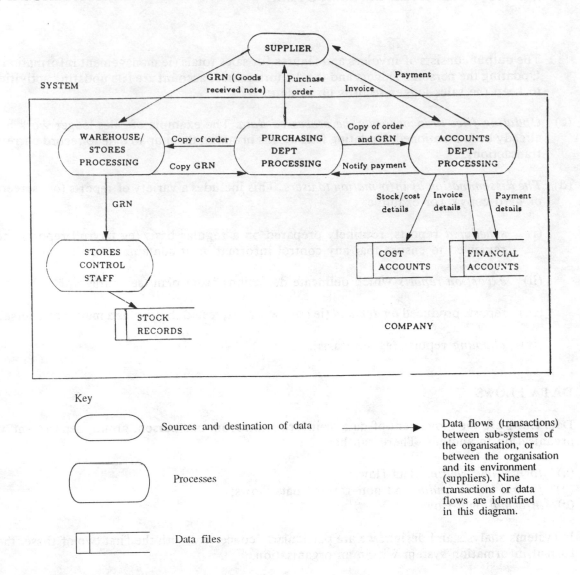

Key

⬭ Sources and destination of data

▭ Processes

▱ Data files

Data flows (transactions) between sub-systems of the organisation, or between the organisation and its environment (suppliers). Nine transactions or data flows are identified in this diagram.

4. TYPES OF INFORMATION

Types of management information required

4.1 A manager needs to know, basically, three things:

(a) What are his resources? (Finance, stocks of raw materials, spare machine capacity, labour availability, the balance of expenditure remaining for a certain budget, target date for completion of a job.)

(b) At what rate are his resources being consumed? (How fast is his labour force working, how quickly are his raw materials being used up, how quickly are other expenses being incurred how quickly is available finance being consumed?)

(c) How well are the resources being used? (How well are his objectives being met?)

4.2   A manager uses resources in the light of information given to him. The board of a company decides how much of available funds should be allocated to any particular activity, and the same problem faces the manager of a factory or department, or even a foreman (ie which machines should he use, which men should he put on certain jobs etc). Having used information to decide what should be done, a manager then needs feedback (or else control information from the environment) to decide how well it is being done.

Levels of information

4.3   Information *within* an organisation (as distinct from information provided by an organisation to external users, such as shareholders, the general public, pressure groups, competitors, suppliers, customers etc) can be analysed into three levels.

(a)   *Strategic information* is used by senior managers to plan the objectives of their organisation, and to assess whether the objectives are being met in practice.

Such information includes overall profitability, the profitability of different segments of the business, future market prospects, the availability and cost of raising new funds, total cash needs, total manning levels and capital equipment needs etc. Much of this information must come from environmental sources, although internally generated information will always be used. Strategic information will be used for the management decision-making previously described as *strategic planning*.

(b)   *Tactical information* is used by middle management.

Such information includes productivity measurements (output per man hour or per machine hour) budgetary control or variance analysis reports, and cash flow forecasts, manning levels and profit results within a particular department of the organisation, labour turnover statistics within a department, short-term purchasing requirements etc. A large proportion of this information will be generated from within the organisation (ie as feedback) and is likely to have an accounting emphasis. Tactical information is usually prepared regularly - perhaps weekly, or monthly (whereas strategic information is communicated irregularly) and it is used for the decision-making previously referred to as 'management control'.

(c)   *Operational information* is used by 'front-line' managers such as foremen or head clerks to ensure that specific tasks are planned and carried out properly within a factory or office etc.

In the payroll office, for example, operational information relating to day-rate labour will include the hours worked each week by each employee, his rate of pay per hour, details of his deductions, and for the purpose of wages analysis, details of the time each man spent on individual jobs during the week. In this example, the information is required weekly, but more urgent operational information, such as the amount of raw materials being input to a production process, may be required daily, hourly, or in the case of automated production, second by second. Operational information relates to the level of decision-making previously referred to as *operational control*.

4.4   The amount of *detail* provided in information is likely to vary with the purpose for which it is needed, and operational information is likely to go into much more detail than tactical information, which in turn will be more detailed than strategic information.

4.5 What is information to one level of management or one department may be raw data (needing to be processed) to another. A foreman, for example, will check the output of each of the men or machines within the area of his responsibility but his superior may only wish to know about the performance of the section as a whole.

Planning, operating and control information

4.6 Another way of categorising information is into planning, operating and control information.

   (a) *Planning information* is the information that is needed to formulate plans, and consider alternative courses of action. It will include:

   (i) forecasts (eg demand forecasts, forecasts of increases in prices and wages costs etc);

   (ii) estimates of environmental conditions, such as likely actions by competitors, possible legislation by the government etc.

   (b) *Control information* is the information which provides a comparison between actual results and the plan. Control information cannot exist without a plan or target. Feedback is the major element in control information, and it is often very detailed. Frequent criticisms of control information are that:

   (i) it arrives too late to be of any use;

   (ii) it contains information about matters outside the control of the person who receives it;

   (iii) the person receiving it does not rely on it, perhaps because he or she suspects it of being inaccurate or incomplete.

   (c) *Operating information* is information which is needed for the conduct of day-to-day operations. It will include much 'transaction data' - ie data about customer orders, purchase orders, cash receipts and payments etc. Operating information must usually be consolidated into totals in management reports before it becomes management control information.

Past, present and future information

4.7 A third useful categorisation of information is between past, present and future information.

   (a) *Past information*. This is *record keeping*, the storing of information about what has been done or what has happened in the past. This historical information will subsequently be used again at some time in the future. Much past information is information of a transaction processing nature.

   (i) In the case of a company, there is a statutory requirement of the Companies Act for a company to maintain proper accounting records of past transactions.

   (ii) Records that are kept of past transactions might be used to generate further routine operations at a later date. For example, a record of a sale to a customer, and details of the invoice sent out, will be kept, and if the customer does not pay on time, a statement or reminder will be sent out, chasing payment.

(b) *Present information*. This is information about what is happening now, so that decisions can be taken about what, if anything, to do next. Present information is therefore most readily associated with *control information*, which is the feedback in a management information system.

(c) *Future information*. This is *forecasting information* about what is expected to happen in the future. It is most readily associated with planning decisions, possibly for a budget, but also for longer term strategic information. Future information is also likely to include a significant proportion of environmental information, because the future of any organisation will not be secure unless it continues to adapt to changes in its environment.

4.8 Past information should be the most accurate of the three categories, and future information the least accurate of the three. The degree of accuracy expected from information should therefore vary according to whether it is past, present or future.

Information for programmed and non-programmed decisions

4.9 Automatic decision making in a computerised control system means that the elements of some (or all) of the factors needed to make the decision have been programmed into the computer, thus allowing the computer to chose 'automatically'.

A computer is capable of making routine decisions (eg re-ordering stock) which are called *programmed decisions* and which almost invariably relate to *operational control*. Any decision which requires management judgement on qualitative data (as well as quantitative data) will be a *non-programmed decision*, so that automatic decision making would not be appropriate in these cases.

5. THE GENERAL CHARACTERISTICS OF GOOD INFORMATION

Other general characteristics of information

5.1 Information has certain other general characteristics.

Information must have a *purpose*, otherwise it is useless and valueless. It might have an immediate purpose or, as we have seen, it might be filed away for future use, even if it is just being held on the off-chance that it might be needed on day.

When information is used, it should be good enough to fulfil its purpose. In other words the information available to the information-user should enable him to do his job (eg make his decision) well and competently. Whether information fulfils its purpose adequately will depend on:

(a) whether it is *relevant*;
(b) whether it is *complete*;
(c) how *accurate* it is;
(d) whether it is *clear* to the user (lack of clarity is known as *noise*);
(e) whether the information-user has *confidence* in the information, or whether he is inclined to mistrust and disbelieve it.

5.2 Since information should have a purpose, there ought to be a clear idea of *who needs it*. The information-users must be identifiable.

5.3 *Volume*. The information available to an information-user might vary in volume as well as scope. It is difficult for manual data processing systems to cope with very large volumes of information. *Reporting by exception* (*exception reporting*) is where information highlights unusual occurrences or where performance differs significantly from budget. This reduces the volume of material necessary to convey this control information.

5.4 *Timeliness*. Information might be communicated when it is needed, or it might be delayed. Some information is needed at once whereas other items of information are not needed for some time and so must be filed away until later.

5.5 *Channel of communication*. Information can be communicated in a number of different ways. A path or medium by which information is transmitted is known as a communication channel. Some examples are:

    (a) written reports;
    (b) telephone conversations;
    (c) management meetings;
    (d) informal discussions;
    (e) transfer of data by computer;
    (f) broadcasting or announcing system;
    (g) factory notice board;
    (h) company journal or magazine.

5.6 *Direction of information flow*. Information should be sent to the right level in the management hierarchy.

5.7 *Cost*. Data costs money to collect and process. Information costs money to communicate and file away. The cost of having information is therefore an important characteristic of an information system because each feature or part of an MIS should not cost more than it is worth.

5.8 Good information can be summarised as information which is:

    (a) relevant;
    (b) complete;
    (c) accurate;
    (d) clear;
    (e) inspiring confidence;
    (f) of manageable volume;
    (g) timely;
    (h) well communicated;
    (i) sent to the right level; and
    (j) worth more than it costs.

6. THE VALUE OF INFORMATION

6.1 Information should have some value, otherwise it would not be worth the cost of collecting and filing it. The benefits obtainable from the information must also exceed the costs of acquiring it, and whenever management is trying to decide whether or not to produce information for a particular purpose (eg whether to computerise an operation or to build a financial planning model) a cost/benefit study ought to be made.

6.2 For information to have value, it must lead to a decision to take action which results in reducing costs, eliminating losses, increasing sales, better utilisation of resources, prevention of fraud (audit requirements) or providing management with information about the consequences of alternative courses of action.

6.3 Deciding whether it is worthwhile having more information should depend on the marginal benefits expected from getting it and the extra costs of obtaining it. The benefits of more information should be measured in terms of the difference it would make to management decisions if the information were made available. More information is only worthwhile if it might make the user/decision-maker change his or her mind from what it would otherwise have been if the extra information had not been there.

6.4 Since the incremental cost of obtaining extra quantities of information will eventually exceed the marginal benefits derived from them, there will inevitably be a limit to the economic size of a management information system.

6.5 The greater the *accuracy* of information provided, the more it will cost. At high levels of accuracy, it is probable that the marginal costs of the extra accuracy will exceed its marginal benefit value. It is most likely, therefore, that management will be satisfied with imperfect information and would not expect perfection.

6.6 The value of information must also relate to the *frequency* of its provision, and to the level in the management hierarchy where it is sent and used:

    (a) front line supervisors need more regular control information - perhaps weekly or daily;

    (b) middle managers and senior managers might need information less frequently, say monthly, half-yearly or yearly.

Information as a strategic resource

6.7 With the development of computer systems, and the ability of companies to hold large quantities of readily-accessible data on database files, there has been a growing awareness of the value of information as a strategic resource, to develop existing businesses or to create new businesses.

'In certain circumstances, information technology has enabled companies to change the entire structure of their industry. This is already happening in banking for example, with developments like automated teller machines.... Other companies have found that computers enable them to actually create new industries and markets. Albeit cautious in this regard,

Marks and Spencer is using the database of quality purchasers it has gathered from its recent entry into the credit card business to enable it to move into the catalogue business' (*Which Computer?* January 1987).

Exercise

Information may be quantitative or qualitative. Quantitative information is measurable in numerical terms, such as money or physical quantities (hours, weight, volume etc) and qualitative information is difficult or even impossible to measure in quantitative terms. Qualitative information is often concerned with attitudes. List examples of qualitative information which you think might be important to a manager in a typical business organisation. Why do you think they are important?

Solution

Examples of qualitative information include employee morale, motivation, customer loyalty, attitudes of the general public and goodwill. Poor employee morale might lead to an increase in labour turnover and the cost of training and recruitment. Poor motivation might lead to lower productivity and cost output. Try to think of circumstances in which possession of the other types of information listed might also be important.

---

7. THE SOURCES OF INFORMATION

7.1 Information comes from sources both inside and outside an organisation, and an information system should be designed so as to obtain all the relevant information from whatever source.

7.2 Gathering data/information from inside the organisation involves:

(a) establishing a system for collecting or measuring data - eg measuring output, sales, costs, cash receipts and payments, asset purchases, stock turnover etc. In other words, there must be established procedures for what data is collected (how frequently, by whom, by what methods etc) and how it is processed, and filed or communicated;

(b) relying to some extent on informal communication of information between managers and staff (eg by word-of-mouth, at meetings etc).

7.3 Obtaining information from outside the organisation might be entrusted to particular individuals, or might be 'informal'.

Formal collection of data from outside sources include the following:

(a) a company's tax specialists will be expected to gather information about changes in tax law and how this will affect the company;

(b) obtaining information about any new legislation on health and safety at work, or employment regulations, must be the responsibility of a particular person - eg the company's legal expert - who must then pass on the information to other managers affected by it. For example, the government recommended that companies registering under the Data Protection Act should appoint a data registration officer with the responsibility for finding out what the company had to do to register properly and then to keep registered details accurate and up to date;

(c) research and development work often relies on information about other research work and development work being done by other companies. An R & D official might be made responsible for finding out what he can about what R & D is going on outside the company;

(d) marketing managers need to know about the opinions and buying attitudes of potential customers. To obtain this information, they might carry out market research exercises.

Informal gathering of information from outside sources goes on all the time, consciously or unconsciously, because the employees of an organisation learn from newspapers and television reports what is going on in the world around them.

8. COMPUTERS AND INFORMATION PROCESSING

8.1 The description of information processing (data processing) in the paragraphs above is applicable to 'manual' or 'clerical' office systems as well as to computer systems. However, computers are a it is important to be aware of the reasons why computers process information 'better' than a manual system.

*Functions of computers
in information processing*

1   To process information more quickly.
2   To handle bigger volumes of processing.
3   To undertake complex processing.
4   To process information more reliably – ie with less chance of errors and mistakes.
5   To process information at less cost than a manual system.
6   To improve the scope and quality of management information.

8.2 It has already been suggested to you that data processing is essentially the same, no matter whether it is done manually or electronically. There are differences, however, and these can be listed as follows:

(a) *Speed:* computers can process data much more quickly than a human. This means that a computer has a much higher productivity and so ought to be cheaper for large volumes of data processing than doing the work manually. As computer costs have fallen, this cost advantage of the computer has become more accentuated.

The ability to process data more quickly means that a computer can produce more timely information, when information is needed as soon as possible.

(b) *Accuracy:* computers are generally accurate, whereas humans are prone to error. The errors in computer data processing are normally human errors (errors in the input of data) although there can be software errors (errors in the programs) and hardware errors (faults or breakdowns in the equipment itself).

(c) *Volume and complexity:* as businesses grow and become more complex, their data processing requirements increase in volume and complexity too. More managers need greater amounts of information. More transactions have to be processed. The volume of DP work is often beyond the capability of even the largest clerical workforce to do manually. Clearing banks, for example, would be unable to function nowadays without electronic data processing to ease the demands on their workforce.

(d) *Human judgement:* oddly enough, perhaps, although a computer can handle data in greater volumes, and do more complex processing, the 'manual' or 'human' method of data processing is more suitable when human judgement is involved in the work.

8.3 Information processing can be divided into two broad categories:

(a) transactions processing; and
(b) management information systems.

As the terms imply, transactions processing involves the routine handling of data transactions, often 'clerical' work, whereas management information involves the formulation of information for managers to use.

9. TRANSACTION PROCESSING SYSTEMS

9.1 Transaction processing systems could be said to represent the lowest level in a company's use of information systems. They are used for routine tasks in which data items or transactions must be processed so that operations can continue. Handling sales orders, purchase orders, payroll items and stock records are typical examples.

9.2 Transaction processing systems generally contain at least two categories of files:

(a) a file (or files) of master records; and
(b) a file of transactions to be used in updating the master records.

Consider a bank: the master records would consist of some identification data, historical transactions and the current balance for all the accounts; the transactions file would consist of a day's transactions and would include deposits, withdrawals, cheques, direct debits, bank charges etc. The transactions file would then be used to update the master file records of customer accounts.

9.3 A *file* of transactions could start off as a pile of forms on a clerk's desk, eg a pile of invoices from suppliers. These transactions would be processed to update the suppliers' accounts in the purchase ledger.

9.4 Most organisations generate a large volume of transactions which need to be processed efficiently and effectively. Computerised transactions processing systems have clear cost and performance advantages over manual systems for all but the most trivial applications. Small businesses are using microcomputers to provide these functions just as larger companies earlier acquired mainframe computers for these purposes.

9.5 Transactions processing systems provide the *raw material* which is often used more extensively by management information systems, databases or decision support systems. In other words, transactions processing systems might be used to produce management information, such as reports on cumulative sales figures to date, total amounts owed to suppliers or owed by debtors, total stock turnover to date, value of current stock-in-hand, and so on, but the main purpose of transaction processing systems is operational - ie as an integral part of day-to-day operations.

10. MANAGEMENT INFORMATION SYSTEMS (MIS)

10.1 An information system, or management information system (MIS) is defined as 'a computer system or related group of systems which collects and presents management information relating to a business in order to facilitate its control'   (CIMA: *Computing Technology*).

An MIS can be distinguished from a data processing system (DPS) or transactions processing system which is a system for processing routine operational data.

10.2 An alternative definition of a management information system is 'an information system making use of available resources to provide managers at all levels in all functions with the information from all relevant sources to enable them to make timely and effective decisions for planning, directing and controlling the activities for which they are responsible.'

10.3 Management information is by no means confined to accounting information, but in practice accounting systems are often more formally constructed and well developed than the rest of the information system of a business enterprise.

10.4 A management information system is therefore a system of providing and communicating information which will enable managers to do their job. Since managers must have information, there will always be a management information system in any organisation.

Information systems: planned and unplanned systems

10.5 Management uses information for decision making and control, therefore every company must have an information system of some kind. Most management information systems are not designed, but grow up informally, with each manager (depending on his drive and initiative) making sure that he or she gets all the information considered necessary to do the job. It is virtually taken for granted that the necessary information flows to the job, and to a certain extent this is so. Much accounting information, for example, is easily obtained, and managers can often get along with frequent face to face contact and cooperation with each other. Such an informal system works best in small companies, but is inadequate in a large company, especially one which spreads over several industries, areas or countries.

10.6 You might well have had experience of an inefficient and unplanned information system in your own job. A symptom of a bad MIS is when people complain, half-jokingly at times but half in earnest, that they are 'working in the dark' and 'no-one tells us about anything around here'. The consequences of a poor MIS might be dissatisfaction amongst employees who believe they should be told more, a lack of understanding about what the targets for achievement are and a lack of information about how well the work is being done.

10.7 Some information systems are designed, ie planned, often because the introduction of computers has forced management to consider its information needs in detail. This is especially the case in large companies.

10.8 Management should try to design the management information system for their enterprise with care. If they allow the MIS to develop without any formal planning, the MIS will almost certainly be inefficient because data will be obtained and processed in a random and disorganised way and the communication of information will also be random and hit-and-miss. For example, without formal planning and design of the MIS:

(a) some managers will prefer to keep data in their heads and will not commit information to paper. When the manager is absent from work, or is moved to another job, his stand-in or successor will not know as much as he could and should about the work because there would be no information to help him;

(b) not all data is collected and processed that ought to be, and so valuable information that ought to be available to management would be missing from neglect;

(c) information is available but not communicated to the managers who are in a position of authority and so ought to be given it. The information would go to waste because it would not be used. In other words, the wrong people would have the information;

(d) information is communicated late because the need to communicate it earlier is not understood and appreciated by the data processors.

10.9 Whether a management information system is formally or informally constructed, it should have certain essential characteristics:

(a) the functions of individuals and their areas of responsibility in achieving company objectives should be defined;

(b) areas of control within the company (eg cost centres, budget centres) should also be clearly defined;

(c) information required for an area of control should flow to the manager who is responsible for it. It is not possible to consider a management information system without considering the management structure of the organisation.

Decision support systems (DSS)

10.10 Decision support systems are a form of management information system. Decision support systems are used by management to aid in making decisions on issues which are unstructured.

10.11 These complex problems are often very poorly defined with high levels of uncertainty about the true nature of the problem, the various responses which management would undertake or the likely impact of those actions. These highly ambiguous environments do not allow the easy application of many of the techniques or systems developed for more well defined problems or activities. Decision support systems are intended to provide a wide range of alternative information gathering and analytical tools with a major emphasis upon flexibility and user-friendliness.

10.12 The term 'decision support systems' or DSS is usually taken to mean *computer* systems which are designed to produce information in such a way as to help managers to make better decisions. (The term was first coined in the late 1970s by Peter Keen, a British systems specialist.)

10.13 Decision support systems do not make decisions. The objective is to allow the manager to consider a number of alternatives and evaluate them under a variety of potential conditions. A key element in the usefulness of these systems is their ability to function interactively. This is a feature, for example, of spreadsheets, which are described in a later chapter. Managers can use these systems often develop scenarios using earlier results to refine their understanding of the problem and their actions.

10.14 A decision support system integrates many of the functions supplied by information systems so that managers may use them more easily and on a wider range of both structures and unstructured problems.

Executive information systems (EIS)

10.15 An executive information system is an 'information system which gives the executive easy access to key internal and external data' (*Management Accounting*, January 1989). EISs have been made possible by the increasing cheapness and sophistication of microcomputer and network technology. An EIS is likely to have the following features:

(a) provision of summary-level data, captured from the organisation's main systems (which might involve integrating the executive's desk top micro with the organisation's mainframe);

(b) a facility which allows the executive to "drill-down" from higher or summary levels of information to lower, more detailed information, if this is required;

(c) data manipulation facilities (eg comparison with budget or prior year data, trend analysis);

(d) graphics, for user-friendly presentation of data;

(e) a template system. This means that the same type of data is presented in the same format, irrespective of changes in the level of information required, eg sales figures both at a country-wide and at a branch level.

10.16 The basic design philosophy of executive information systems is that they should:

(a) be easy to use ('idiot-proof' not just user-friendly) as an EIS may be consulted during a meeting, for example;

(b) make data easy to access, so that it describes the organisation from the executive's point of view, not just in terms of its data flows;

(c) provide tools for analysis (including ratio analysis, forecasts, what-if analysis, trends);

(d) provide presentational aids so that information can be conveyed 'without bothering the executive with too many trivial choices of scale, colour and layout'.

10.17 Many of the features described can be provided by some of the systems later described in this text. Spreadsheets, for example, provide what-if analysis. However, an EIS is not only a tool for analysis, but also a tool for interrogating data (drilling down, as mentioned above).

Expert systems

10.18 Artificial intelligence is the concept that computers can be programmed to carry out certain logical processes which are normally associated with human intelligence rather than with 'machines', such as learning, adaptation and self-correction.

The main area of development in artificial intelligence is with *expert systems*.

10.19 Expert systems describe computer programs which allow users to benefit from expert knowledge and information, and also advice.

An expert system is therefore a program for which the master/reference file holds a large amount of specialised data, eg on legal, engineering or medical information, or tax matters. The user keys in certain facts and the program uses its information on file to produce a decision about something on which an expert's decision would normally be required. For example:

(a) a user without a legal background can obtain guidance on the law without having to consult a solicitor - for example, on property purchase matters, or for company law guidance;

(b) a user without much tax knowledge could consult an expert system for taxation for guidance on particular matters of tax;

(c) as a non-business example, a non-medical user can obtain an expert medical diagnosis about a patient without having to consult a doctor or a surgeon etc.

10.20 Expert systems can give factual answers to specific queries, but they can also indicate to the user what a decision ought to be in a particular situation, and in this respect, expert systems can be a form of decision support system for managers.

10.21 Expert systems contain *rules* which indicate that if x, y and z are the case, then the appropriate course of action is q. As such, they are ideal for automating relatively formalised bodies of knowledge (eg tax law), or company rule books. However "to the extent that companies want increasingly to tap the initiative and independence of their staff they will find the other big trends of the 1980s - towards networks of powerful workstations with user-friendly, liberating software - more appealing" *(Financial Times* 20 March 1989).

The program's 'rules' can be changed and its 'knowledge' can be updated.

10.22 Applications of expert systems include:

(a) in some database systems, to speed up the process of retrieving data from a database file;

(b) diagnostic systems, to identify causes of problems - eg in production control systems, or in medical aplications;

(c) in some decision support systems, to provide advice to a decision maker. Expert systems can give facts, but they can also indicate to the user what a decision ought to be in a particular situation, and in this respect, expert systems can be a form of decision support system for managers in business.

10.23 Expert systems can be written from scratch, in specialised artificial intelligence programming languages such as PROLOG or LISP.

Alternatively, an expert system can be bought off-the-shelf as a 'shell' - ie a package which is empty of information but with a rule structure already in place.

Yet another way of obtaining an expert system is to buy a package which has already been developed for a particular application (often with the software house having taken an expert system shell and then developed the shell to a specific use). For example, expert systems have been provided for:

(a) Data Protection Act advice (Data Protection Act Advisor, from Helix Expert Systems);
(b) advice to farmers on fungal disease control (Counsellor, from ICI);
(c) providing tax advice.

11. INFORMATION TECHNOLOGY AND COMPETITIVE ADVANTAGE

11.1 In the earlier discussion about the value of information, it was mentioned that information has a value, which can sometimes be quantified. If the value of information is greater than the cost of providing it, then it is worth acquiring. If information costs more to produce than the economic benefits derived from it, then there is no point in producing it.

11.2 This issue is particularly pertinent when considering the substantial amounts of money and management time invested by large organisations in information systems. However, there are two complicating factors.

(a) The information system is used to produced a wide variety of information. The cost of an individual item of information is not always easy to quantify. For example, if a manager uses an EIS to enquire into the company's database, what is the cost of this enquiry?

(i) The information is already existent anyway, as it is used for a number of different purposes. It might be impossible to predict how often it will by used, and hence the economic benefits derived from it.

(ii) The information system which is used to process these requests has also been purchased. Its cost is largely fixed.

(b) Just as the costs of an item of information are harder to assess than might appear superficially, so too the benefits are often hard to quantify. While no-one doubts that information is vital, it is not always easy to construct an economic assessment of the value of information.

(i) A monthly variance analysis will only generate economically consequential decisions if there is some control failure leading to variances, and control failures are not easy to predict.

(ii) The economic consequences of a decision are not always easy to predict.

1: INFORMATION: THE ROLE OF COMPUTERS

11.3 Just because costs and benefits cannot be quantified does not mean that they are fictitious. While organisations often complain about the poor value they receive from information systems, this does not stop them installing them.

11.4 An area where information technology and information systems are felt to give the organisations which use them substantial benefit is in giving the owner competitive advantage over other organisations.

11.5 *Competitive advantage* can be defined as that factor or factors which:

(a) encourages customers to prefer your products and services over someone else's;

(b) on a sustained basis (ie the search for competitive advantage does not lead to bankruptcy, cash crises, organisational failure).

11.6 The state of competition in a particular market is determined by five major factors. These are as follows.

(a) Suppliers (who can force up costs)
(b) Customers (who choose between your product's and a competitor's)
(c) The threat of new entrants to the market (more competition for resources and customers)
(d) The threat of substitute products
(e) The behaviour of competitors

11.7 What is the role of Information Technology in securing competitive advantage? Firstly, an organisation can ask itself the following four questions?

(a) *Can IT build barriers against competitors?* An example is an airline booking service. Let's take a fictitious airline: British Transatlantic Airways (BTA). A passenger wishes to fly BTA from the UK to New York, and then from New York go to Minneapolis. BTA is forbidden to make internal flights in the USA. However, several American airlines fly from New York to Minneapolis. BTA's booking system is interlinked with that of *one* other American airline, whose flights are always chosen for connections by the BTA booking system. The IT system is thus a barrier to competition, as alternative flights from New York to Minneapolis are not offered.

(b) *Can IT capture customers* by making it too expensive to change? Once a bank customer has gone to the effort and expense of installing a home banking system, he or she is unlikely to make a decision to change banks (to another system).

(c) Can IT give an organisation more power in relation to its suppliers? Efficient stock control systems (eg just-in-time) might make an organisation more dependent on efficient suppliers.

(d) Can IT generate new products or services? An example in the financial service sector is Automated Teller Machines.

11.8 A leading theorist on this subject, Michael E Porter, has written that an organisation can have three basic strategies for obtaining competitive advantage. These, and the uses of IT in obtaining them, are outlined below.

(a) *Overall cost leadership* (become the most cost efficient producer). IT can reduce costs by:

    (i)   reducing labour costs (eg production control systems, clerical work);

    (ii)   reducing manufacturing costs by efficient scheduling etc (eg computer integrated manufacturing, better monitoring of raw materials usage to reduce wastage).

(b) *Product differentiation* (making a unique product or a product which appears different from your competitors', and hence more attractive). Information technology can be used to:

    (i)   design new products speedily (computer aided design);

    (ii)   enable customisation of a product to a customer's particular specification (computer integrated manufacturing);

    (iii) differentiate the product by using IT-based components to make it unique (eg Automated Teller Machines, when they were first introduced although they are now standard).

(c) Find a *market niche* (ie a group of consumers whose needs are not satisfied).

    (i)   Use sales data to identify customer preferences and spot unusual trends.
    (ii)   Use IT to analyse market research and statistical information.

12. CONCLUSION

12.1 Whenever an information system is designed, the characteristics and qualities of the system and its information need to be considered.

(a) *Why? - ie its purpose.* Transaction processing, management information system, decision support system? The information must be relevant, complete and accurate enough for its purpose, without going into unnecessary detail.

(b) *Who?* Who needs the information? Office clerks, supervisors, middle managers, senior executives? How many people need it, and so should a database system or a multi-user or network computer system be used?

(c) *When?* When is the information needed, and so how promptly must it be gathered and accessible?

(d) *Where?* Where should the information be processed, and where should the files be held?

(e) *How?* How should the information be processed? How, in what form, should the 'output' be produced for subsequent use?

(f) *What?* What information is needed? What must it do to achieve the qualities desired of it?

(g) *How much?* The costs of the information system should be outweighed by its benefits.

TEST YOUR KNOWLEDGE
The numbers in brackets refer to paragraphs of this chapter

Explain the following terms.

1   Information processing. Data processing. (1.7)

2   Strategic information. Tactical information. Operational information. (4.3)

3   Noise. (5.1)

4   Exception reporting. (5.3)

5   Transactions processing. (9.1)

6   Management information system. (10.1, 10.2)

7   Decision support system. (10.10)

8   What are the three main strategies for winning competitive advantage? (11.8)

Now try questions 1 and 2 at the end of the text

Chapter 2

FILE AND DATABASE CONCEPTS

This chapter covers the following topics.

1. Files, records, fields and characters
2. Transaction files, master files and reference files
3. Key fields
4. Codes
5. Data processing operations involving files
6. File organisation
7. File access
8. Application-specific and database files
9. An introduction to databases
10. Databases

Tutorial note. Database concepts are usefully discussed in the context of files generally. File design is part of the Paper 11 examination syllabus. Some material may be familiar to you, if you were not exempt from Paper 6.

---

1. FILES, RECORDS, FIELDS AND CHARACTERS

1.1 A *file* is a collection of data records with similar characteristics.

Examples of files are a sales ledger, stock records and a correspondence folder.

All files have a name, number or title to distinguish them from other files. In the case of a manual file, the title is often printed or written on the front of the file. In the case of a computer file, the file title is included as data on the file, as a 'header label' or 'identification label'.

1.2 A *record* consists of data relating to one logically definable unit of (business) information.

A collection of similar records makes up a file.

(a) the records for a sales ledger file consist of customer records (or 'customer accounts')
(b) a stock file consists of records for each stock item.
(c) letters and memos are the records in a correspondence file.

1.3 Records consist of *fields* of information. A field of information is an item of data relating to a record. For example, a customer record on the sales ledger file will include the following fields:

(a) name;
(b) address;
(c) customer reference number;
(d) balance owing; and
(e) credit limit.

1.4 A field consists of *characters* (eg letters, numbers) which themselves are composed of bits, (binary digits, 0 or 1).

2. TRANSACTION FILES, MASTER FILES AND REFERENCE FILES

2.1 In some systems, files can be classified into transaction files, master files and reference files.

2.2 A *transaction file* is a file containing records that relate to individual transactions that occur from day to day. The transaction records must all be processed.

When a company sells its goods day-by-day, the accounts staff might record the sales in a sales day book, which lists the sales made on that day, for which invoices have been issued. Eventually these transactions in the sales day book will be transferred ('posted') to the personal accounts of the individual customers in the sales ledger. The sales day book entries are examples of transaction records in a transactions file.

2.3 A *master file* is a file which shows a cumulative position. This means that it contains the following.

(a) *Transactions data* which is built up over time. For example in a purchase ledger system transaction data for each supplier, itemising purchases, purchase returns and payments to the supplier, would be collected over a period, so that the history and current account balance are shown.

(b) *Reference data*. This is normally altered (updated) infrequently. For example, in a purchase ledger system 'standing' reference data for each supplier including supplier name and address, reference number, amount currently owed etc.

2.4 A *reference file* or index file is a file containing reference data, which is normally altered (updated) infrequently. It contains no transaction data. Examples of a reference file are:

(a) a price list;
(b) manuals of company regulations and procedures.

Temporary files and permanent files

2.5 Files of data/information might be temporary or permanent. Master files and reference files are usually permanent, which means that they are never thrown away or scrapped. They will be updated from time to time, and so the information on the file might change, but the file itself will continue to exist.

A temporary file is one that is eventually scrapped. Many transaction files are held for a very short time, until the transaction records have been processed, but are then thrown away. Other transaction files are permanent (eg a cash book) or held for a considerable length of time before being scrapped.

3. KEY FIELDS

Fields length

3.1 The length of a field could be as short as one character (and with some records, a field might be missing altogether).

(a) A *fixed length field* is a field whose length is a fixed number of characters for every record on the file. For example, stock records might include an item for supplier identity code number. This field might be a fixed length field of six characters, say, for every stock record item.

(b) A *variable length field* is a field which varies in its number of characters from one record to another. On a sales ledger file, for example, variable length fields might include:

(i) customer name;
(ii) address.

Key fields

3.2 Records on a file should contain at least one *key field*. This is an item of data within the record by which it can be *uniquely* identified.

(a) The key field in a *transaction record* is the item of data which will be used to identify the *master file record* with which it should be associated.

(b) The key field in a *master file record* is the item of data by which the record in the file is *sequenced* or *indexed*, for retrieval purposes.

Example: sales ledger system

3.3 Suppose that in a sales ledger system, all the invoices issued on a particular day are listed in the sales day book, and a sales ledger clerk must now post these transactions from the sales day book to the sales ledger. The entries in the sales day book might include, for example:

Date	Address name	Account	Invoice number	Amount number	
31.8.X7	J Smith	8 High St	2420	3245	£242.00
31.8.X7	B Brown	4 Low Rd	3176	3246	£823.64
31.8.X7	T Jones	7 Middle Way	2883	3247	£150.20

What would the key field be in each transaction?

Solution

3.4 In a *manual processing system,* the key field might be customer name, and the personal accounts for each customer in the sales ledger would be held in alphabetical order.

In a *computer processing system,* and in some manual systems, the key field would be the account number. After all, there might be two different customers called J Smith and it is safer to give each customer a unique account number to identify him by.

3.5 The sales ledger records would use the same key field (customer name or account number) so that a transaction record can be 'paired' or matched with its corresponding master file record.

Exercise

What might be the records, record fields and key record field in a payroll master file?

Solution

The amount of information held on the payroll master file will depend on whether some employee information is held on another file or on the payroll file - eg is a person's home address, annual holiday entitlement and sickness history recorded on a personnel file or added to the payroll file record? And is the gross pay (and overtime rate etc) for a grade of worker included on a separate pay scales file, or is an individual's gross pay rate kept on the payroll file record itself? etc. The solution below is merely intended to give you an idea of what might be included on the payroll file. It is not a unique 'correct' solution, nor is it necessarily comprehensive.

Payroll file. The records relate to individual employees. The fields in each record might be:

> Employee number - key field
> Name
> National Insurance number
> Department code
> Gross annual pay (salaried employees)
> Hourly rate (wage earners)
> Income tax code
> Pension deductions
> Union membership contributions
> Other deductions (voluntary subscriptions)

Pay details for the year to date:
Gross pay to date;
Income tax to date;
National Insurance to date;
Other deductions to date;
Cumulative entitlements for the year to date;
Holiday pay.

---

4. CODES

4.1 In manual systems of data processing, items of data are often coded. Coding saves time in copying out data because codes are shorter than 'longhand' descriptions. For the same reason, and also to save storage space, computer systems make use of coded data.

4.2 The CIMA's Computing Terminology makes a reference to the storage-space-saving aspect of codes, by defining a code as 'the use of characters for coded representation of particular items within a system, eg a Customer Account Code in a sales ledger. The use of such coded representation facilitates input and reference procedures and optimises the use of storage space'.

4.3 In business systems, some examples of codes in files are:

(a) customer account numbers (codes);
(b) nominal ledger account numbers (codes);
(c) employee reference numbers (codes);
(d) stock item codes;
(e) department identity codes.

4.4 It is quite common for key fields to be coded items. The examples of codes in the list above would be likely to be the key field items in a sales ledger system, nominal ledger system, payroll system, stock system and personnel records system respectively.

5. DATA PROCESSING OPERATIONS INVOLVING FILES

5.1 Files are used to store data and information that will be needed again at some future time (eg next week, next month, next year etc) or provide data or information for current use.

The main types of data processing operations involving files are:

(a) updating
(b) maintenance
(c) retrieval, enquiry or interrogation

2: FILE AND DATABASE CONCEPTS

File update

5.2 *Updating* a file is a process whereby a data file in a system is brought up-to-date by interaction with other file(s).

For example, a file of receipts into stock and issues from stock might be processed periodically, say every week or month, to bring the records of stock-in-hand on the master Stock File up to date.

Updating usually involves processing records on a transaction file and in doing so, updating the corresponding records on a master file. *Transaction records* and corresponding *master file records* must be matched so that processing to update the master file record can take place.

5.3 The information in the master file will eventually be used for other processing work. For example, the sales ledger might be used to produce monthly statements for customers.

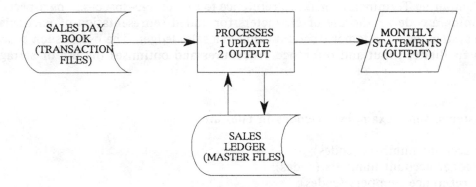

5.4 Sometimes, data processing involves bringing two or more master files together. An example would be a stock re-ordering system in which:

(a) the stock file data is used to identify which items of stock need re-ordering, and what the re-order quantities should be;

(b) the purchase ledger file or supplier file provides data about which suppliers can supply the stock items to be ordered.

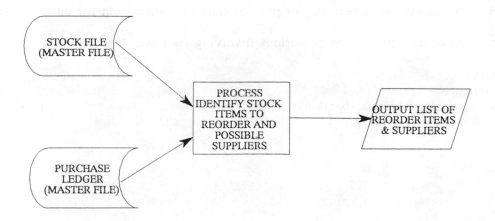

28

5.5　To familiarise yourself with the idea of how files are used you might like to think of a job that you do yourself involving files, and identify:

(a)　input 'transaction' records - ie the transactions file;

(b)　master files or reference files used;

(c)　the nature of the process;

(d)　the nature of the output.

5.6　In particular, try to recognise that in many jobs, data processing involves using two or more files. Indeed, the term 'update' means 'a process whereby a data file in a system is brought up-to-date by interaction with other file(s).' *('Computing Terminology' CIMA)*

File maintenance

5.7　*File maintenance* is the process of keeping standing data on a master file or reference file up-to-date. These items of data are rarely changed. Examples would be:

(a)　changes to prices on a price list;

(b)　changes to a payroll file to include new employees, delete employees who have left the organisation, change an employee's tax code or work grade etc;

(c)　changes to a stock master file to insert new items now being stocked, or delete obsolete items no longer stocked. Alternatively, to change the stock re-order level of an item.

File enquiry

5.8　A file enquiry or file interrogation involves obtaining and *copying* information from a file. This extracted data or information might be copied from the file without any processing (except for some text editing), or alternatively, might be processed to produce some information as output for the user.

File enquiry involves copying out records (or parts of records) *without* altering what is held on file. For example, if there is a file enquiry to list all the stock items on a Stock File and the current stock balance for each item, the program would arrange for the information to be obtained from the file without altering the file in any way.

Retrieval of data

5.9　Data on a file has to be retrieved when it is needed. The purpose of *key fields* is to help with the retrieval of data on a master file.

5.10　There is an important difference between retrieving records on a transaction file and retrieving records on a master file. All the records on a transaction file must be processed, and so it is necessary to work through all the transaction records, one at a time, until every one has been dealt with.

Not all the records on a master file will be wanted for processing or updating every time. It could be a time consuming task to work through every master file record looking for the records required for processing. Retrieving data will be simpler, in manual processing systems, and many computer processing systems too, if the individual master file records can be located, so that if we wish to update the master file record of customer number 1234 in the sales ledger, for example, we can go direct to this record in the file, without having to look through every account in the file until we come across the one we want.

5.11 The distinction between retrieving data on a transaction file and a master file is therefore that it is helpful to have a system for retrieving individual master file records, whereas it does not matter so much for transaction file records, since all of these will have to be processed anyway.

The need to retrieve data from a file leads us to the concept of file organisation.

6. FILE ORGANISATION

6.1 File organisation refers to the way in which records are held on a file, with a view to the retrieval of data/information.

'With any file, regardless of the medium used to hold it, some method is needed by which a record can be located when it is desired to retrieve it. For this purpose it is necessary to give each record in the file a key field by which it can be identified . . . The relationship of the key fields in consecutive records is termed the file organisation.'

(Daniels and Yeats *Basic Training in Systems Analysis*)

File organisation might be:

(a) unordered;
(b) sequential; or
(c) random.

Unordered (or serial) file organisation

6.2 A file has an unordered organisation if the records are in no particular order or sequence on the file. Transaction files may have an unordered organisation. Unordered organisation is *not* the same as random organisation.

Sequential file organisation

6.3 A file's organisation is sequential if the records on the file are in a logical sequence according to their key field - eg in alphabetical order, or in numerical order. New records must be placed into their correct position in the file, and records which follow 'pushed back' to make room for the new records.

6.4 In computer systems this could lead to a large number of 'accesses' ie (moving each record in turn one position back in the file).

To get round this problem, it is usual to leave spaces on a sequential file, to allow room for new records. This is done by grouping records together in 'buckets' with each bucket starting part-filled with records and part-empty for new additions. After a while, when the empty spaces start to fill up, the file will be given a spring-clean, and records regrouped into new buckets with spaces. This process of tidying up the file is called *housekeeping*.

Random file organisation

6.5 Random file organisation is a bit more difficult to understand. When we say that a file has a random organisation, we don't mean that the records are held anywhere on file, as the term 'random' might lead you to suppose. With random organisation, records are put on file:

(a) either in some way that corresponds to a key field value, which is 'calculated' from data on the record when it is filed;

(b) or by means of an index. When a record is put on file, its key field is listed sequentially in an index, which shows the 'address location' on file where the record is to be placed. An index on a computer file is similar in principle to an index at the back of a book.

Looking at the records on file, in sequence, would give you no idea as to why they are located where they are - hence the term 'random' organisation.

7.   FILE ACCESS

7.1 File access means locating individual records on the file. The way in which a file can be accessed will depend on how the file is organised, but access might be:

(a) serial access;
(b) sequential access; or
(c) direct access (indexed sequential or random).

Serial access

7.2 The *only* way of retrieving records from an unordered file is to start at the first record on the file, then go on to the next record, and the next, and so on through to the end of the file. This is known as serial access.

(a) With transaction files, serial access of an unordered file will often be suitable, because every record on the file has to be processed.

(b) With master files, serial access to locate records would be very time consuming and so very inefficient. Master files should never have an unordered file organisation!

Sequential access

7.3 With sequential access, the records on the file must be organised sequentially. Sequential access is the access of records on a sequentially organised file, *without* using an index. Sequential access is faster than serial access for two reasons:

(a) Since records on a sequentially organised file are in key field order, once the particular record has been located, there is no need to check serially through the rest of the file, in case there is another record on file with the same key field number;

(b) There is a method of locating records on a sequential file, known as *binary search*, which means that individual records can be located more quickly than with serial access.

Direct access

7.4 Both indexed sequential access and random access are methods of locating an individual record in a file directly, without having to look through any other records first. They are both methods of *direct access*.

(a) *Indexed sequential access* is direct access to records that are held in a key field order in file - ie are filed sequentially - *using an index* to locate individual records directly.

   (i) Both the records on file and the index must be held in sequence, and new records must be placed in their correct position on the file, and their correct place on the index.

   (ii) Indexed sequential access is often faster than sequential access, because any record can be located by reference to the index, which gives its specific address location on file.

(b) *Random access* refers to the retrieval of data from a randomly-organised file.

   (i) The method of random access will depend on the method used to put records on to the file in the first place - ie

     (1) by calculating a key value from data on the record;
     (2) or by reference to an index.

   (ii) Random access, especially when used with a powerful computer and calculating the address location of a record from its key 'search' value, can be very fast.

8. APPLICATION-SPECIFIC AND DATABASE FILES

8.1 In our discussion of files so far, we have looked at:

(a) how files are structured (files, records, fields);
(b) how they can be processed (update, enquiry, retrieval);
(c) how records are physically organised on a file (unordered, sequential, random);
(d) how records are accessed (serial, sequential, direct);
(e) what sort of files there might be (master file, transaction file).

8.2 You might of noticed, however, that each of the files we have discussed processes only one sort of data. A payroll file processes only payroll data, a stock file only stock data, and so forth.

8.3 An organisation might end up with separate files and processing systems for:

(a) payroll;
(b) sales ledger;
(c) purchase ledger;
(d) stock control;
(e) nominal ledger;

(f) budgeting;

(g) financial modelling ; and

(h) job costing.

8.4 A separate file of data is maintained for each of these applications. However, in many cases the underlying data used by each application might be the same. A major consequence is that data items are duplicated in a number of files. They are input more than once (leading to errors and inconsistencies) and held in several files (wasting space).

For example, data relating to the hours an hourly-paid employee has worked on particular job is relevant to:

(a) the payroll system, as the employee's wages will be based on the hours worked;

(b) the job costing system, as the cost of the employee's time are part of the cost of the job.

8.5 Each file is only used by one application. Such a file is known as an application-specific file. The disadvantages of application-specific files are:

(a) data is duplicated (*data redundancy*);

(b) data can only be used in a limited way (ie the payroll system is a program which only uses payroll data to produce output which has been determined in the program; other than simple file enquiries, you'd have to write a computer program to select certain items of data which share one characteristic in common).

8.6 The problem of data redundancy is overcome, partly, at least by an *integrated system*. An integrated system is a system where one set of data is used for more than one application.

8.7 In an accounting context, it might be possible to integrate parts of the sales ledger, purchase ledger, stock control systems and nominal ledger systems, so that the data input to the sales ledger updates the nominal ledger automatically.

8.8 Moreover, some of the more advanced decision support and executive information systems (as described in Chapter 1) might be integrated with the system, so that data can be downloaded automatically from the accounts system. The advantage of this is that data from the accounting system does not have to be to transcribed by manually to the new application.

8.9   A diagram of an integrated accounting system is given below.

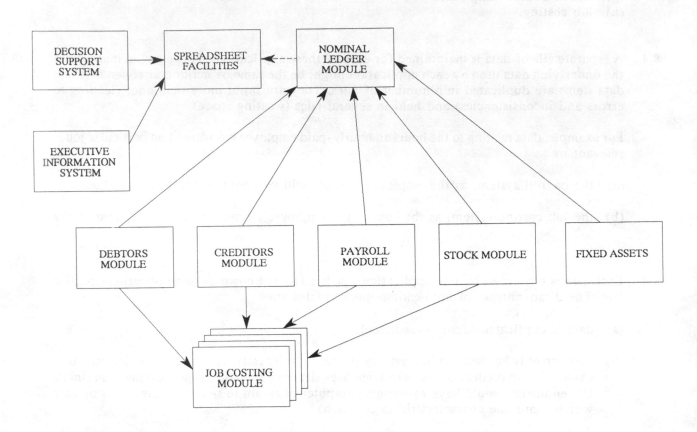

8.10   There are other types of integrated system available. Some types of integrated system combine
       two or more general purpose packages. A *general purpose package* is software which presents the
       user with a number of tools or facilities. A spreadsheet enables the user to construct
       financial models. A word processor package provides facilities for text editing. (You should
       note that a word processed document is a type of computer file, as is a spreadsheet model.
       These are discussed in later chapters). A software package like Lotus Symphony enables
       spreadsheet data to be transferred automatically to the word processor.

8.11   The integrated systems approach, where different applications update each other, is a half way
       house, as it were, between a system based on separate application-specific files and a database
       approach.

8.12   Broadly speaking a database is a file of data organised in such a way that it can be used by
       many applications. Recall the example noted in Paragraph 8.4 above.

       (a)   The employee's hours are input twice, once to the payroll application, once to the job
             costing system, in a non-integrated system of application specific files.

       (b)   In an integrated system, the data would have been input to the payroll application. The
             payroll application would have been used to update the job costing application.

(c) In the database approach, the data is also input once only, but not to any of the applications. Rather, it is input to a pool of data, the database, to which the payroll programs and job costing programs have equal access, or indeed any other enquiry or application.

8.13 This diagram might make this more clear. It deals with a stock control, sales order and purchases applications.

(a) Application-specific systems

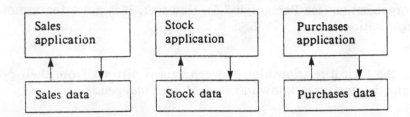

(b) Integrated systems

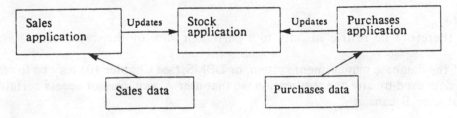

(c) Data base

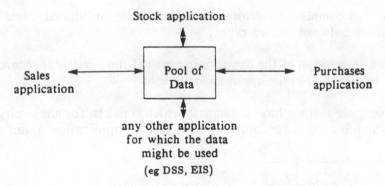

8.14 There are a number of important facts to note about databases. Databases are described in detail below, as the database approach to storing and handling data is becoming widely adopted in many business areas. However, as a database is a particular type of file, certain salient features are noted below. Remember that the basic unit of data on a file is a record, which consists of related fields or sub-items of data.

9.   AN INTRODUCTION TO DATABASES

9.1   When a record is placed on a storage device, such as a disk, it becomes a *physical record*. There is some location on the disk which physically contains the data.

9.2   *Logical records* can be distinguished from physical records. The logical relationship between records on a file may bear no relation to the exact physical location where those records are stored: record A can be be in position 120 on the storage medium, record B on position 77, record C on position 666, or whatever. The logical relations between the records in this case is that they are in alphabetical sequence, logically, but not physically. This is a feature of any random file organisation (see Paragraph 7.5). However, it is not a feature of serial or sequential file organisation.

9.3   This concept, that the logical relationships between data is distinct from their position on the storage medium, is sometimes known as *logical data independence*.

9.4   It is often the case that certain data must remain confidential, and it is nearly always the case that in any database, no one application will need to access *all* types of data.

9.5   Users can therefore be restricted only to a particular *view* of the database.

One task of the database management system, or DBMS, (see Chapter 10) may be to restrict the amount of data used by any one application, so that user A, say, cannot access certain data on the file but user B can.

In database terminology:

(a)   a logical *schema* is a complete description of the database, in logical terms (eg record types, relationships between record types)

(b)   a *sub-schema* is a description of the database in terms of the *particular* records and data items required by any *particular application*, or user.

Thus, for example, suppose that we have a database which consists, for simplicity's sake, of just eight records, which is accessed by only two applications, application A and application B.

1	2	3	4	5	6	7	8

The DBMS may allow application 'A' to use records 1, 2, 3, 7, 8 only and application B to use records 4, 5, 6, 7, 8 only.

9.6   The *physical model* of the database describes the physical construction of the databases (eg how record *address* locations are calculated, in a random access file).

9.7   Data *independence* (ie separation of data items from the applications which process them) is therefore maintained by:

(a) separation of physical and logical models;

(b) different subschemas for different users.

9.8 The concept of file enquiry and file updating was mentioned earlier, as being two distinct operations. In a database system this is not necessarily the case. It is possible to access a record, according to the criteria you choose, alter it at will with relative ease. You do not *need* a file of transaction data to be run in conjunction with a master file. A database system therefore requires a random or indexed-sequential file organisation, which must be accessed directly.

10. DATABASES

10.1 The definition given by the CIMA (Computing Terminology) refers to the strict and looser meanings of database and DBMS, as follows.

(a) *Database.* 'Frequently a much-abused term – in its strict sense a database is a file of data structured in such a way that it may serve a number of applications without its structure being dictated by any one of those applications, the concept being that programs are written around the database rather than files being structured to meet the need of specific programs. *The term is also rather loosely applied to simple file management software.*'

(b) *Database management system (DBMS).* 'Technically, a system which uses a database philosophy for the storage of information. In practice this term is often used to describe any system which enables the definition, storage and retrieval of information from discrete files within a system. Thus many simple file-handling systems are frequently referred to as 'database systems'.'

10.2 The database approach can be summarised diagrammatically:

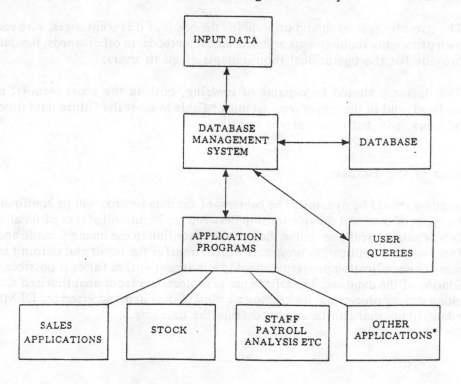

10.3 A DBMS is central to the operation of a database. It is the software that:

    (a) builds the database files;
    (b) manages the database;
    (c) provides access for application programs to the data on the database files.

    Databases must be accessible directly, and so the file medium for a database must be a direct access medium - ie magnetic disk.

10.4 As a general purpose system, the database approach can be used for a wide variety of functions. A database is perhaps distinguished by what can be done with the data it contains. Whereas a spreadsheet deals with modelling, a database system deals with information storage and retrieval and filing. A database approach is advantageous because:

    (a) data can be sorted in a variety of ways to suit different users;
    (b) a database can be interrogated without the need for a massive processing operation;
    (c) it is easy to sift out *relevant* data for a processing operation using specified criteria;
    (d) it provides administrative convenience.

The objectives of a database system

10.5 A database should have four major objectives.

    (a) It should be *shared*. Different users should be able to access the same data in the database for their own processing applications, and at the same time if required.

    (b) The *integrity* of the database must be preserved. This means that one user should not be allowed to alter the data on file so as to spoil the database records for other users. However, users must be able to update the data on file, and so make valid alterations to the data.

    (c) The database system should provide for the needs of different users, who each have their own processing requirements and data access methods. In other words, the database should provide for the operational requirements of all its users.

    (d) The database should be capable of *evolving*, both in the short term (it must be kept updated) and in the longer term (it must be able to meet the future data processing needs of users, not just their current needs).

Administration of the database

10.6 The database should be dynamic. The contents of the data records will be continually changing, and the types of data and the relationship between the items will also occasionally change. The DBMS will automatically re-index the records according to the changes made and provide the interface with the application programs which transfer the input and output to and from the database. The application programs should be independent, as far as is possible, of the actual organisation of the database. The DBMS has to protect data from unauthorised access and from corruption during processing. By keeping a record of data items accessed the DBMS can identify redundant items that can be removed from the database.

10.7 A *database administrator* will often be appointed to look after the structure, physical storage and security of the data in the best interest of all users. He is responsible for:

(a) maintaining the database, including the addition of new data;
(b) maintaining a dictionary describing the data items;
(c) maintaining manuals for users describing how to use the facilities of the database;
(d) overseeing the security of the database and maintaining individual privacy;
(e) ensuring that the requirements of the Data Protection Act 1984 are complied with.

Data analysis; entity modelling

10.8 A database must be structured in such a way that users of the system can access and process data in all the ways they want. Unless the database is properly structured, this will not be possible.

The person creating the database file must first carry out an analysis of all the *data* for processing and filing, because a full and accurate analysis of data in the system is crucial to the construction of complete and workable database files. Data analysis involves:

(a) identifying what data is available and needed;
(b) where it originates;
(c) how it is used;
(d) when it is needed.

Entity modelling

10.9 One approach to data analysis is *entity analysis*. An *entity* is an item (a person, a job, a business, an activity, a product or stores item etc) about which information is stored. In single application systems (such as a sales ledger system, a payroll system, a purchase ledger system) a record will be made about an entity. In a sales ledger system, records will be made about customers. A customer is an entity, and all customers can be referred to as an *entity set*. Similarly, in a payroll system, records will be made about employees. An employee is an entity, and all employees together can be referred to as an entity set.

You may prefer to think of an entity as a record.

10.10 Each record in the file will then be given *attributes*. An attribute is a characteristic or property of an entity. For a customer, attributes include customer name and address, amounts owing, date of invoices sent and payments received, credit limit etc. For a stores item, attributes include stock number, description, quantity, size, colour, supplier, balance in stock, reorder level, reorder quantity etc.

You may prefer to think of attributes as fields in a record.

10.11 For any entity or entity set, we can also identify *relationships* between attributes. There are also relationships between entities. Here are some simple examples. The diagrams are called *Bachmann* diagrams.

(a) An address book is an example of where there are *no relationships*, as it is simply a list of records. The *entity* is the person whose address is stored. The *attribute* in a record is a person's address.

(b)

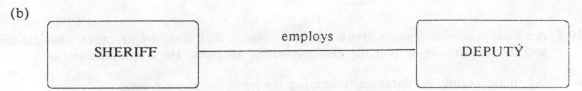

There is the relationship *employs* between the sheriff and the deputy. It is a *one-to-one* relationship because the sheriff employs only one deputy.

(c)

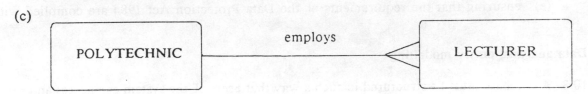

The polytechnic employs a large number of lecturers. The relationship is *one-to-many*.

(d)

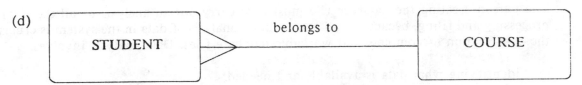

Many students belong to one course. The relationship is *many-to-one*.

(e)

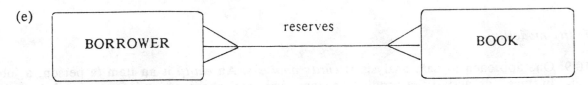

A large number of borrowers wish to reserve a large number of books. The relationship is *many-to-many*.

Data structures

Hierarchical data structures

10.12 Let us consider further how we can structure our data. Many relationships are one-to-many or many-to-one relationships. Such relationships can be expressed conveniently in a hierarchy. Each data item is related to only one item above it in the hierarchy, but is related to any number of data items below it. (Hierarchies are sometimes referred to as parent-child structures.)

For example, if a large multinational bank built up a database of all its branches throughout the world, it might be structured in layers as follows:

(a) continent;
(b) country;
(c) region;
(d) county;
(e) town; and
(f) district.

10.13 In another example a simple hierarchical relationship could be expressed between work in a department, individual jobs within the department, and individual transactions carried out by each job-holder. The data is organised hierarchically. Access to the data is achieved by splitting up the search into levels, thus reducing the amount of search time needed within the computer and so speeding up access times. In this example, the search for data about a transaction would be split into a search for the department, then a search for the job within the department and then a search for the individual transaction within the job.

10.14 The biggest drawback to a file organised with a hierarchical data structure is that the user is limited in the number of ways he or she can look for records because the file organisation makes it much easier to search for certain items in the file records than for others.

Network structures

10.15 We can express many-to-many relationships in a *network data structure*. This is like a hierarchical structure but any data item may be related to any number of other data items, and so a hierarchical tree structure does not exist.

10.16 Whereas a hierarchical data structure only allows a one-to-many relationship between data items, a network database is a database in which the logical data structure allows many-to-many relationships.

10.17 Hierarchical and network *data structures* have been incorporated in hierarchical and network *databases* which used a *pointer-based system* to implement them. This meant that an enquiry had to *navigate* through a number of records to obtain its object. It also meant that it was very hard to alter the database in any way as altering one 'pointer' might have meant altering many more.

The relational model

10.18 A way of *expressing* many-to-many and one-to-many relationships is in the *relational* model. A relational model organises data elements in a two dimensional table consisting of rows and columns.

A row represent a record, and columns represent parts of a record. A row is sometimes called a *tuple* and a column is sometimes called a *domain*.

Column name

	1 Number	2 Name	3 Title	4 Salary	5 Department
Row 1					
2	79	VOLTAIRE	Manager	28,000	4
3	81	ROUSSEAU	Executive	31,500	4
	92	DIDEROT	Clerk	7,000	2

Primary key

Any data element can be recognised by its record number or field name. The primary key is used to identify a record.

In our example, employees Voltaire and Rousseau both belong to department '4'. There is thus a *many-to-one* relationship between, on the one hand, Voltaire and Rousseau and, on the other, their departments: an employee can only belong to one department, but one department can employ a number of employees.

10.19 Entity analysis, attribute analysis and the analysis of relationships between attributes, and more especially between entities, are all important in the data analysis work for relational database design. The structure of a relational database is modelled on this entity basis.

10.20 In the relational model the relationships between entities can be simplified to the point where all the data for an entity can be regarded as residing in tables, with each column representing an attribute and each row having a key by which it can be uniquely identified. The relationships between these entity types and attributes would be expressed in the form of a table, allowing users of the database management system to extract data in whatever way they want by specifying the relationship or attributes which they want information about.

10.21 A matter of concern for the designer of a database will be what data items should be grouped together in a single record. A variety of ways of grouping data items will be possible, but some will obviously be better than others. Among the objectives in designing a database are

(a)   to eliminate unnecessary *redundancy* (ie duplication of items);
(b)   to reduce the need for restructuring if new types of data arise;
(c)   to separate logically distinct aspects of the data so that modifications which concern only one area can be made without affecting other areas.

10.22 To achieve these objectives a step-by-step process of *normalisation* is used in which a set of related data fields are refined into new sets having progressively simpler and more regular structure.

Normalisation is a term used in the design of relational database systems, to describe the process of reducing complex relationships to a simpler and more regular two-dimensional tabular form. Normalisation is sometimes called *relational data analysis*.

Summary: data structures and databases

10.23 Perhaps a summary would be useful here.

(a)   Hierarchical and network *databases* were often implemented on a *pointer-based* system, and a transaction had to 'navigate' through other data in the system before the required record was reached. The structure of the file is contained in the data items themselves.

(b)   In a relational database, the structure of the file is independent of the actual data. The relationships between different entity types have been determined at the outset, and are not embodied in the records themselves. The logical associations between different types of data are achieved, not by pointers, but by having common information in different tables (ie a link).

10.24 Once the data analysis for a database file has been completed, a database system can be developed. An organisation might use a database software package to do this, with a flat file, multiple file, network or relational database package, as required.

The data dictionary

10.25 A data dictionary is a feature of many database systems. As the term might suggest, it provides a method for looking up the items of data held in the database, to establish:

(a) a list of the entity, attribute and relationship types;

(b) a list of all the functions which use data about each entity type;

(c) how to *access* the data in whatever manner is required (a data dictionary is sometimes called a data directory);

(d) what the data codes and symbols mean.

It can also store standard subroutines.

10.26 Definitions of data dictionary are:

(a) 'An index of data held in a database, used to assist in maintenance and any other access to the data.' (The British Computer Society: 'Glossary of Computing Terms');

(b) 'A facility that allows the definition of data items in a unique and organised manner for subsequent use in a variety of systems in a business.' (CIMA: 'Computing Terminology').

10.27 A data dictionary is simply a list or record of each data store in the system, and each data flow in the system showing what items of data they contain.

The usefulness of a data dictionary

10.28 A data dictionary provides a description of the data which is used by a program. It provides this information in order to minimise the number of problems which might arise due to mis-understandings about what the data is, how it is organised or what is to be done with it.

10.29 The data dictionary is a form of technical documentation, it ensures that everyone in the organisation defines and uses the data consistently. This consistency is extremely important for large projects which involve several programmers. The opportunity for mis-understandings is so high that the data dictionary becomes essential. From time to time programs are updated or modified. Where this is necessary a data dictionary can quickly acquaint the programmer with the existing data, its structure and uses.

10.30 A data dictionary helps with systems analysis, systems design and systems maintenance.

(a) During systems analysis, a data dictionary helps the analyst to organise his information about the data elements in the system, where they come from, where they go to, and even whether any key data elements are missing.

(b) During systems design, a data dictionary helps the analyst and programmers to ensure that no data elements are missed out if they are really needed.

(c) Once the system is operational, and an amendment is required to a program, a data dictionary will help the programmer to understand what each data element is used for, so that any amendment he makes does not 'spoil' other parts of the program.

10.31 Data dictionaries have been found so useful that software packages which automate the creation of dictionaries have been developed. The creation of this reference material is tedious and the availability of a computer tool which can determine basic information about the data has increased their use. These packages will provide the basic information about the variables' names, their structure and perhaps the places in the program where they are used. This information can readily be extracted from the program without any human involvement. A full dictionary entry would require some additional information only available from the user. For example, a simple variable name may not contain sufficient information to intelligibly identify a particular piece of data. The software packages require that the user provide this additional information.

10.32 A data dictionary is a simple, easy to use tool which has significantly eased the communications needed in large projects and maintenance work. Its role has expanded so it is now an integral tool of systems *design*.

11. CONCLUSION

11.1 A file is a collection of records with similar characteristics.

11.2 Each record is uniquely identified by a key field.

11.3 In some systems, master files are updated by transaction files.

11.4 In Chapter 1, we discussed, briefly, the use of information as a resource of the organisation. This idea has its physical manifestation in the database approach to storing information. The database is, in fact, a resource of data for the application programs, user queries, EISs, DSSs and other systems to draw on.

TEST YOUR KNOWLEDGE

The numbers in brackets refer to paragraphs of this chapter

1   Distinguish between a record, a field and a character. (1.1, 1.2, 1.4)

2   Distinguish between a master file, a transactions file and a reference file. (2.2, 2.3, 2.4)

3   Distinguish between a variable field and a fixed field. (4.1)

4   What is a key field? (3.2)

5   What is file updating? (5.2)

6   What is file maintenance? (5.7)

7   List the three basic methods by which records can be organised on a file. (6.1)

8   List three ways by which records can be accessed. (7.1)

9   What is an integrated system? (8.6)

10   What, in general terms, is a database? (8.12)

11   What is data independence? (9.9)

12   What are the functions of a DBMS? (10.3)

13   Distinguish between hierarchical and network data structure. (10.12, 10.15)

14   What is the relational model? (10.18)

15   What is a data dictionary? (10.25) How is it useful? (10.28)

Now try questions 3 and 4 at the end of the text

Chapter 3

REVISION CHAPTER: COMPUTER HARDWARE AND THE OPERATING SYSTEM

This chapter covers the following topics.

1. Definition of a computer
2. The Central Processing Unit (CPU)
3. Mainframes, minicomputers and microcomputers
4. The choice of input
5. Direct data entry with VDU and keyboard
6. Encoding to disk or tape
7. Direct input devices
8. The choice of output
9. Printed output
10. Computer output on microform (COM)
11. The choice of backing storage
12. Magnetic disk storage
13. Magnetic tape storage
14. Optical and other storage media
15. Operating systems software and utilities

Tutorial note. Use this chapter for revision if you have sat Paper 6 (Elements of Information Systems). If you were exempt from that paper, this chapter should give you a basic grounding in computer equipment and operating systems. Moreover, this paper does contain questions relating to hardware etc, though from a 'design' angle.

---

1. DEFINITION OF A COMPUTER

1.1 The British Computer Society's definition of a computer is 'a machine that, under the control of a stored program, automatically accepts and processes data, and supplies the results of that processing'.

1.2 The basic components of a computer's *hardware* consist of the following.

(a) *Input devices*. These accept input data for processing.

(b) *External storage devices* (backup, secondary). These hold data or information on file until it is needed for processing. Processed data may also be put on to an external storage file.

(c) *Output devices*. These accept output from the data processing device and convert it into a usable form. The most common output devices are printers (which print the output on paper) and screens (which display the output).

Note that input devices, external storage devices and output devices are often referred to collectively as *peripherals*.

(d) *Processing device*. The computer has a *central processor*, which performs the data processing, under the control of the stored program(s), by taking in data from input devices and external storage devices, processing it, and then transferring the processed information to an output device or external storage device.

The term 'computer system' refers to the central processor together with its associated peripheral equipment – ie the input, output and storage devices.

1.3 The links between these devices can be shown diagrammatically, as follows.

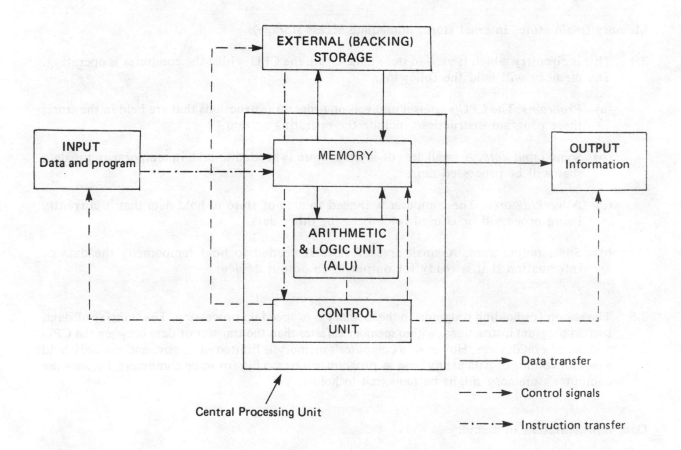

2. THE CENTRAL PROCESSING UNIT (CPU)

2.1 The CPU is the 'brain' of the computer. It is a collection of electronic circuitry and registers that carries out the processing. The CPU is divided into three areas, the control unit, the arithmetic logic unit, and memory. The set of operations that the CPU performs is known as the *instruction set*, or repertoire, and this determines in part the speed at which processing can be performed. *Reduced Instruction Set Computer* (RISC) chips are very fast as they construct complex instructions as a string of simple ones.

3: REVISION CHAPTER: COMPUTER HARDWARE AND THE OPERATING SYSTEM

The control unit

2.2 This improvises the execution of program instructions under operating system direction, and accesses peripheral (input and output) devices. The control unit sends out *control signals*, coordinated by a clock: the number of pulses (cycles) produced per second is an indication of processing speed, and is usually measured in megahertz (MHz). One MHz is one million pulses (cycles) per second.

The arithmetic and logic unit (ALU)

2.3 This is the part of the CPU where the arithmetic and logic operations are carried out, eg:

(a) arithmetic (eg add, subtract, multiply, divide);
(b) comparison;
(c) branch, (a branch instruction changes the order of program instructions);
(d) movement of data.

Memory (main store, internal store, immediate access storage)

2.4 This is circuitry which is used to store data within the CPU whilst the computer is operating. The memory will hold the following.

(a) *Programs*. The CPU's control unit acts on program instructions that are held in the store; these program instructions include the operating system.

(b) Some *input data*. A small area of internal store is needed to take in temporarily the data that will be processed next.

(c) A *working area*. The computer will need an area of store to hold data that is currently being processed or is used for processing other data.

(d) *Some output data*. A small area of store is needed to hold temporarily the data or information that is ready for output to an output device.

2.5 The reason for holding programs in the memory is to speed up processing. The transfer of data, such as program instructions, within memory is faster than the transfer of data between the CPU and peripheral devices. However, a computer's memory is limited in its size, and can only hold a certain volume of data at any time. A program can be too big for some computers, because the computer's memory might be too small to hold it.

Data representation in memory

2.6 A digital computer holds data in its memory, and *characters* (letters, numbers and other symbols) are represented in binary digits or *bits*. A group of eight bits is known as a byte.

A computer's operations depend on simple circuits which can be switched ON or OFF. These two states can be conveniently expressed by the numbers 1 and 0 respectively. Any piece of data or instruction must be *coded* in these symbols before processing can commence.

(a) Numbers and letters can be represented in the CPU by codes (eg ASCII, EBCDIC) , or in ordinary binary arithmetic. ASCII codes are more commonly used for commercial applications, eg for representing stock item codes, customer codes, invoice numbers, invoice values, delivery note numbers etc.

(b) There are different codes for capital letters and for small letters, so that a total of 52 code numbers are used to represent the alphabet. Some examples of ASCII codes are:

A	01000001
B	01000010
3	00110011
4	00110100
?	00111111

Address locations and instructions

2.7 Every computer memory has a system of numbered address *locations*. Data is stored (written) and retrieved (read) by reference to its appropriate address in the memory. Each store contains *several* bits, and this is the *minimum* number of bits that can be addressed in one go (the minimum addressable unit of memory is referred to as a *word*).

Integrated circuit (IC) store

2.8 The memory in a CPU is often built with integrated circuits, which consist of transistors and their interconnecting patterns on an extremely small scale. Many circuits are now mass produced on square chips of silicon, and so are very cheap to make. In some modern microcomputer systems, the *microprocessing unit* (MPU) contains all the elements of a computer - arithmetic and logic unit, control unit, and the input/output interface - on a single chip. Some microcomputers (eg Compaq's EISA) use two for the extra processing capacity.

(a) With IC store, much more data can be held on a single, small chip. The storage capacity of machines is higher and their physical size smaller than in the past.

(b) They have reduced the hardware cost of the CPU *dramatically* and introduced an age of a mass user market for computers as a result.

(c) The IC chip is mounted on a carrier unit which in turn is 'plugged' on to a circuit board with other IC chips, each with their own functions. In addition to storage and computing, ICs are used to control the activity, timing, input, output etc of the CPU.

2.9 A distinction is made between different types of memory.

(a) ROM: *Read only memory* (ROM) is a memory chip into which fixed data is written permanently at the time of its manufacture. New data cannot be written into the memory, and so the data on the memory chip is unchangeable and irremovable. The data on an ROM chip will consist of items of software.

ROM is also described as 'non-volatile' memory (ie its contents do not disappear when the computer's power source is switched off). A computer's start-up program, known as a 'bootstrap' program, is always held in a form of a ROM.

(b) PROM is *programmable ROM*. ROMs are supplied by the manufacturer already programmed during the last stage of chip manufacture. With a PROM, the chip is provided for the *user* to program. Special equipment is needed, and it is not normally alterable.

(c) EPROM: *Electronically programmable* ROM differs from PROM in that the program data (ie software) written on to the memory can be erased and new data written (with special equipment). In an EAROM (electronically alterable ROM) the old contents do not have to be erased first.

(d) RAM: Random access memory (RAM) is memory that is directly available to the CPU. Data can be written on to or read from random access memory. RAM can be defined as 'memory with the ability to access any location in the memory in any order with the same speed'. Random access is an essential requirement for the main memory of a computer.

RAM in microcomputers is 'volatile' which means that the contents of the memory are erased when the computer's power is switched off.

2.10 A *cache* memory is used to speed up processing, as it contains data drawn from main memory before processing.

Memory expansion: extension boards

2.11 Many microcomputers offer the user the option to increase the size of their Random Access Memory. The reason for wanting more RAM would be to:

(a) use longer programs; and/or
(b) have more memory for data.

Memory can be expanded in the following ways.

(a) *An expansion slot* allows the extra RAM storage device to be 'plugged in' to the microcomputer's CPU, so as to become a part of the computer's main memory.

(b) An extension card or board fulfils the same function, but fits inside the microcomputer 'box' itself. A microcomputer may have space inside it to accept extra printed circuit boards, to enhance its storage size or processing capabilities. A *RAM card* is one example of an extension card that might be inserted. Another example is a *graphics card*, which gives a microcomputer the ability to process graphics software, and present graphics images on a VDU screen.

2.12 The processing capacity of a computer is in part dictated by the size of its memory. Memory size is calculated in Kilobytes (1 kilobyte = 1,024 bytes) and megabytes (1 megabyte = 1,024 x 1,024 bytes). So a computer described as having a 640K RAM memory has, in addition to ROM, a random access memory of 640 x 1,024 bytes = 655,366 bytes.

Multitasking (multiprogramming)

2.13 As the CPU works at vastly faster speeds than any peripheral device, CPU time is wasted to the extent that processing times are dependent on the speeds of these peripheral units. Wasted CPU time can be reduced by the simultaneous use of more than one peripheral device (simultaneity), so that the CPU can be receiving some input A from one or more peripheral devices, processing data B and sending output C to one or more peripherals all at the same time.

In spite of simultaneity, a computer's CPU is still idle for a large part of the time. Multitasking (sometimes called multiprogramming) enables several programs to share the use of the CPU and take up the under-used capacity.

A distinction between multitasking and multiprogramming (definitions taken from the CIMA *Computing Terminology*) is that:

(a) multitasking is 'the performance of more than one task concurrently by one user on a computer system' whereas;

(b) multiprogramming is 'a technique whereby use of the CPU is optimised through the interleaved execution of a number of separate programs.'

2.14 Some programs will be *peripheral bound*, requiring considerably more input/output time than CPU time, while others will be *CPU bound*, requiring more CPU time than input/output time. The programs used in a multiprogramming or multitasking operation should ideally comprise a mix of peripheral bound and CPU bound programs which can be allocated a priority sequence.

2.15 With a large number of programs and peripheral units, the CPU can be kept occupied for almost 100% of the time. This needs a suitable operating system, whose functioning in turn requires:

(a) sufficient memory to hold *all* programs; *and*

(b) the data which is to be processed by each program;

(c) that one program must not be allowed to overlap into store allocated to another;

(d) *store protection*. (A user must not be allowed access to parts of main storage not allocated to his program and data);

(e) *priority ratings* for each program. The highest priority program (usually the most peripheral bound) is allowed to use the CPU whenever it requires to do so (eg after an input/output transfer). When the program can no longer use the CPU, the operating system allocates processing time to the next program in line. Whenever a higher priority program is ready to use the CPU, the operating system *interrupts* the lower priority program and passes control to the higher priority one;

(f) *special control programs*. The operating systems software must be designed to cope with the problems of multiprogramming or multitasking - controlling all peripherals and the use of the CPU by priority procedures.

3: REVISION CHAPTER: COMPUTER HARDWARE AND THE OPERATING SYSTEM

3. MAINFRAMES, MINICOMPUTERS AND MICROCOMPUTERS

3.1 Computers can be classified as follows, although the differences between these categories can quite vague.

    (a) supercomputers;
    (b) mainframe computers;
    (c) minicomputers;
    (d) microcomputers;

Supercomputers

3.2 A supercomputer is used to process very large amounts of data very quickly. They are particularly useful for occasions where high volumes of calculations need to be performed.

Mainframes

3.3 A *mainframe computer* is a large computer in terms of price, power and speed. It will probably:

    (a) cost over £1,000,000;
    (b) have a wider variety of peripheral devices than are found with smaller computers;
    (c) require an airconditioned room, or even water cooling;
    (d) support more users than most smaller computers (eg 500 terminals simultaneously);
    (e) deliver processing power of at least ten MIPs up to a maximum of around 100 MIPs;
    (f) have a large memory, and be able to control a database of 10 gigabytes;
    (g) handle a mixed computing workload (eg on-line and batch processing simultaneously);
    (h) 'pipeline', or preprocess, instructions so that they are executed quickly.

3.4 Many organisations do not need mainframe computers for their data processing, because they would be too big and expensive to justify the volume of processing that is needed.

Minicomputers

3.5 A *minicomputer* is a computer whose size, speed and capabilities lie somewhere between those of a mainframe and a microcomputer. The term was originally used before microcomputers came along, to describe computers which were cheaper but less well-equipped than mainframe computers (which had until then been the only type of computer available). The advent of more powerful chips means that some 'superminis' can run more powerfully than small mainframes.

3.6 With the advent of microcomputers and with mainframes now being physically smaller than in the past, the definition of a minicomputer has become rather vague. There is no adequate definition which distinguishes between a microcomputer and a minicomputer. Price, power and number of users supported have been used to provide distinguishing features, but these differences have tended to erode as microchip technology has progressed.

3: REVISION CHAPTER: COMPUTER HARDWARE AND THE OPERATING SYSTEM

Microcomputers

3.7 An independent 'free-standing' *microcomputer* consists of three major components (plus a printer, which is a 'peripheral' device):

(a) The *basic module* consists of one or two floppy disk drives and/or an integrated hard disk unit. It can also act as a pedestal for the video display.

(b) The *keyboard* is connected to the system via a plug connection to the basic module. On newer machines keyboards are attached by coiled cables (like a telephone) which allows the keyboard, module and screen to be moved around in relation to each other according to available space and the user's comfort.

A *mouse* - a device used in on-screen graphics and sometimes as an alternative to using the keyboard to input instructions - is attachable either to the basic module via another socket or sometimes to the keyboard.

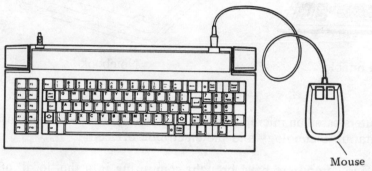

Mouse

(c) The *visual display unit* This displays input or output items, as letters and numbers etc or in graphical or 'picture' form. It may display in colour, or 'black and white', and, like a television set, has 'contrast' and 'brightness' controls. The screen is usually adjustable in all directions ie. tilt, swivel etc. so that it can be placed where the user can see it without eye or neck strain.

Portable computers and laptops

3.8 As you will have gathered, miniaturisation is the key technological development governing usage. Some computers are now portable. Three categories of portable computer have developed:

(a) small PCs without batteries which are simply carried from location to location (sometimes referred to as lunchboxes);

(b) 'laptop' machines, which can be used on the plane, train etc; and

(c) 'handhelds', or pocket computers.

3.9 The largest group at present is the laptop category. A laptop normally:

(a) is powered with a rechargeable battery;
(b) uses $3\frac{1}{2}$" floppy disks for storage;
(c) uses liquid crystal (or gas plasma) screen display;
(d) is about the size of a telephone directory;
(e) is compatible with desktop machines running the same program (eg spreadsheets);

(f)   is often fitted with a modem (see later chapter) so that it can be connected to the telephone network.

For people using computers away from their office (eg sales people), laptops are a tool to help market their wares.

| Portable | Notebook | Palmtop |

3.10   Computers based on microprocessors are a central feature of many of the major developments in information technology and the electronic office.

(a)   Microcomputers have brought computing into the 'local' office environment;

(b)   Word processing systems, now very common, are based on microcomputers;

(c)   Local area networks and other distributed data processing systems rely on microcomputers;

(d)   The 'mass' production of standard software packages has made software cheaper and therefore more available to users. The widespread use of microcomputers is an essential prerequisite for mass-produced software packages.

Thanks to the miniaturisation of processing power, it is likely that the old distinction between mainframes, minis and micros will erode. IBM, which dominated the mainframe market, reported in 1989 that its revenues from micros exceed its revenues from mainframes.

'Mainframe sales are being hurt furthermore by the emergence of small inexpensive computers able to take on tasks normally run on mainframes' (*Financial Times*, 16 November 1989).

Computers for different uses

3.11   So far, we have examined the different kinds of computer in isolation, as if a an organisation were considering the purchase of either a mainframe system or a mini system or a micro system. In practice, however, many organisations will have a variety of computer systems.

3.12   For example, an organisation may maintain a large *mainframe* system to drive the processing of the many transactions that occur every day. On the other hand some employees may use a microcomputer (eg for spreadsheet modelling). If a bank employs sales representatives to market pensions in the clients' homes, then personnel may use a *laptop* computer. If you recall, Chapter 1 described an Executive Information System - the executive will use the processing power of a micro, but will obtain the data from the organisation's database which might be held on a mainframe.

3.13 Many small computer users will find as time progresses that they need more powerful computing facilities to carry out more and more processing. There are three ways to upgrade a computer system:

(a) buy a computer that is initially too large for the user's requirements and so provide capacity for expansion;

(b) buy equipment that can be upgraded on site - ie by adding more peripherals, or adding modular units to the CPU, (extension cards etc);

(c) purchase a new machine similar to the first when processing demand reaches the stage that more computing power is needed. This option exists because of the low costs of micro hardware and has the advantage of providing a back-up facility in the case of a breakdown. This is a route that many users will take, especially with the development of local area networks (LANs) which allow users to plug in extra machines in different offices to an existing system.

4. THE CHOICE OF INPUT

Stages of input

4.1 In previous chapters, it was noted that any computer system, whether it be a large mainframe application or a simple microcomputer, processes data in the same basic stages. There are several steps in the input process.

4.2 *Data origination*. Data items for processing might be originated in a number of ways. For example, a customer of a bank may wish to pay for a meal, and to do so writes out a cheque. The act of paying for the meal is the transaction that gives rise to data which must be recorded in the customer's and the restaurant's bank accounts.

4.3 *Transcription*. The CPU, you will recall, is basically a complex collection of electronic circuits which can be ON or OFF. Data to be processed must be converted to this form. In short, data must be *machine-sensible*, otherwise it cannot be processed.

For example, if you receive a purchase invoice and you want to ensure that this expense is recorded on your computer system, you cannot simply stuff the paper into the machine.

Data has to be *transcribed* into machine-sensible form. In this case, you might simply type in the details into your computer. The transcription occurs by the fact that the letters and numbers you type in at the keyboard correspond to a sequence of electronic pulses directed to the circuitry of the machine.

4.4 *Data capture*. In many cases, transcription is avoided, by a process of *data capture*, where data is recorded in such a way as to be directly convertible into a machine-sensible form without any human intervention. In many situations, data capture or transcription occur far away from the main computer, and data has to be *transmitted* to where it is to be processed.

4.5 *Input*. Data is transferred to the computer's memory for processing.

3: REVISION CHAPTER: COMPUTER HARDWARE AND THE OPERATING SYSTEM

The factors to consider in choosing a method of data capture and input

4.6 Data collection can be:

(a) *time-consuming*, especially when a large volume of data must be input for processing;

(b) *costly* because of the labour time needed to collect, transmit, prepare and input the data and also because of the costs of the equipment and data documents and files needed to do the work;

(c) *error prone*, especially where the collection of data is done largely by manual methods;

(d) *inconvenient*, especially when data has to be despatched, perhaps by security van, to a distant computer centre where it will be processed by a mainframe computer, and then returned with the output information, also perhaps sent by security van.

4.7 There is a wide range of input methods, each one having its own advantages and disadvantages. From the descriptions given in this chapter you should be able to formulate your own ideas on the advantages and disadvantages of each method and you may be required in your examination to select the most suitable data input method in a particular situation. Factors you should consider, however, are:

(a) *suitability for the application.*

(b) the *timing requirements* of the system (response times required);

(c) the *volume of data.*

(d) the *accuracy* required.

(e) the *cost* of the method chosen as compared with the benefits to be derived, including building (room) cost, machinery cost, operator cost, media cost;

(f) the possibility of using *turnround* documents for data capture and the benefit of OCR methods.'

5. DIRECT DATA ENTRY WITH VDU AND KEYBOARD

5.1 Direct data entry methods have been developed so that input can be fed directly into a computer using a keyboard. As input is at normal typing speed their use is normally restricted to low volume applications, file enquiry, and update in real-time systems (which are described in a later Chapter) and the control of computer operations. These input devices double up as computer output devices as well. The principal direct entry terminals with a keyboard are:

(a) keyboards with a limited visual display facility;
(b) VDUs with keyboard.

5.2 *Keyboard terminals with limited screen display.* These simple terminals will have a small single or multiple line screen. They are used for data collection and input and are particularly useful in stock control (eg a terminal in the stockroom), and work in progress control etc in industrial organisations.

5.3   VDU and keyboard can be used as media for direct data entry as:

(a) terminals connected to a mainframe or minicomputer;
(b) an integral part of a microcomputer installation.

Keyboard layout and functions

5.4   You may be familiar with the basic QWERTY typewriter keyboard. A typical computer keyboard is a development of the QWERTY design. A basic keyboard includes the following.

(a) *Ordinary typing keys* used to enter data or text.
(b) A *numeric key pad* for use with the built-in calculator.
(c) *Cursor control keys*, which may be incorporated into the numeric section.
(d) A number of *function keys* for use with the system and application software.

5.5   In addition to the function keys, there are special keys that must be used to communicate with the operating programs, to let the computer know that you wish to enter or have finished entering a command, correct a command etc. Nothing appears at the cursor point when these keys are used, but they *affect* operations on screen.

(a) *Return or Enter key*. All commands direct to the system must be 'entered' with this key - to let the machine know that you have finished typing your command and wish it to be executed.

(b) *Escape key*. This key can be used when, for example, you wish to exit from a procedure, although it can be used like a command. In a menu-based system it might refer you to a previous menu in the hierarchy.

(c) *Control key*. This tells the machine that a control is about to be entered, in systems which use codes to issue instructions.

(d) There may be another special key or combination which can be used as a command to reach an alternative keyboard: there is no room on the QWERTY for characters such as accents, foreign alphabets, mathematical and scientific signs etc. so an invisible keyboard can be programmed to contain eg:

$\mu \; \theta \; \delta \; \eta \; \alpha \; \beta \; \gamma \; \chi \; \Sigma \; \sigma \; \propto \; \dot{\iota} \; @ \; \varsigma$ etc.

The VDU screen

5.6   A VDU screen (or *monitor*) displays text and graphics. Monitors are either cathode ray tubes, liquid crystal displays or gas plasma display.

(a) The screen's *resolution* depends on the number of pixels. A pixel is a pictorial element - a 'dot' on the screen, as it were. The fewer the pixels on screen, the larger they will be: the resolution of any picture will be low. More and smaller pixels enable detailed high-resolution display. High resolution monitors currently available include 1024 (horizontal) x 768 (vertical). Currently, many PCs have a resolution of 640 x 480. (This is the resolution offered by IBM's VGA standard). Higher resolution requires more processing power. 'Graphics only became truly viable with the introduction of fast processor chips like the Intel 80386'.   (*Which Computer?* November 1989)

(b) The user must 'pan' up, down or sideways to view a different piece of text.

(c) A *wrap-around* facility enables it to display a line of text that is too long to be displayed on the screen as one line in its entirety. *Scrolling* occurs when the screen is full of text: the computer moves each line of text up one line, thus removing the first line from view, so that text input can continue on the bottom line.

The advantages of direct keyboard input

5.7 By far the most significant advantage of direct input via keyboard is that a computer user can have *interactive processing* using a keyboard and VDU. Interactive processing is when data can be input to a computer, output information received quickly, and where appropriate further input keyed in and output received. The computer user gets the information he or she wants 'instantly'. This is described in another chapter.

5.8 The other advantages of keyboard input are that:

(a) the person keying in the data can be in a location far away from the computer itself, with the keyboard terminal linked to the computer by telephone link or private wire. The source document never has to leave the computer user's office and so the data is always under the user's own control;

(b) the person keying in the data can check it on the VDU screen before inputting it to the computer. Any keying errors, or even errors in the data itself, might be identified and corrected on the spot.

(c) keyboard input is convenient for *small volumes of data* when the time taken up by data input is only short. Most microcomputer systems in offices use keyboard and VDU for data input.

The disadvantages of direct keyboard input

5.9 (a) It is unsuitable for large volumes of transaction data. Keying in takes a long time (in computer terms), and when a keyboard terminal is on-line to a computer, the CPU is idle for much of the time. Input via tape or disk makes much better use of the computer's processing capabilities, and processing is much faster as a result.

(b) Keyboard input is likely to be error-prone because the only data verification that can be done is a visual check of the data on the VDU screen before input.

(c) There might be security problems. Keyboard terminals are less 'secure' than a computer centre, and there is a possibility that unauthorised users can gain access to a keyboard terminal in an office (or that unauthorised people can gain access from their own personal terminal to someone else's computer). Security measures which try to deal with this problem are described in a later chapter.

6.   ENCODING TO DISK OR TAPE

6.1   Encoding to disk or tape, like direct data entry, involving the use of keyboards. The difference is that here, processing is *not* interactive. Data is copied from source documents and be written on to a magnetic disk or a magnetic tape from a keyboard or terminal. This process is called *encoding*. Encoding can be done in either of two ways:

(a)   'on line' to a computer, so that the keyboard input is encoded on to a disk, a floppy disk, a magnetic tape (cartridge or reel) depending on the configuration, via the computer; or

(b)   'off line' using special key-to-disk encoding equipment.

In both cases, the data (probably transaction data) that is encoded on to the disk will be re-organised (eg sorted) before input to the 'main' processing progam(s).

6.2   Generally, key-to-disk encoding systems are multi-station systems comprising a number of keyboard/VDU terminals on-line to a small computer.

6.3   The procedure is as follows.

(a)   Data is keyed in, *validated* (to identify inconsistences or errors in *input data*) and formulated on the VDU screen (detected errors are indicated on the screen) and when accepted, written on to the magnetic disk.

(b)   *Verification* is carried out by another operator at any other key-station. Verification is the process of checking that data resulting from a transmission or copy operation is *identical to source data*.

(c)   Completed batches are grouped together to create the complete transaction file which is written from the working disks to another disk (or a magnetic tape).

(d)   This disk is *then* used as the input for the computer application program on the main computer.

6.4   Key-to-disk encoding is suitable for data input preparation in systems where large volumes of data are input for processing.

7.   DIRECT INPUT DEVICES

Document reading methods

7.1   Copying manually-prepared data into a computer-sensible form such as disk or tape is costly in manpower, time and accuracy. Document reading methods of data collection involve the use of a source document that both humans and computers can read. The data on the source document might be pre-printed, or added later by manual processing, but in either case the source document itself is fed in to the computer. Data transcription and verification become unnecessary. A document reader is an input device which reads marks or characters made in predetermined positions on special forms. The character/mark recognition methods described below are:

(a) magnetic ink character recognition (MICR);
(b) optical character recognition (OCR);
(c) mark sensing and optical mark reading (OMR);
(d) bar coding.

Magnetic ink character recognition (MICR)

7.2 MICR is 'the recognition by a machine that reads special formatted characters printed in magnetic ink'.   (CIMA *Computing Terminology*)

Using ink which contains a metallic powder, highly stylized characters (eg as on a cheque) are encoded on to documents by means of special typewriters. The document must be passed through a magnetic field before the characters can be detected by a suitable reading device.

7.3 The largest application of MICR is the banking system. Cheques are *pre-encoded* with the customer account number, branch code and cheque number and, after use, *post-encoded* with the amount of the cheque. The main advantage of MICR is its accuracy, but MICR documents are expensive to produce, and so MICR has only limited application in practice.

Optical character recognition (OCR)

7.4 The CIMA's Computing Terminology defines OCR as 'a method of input which involves a machine that is able to read characters by optical detection of the shape of those characters'.

7.5 Optical (or laser) scanners can read printed, typed (or even block hand written) documents at up to 300 pages per hour. They recognise the characters, convert them into machine code and record them on to the magnetic medium being used (or directly input the data to the CPU). Most machines still require particular typefaces, examples of which are OCR - A and OCR - B (ECMA 11).

7.6 The advantage of OCR over MICR is that the computer can read ordinary typed or printed text, provided that the quality of the input document is satisfactory. (Note: this is why banks cannot use OCR for cheques. Cheques would often be too crumpled for reading by OCR methods.)

Mark sensing and optical mark reading (OMR)

7.7 *Mark sensing* is generally used for numeric characters. Values are denoted by a pencilled (graphite) line or cross in an appropriate box, whose position represents a value, on the preprinted source document (or card). The card is then read by a device which senses the graphite mark in each box using an *electric current* and translates it into machine code.

7.8 *Optical mark reading* is similar, except that the reading device uses an artificial light source and the marks can be made with biro or ink as well as with pencil. An application in which both methods are used (particularly OMR) is the recording of gas and electricity meter readings by meter readers on to preprinted documents. Once the readings are made, the documents are input to the computer using an OMR reading system.

Bar coding

7.9 A bar code reader is 'a device reads documents which contain bar codes - these are groups of marks which, by their spacing and thickness, indicate specific codes or values. Such devices are now commonly seen as an input medium for point of sale systems in supermarkets - many products now carry bar coding on their labels.' (CIMA Computing Terminology)

7.10 When a customer buys bar coded items and takes them to the check-out to pay, the shop assistant will use a bar code reader which transmits the bar coded data to a central CPU in the store. The computer then provides the price of the item being purchased (from a price list on the Stock File) and this is output to the cashier's check-out point. The total cost of all the purchases is similarly calculated, and the customer sees what he or she must pay on a small display screen, and receives a printed receipt. At the same time, the data about the purchases that have been read into the computer from the bar codes can be used to update the Stock File and record the sales data for management information purposes.

7.11 Here is the bar code for a well known drinks product.

5 000136 998634

7.12 OCR and OMR methods of optical character recognition can make use of a *turnround document*. A turnround document is a document that is initially produced by computer. It is then used to collect more data and then re-input to the computer for processing. Examples of turnround documents are as follows.

(a) OCR. Similarly, credit card companies include a payment counterfoil with their computer-produced bill - eg Access and Visa - which will then be used for inputting payment data to a computer.

(b) OMR. Multiple choice examination papers. An examining body that stores multiple choice questions on a computer file can produce examination papers by computer. Candidates are then asked to tick the correct answer, and the position of the answer mark will be detectable by OMR reader, and so the examination paper can be marked by computer.

7.13 The advantages and disadvantages of document reading methods are summarised below.

(a) Document reading methods reduce human 'intrusion' into data capture and cut out the need to transcribe manually-prepared data on to a computer-sensible input medium. This saves time and money and also reduces errors because it cuts out all data preparation errors and also, in the case of pre-printed documents such as cheques, many data recording errors too.

(b) Direct input to the CPU is possible when equipment is on-line.

(c) It is relatively easy to train staff to use this equipment.

(d) The main drawback to turnround documents is their limited application. There are not many situations where an organisation can produce a document which can then be used for subsequent data input.

The telephone as an input device

7.14 Many computer systems are connected by the telecommunications network, outlined in a later chapter, but here we will consider the use of the telephone handset itself as an input device. This is most common in the banking sector.

7.15 *Telephone banking,* by which a customer deals with his or her bank not through a branch network but over the phone, has had a quite a long history. Most telephone enquiries to these systems are fairly routine (eg order a bank statement). Rather than employ staff to process these routines requests banks have tried to save money by automating this facility, by using the keypad on the telephone and a voice response unit.

7.16 The customer may use the keypad to issue simple coded instructions over the phone. The customer telephones the bank, and receives a prerecorded message which asks the customer to use the keypad to key in some sort of identification number. The prerecorded message is controlled by a *voice responder*. This accepts data punched in from a keypad, and is capable of arranging words and phrases from a small library into coherent messages (similar to the speaking clock).

Card reading devices

Magnetic stripe card

7.17 Magnetic stripe cards have been widely distributed over the past decade, so that almost every person with a bank or building society account can use one. The use of magnetic stripe cards in automated teller machines is considered further in the chapter on the electronic office.

(a) The standard magnetic stripe card is rectangular in shape, about 8.5cm by 5.4 cm in area, and about 1mm thick.mts

(b) One face of the card contains the name of the issuer, the payments system the card applies to (eg VISA), and often a hologram image (eg a bird on VISA cards) for security purposes. The customer's name, the card number and the card expiry date also appear (in embossed form, so that the details can be printed on to credit card payment slips).

(c) However, none of this surface information is strictly necessary for data input to a computer system. All the machine-sensible data is contained on the back, on a magnetic stripe, which is a thin strip of typical magnetic recording tape, about 1.2cm wide stuck to the back of the card.

(d) The magnetic card reader converts this information into directly computer-sensible form.

3: REVISION CHAPTER: COMPUTER HARDWARE AND THE OPERATING SYSTEM

Smart cards

7.18 Smart cards are similar to magnetic stripe cards in that information is held on a plastic card for the customer to use at will. However, the technology by which this is achieved is quite different. Smart cards are much more versatile than magnetic stripe cards. They are currently most widely used in France.

    (a) A smart card is a plastic card in which is embedded a microprocessor chip. The microprocessor has an electronically programmable read-only memory (EPROM).

    (b) The smart card can contains a great deal more information than a magnetic stripe card. Not only does it contain basic account details, but also a memory and a processing capability.

    (c) The smart card is used in a similar way to a magnetic stripe card for making payments.

    (d) One of the principal economic advantages of smart cards over magnetic stripe cards is that they are much harder to duplicate, and so are more secure. On the other hand, it is more expensive to produce.

Electronic point of sale (POS) devices

7.19 More and more large retail stores are introducing electronic point of sale devices which act both as *cash registers* and as terminals connected to a main computer. This enables the computer to produce useful management information such as sales details and analysis and stock control information very quickly. Many use bar coding, as described earlier, or direct keyboard entry.

A fully itemised, accurate and descriptive receipt can be produced for the customer, who will also feel the benefit of faster moving queues at the checkout. Management will obtain more information more quickly than was ever possible before, in particular:

    (a) immediate updating of stock levels;
    (b) identification of fast-moving items for reordering, hence avoidance of stock-outs;
    (c) sales information.

The provision of immediate sales information (eg which products sell quickly), perhaps analysed on a branch basis, permits great speed and flexibility in decision-making (certainly of a short-term nature), as consumer wishes can be responded to quickly.

7.20 The banks are currently introducing EFTPOS systems (Electronic Funds Transfer at the Point of Sale). These are systems for the electronic transfer of funds at the point of sale. Customers in shops and at petrol stations can use a plastic card (eg a credit card) to purchase goods or services, and using an EFTPOS terminal in the shop, the customer's credit card account or bank account will be debited automatically. EFTPOS systems combine Point of Sale systems, which many retail organisations now use, with electronic funds transfer. EFTPOS is considered further in the chapter on the electronic office.

Scanners

7.21 Scanners *could* be seen as a form of very advanced OCR in that they are a means of inputting documents to a computer system. A document is fed into the scanner which passes a light band along the page. The pattern is transferred to the computer. Some scanners *only* recognise sharp distinctions between black and white. Other scanners can detect shades of grey: the Apple scanner can distinguish several shades, and so scans pictures as well as text.

7.22 Some scanners are used simply for document image processing (DIP). Alternatively they might be used in desk top publishing (DTP) to input the image to the desk-top published document. An 80386-based or fast 80286-based machine with a hard disk is essential for scanning work. Scanning text and images uses up a great deal of processor capacity.

Exercise 1

Attempt a brief solution to the following question.

Consider the following two separate situations:

(a) A TV rental company has several thousand customers who are expected to make monthly payments of rent at branch offices of the company. Records of all the customers are kept on a Head Office computer and these records require monthly updating with data relating to customer payments.

(b) An engineering company manufactures a wide range of standard products in large volume. Products are made from a variety of components, each of which undergoes a series of manufacturing operations prior to final assembly. For input to computerised work-in-progress, stock control and operator bonus calculation systems, the company needs to capture data relating to the quantities of components passing through specified operations in the manufacturing departments.

Describe the method you would propose to capture data in each of the above systems.

Solution

(a) TV rental company:
A system of on-line remote terminals from branches to the head office computer would be too expensive and perhaps technically difficult (depending on the number of branches). A batch processing system would seem suitable.

Suggestion. Customers should have payment books, with tear-out coupons for each monthly payment. The coupon could be an OCR document, which is handed in to the branch when the monthly payment is made, batched and despatched to the head office computer centre. An OCR reader would read the payment data from these documents on to disk or tape.

(b) Engineering company:
A card and badge transmission system could be used. There would be a card for each job, acting as a job ticket. The plastic badge would identify the factory operative.

Transmitters should be located in different departments in the factory: operatives would insert their badge and the job card, and key in details such as whether he is starting or has finished work on the job. The data would then be transmitted to the computer department, where it would be either written (off-line) on to a tape, or else input directly to the CPU for immediate processing.

---

8. THE CHOICE OF OUTPUT

8.1 As with choosing an input medium, choosing a suitable output medium depends on a number of factors, which you should bear in mind when we go on to consider each type of output in turn. These factors are:

(a) bearing in mind that a VDU is an output device, is a *'hard' copy* of the output required; in other words, is a printed version of the output needed? If so, what quality must the output be?

   (i) if the output includes documents that are going to be used as OCR turnround documents, the quality of printing must be good;

   (ii) if the information will be used as a working document with a short life or limited use (eg a copy of text for type-checking) then a low quality output on a dot matrix printer might be sufficient;

(b) the *volume* of information produced. For example, a VDU screen can hold a certain amount of data, but it becomes more difficult to read when information goes 'off-screen' and can only be read a bit at a time;

(c) the *speed* at which output is required. For example, to print a large volume of data, a high speed printer might be most suitable to finish the work more quickly (and release the CPU for other jobs);

(d) the *suitability* of the output medium to the application - ie the purpose for which the output is needed;

   (i) a VDU is well-suited to interactive processing with a computer;

   (ii) a graph plotter would be well-suited to output in the form of graphs;

   (iii) output on to a magnetic disk or tape would be well-suited if the data is for further processing;

   (iv) large volumes of reference data for human users to hold in a library might be held on microfilm or microfiche, and so output in these forms would be appropriate;

(e) *cost:* some output devices would not be worth having because their advantages would not justify their cost, and so another output medium should be chosen as 'second best'.

9.   PRINTED OUTPUT

Impact printers

9.1   In a *daisy wheel printer*, fully formed print characters are positioned at the end of long stems, which protrude from a central wheel. This gives the impression of a daisy-like flower, with a solid round centre and petals sticking out all around it - hence the name of the printer. Daisy wheel printers have now been widely superseded by most other types of printer. They are slow and noisy although they provide a better quality of print than dot matrix printers.

9.2   A *dot matrix printer* has a head containing a series of steel pins or 'needles'. Characters are constructed by pressing a combination of these pins against the print ribbon, and so on paper each character appears as a matrix of small dots. It depends on which combination of pins is fired as to which character appears.

(a)   The dots can be placed anywhere on paper, and so it is possible to *produce graphics* as well as characters. Their main drawback is the low-resolution of their printed characters, which is unsuitable for many forms of printed output.

(b)   Most dot matrix printers can also be used to print better quality print (known as NLQ - *near letter quality*). This is still not up to daisy-wheel standard but it is acceptable for many users.

Non-impact printers

9.3   *Laser printers* print a whole page at a time, rather than line by line. Unlike daisywheel and dot matrix printers, they print on to individual sheets of paper (the same as photocopiers do) and so they do not use 'tractor fed' continuous computer stationery.

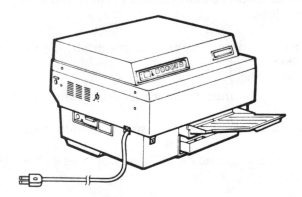

9.4   The resolution of printed characters and diagrams with laser printers is very high - up to 600 dots per inch - and this high-quality resolution makes laser printing output good enough to be used for professional printing. Typically, a desk-top laser printer will print about 8 or 10 A4 pages per minute, although faster speeds are possible.

9.5   Laser printers are a microprocessor in their own right, with RAM memory for storing data prior to printing. There are several distinct advantages of laser printers.

(a)   They can be used to combine different 'fonts' - eg italics, bold characters etc - and a wide range of characters, including mathematical symbols, Greek letters etc.

(b)   They can be used to produce graphics and logos as well as characters. A firm can therefore produce letter-heads as well as the letters themselves on to blank paper using a laser printer.

(c)   They are quiet, because unlike daisy wheel and dot matrix printers, laser printers are not 'impact' printers which rely on the striking of hammers or pins.

9.6   The cost of laser printers is higher than daisy wheel and dot matrix printers but, if local area networks develop sufficiently, it is quite possible that several terminals will opt to share a single laser printer.

9.7   There are two types of *thermal printer*.

(a)   Some work by heating thermally-sensitive paper with a printhead to form characters.

(b)   An alternative form of thermal printer, a thermal transfer printer, uses a special printing ribbon with heat-sensitive ink, which melts on to the paper when either the hot printhead touches it, or an electric current is run through the ribbon.

A type of thermal printer for *portable computers* has been manufactured by CANON, and it is called a *bubblejet* printer. The print head heats up the ink and deposits it on paper. The inkhead and cartridge are removed when the ink runs out.

9.8   Inkjet printers, as their name suggests, work by sending a jet of ink on to the paper to produce the required characters. They are quiet and fast, but they need special paper that can soak up the ink as quickly as it is squirted on to it, to avoid smudging and produce good quality copy.

10.   COMPUTER OUTPUT ON MICROFORM (COM)

10.1   COM is a form of computer output whereby instead of printing the output on to paper, it is projected on to a cathode ray tube and then photographed into a very much reduced form - ie into a microform. (Alternative methods of producing COM involve laser beam, electron beam or optical fibre technology.)

The microform is readable, but not to the unassisted naked eye, and a *magnifying reading device* (with a viewing screen) is needed by users. To assist the user in finding the records on the microform, 'eyeball' characters - ie letters or numbers visible to the eye without magnification - are created on the microform.

Microfilm is a continuous strip, with images formed in frames one at a time all along the strip of the film. *Microfiche* on the other hand, consist of separate sheets of film (at least three times wider than microfilm) each sheet containing over 100 frames or 'pages' of information.

When microform is produced by computer, it may be produced either on-line or off-line. When it is produced on-line there is a microform-producing peripheral device on-line to the CPU, whereas off-line production involves producing a magnetic tape (or disk) by the CPU and using the tape as input to an off-line microform-producer.

10.2 Both systems have the following advantages over printed output:

(a) large volumes of information can be condensed into a very small physical space so that savings in storage space can be considerable where printed matter would otherwise have to be kept for fairly long periods of time;

(b) microform therefore provides a suitable storage medium for *archive information* or *reference information;*

(c) microform frames or pages can be reproduced on paper in an enlarged, readable form, if required.

Exercise 2

The *quality* of output is an aspect of computer systems which should not be overlooked whenever a new system is bought or developed. Good quality output is desirable for both screen display and printed hard copy. Attempt a brief solution to the following problem.

'The quality of screen display or printed output produced by a system will largely determine the acceptability of the system from a user's point of view.'

Explain, with examples, what constitutes good display or output for each of the following in a sales order processing/stock control/customer invoicing system.

(a) A data entry clerk dealing with enquiries and transaction entry via a VDU terminal.

(b) An accounts supervisor receiving printed information to monitor customer payment performance.

(c) A customer in receipt of invoices and statements.

Solution

(a) User-friendly screen displays.

   (i) For enquiries, 'pull-down' menus for the keyboard operator to read and follow, or prompts (ie instruction and response in an interactive dialogue). Clear presentation of records on screen in response to enquiries.

   (ii) For transaction input. Pull down menus and formatted screens.

(b) Carefully formatted reports which avoid excessive detail, and highlight exceptional situations which warrant further investigation.

   If tabulated data is needed, clear table headings and column headings, sub-totals where appropriate, and column/row totals.

(c) Pre-printed stationery. Letter-quality printing. Possibly an OCR turn-round document. This output leaves the organisation and goes out to customers, and so there is the company 'PR' or image to consider.

---

11. THE CHOICE OF BACKING STORAGE

11.1 You may like to consider *where* storage media are most appropriate. A rule of thumb, which indicates some initial matters to consider it outlined below.

(a) Magnetic disks offer:

    (i) fast access times in addition to serial, sequential access;
    (ii) direct access to data;
    (iii) suitability for multi-user environments.

Magnetic disk storage is therefore the predominant storage medium in most commercial applications currently. Direct access is essential for many commercial applications (eg databases) and in addition speed is necessary for real-time applications.

(b) Magnetic tapes offer:

    (i) cheap data storage;
    (ii) portability;
    (iii) serial or sequential access only.

As other file storage media have fallen in price, and as applications requiring direct access are used frequently, magnetic tape (in reel or cassette from, for micros) is most valuable as a backup medium, on to which the contents of a disk file can be dumped at the end of every day, or period of processing.

(c) Optical disks offer:

    (i) capacity to store vast amounts of data;
    (ii) slower access speeds than magnetic disks;
    (iii) direct access, or emulation thereof, in some technologies.

They are most suitable for backup archiving, or keeping old copies of files which might need to be retrieved. However, the technology behind optical drives is still in development, and it may not be too long before they are a viable alternative to magnetic disk drives for most application.

11.2 The problems of using magnetic storage devices will be covered fully in the chapter on security and controls but it is useful to list the main considerations here:

(a) physical security;

(b) how to avoid processing the wrong file;

(c) how to prevent or correct corruptions of the file due to hardware or program faults;

(d) keeping the files in a safe environment. If brought close to a magnetic field, data on a file will be totally corrupted. Files are also susceptible to humidity and dust, and must therefore be kept in safe, controlled surroundings;

(e) magnetic tapes need to be run at least once per year to preserve the data on them;

(f) the danger of losing data is so great that there should be multiple copies ('back-up files') of files containing valuable data.

12.   MAGNETIC DISK STORAGE

12.1 The most commonly used backing storage medium with computers is magnetic disk.

A magnetic disk consists of a flat circular disk, which is covered on both sides with a magnetic material. Data is held on a number of circular, concentric tracks on the surfaces of the disk and is read or written by rotating the disk past read/write heads, which can write data from the CPU's memory on to disk, or can read data from it for input to the CPU's memory. The mechanism that causes the disk to rotate is called a *disk drive*.

12.2 An *exchangeable disk pack* is a pack of hard magnetic disks. It is commonly used in larger computer systems.

Winchester disks

12.3 With the growth of minicomputer systems in recent years it became necessary to develop a hard magnetic disk storage medium which was less expensive than the six-disk exchangeable disk pack but still had substantial storage capacity and offered direct access. To enhance the appeal of minicomputer and microcomputer systems, and to provide storage facilities in addition to the generally-used flexible disks (or relatively low capacity), smaller *hard disks* (often called Winchester disks) have been developed.

12.4 Hard disks with a microcomputer might be:

(a)   *external*. These sit alongside the computer in an extra 'box' with its own power supply;
(b)   *internal*. These are incorporated inside the microcomputer itself. Internal hard disks tend to have less storage space than external disks.

Floppy disks

12.5 Although microcomputers will often have a hard disk drive, they will also have one or two floppy disk drives too. The *floppy disk* provides a cost-effective means of on-line storage for small business computer systems. Floppy disks are used in the smallest microcomputer systems as well as with minicomputers, and are particularly useful in providing a means of decentralised processing.

12.6 A floppy disk is an exchangeable circular, flexible disk (typically $5\frac{1}{4}$ inches or $3\frac{1}{2}$ inches in diameter) which is held permanently in a square paper sleeve. The sleeve cover contains an identification label for recognising the disk and its contents. The sleeve has openings for moveable combined read/write heads to enter, for the drive spindle, and for index/sector hole sensing. The disk is inserted into the disk unit in its sleeve. Access times are slower than with 'hard disks'.

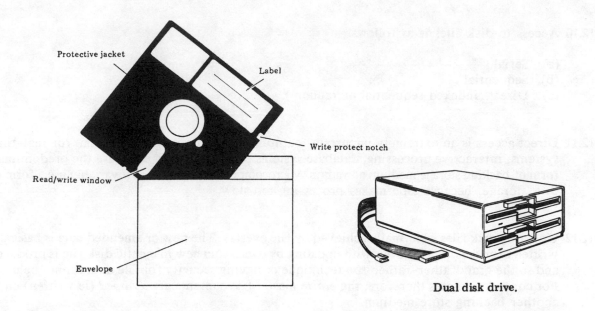

Dual disk drive.

12.7 Floppy disks do not require special storage conditions, and indeed, they are often stored/filed in open trays. However, data on them can be easily corrupted. In particular, they are subject to physical wear, because the read/write head actually comes into contact with the disk surface during operation. This is not the case with other types of disk. Because they can be left lying around an office, they are also prone to physical damage, such as having cups of tea spilled over them. As the disks tend to be less reliable than hard disks administrative procedures should be instituted to protect them (eg using steel filing cabinets, careful handling etc).

Floppy disks and hard disks: summary

12.8 The price of hard disks has fallen dramatically since the mid 1980s, and the price differential between microcomputer systems with twin floppy disk drives and systems with a hard disk has now almost disappeared.

Compared to floppy disk drives and floppy disks, hard disk has the advantages of:

(a) more storage. A 100 Mbyte hard disk holds as much data as 55 standard IBM floppy disks;
(b) quicker data access, thus reducing waiting time for the user;
(c) greater mechanical reliability. Floppy disk drives are more prone to breakdown.

File organisation and access with magnetic disks

12.9 The record organisation on a disk may be one of the following.

(a) Unordered.
(b) Sequential.
(c) Random.

71

12.10 Access to disk files is as follows.

    (a) Serial
    (b) Sequential.
    (c) Direct (indexed sequential or random).

12.11 Direct access is an extremely important feature of disk storage. It is essential for real-time systems, interactive processing, database systems etc. This is why disks are the predominant form of backing storage medium nowadays. Microcomputers in the office invariably use a form of disk storage, because tape makes processing too slow.

12.12 Updating disk files is normally achieved by file overlay. The new or amended data is basically written over the old. However, with updating by overlay no new magnetic disk file is produced and so the grandfather-father-son technique of having security for file data cannot be used. For control purposes therefore, the entire master file contents are *dumped* (ie written) on to another backing store medium.

13.   MAGNETIC TAPE STORAGE

13.1 Magnetic tape consists of a strip of plastic tape coated with a magnetic material deposited in grains, each of which may be magnetised in one of two possible directions. To each of the directions, the significance 0 or 1 is attached which means that data can be written, stored, and read on to tape. As with domestic audio tape, a recording can be erased and the tape used for a completely different purpose.

Magnetic tape cartridge and cassette

13.2 The development of microcomputer systems has led to the use of magnetic tape in cartridge form as a backing storage medium.

They are similar to but larger in size than a normal audio cassette (being $\frac{1}{4}$" wide) and are 300-600 feet long. They have a capacity of up to 60 Megabytes, depending on size and format. Cartridges are being used increasingly in 'streaming mode' to provide a back-up file copy for data held on Winchester disks.

Fast tapes which can be used to create a back-up file very quickly are known as *tape streamers*.

File organisation, file access and processing with magnetic tape

13.3 An important feature of magnetic tapes is that:

    (a) file organisation *must be* either serial or sequential;
    (b) file access *must be* serial or sequential.

It is impossible to have direct access with magnetic tape, and so indexed sequential file organisation or random organisation are similarly impossible.

13.4 Since magnetic tape must be accessed serially or sequentially, it follows that magnetic tape as a file storage medium is only usable in certain circumstances:

    (a) for a transaction file, when every record on the file will be processed in turn;

    (b) for a master file, when the 'hit rate' is high enough to make sequential processing efficient, ie quicker than direct processing. The tape master file must be organised sequentially.

13.5 Another important feature of magnetic tapes is that the same physical tape cannot be used to input data and receive output data in the same process.

Magnetic tape security

13.6 Magnetic tapes can get lost, or the data on them can 'get corrupted'. Any computer system should provide for the security of its master file data, to prevent a disastrous loss of a complete file. With magnetic tapes, the method of updating a magnetic tape master file by producing a new carried forward tape provides a means of data security. The brought forward tape and the relevant transaction tape can be kept for two or three generations to safeguard against the loss of data on a current file.

The *grandfather-father-son* technique allows for files to be reconstructed if a disaster should occur. Once the stipulated number of generations has passed, the former 'grandfather' tape can be purged and used again for other processing.

14. OPTICAL AND OTHER STORAGE MEDIA

Optical storage

14.1 Optical technologies are slowly being introduced into computer systems. Optical disks are now being used for data storage, in three possible ways:

    (a) as backup;

    (b) as a general purpose hard disk;

    (c) as a medium for document storage and retrieval (eg in a *document image processing* system), as described elsewhere in this text.

14.2 Optical technology is similar in principle to the Compact Disk used for audio recording. There are three basic types of optical disk: CD-ROM, WORM and magneto-optical.

14.3 *CD-ROM* was first introduced in the mid-1980s. It is a read-only technology. This means that all data is implanted into it at manufacture, in the same way as music is recorded on to a compact disk. Effectively, a CD is produced from a master copy, by a process of injection moulding (like casting a bronze statue). Users can only retrieve information. They cannot write their own. It is used primarily as a medium for *publishing* large amounts of data.

14.4 *WORM (Write once read many times)* devices are more advanced than CD-ROM to the extent that users can write to them what data they require. However this data can never be erased. Most WORM devices are written in *sequence*, although manufacturers have gone to great lengths to make them emulate (imitate) random-access devices. Rather than arrange data in concentric tracks, data on many WORM devices is written into one long continuous *spiral*. Access is therefore sequential. However, as their storage is so vast, many manufacturers try to ensure that they emulate random access as far as possible.

14.5   It is not possible to erase data on a WORM device. Instead, if it is used to contain variable data, one or more versions of the file may be kept on the disk. Some manufacturers make a virtue out of this necessity by advertising a *history facility* (ie the ability to look up old versions of the file) on disk. WORM devices are ideal for archiving very large amounts of data (eg where permanent records are required by legal or taxation authorities).

14.6   *Magneto-optical disks* are *erasable*. These comprise a magnetised recording medium sandwiched between two plastic disks. The contents of the disk can be altered magnetically *at high temperatures*. The area to be altered is heated by a *laser*, and then its magnetic charge is reversed, a state in which it remains when cooled down.

Bits are therefore represented by changed magnetic orientations (positive or negative) in the disk.

14.7   The main advantage currently enjoyed by optical disks over other storage media is that very large volumes of data can be stored in one space. One writer has indicated that, in terms of volume, it costs about 100 times less per megabyte than magnetic disk storage. However, before purchase, an organisation has to make sure that its data storage requirements are sufficiently vast to warrant it.

Other storage media

14.8   The backing storage media dealt with above are the principal ones used in modern computer systems. Examples of other backing storage media are:

(a)   *Magnetic drums* are another form of direct access device. They are now 'old-fashioned' but are sometimes used for files in a system where *extremely fast* access times are required, with low volumes of data.

(b)   *Magnetic cards* which have a slower access time than disks, but this is off-set by their very large capacity. A typical unit consists of a magazine holding a number of cards, a transport mechanism and a read/write station. Most modern systems do not use magnetic cards for backing storage and they are now virtually obsolete.

Backing stores for very small computers

14.9   (a)   *Silicon (RAM) disk.* This is a silicon chip which acts as a disk. Some portable/laptop computers use a memory-board mounted with a number of RAM chips which 'plug in' to the computer.

This is *volatile* memory and must be sustained by a small built-in battery.

(b)   *U/V EPROM*, developed for the PSION organiser, is non-volatile memory which can be erased by sustained exposure to ultraviolet light. Flash EPROM, a very recent development by INTEL, erases data with an electrical charge.

There are responses to the problem of miniaturisation. The *technological* distinction between *immediate access store* and *backing store* is eroding.

'What is needed is a source of non-volatile memory that you can write to on the fly an infinite number of times, that is physically small, and that offers very high capacity. Needless to say it has to be inexpensive.' *(Which Computer*, February 1990).

15. OPERATING SYSTEMS SOFTWARE AND UTILITIES

15.1 An operating system is like a 'silent partner' for the computer user, providing the interface between the computer hardware and both the user (via keyboard) and the other software. An operating system or operating software can be defined as 'a program or set of programs which provide the 'bridge' between applications software and the hardware. For example, access to data files held on disk during the process of a business application would be managed by the operating system. Operating systems normally include a number of utility programs in addition to the control software. Operating software is sometimes referred to as Systems Software' (CIMA: *Computing Terminology*).

15.2 There has been little standardisation amongst mainframe and mini computers with manufacturers producing operating systems software machine-specific their own hardware eg IBM-OS/VS; ICL - VME; Honeywell - GECOS etc) and it is not possible within this text to discuss particular systems in detail.

15.3 With microcomputers the situation is quite different. Operating software is not machine-specific as manufacturers can build computers which run on an operating system used on another machine.

MS-DOS (Microsoft-Disk Operating System), or variants of it is widely used for 16-bit microcomputers that are clones of the IBM-PC. As it was used for stand-alone computers, there have been some worries that it was not suitable for multitasking (see below) or networking. (The running of networks requires software to control the interaction between the various machines).

15.4 An OS will typically perform the following tasks.

(a) Initial set-up of the computer, when it is switched on. This is achieved by the boot (or *bootstrap)* program, which is normally resident in ROM. It summons the rest of the OS from backing storage into RAM.

(b) Checking that the hardware (including peripheral devices) is functioning properly.

(c) Calling up of program files and data files from external storage into memory.

(d) Opening and closing of files, checking of file labels etc.

(e) Assigning program and data files from memory to peripheral devices.

(f) Maintenance of directories in external storage.

(g) Controlling input and output devices, including the interaction with the computer operator or user. Operating systems are said to manage the *user interface*.

(h) Controlling system security (eg monitoring the use of passwords).

(i)   Handling of interrupts (program abnormalities, machine failure etc).

(j)   Checkpoint procedures. If there is some catastrophe, the entire contents of memory can be dumped to a storage device and printed for investigation. Sometimes checkpoint programs will be implemented dumping memory contents on to a disk as a matter of routine, so that if processing is interrupted, it can be continued from the checkpoint.

(k)   Managing multitasking and multiprogramming (see below).

(l)   Many operating systems software contain *utility* programs, which can be accessed by the user through interaction with the operating system. These are described below.

Utilities

15.5   A utility program is defined in the CIMA's *Computing Terminology* as 'a program which performs a function that may be required by a number of other programs or in a number of circumstances, eg a sort utility or a file copy utility.'

Whilst strictly speaking a utility is not part of the OS, utility programs are provided with OS software. MS-DOS, for example, includes a number of utilities. A utility does not deal with the specific *contents* of a file, but rather operates on files as whole units.

15.6   Examples of utilities include the following.

(a)   File conversion (ie transferring data or program files from one output or storage medium to another).

(b)   File copying (ie producing a backup file or files eg MS-DOS allows you to copy files from hard disk to floppy disk eg COPY).

(c)   Memory dumping, as part of a checkpoint program, mentioned above.

(d)   copying whole disks (DISKCOPY in MS-DOS).

(e)   Making directories (MKDIR in MS-DOS).

(f)   Listing file or directors (eg the MS-DOS command DIR A:\ means list all file son the disk in drive A).

(g)   Comparison of the contents of two disks, if one has been copied from another.

(h)   Deletion of files (DEL {file name} in MS-DOS).

(i)   Sending files to a printer, or output device.

(j)   Renaming a file (REN {file name} in MS-DOS).

(k)   Sorting data by key-field sequence in some cases.

16. CONCLUSION

16.1 This chapter has briefly described some of the principal elements of a computer configuration.

16.2 You may be asked to select the hardware and operating system for a particular computer configuration in the exam.

TEST YOUR KNOWLEDGE
The numbers in brackets refer to paragraphs of this chapter

1   What is meant by ROM and RAM? (2.9)

2   Why might a business want a mainframe (rather than a smaller) computer? (3.3)

3   Explain the following terms.

    (a)   Data capture (4.4)
    (b)   Encoding (6.1)
    (c)   Document reader (7.1)
    (d)   Resolution (5.6)
    (e)   Smart card (7.18)
    (f)   Laser printer (9.5)

4   What is a floppy disk? (12.5)

5   What is a WORM device? (14.4)

6   What is a RAM disk? (14.9)

7   List the tasks typically performed by the operating system. (15.4)

Now try question 5 at the end of the text

Chapter 4

DISTRIBUTED PROCESSING AND NETWORKS

┌───┐

This chapter covers the following topics.

1.   Centralisation or decentralisation
2.   Data transmission
3.   ISDN
4.   Protocols
5.   Computer-to-computer links
6.   Stand-alone computers
7.   Multi-user systems
8.   Distributed processing and networks
9.   Selecting the right configuration

└───┘

1.   CENTRALISATION OR DECENTRALISATION

1.1   An important design issue is whether the information processing system ought to be centralised or decentralised.

1.2   *Centralised processing* means having the data/information processing done in a central place, such as a computer centre at head office.

Data will be collected at 'remote' offices and other locations and sent in to the central location, by post, by courier or by telecommunications link (eg links from remote terminals to the central computer).

At the central location there will be:

(a)   a central computer, possibly a large mainframe computer;
(b)   central files, containing all the master files and reference files for the system.

Processing could be in either batch processing mode or on-line.

1.3   *Decentralised processing* means having the data/information processing carried out at several different locations, away from the 'centre' or 'head office'. Each region, department or office will have its own processing systems, and so:

(a)   there will be several different and unconnected computers in the various offices;

(b) each computer will operate with its own programs and its own master files and reference files.

Sometimes this is referred to as *distributed processing*.

1.4 Centralised and decentralised processing are two extreme forms of processing system, but it is useful to contrast their main advantages and disadvantages.

	Centralised processing	*Decentralised processing*
Advantages		
	1 One set of files. Everyone uses the same data and information	1 Each office can introduce an information system specially designed for its individual needs.
	2 Better security/control over data and files	2 If data originates locally it might make sense to process it locally too.
	3 Head office in a better position to know what's going on.	3 Each office has control over its own files and data.
	4 An organisation might be able to afford a central computer which is very large, with extensive processing capabilities that smaller 'local' computers couldn't carry out.	4 Like to be easy/quick access to information when it is needed.
		5 Any breakdowns in the system are restricted to just one part of the system.

	Centralised processing	*Decentralised processing*
Disadvantages		
	1 Local offices might have to wait for data to be processed centrally, especially if processing is done by batches.	1 Many different and unco-ordinated information systems will be introduced.
	2 Reliance on head office. Local offices have to rely on the central processing unit to provide the information they need.	2 Decentralisation encourages lack of co-ordination between departments.
		3 One office might be unable to obtain information from the information system of another office.
	3 If the central computer breaks down, or the software develops a fault, the entire system goes out of operation.	4 There might be a duplication of data, with different offices holding the same data on their own separate files.

1.5 Thankfully, information systems don't have to be entirely centralised or entirely decentralised, and a suitable mixture of centralisation and decentralisation can be used.

4: DISTRIBUTED PROCESSING AND NETWORKS

> (a) Local offices can have their own local systems, perhaps on microcomputer, and also input some data to a centralised processing system.
>
> (b) Computer systems can be networked, and there might be:
>
> > (i) a multi-user system;
> > (ii) a distributed data processing system in a local area network (LAN) or wide area network (WAN).

2. DATA TRANSMISSION

2.1 Data transmission is 'is the process of using a data link' (British Computer Society).

When all data processing is done in the same office, no serious problem should arise with the transmission of data between input and output devices and the CPU. The equipment will be joined together by internal cable.

2.2 A data transmission link might link up:

> (a) a computer and a remote terminal (keyboard and VDU). A computer may have a number of remote terminals linked to it by data transmission equipment;
>
> (b) two computers located some distance from each other (eg. a mainframe and a microcomputer, which would use the link to exchange data);
>
> (c) several processors in a network, with each computer in the network able to transmit data to any other.

Who provides the telecommunications link?

2.3 In the UK, British Telecom and Mercury provide services for the transmission of data (although no longer the supply of some of the equipment used) and can supply public or private lines *for direct data links*.

> (a) *Public lines* use the ordinary telephone network and the cost is dependent upon the service used and the time the telephone link is maintained (as for any ordinary telephone call).
>
> (b) *Private lines* (or leased lines) also use the telephone network but a special line is provided at a fixed charge per annum.

2.4 The amount of data that can be sent down a telecommunications line is in part determined by the bandwidth. *Bandwidth* is the range of frequencies that the channel can carry. Frequencies are measured in cycles per second, or in Hertz:

> (a) narrow band (up to 300 Hertz);
> (b) voice band (300-3,000 Hertz);
> (c) broad band (over 3,000 Hertz).

The wider the bandwidth, the greater the number of messages that a channel can carry at any particular time. Broad bandwidth enables messages to be transmitted simultaneously.

Bit serial and bit parallel transmission

2.5   Data transmission can be either *bit serial transmission* or *bit parallel transmission*. In bit serial transmission, each bit making up a character is sent one after the other down the line. In a bit parallel transmission, eight lines are required as each bit in a byte is transmitted at the same time over its own channel. Bit serial transmission is the most common method. The number of bits transmitted per second is referred to as *baud rate*.

Data switching

2.6   When the computer user has a number of computers (and terminals) which will transmit data to each other in an irregular and unpredictable way, it would be too expensive to rent dedicated private lines for direct data links. Instead, a data switching arrangement is used. A *switch* is a device for opening, closing or directing an electric circuit. A telecommunications link is a circuit like any other: when you are speaking to someone over the telephone a circuit exists between the two devices. In the telephone network, switches connect one set of lines to another.

2.7   *Circuit switching* occurs when the connection is maintained until broken at one end. If data is sent simply by circuit switching, the line between the sender and the recipient must be open for the duration of the message. As much data transmission is irregular, this is a wasteful use of the telephone line. Gaps in transmission of your message, when the line is idle, could be used by somebody else. Similarly, you may wish to transmit your data at a time when there is nobody on the other end of the line to receive it. *Message switching* requires no direct physical connection between sender and receiver before communication can take place, as the message is stored on a central computer or switching station before being forwarded to another switching station and ultimately to its destination. A message can be sent even though the destination is not able at that time to receive it. (It is also known as the *store-and-forward* technique).

2.8   Finally, data can be sent over a *packet switching* system. The PSN (UK Public Packet Switched Network) is run by British Telecom.

   (a)   A data message is *divided* up into packets of data of a fixed length, usually 128 bytes, and transmitted through the network in these separate packets. Each packet contains control data, which identifies the sender of the message and the address of the recipient. The first packet opens a route (or *virtual circuit*) from source to destination, which the others will follow.

   (b)   The PSN is a network of processors. Each processor receives packets of data from another processor in the network, and redirects them to the next processor along the chain to the eventual recipient.

   (c)   At the 'local' end of the PSN link (ie. the end near the recipient of the message) the packets of data are reassembled into their full message, which is transmitted to the recipient. If terminals are asynchronous, they will be connected to the packet switching network by a packet assembler/disassembler (PAD).

   For example, say source A sends a message to destination B, and source Y sends a message to destination Z. Each message is split into two packets.

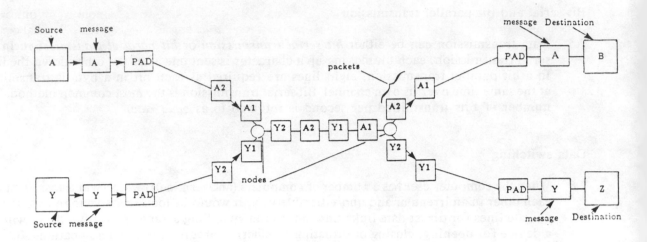

Simplex, duplex and half duplex transmission

2.9 There are three modes of transmission each of which will require different types of equipment (at increasing cost). These are:

(a) *simplex* - transmission in one direction only; eg. a computer can be used to send out messages to a terminal (eg. a remote printer or screen) but the terminal cannot send data back;

(b) *half duplex* - transmission in both directions but not simultaneously;

(c) *full duplex* - transmission in both directions simultaneously.

Synchronous and asynchronous data transmission

2.10 Data transmission can be asynchronous or synchronous.

(a) With *asynchronous transmission*, one character at a time is sent. Each character is preceded by a start bit and ended by a stop bit with the bits of the character coming in between. The receiving device at the end of the line recognises a start signal which activates a clock and then reads the bits that follow until it comes to the stop signal which turns the clock off. *Microcomputers* normally use asynchronous transmission (since its RS232C serial communications port is an asynchronous device). Asynchronous transmission is efficient and economical provided that very large quantities of data are not being transmitted.

(b) With *synchronous transmission*, data is transmitted between the sending and receiving machines at a constant rate, and so there is no need for start signals and stop signals between each character that is transmitted. The rate of transmission is controlled by a clock, which is usually the computer's internal clock. Synchronous transmission is less error-prone than asynchronous transmission. However, it needs more expensive equipment. Many *mainframes* normally use synchronous transmission, and can only communicate in the asynchronous mode by adding special items of equipment.

(c) One type of synchronous data transmission is BISYNC (binary synchronous communication) developed by IBM for communication between a mainframe and terminals. Special control characters are used to control the message. Synchronisation *characters* begin a message, followed by header, text and end of text characters.

Data transmission equipment

Modems and acoustic couplers

2.11 You will remember that computer equipment stores and uses data in discrete *digital* (or 'bit') form. Much of the telephone network, however, still handles data in *analog* or wave form. For data transmission in analog (or 'wave' form) through the telephone network to be possible, there has to be a device at each end of the telephone line that can convert (modulate) the data from digital form to wave form, and (demodulate) from wave form to digital form, depending on whether the data is being sent out or received along the telephone line. This converting of data is done by devices called modems. There must be a modem at both ends of the telephone line.

2.12 An acoustic coupler is a form of modem. It is used to link the user to the telephone network via his telephone handset (which fits into rubber cups in the coupler) to establish the communications link.

Multiplexors

2.13 In some computer systems, several terminals or local micros share the same data link. A multiplexor is used where it is necessary to send data from several sources down a single line at the same time. It codes the data in a special way so that it can be sorted out at its destination. Where a number of terminals are linked to the control computer, the multiplexor is an essential piece of hardware handling the input/output and reducing line charges (as only one line, rather than several, is necessary).

2.14 A multiplexor may be defined as a device that enables a computer to receive data or transmit data through a number of *channels* at the same time. It is a device that permits several independent signals to share a common signal path. One of the functions of a multiplexor is to stop the data from one source being mixed up with the data from another. The same task could be done by a 'front end processor' which would in effect be acting as a multiplexor. In *time division multiplexing*, a device is allocated specific time slots in which to use it. In *frequency division multiplexing*, the transmission medium is divided into a number of channels of smaller bandwidth.

Line concentrator

2.15 This is a device that enables several terminals to make efficient use of a common data communications link. It combines input lines whose total bandwidth (see paragraph 1.6) is greater than that of the output line. It might be used to handle data in blocks of packets.

4: DISTRIBUTED PROCESSING AND NETWORKS

3. ISDN

3.1 There have been a number of technological advances in data transmission technology. Both British Telecom and Mercury have announced *digital* telecommunications networks. BT's service is called *Integrated Systems Digital network (ISDN)*, and involves the conversion of *analog* to *digital* circuits using digital switching equipment and an agreed set of technical standards. As these networks develop, the telecommunications system will be able to handle from one workstation voice, data, images and text.

3.2 Data can be transmitted six times as fast over ISDN than over normal telecommunications links (but more slowly than a high bandwidth line). ISDN is considered further in the chapter on the electronic office.

4. PROTOCOLS

4.1 One of the big problems in transmitting data down a public or private telephone wire is the possibility of distortion or loss of the message (or 'noise'). There needs to be some way for a computer to:

(a) detect whether there are errors in data transmission (eg loss of data, or data arriving out of sequence, ie in an order different from the sequence in which it was transmitted);

(b) take steps to recover the lost data, even if this is simply to notify the computer or terminal operator to telephone the sender of the message that the whole data package will have to be re-transmitted. However, a more 'sophisticated' system can identify the corrupted or lost data more specifically, and request re-transmission of only the lost or distorted parts.

The mechanism used to detect and usually then to correct errors is known as a *communications protocol*.

4.2 Protocol is defined as 'an agreed set of operational procedures governing the format of data being transferred, and the signals initiating, controlling and terminating the transfer.'
(British Computer Society).

4.3 One set of protocols has been developed by the International Standards Organisation (ISO). It is known as *open systems interconnection (OSI)*. Protocol was divided into seven functions in a *seven-layer reference model*.

(a) The *physical layer* deals with electromechanical and other matters, to ensure that physical connections can be made.

(b) The *data link layer* provides *functional* and procedural means to ensure that reliable communications links are set up.

(c) The *network layer* ensures that individual messages are switched and routed properly though the network.

(d) The *transport layer* ensures that the previous three layers are used properly so that messages are clear and arrive in the right order.

(e) The *session layer* deals with users opening and closing communications between two computers.

(f) The *presentation layer* provides standard formats for the interpretation of data, enabling different terminal and computer equipment to communicate.

(g) The *application layer* deals with the interconnection of user programs and applications, where the user decides what data is to be sent.

This is only a model, and is not universally adopted. Rather it indicates the types of protocols that are needed. It is part of a customer driven trend towards open rather than proprietary systems.

5. COMPUTER-TO-COMPUTER LINKS

5.1 One computer can be connected to another computer, or to several other computers (depending on the size of computer). These computer-to-computer links might be via internal cable (and so 'local') or via a data transmission link, so that geographically distant computers can be made to communicate directly with each other.

5.2 Why should computers need to communicate directly with each other?

(a) Two or more computers can share the data processing work.
(b) One computer can obtain data or programs from another computer's files.
(c) Database systems can be made more versatile and useful when several computers have access to the same database.

5.3 Mainframes can be linked directly to each other, but more common types of computer-to-computer links are micro-to-mainframe or micro-to-mini and micro-to-micro, in some form of *network* configuration.

5.4 There is quite a considerable amount of variation in the way that computer configurations are assembled.

6. STAND-ALONE COMPUTERS

6.1 A computer configuration might consist of a stand-alone computer with its peripheral equipment and one user, a computer whose peripheral equipment includes several terminals for several different users, or networks of inter-communicating computers with shared files.

Let's now look in a bit more detail at some of these typical configurations.

6.2 Stand-alone computers are used:

(a) when the data processing requirements can be handled by one user with one computer. Office microcomputers are often stand-alone machines for use by individuals, eg for developing a personal spreadsheet model;

(b) when the data processing is centralised - eg with very large volumes of transaction data being handled by a mainframe, or with a centralised minicomputer being used for the processing requirements of a department (eg an R & D department).

7. MULTI-USER SYSTEMS

7.1   With mainframe computers, minicomputers and larger microcomputers, several users, each with their own VDU and keyboard, might be connected to the same computer, with the ability for all the users to carry out processing work simultaneously. Computer configurations of this type are called *multi-user systems.*

Multi-user means 'access to a system by a number of users, apparently simultaneously, but in practice processed successively according to defined priorities for that system.' (CIMA Computing Terminology)

7.2   With a multi-user system, the central computer can be linked up to several terminals and the CPU allows several programs to be run at the same time and accessed by different users.

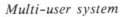

Multi-user system

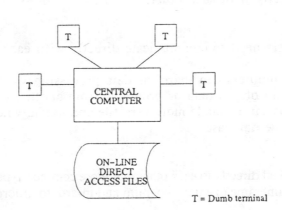

T = Dumb terminal

(a) The terminals are *dumb* terminals, which means that they do *not* include a CPU and so cannot do independent data processing. A dumb terminal relies on the central computer for its data processing power.

(b) The terminals in a multi-user system might be:

(i) in the same room or same building as the central computer, connected to the computer by internal cable; or

(ii) geographically distant from the central computer, in which case the terminals are connected to the central computer by an external data link, usually provided in the UK by British Telecom.

(c) Terminals can be used:

(i) for interactive computing with the central computer; or

(ii) to input data ('transactions' data) into the computer from a remote location. *Remote access* describes access to a central computer installation from a terminal which is physically 'distant'. The term *'remote job entry'* is used to describe a method of processing in which the computer user inputs his data, and often his programs too, to the computer from a remote terminal.

7.3

> *The benefits of multi-user systems*
>
> (a) More departments or sections can have access to the computer, its data files and its programs. This improves the data processing capabilities of 'local' offices.
>
> (b) By giving departments more computing power and access to centralised information files, multi-access systems also make it easier for an organisation to *decentralise* authority from head office to local managers.
>
> (c) The speed of processing, for both local offices and head office, is very fast.
>
> Local offices retain their input documents, and do not have to send them to a remote computer centre for processing.

7.4 Multi-user systems can be contrasted with office systems which use 'stand-alone' microcomputers. Like stand-alone micros, multi-user systems allow 'local' offices to benefit from the scope, speed, complexity and reliability of processing with computers, and the improved quality of management information.

Multi-user systems have advantages over stand-alone microcomputers, however, because all users can share the same (large) files and (large) programs of the central computer.

8. DISTRIBUTED PROCESSING AND NETWORKS

8.1 *Distributed processing* is a term defined by the National Computer Centre as a system in which there are several autonomous but interacting processors and/or data stores at different geographical locations linked over a communications network. In other words, distributed processing links several computers together:

(a) a mainframe computer with microcomputers as intelligent terminals;
(b) with stated peripheral equipment;
(c) with files either held centrally or at dispersed sites.

An example of a distributed processing system is the *Integrated Banking System* (McDonnell Douglas Information Systems International) which runs off DEC VAX minicomputers.

8.2 There is some flexibility in such computer system design, but the key features of distributed processing are as follows.

(a) Computers distributed or spread over a wide geographical area.

(b) A computer in the system can access the information files of other computers in the system.

(c) The ability for computers within the system to process data 'jointly' or 'interactively'.

(d) *Processing* is either carried out centrally, or at dispersed locations.

(e) *Files* are held either centrally or at local sites.

(f)   *Authority* is decentralised as processing can be autonomously performed by local computers under local management.

8.3   One form of distributed data processing system is illustrated below:

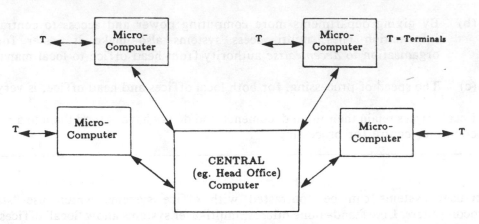

The reasons for wanting mainframe to microcomputer links

8.4   There are three main reasons for wanting to link a desk-top microcomputer to a mainframe computer, instead of relying on stand-alone microcomputers for the organisation's data processing.

(a)   Opening a communications link between a micro and a 'host' mainframe allows the micro user to run programs on the mainframe, using the micro as a terminal.

(Having the micro as a terminal saves the user having two screens and keyboards on his or her desk, one screen and keyboard for a micro to do local processing, such as spreadsheet modelling and word processing, and the second screen and keyboard being a dedicated terminal link to the mainframe.)

(b)   When the computer user writes software for the mainframe computer, a microcomputer can be used to create and debug programs on the micro using the micro's 'text editor' software.

Mainframe time is expensive, and so creating and testing programs on a micro first is cheaper and often more convenient. When the program has been written and de-bugged on a micro, it can be transferred to the mainframe and then used operationally.

(c)   *With the right software* to link the micro and host mainframe, data can be exchanged between them - eg giving the micro access to the mainframe's database files, and integrating the organisation's data processing system.

Local area networks or 'networked micros'

8.5   Distributed processing systems are usually referred to as a network.

A local area network (LAN) is a system of interconnecting *micros* (2-20 in number, but sometimes more) and other devices over a small area, typically within a few hundred metres.

8.6 Several sorts of networks exist, giving a variety of speed/cost/capacity trade-offs; essentially, the faster the data transfer round the network, the more expensive the system.

The British Computer Society's definition of a *local* area network states that the distinctive characteristic is that systems are linked by *direct cables* eg *Ethernet*, rather than via telecommunications lines. This means that a LAN:

(a) will usually be located on a single site;
(b) does not need modems.

This characteristic of LANs distinguishes it from *wide* area networks.

8.7 Most LANs include a *server* computer (or *'file server'*). As its name implies, it serves the rest of the network:

(a) offering a generally-accessible hard disk file for all the other micros in the system;
(b) sometimes offering other resources, such as a shared printer for the network.

8.8 Networks can interface with users in two ways.

(a) The *file server* model. In this way, the server sends *entire* files down the network to users. This means that a file might be temporarily unavailable to other users. However information and applications are shared without being duplicated.

(b) The *client-server* model works in a different way. The server machine does not transfer entire files to the workstation on the network. Instead, it only sends the data requested.

Network topologies

8.9 Basically, there are three types of LAN system configuration:

(a) broadcast or linear bus systems;
(b) a ring;
(c) a star network.

Network topology means the physical arrangement of *nodes* in a network. A node can be a computer, or a peripheral device such as a printer. Some networks drive data round in packets.

8.10 In a bus *structure*, messages are sent out from one point along a single *bus*, and the messages are received by other connected machines. Messages identify the intended recipient, and machines only receive messages which contain their unique identifying code.

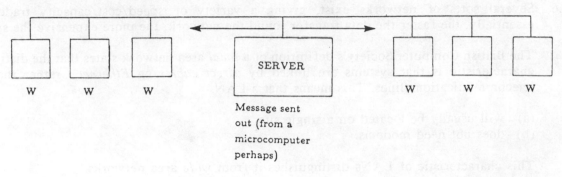

W = Workstation

8.11 In a *ring system*, the cable in the network, and the microcomputers in it, are joined in a ring. There may or may not be a server.

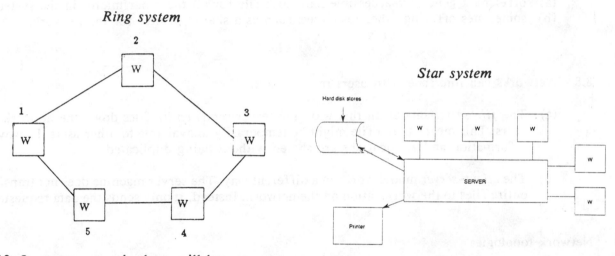

8.12 In a *star network*, there will be:

(a) a central disk file and program store, controlled by a dedicated microcomputer;
(b) a cable linking this control microcomputer to the other micro-computers.

Extra micros can be 'plugged in' to the system. The *Ethernet* system uses *transceivers* attached to coaxial cable to do so. 'The system works in a similar fashion to a ring main circuit for domestic electricity supply. Thus the central consumer unit provides a cable which loops round the house, with power outlets provided at appropriate points. The consumer is then able to plug in appliances at power points as he chooses and, within reason, where he chooses. With a networked computer system, the user is able to plug in additional processing power at any point on the data highway as required.' (*Make a Success of Microcomputing in Your Business* Pannell, Jackson, Lucas).

Why have LANs become so popular?

8.13 Local area networks have been successful for a number of reasons.

(a) Microcomputers of sufficient power and related software (eg Unix) have been developed, so that network applications are possible. An example in Kindle Software's *Bankmaster* which runs in a branch or back office on a server linked to micros or a LAN. It can handle one to one million accounts.

(b) Networks have been made available to computer users at a fairly low price. Some computer users who could not afford a mainframe or minicomputer with terminal links have been able to afford a LAN with microcomputers and software packages.

(c) Networks provide important advantages for the computer user.

(i) Data files can be shared by all the micros/terminals in the network. With stand-alone micros, each computer would have its own data files, and there might be unnecessary duplication of data. A system where everyone uses the same data will help to improve data processing and decision-making. The value of information increases with its availability.

(ii) Each micro/terminal in a network can do the same work. If there were separate stand-alone micros, micro A might do job 1, micro B might do job 2, micro C might do job 3 and so on. In a network, any micro, (A, B or C) could do any job (1, 2 or 3). This provides flexibility in sharing work-loads. In a peak period for job 1, say, two or more people can share the work without having to leave their own desk.

(iii) Peripheral equipment can be shared. For example, in a LAN, five micros might share a single on-line printer, whereas if there were stand-alone micros, each micro be given its own separate printer.

(iv) LANs can be linked up to the telex network, thus adding to the processing capabilities in an office.

In summary, networks offer the computer user an efficient system of data processing at a reasonable cost.

Wide area networks (WANs)

8.14 Wide area networks are networks on a wide geographical scale. WANs use minicomputers or mainframes as the 'pumps' that keep the data messages circulating, whereas shorter-distance LANs normally use microcomputers for this task. A wide area network is similar to a local area network in concept, but the differences are:

(a) the geographical area covered by the network;

(b) WANs will send data over telecommunications links, and so will need modems. LANs, in contrast, will use direct cables only for transmitting data;

(c) WANs will often use a larger computer as a file server.

WANs will often be larger than LANs, with more terminals/computers linked to the network. This need not be the case, however.

Network protocols

8.15 Protocol was mentioned earlier in the context of open systems interconnection, and the seven layer reference model was described. The OSI model exists to ensure that different computing environments can be connected. You may have realised that OSI is relevant to the success of networks, too, especially Wide Area Networks.

Network architectures are being designed with OSI in mind. *Appletalk* is provided for Apple networks, for example. *Netware* is provided for others. The trend is towards modular definitions of each of the levels (ie each layer in the OSI seven-layer reference model is represented by a separate software module).

8.16 Some sort of OS is needed to control the interaction and communication between the various machines in a LAN or WAN. Put crudely, there are two approaches to this problem.

(a) A separate networking operating system that 'sits on top' of the operating systems of the individual microcomputer. As MS-DOS was designed purely for personal computing, this is the solution necessary when machines using MS-DOS are to be linked. An example of network OS is Novell's *Netware*.

(b) An operating system in which networking facilities are an integral part of the design. An example of such an OS is Unix (which comes in a number of variants).

(c) An OS of a LAN environment may include the following features:

(i)   electronic mail;
(ii)   support of more than one file server;
(iii)   use of the file server as a workstation;
(iv)   use of any workstation on the network to be a file server;
(v)   designation of a single network administrator to control the network;
(vi)   monitoring of traffic between workstations:
        (1)   reporting users logging on to the system;
        (2)   logging errors;
        (3)   logging shared resources;
(vii)   provision of security features eg:
        (1)   passwords (to identify users);
        (2)   passwords (to restrict access to particular files);
(viii) support of a variety of network hardware systems (eg Ethernet);
(ix)   ability to connect to other LAN systems.

9.   SELECTING THE RIGHT CONFIGURATION

The choice of system: stand-alone computers, multi-user system or a network?

9.1 Should an organisation buy stand-alone microcomputers, a multi-user system or a network? The following general guidelines might be helpful.

(a) If large numbers of documents need to be created or if large files are involved (eg a database) then a hard disk computer should be used.

(b) If three or four computer users need access to the same data, to avoid the duplication of files, a multi-user system or network would be suitable.

(c) If six or more people need to be linked together, the organisation can choose between:

(i)   a distributed processing system. (eg LAN);

(ii)   a multi-user system which links terminals with each other, but relies on a central computer for all the processing.

(d)   If a manager needs information from external information services, such as Reuters or Topic, then it may be suitable for him or her to have a multi-function terminal. This can be used as:

(i)   a personal computer;
(ii)   a terminal linked to the company's mainframe computer;
(iii)   a terminal for accessing the external information services;
(iv)   a telephone.

(e)   If a senior manager wants a personal desk-top computer, a computer which is also linked to the company's mainframe might be suitable (eg for DSS or EIS applications).

(f)   Employees who travels out of the office regularly might wish to use a portable or laptop computer (battery-operated), but one which can download data to a microcomputer.

(g)   If an organisation needs a large computer for processing data (eg because of the complexity of the processing or the large volume of transactions) it will need a mainframe or minicomputer, probably with on-line access from remote terminals (ie a form of multi-user system).

Switching from stand-alone micros to multi-user or a network system

9.2   If a computer user decides to switch from having stand-alone microcomputers in the office to a multi-user system or a local area network, the changeover involves more than just adding in the extra cables.

(a)   The system will need appropriate software.

(i)   Stand-alone micros usually come with an MS-DOS or PC-DOS operating system, but moving to multi-user operation means either taking a multi-user operation system like Unix, or a network system, such as Novell or 3 Comm.

(ii)   The user will then have to buy applications software packages to go with the system. For example, a leading multi-user software package for an accounts system is called Multisoft, which can be run with the Xenix operating system (a UNIX variant).

(b)   If the stand-alone micros use floppy disks, the multi-user system or network will need a hard disk.

The advantages and disadvantages of distributed processing and networks

9.3   Because the increase in power of micro and mini computers has corresponded with a fall in their costs, many organisations are now reversing the previous tendency towards centralisation of data processing on large mainframe computers.

The advantages of using a distributed processing system compared with having a stand-alone centralised mainframe computer are as follows.

(a)   Greater flexibility in system design. The system can cater for both the specific needs of each local user of an individual computer and also for the needs of the bank as a whole, by providing communications between different local computers in the system.

(b) Since data files can be held locally, data transmission is restricted because each computer maintains its own data files which provide most of the data it will need. This reduces the costs and security risks in data transmission.

(c) Speed of processing for both local branches and also for the central (head office) branch.

(d) There is a possibility of a *distributed database*. Data is held in a number of locations, but any user can access all of it for a global view.

(e) The effect of breakdowns is minimised, because a fault in one computer will not affect other computers in the system. With a centralised processing system, a fault in the mainframe computer would put the entire system out of service.

(f) The fact that it is possible to acquire powerful micro-computers at a 'cheap' price enables an organisation to dedicate them to particular applications. This in turn means that the computer system can be more readily tailored to the bank's systems, rather than forcing the bank to change its systems to satisfy the requirements for a mainframe computer.

(g) Decentralisation allows for better localised control over the physical and procedural aspects of the system.

(h) Decentralised processing may facilitate greater user involvement and increase familiarity with the use of computer technology. The end user must accept responsibility for the accuracy of locally-held files and local data processing.

(i) There is no need for costly air-conditioning or filtration units or for high voltage electricity supplies.

9.4 Distributed processing has certain disadvantages, some of which might be overcome by future technological developments.

(a) Mini computers and microprocessors have not had a large storage capacity in the past, and the high-level language programs needed for distributed processing have used up much of the storage capacity available. This disadvantage is now being eliminated by the development of more powerful small machines.

(b) There may be a duplication of data on the files of different computers. If this is the case, there may be some unnecessary storage costs incurred.

(c) A distributed network can be more difficult to administer and to maintain with service engineers.

(d) The items of equipment used in the system must, of course, be compatible with each other.

Networks and systems design

9.5 When a systems analyst designs a distributed data processing system, he or she must consider the following points:

(a) Should the *files* be held centrally; or should there be distributed files around the system?

(i)   Will 'local' files reduce the volumes of data transmission between computers so as to provide large savings in data transmission costs?

(ii)   Do the different 'local' computer users all require access to common data, in which case a central file would avoid duplication of records?

(iii)   Is there a 'natural' way of dividing the data into local groups, so that each local computer has its own logical grouping of records?

(iv)   Would there be adequate security for locally-held files, compared with the security available for a central file?

(v)   Who is responsible for amending or updating records? If files are held locally, does the responsibility for updating the files belong to the staff who use that local computer, or not?

(vi)   How often must the files be updated?

(b) Is distributed data processing suitable for the system, or would a stand-alone central mainframe computer, a multi-user system, or separate stand-alone micros be more efficient?

(i)   Do the local user departments require large amounts of data processing with a quick turnround of data? If so, local processing facilities would seem appropriate, although a multi-user system could also do the job.

(ii)   Can the local processing requirements be met entirely by local files? If so, stand-alone microcomputers might be more suitable than distributed processing. Is some transfer of data required between different local end-users? If so, distributed processing would perhaps be more appropriate than stand-alone micros.

(iii)   Is there a security risk in transmitting data over communications links?

(iv)   Would the failure of a stand-alone central mainframe computer create unacceptable delays for data processing in the system? If so, distributed processing would probably be preferable to centralised processing, since the failure of one computer in the system would not affect all the system.

(c) Which system is *cheaper* to install and operate - a centralised mainframe computer, a multi-access system, a distributed system or stand-alone micros?

(d) Is there any advantage in having a common central file (database) with separate local data processing facilities?

Exercise

Consider a large group of companies which all have access to the head office mainframe computer via local terminals. The IT manager of one subsidiary wants to take over processing responsibility for his own system by installing a network which will be independent of the head office system. List the advantages and disadvantages of this course of action.

Solution

Advantages include:

(a) improved access times;
(b) local control over prioritisation of work;
(c) greater user involvement;
(d) reduced data transmission over public networks;
(e) no service charge payable to the holding company;
(f) local user requirements better catered for.

Disadvantages include:

(a) cost of new system;
(b) need for specialist staff;
(c) disruption during changeover;
(d) no immediate access to holding company files;
(e) co-operation still required to meet head office requirements.

---

10. CONCLUSION

10.1 Data transmission connects items of equipment distant from each other.

10.2 The advantages of using data transmission include:

(a) faster data collection;
(b) more readily available information;
(c) greater availability of computing facilities.

10.3 A multi-user system connects peripheral devices to a single processor.

10.4 Network systems connect several processors, thus making decentralised processing a real possibility.

TEST YOUR KNOWLEDGE

The numbers in brackets refer to paragraphs of this chapter

1 Distinguish between centralised and decentralised processing. (1.2, 1.3)

2 What is data transmission? (2.1)

3 What is packet switching? (2.8)

4 Describe a modem (2.11) and multiplexor. (2.14)

5 What is protocol? (4.2)

6 What is open systems interconnection? (4.3)

7 What is a multi-user system? (7.1)

8 Distinguish between a LAN and a WAN. (8.6, 8.14)

9 Sketch three network topologies. (8.10, 8.11, 8.12)

10 What type of functions might be provided by a network's controlling software? (8.16)

Now try question 6 at the end of the text

Chapter 5

BATCH AND INTERACTIVE SYSTEMS

This chapter covers the following topics.

1. Batch and demand processing
2. Batch processing
3. Interactive processing

---

1. BATCH AND DEMAND PROCESSING

1.1 Computers, input, files and output can be brought together in a variety of different ways to provide a computer system. So how do we set about designing a computer system to do a particular job of data processing?

1.2 Both manual and computer data processing can be divided into two broad types:

(a) batch processing;
(b) demand processing, or transaction processing.

1.3 Batch processing is 'the processing as a group of a number of transactions of a similar kind which have been entered over a period of time to a computer system.' (CIMA *Computing Terminology*).

1.4 For example the payroll work for salaried staff is done in one operation once a month. The payroll line office will be processing a large number of similar transactions, in this case preparing salary statements and arranging to have the salaries paid, and so batch processing methods would apply. To help with organising the work, the payroll office might deal with each department separately, and do the salaries for department 1, then the salaries for department 2, and then department 3, and so on. If this is the case, then the batch processing would be carried out by dividing the transaction records into smaller batches eg one batch per department. This batching of the large number of transactions into smaller groups of transaction records is a feature of batch processing by computer.

1.5 Transactions are therefore collected up over a period of time, perhaps in a transaction file, and will then be dealt with all at the same time. Some delay in processing the transactions must therefore be acceptable - ie in a payroll system, employees must agree to regular weekly or monthly payment.

1.6 Demand processing is the use of an on-line computer system to interrogate or update files as requested rather than batching such requests together for subsequent processing.

(a)   Transactions for processing might arise infrequently, and so it would take too long to build up a batch for processing at the same time. Instead, each transaction would be processed individually as it arises.

(b)   The information user might want to process a transaction immediately, and would not be prepared to accept the *delay* implicit in batch processing. For example:

    (i)   if a final demand to pay an invoice is received, perhaps because the invoice had been overlooked, it might be decided to pay it at once. For example, a threat to cut off the telephone or electricity supply unless an invoice is paid immediately would provoke a company into dealing with the matter urgently;

    (ii)   if a manager asks for some information from the data files - eg a statement of monthly sales figures for the past 3 years, he will usually expect to have the work done on demand;

    (iii)   'ad hoc' requests for information, or recording 'one-off' transactions (such as the purchase of a new building or piece of machinery) would be dealt with as they arise because there will be no like items in the foreseeable future to batch them with.

1.7 *On-line* refers to 'a machine which . . . is under the direct control of the principal *central* processor for that hardware configuration. A terminal is said to be on-line when it communicates interactively with the central processor' (CIMA *Computing Terminology*).

Combinations of batch processing and demand processing in a computer system

1.8 A computer system doesn't have to be 'all batch processing' or 'all demand processing'. A variety of combinations are possible, as follows.

There are four basic types of processing method used with computers.

(a)   *Batch input and batch processing of all data*, so that:

    (i)   all transaction records for file updating or file maintenance are batched for input and processing at the same time;

    (ii)   all file enquiries are also batched for input at the same time.

(b)   *Batch input and batch processing of all transaction data, but with on-line file enquiries*, so that:

    (i)   all transaction records for file updating or file maintenance are batched for input and processing at the same time;

    (ii)   file enquiries can be made 'ad hoc' and individually by means of on-line direct access.

(c) *On-line input (remote job entry), batch processing, and on-line enquiry,* so that:

   (i)   data is input via remote terminals and stored on a computer file without being processed (except perhaps for some simple preparatory processing such as data validation of the input records);

   (ii)   the input data on the temporary transaction file will be periodically, say once a week, used to update the master file, and so updating is done in batch mode;

   (iii)   file enquiries can be made ad hoc and individually by means of on-line direct access from a terminal.

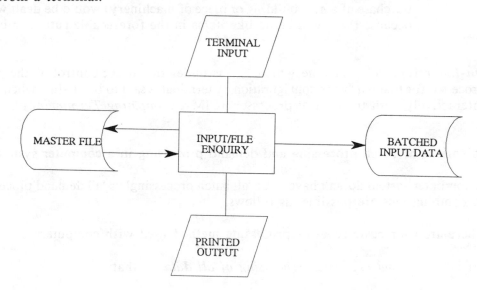

The master file must be kept permanently on-line. It can be accessed for file enquiries and also, if needed, for the preparatory processing and data validation of input data.

The term used to describe batch processing where a user's data (and often the user's programs too) are transmitted to the computer from a remote on-line terminal is *remote job entry.*

(d) *On-line input, on-line (real time) updating and on-line enquiry,* so that:

   (i)   data is input from remote terminals;

   (ii)   the master file is updated when the data is input - ie. at once - so that the master file is up-to-date at all times;

   (iii)   file enquiries can be made ad hoc as and when required.

This is known as *real-time processing*, and updating the master file immediately is a central feature of it. The master file must be on-line to the CPU at all times. This is described in more detail in Section 3 of this Chapter.

2. BATCH PROCESSING

2.1 This type of processing is associated with larger computers, and *bulk volume* processing of transaction data.

2.2 The features of batch input and batch processing are as follows.

(a) Batch input allows for *better control over the input data*, because data can be grouped into numbered batches. The batches are dispatched for processing and processed in these batches, and printed output listings of the processed transactions are usually organised in batch order. If any records go missing - ie. get lost in transit - it is possible to locate the batch in which the missing record should belong. Errors in transaction records can be located more quickly by identifying its batch number. A check can be made to ensure that every batch of data sent off for processing is eventually received back from processing, so that entire batches of records do not go missing.

(b) Bulk volume processing in batch mode allows the processing to be divided into separate stages, where each stage of processing is performed by a separate computer program. Because of the large volumes of data input 'in one go' and the possibly lengthy processing required on the data, it is convenient to split the processing between two or more programs.

If the processing were not split up in this way, the program needed to do all the processing would be long and complex. Long complex programs:

(i) are more prone to error (not even computer programmers are perfect!)
(ii) take up more space in the CPU's internal store. It might even be too big to fit in the computer!

Batch processing example

2.3 Chary Ltd operates a computer based sales ledger. The main stages of processing are:

(a) the sales invoices are prepared manually and one copy of each is retained. At the end of the day all the invoices are clipped together and a batch control slip is attached. The sales clerk allocates the next unused batch number in the batch control book. He or she enters the batch number on the control slip, together with the total number of documents and the total value of the invoices. The control details are also entered in the control book;

(b) the batch of invoices is then passed to the data processing department. The data control clerk records the batch as having been received;

(c) the invoice and control details are encoded, verified, and input to the computer. The first program is a data vet program which performs various checks on the data and produces a listing of all valid invoices together with some control totals. It also produces *rejection listings (exception reports)*;

(d)   the data control clerk reconciles the totals on the batch control slip with the totals for valid and rejected data;

(e)   the ledger update program is run to process the invoice data;

(f)   among the information, the computer prints out the total of invoices posted to the ledger and the data control clerk again reconciles this to the batch totals, before despatching all the output documents to the sales department;

(g)   all rejected transaction records are carefully investigated and followed up, usually to be re-input with the next processing run.

Sketching a batch processing system

2.4   When drawing a diagram of a large batch processing it is usual to show the files used as well as the processes and programs, and so a system can be shown as in the diagram on the following page.

2.5   The programs shown in this diagram are by no means regular programs which appear in *every* batch processing system, but they are indicative of the type of processing done when processing is done in steps or stages.

2.6   There are three basic types of program in more detail:

(a)   validation (or data vet) program;
(b)   sort program (eg prior to a master file update);
(c)   master file update program.

Data validation

2.7   This is done by program, with the computer checking that input data seems to be correct. It has nothing to do with an operator. For example, the computer might receive some data on stock sales and run through a series of validation checks. Data validation always exists in batch processing systems, and usually exists in on-line processing systems too. Validation checks are covered in detail in a later chapter.

Sort programs

2.8   Data will normally be input to a batch processing system in no special order (or serial order, ie origination of data order - eg invoice number order). Where transaction data has not been pre-sorted:

(a)   a sort program will be essentail if the master file is sequentially accessed to sort the transaction data to the same key-field sequence as the master file before updating;

(b)   a sort program will speed up processes of a direct access master file (eg magnetic disk).

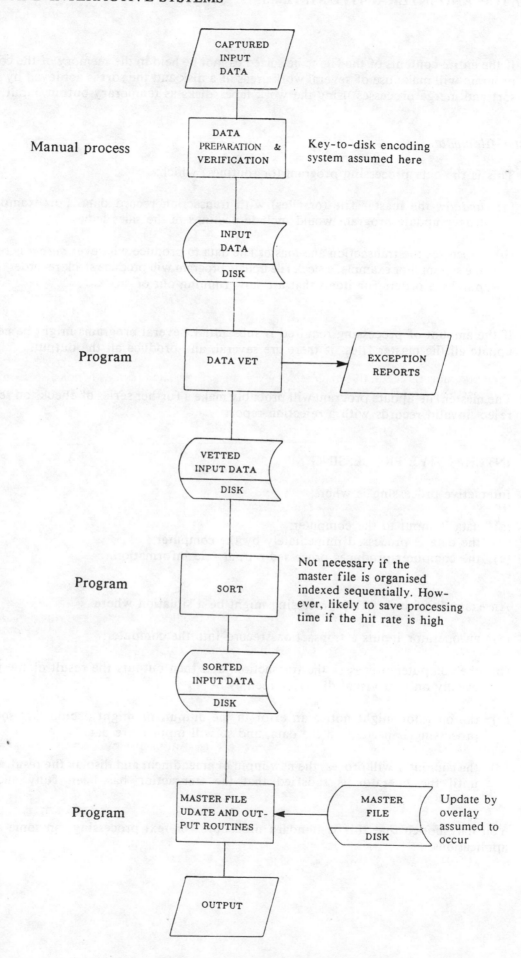

CAPTURED
INPUT
DATA

Manual process

DATA
PREPARATION &
VERIFICATION

Key-to-disk encoding
system assumed here

INPUT
DATA

DISK

Program

DATA VET → EXCEPTION
REPORTS

VETTED
INPUT DATA

DISK

Program

SORT

Not necessary if the
master file is organised
indexed sequentially. However, likely to save processing
time if the hit rate is high

SORTED
INPUT DATA

DISK

Program

MASTER FILE
UDATE AND OUT-
PUT ROUTINES ← MASTER
FILE

DISK

Update by
overlay
assumed to
occur

OUTPUT

2.9 If the entire contents of the file to be sorted cannot be held in the memory of the computer, a program will make use of several work areas of a disk and the sort is achieved by a series of sort and merge processes using the work tapes/disks as temporary output/input files.

Master file update

2.10 This is the data processing program (or routines) which:

(a) *updates* the master file (or files) with transaction record data. For example, a sales ledger update program would include postings to the sales ledger.

(b) processes the transaction and master file data to produce whatever *output* is required by the system. For example, a stock file update program will produce stock re-order demands or purchase orders for items that are now running out of stock.

2.11 If the amount of processing required is substantial, several programs might be necessary to update all the master files, if there are several, and produce all the output.

2.12 The master file update program will probably make a further series of checks on records, and reject invalid records with a rejection report.

3. INTERACTIVE PROCESSING

3.1 Interactive processing is where:

(a) data is input to the computer;
(b) the data is processed immediately by the computer;
(c) the computer produces processed output - ie information.

3.2 An example of interactive processing might be a situation where:

(a) an operator inputs a transactions record into the computer;

(b) the computer processes the transaction, and then outputs the result of the processing, usually on to a visual display screen;

(c) the operator might notice an error in the output, or might decide that some further processing is needed on the data, and so will input more data;

(d) the computer will process the new input or amendment and display the results, and so on, until the operator is satisfied that the transaction has been fully and correctly processed.

You may notice that this is standard procedure for text processing, on some spreadsheet applications.

3.3 Another example of interactive processing is a situation in which an operator wants to carry out several data processing operations on some input data, and the processing is divided into small stages. After each stage of processing, the computer will show the operator the results so far and sometimes even ask the operator in a message (or 'prompt') on the screen what he or she wants to do next. In effect, the processing is carried out by means of the operator and the computer swapping messages with each other or 'talking to each other' and this form of interactive processing dialogue is sometimes referred to as 'conversational mode' of data processing.

Real-time processing, ie. on-line input, processing and file enquiry

3.4 The CIMA's definition of real time processing is 'the *continual receiving and rapid processing* of data so as to be able, more or less instantly, to feed back the results of that input to the source of the data. This may be contrasted with Batch Processing.'

3.5 As each transaction is processed immediately on input (rather than in batches), all the batch processing stages of input, validation (using appropriate data vet checks), updating and output are applied to that one transaction by a single computer program.

3.6 The larger the system and the faster the response times required, the more expensive it is going to be. However the use of real time systems is rapidly increasing and examples include the following.

(a) *The British Airways Booking System (BABS)* is operated by a central computer at Heathrow linked to British Airways agents in the UK, Europe, USA, South America, Australia, etc via a communications network (telephone and satellite). An intending passenger may enquire at an airline office or travel agents for a flight to a particular place on a certain day. The reservation clerk is able to ascertain *immediately* if there is a vacancy, and then make a booking if required to do so. If no seats are available the computer will indicate possible alternatives for the customer's consideration (a travel agent will have access to many airlines' flight details).

(b) *Stock control* (eg in retail outlets). As a sale is made in a department store or a supermarket and details are keyed in on the point of sale terminal, the stock records are updated in real-time. Any customer wishing to buy a product can be informed as to whether the item is available or not (if not, an alternative might be offered). Although the stock files are maintained in real time, other files (eg sales analysis, debtors etc) may be batch processed at a later stage with the accumulated sales details (eg stored on magnetic tape) from each point of sale terminal. The computer can automatically order goods from Suppliers should the stock fall below replenishment level. More and more retail stores (eg. John Lewis, Argos, Key Markets) are introducing systems which incorporate some real-time data processing.

(c) *Banking and credit card systems* whereby customer details are maintained in a real-time environment. There can be immediate access to customer balances, credit position etc and authorisation for withdrawals (or use of a credit card). Real-time banking systems are gradually being introduced in the UK (cash dispensers etc) but are not as widespread as in the USA and some European countries.

5: BATCH AND INTERACTIVE SYSTEMS

Batch and real-time processing in accounting systems

3.7 Real time processing systems are likely to become more common for accounting work in large organisations, using a mainframe computer, given the developments in mainframe computer technology in recent years. Many batch processing systems have on-line facilities, such as on-line input of data with batch processing of accumulated input at a later time. Real time processing of accounts work on a mainframe computer is different from this.

(a) With a typical batch processing system for ledger accounts, there would be:

    (i) a batch input of transactions with data validation and update programs, followed by a journal processing run for the nominal ledger;

    (ii) the production of reports showing *last month's* financial position.

Processing in this way can be time consuming, and reports give information that is soon out-of-date.

(b) With a real time processing system for ledger accounts, there are no schedules or time-scales for the input of transaction data and production of management information.

    (i) Input, data validation and update can be achieved interactively in real time, from the user's remote terminal.

    (ii) The user is in a position to ensure that the files are always fully up-to-date.

    (iii) Reports can be requested at any time, that will show fully up-to-date information.

Real time systems and back-up facilities in case of CPU breakdown

3.8 When a real time system is designed, there are two considerations which are likely to mean that a back-up service will be provided by a stand-by computer. These two considerations are:

(a) Availability of service. If the system requires an unbroken availability of service, there must be a stand-by computer capable of taking over if the first computer breaks down or goes out of service for any other reason.

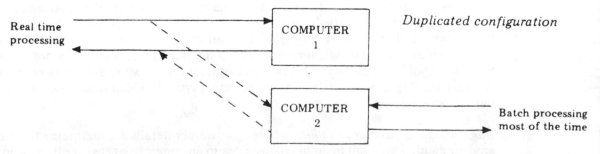

In the event of breakdown of computer 1, the input/output channels (which include access to backing files) are switched to computer 2. This stops batch processing (dumping the store contents), takes over the real-time work, and returns to batch processing only when computer 1 is operational again.

(b)   Response times:

(i)   To keep response times down to an acceptable level during peak periods of use, a second computer might be used to take on some of the data processing work in parallel with the first computer.

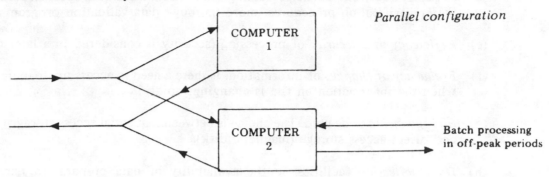

Parallel configuration

COMPUTER 1

COMPUTER 2

Batch processing in off-peak periods

During off-peak periods one computer carries out batch processing, (helping out with real time messages) while the other works in real time. In peak periods both handle the real time applications. Any breakdown of one computer will leave the system operational but with reduced response times.

(ii)   A 'front-ending' arrangement gives the real time system more 'computer power'.

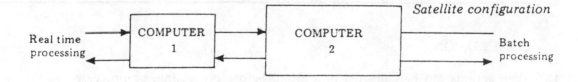

Satellite configuration

Real time processing

COMPUTER 1

COMPUTER 2

Batch processing

The smaller 'front-end' computer handles most real-time messages, referring more complex ones to the larger, mainly batch processing computer. Real-time responses from computer 2 are sent to the operator terminal via computer 1. In the event of failure of computer 2, computer 1 will still be able to cope with most messages.

Exercise

What considerations would you take into account when deciding on the type of processing method, batch processing or demand processing to be used?

Solution

(a)   *Response time required*, when output is time-critical.

(b)   *Volume of processing*. Batch input with batch processing is more suitable for large-volume or routine transactions.

(c) *Availability of computer* (and peripheral device) hardware. Microcomputer systems, for example, are generally associated with keyboard input of transaction or interrogation data and either real-time or small batch processing.

(d) *Accuracy required.* Batch processing lends itself more readily to accuracy checks (eg. better verification procedures, more thorough data validation programming).

(e) *Efficiency* and *security* of processing (security is considered in a later chapter).

(f) *Frequency of changes* of information. Is there a need to access up-to-date files regularly when the information on file is changing rapidly?

(g) *Storage media* to be used. The choice is between sequential access storage (magnetic tape) and direct access storage (magnetic disk).

(h) *Data collection* facilities; ie the availability of data preparation hardware, trained staff, accommodation, telephone lines (if required) etc.

(i) *Cost.* A cost/benefit analysis of various alternative types of processing (including manual methods, or larger/smaller computers) should be carried out.

(j) *Availability of finance* to buy new equipment etc. (although renting, leasing or computer bureau agreements could also be considered).

---

4. CONCLUSION

4.1 Transactions can be collected in a group before processing, or processed as they arise.

4.2 Real-time processing implies that processing is immediate, and that output is sent directly to the user once processing is achieved.

TEST YOUR KNOWLEDGE
The numbers in brackets refer to paragraphs of this chapter

Explain the following terms.

1   Batch processing. (1.3)

2   Demand processing. (1.6)

3   On-line. (1.7)

4   Interactive processing. (3.1, 3.2)

5   Real-time processing. (3.4)

Now try question 7 at the end of the text

Chapter 6

THE ELECTRONIC OFFICE

This chapter covers the following topics.

1. What is office automation?
2. Correspondence: changing techniques
3. Message and data transmission
4. Document image processing (DIP)
5. Office automation and its effect on business

---

1. WHAT IS OFFICE AUTOMATION?

1.1 Office work is generally a matter of information handling and information processing. In spite of the widespread use of the telephone, and even the early developments in computer technology, office work has also been associated with paperwork, and office workers as paper pushers.

1.2 The advance of computer technology and communications technology (ie information technology) has brought nearer the coming of the 'electronic' office which are terms used to describe the way in which the modern office is developing.

(a) Computer technology has developed to the point where an office might have a computer terminal (keyboard and screen) on every desk, with data processed and transmitted by terminal link-up to a computer rather than by means of paper and internal mail.

(The 'workstation' is a term used to described an office manager's desk which has its own integral microcomputer and disk storage, together with readily-available application software.)

(b) A number of microcomputers can be linked together into a small *local area network*. (The hardware features of networks were discussed in Chapter 4).

(c) Office switchboards and *telephone systems* might use electronics. Electronic/digital Private Automatic Branch Exchanges (PABX systems) provide features such as automatic message switching, automatic dialling and call repeating (when a line is engaged), conference calls, diary facilities etc.

(d) Office users can access information provided by an information-supplying organisation using the Prestel service of British Telecom.

(e) Office automation software (eg IBM's *Officevision*) combines electronic-mail and word processing applications.

6: THE ELECTRONIC OFFICE

1.3 The development of the electronic office has meant that office workers do their jobs in a different way. Technological change has brought about job changes and changes in organisation structure. These in turn affect the way that office workers communicate with each other and the 'social' life of office workers and the behaviour of office workers as groups is also undergoing change. According to a report published by the Advisory Conciliation and Arbitration Service in March 1989, the role of the secretary is likely to be enhanced as the technology under his or her supervision becomes more complex.

2.   CORRESPONDENCE: CHANGING TECHNIQUES

2.1 The 'old fashioned' office in which correspondence is typed is being superseded by more modern methods of preparing and/or transmitting letters and other correspondence.

(a)   *Word processing* and *'desk-top publishing'* (whereby the artwork of a text for publishing can be produced within an office environment) are covered in Chapter 8.

(b)   Because of the development of computer systems, it must be questioned whether some correspondence is actually needed on paper. It might be appropriate to hold much information on computer file, whether in magnetic form or part of a *document image processing* (DIP) system which a user can obtain by calling it up on to a VDU screen. Alternatively, records can be held on *microfilm* or *microfiche*.

(c)   *Dictating machines* allow an organisation to:

(i)   save management time, by allowing managers to dictate letters, rather than write them in manuscript, and without the need for shorthand secretaries;

(ii)   spread the workload of typists, who can type from dictating machine tapes at a convenient time to suit their busy and quiet periods.

3.   MESSAGE AND DATA TRANSMISSION

3.1 The telephone is still the most important method of communication in the office, and even in this area, there have been major advances in technology, eg:

(a)   mobile communications (eg cellular radio, 'telepoint')
(b)   office switchboards (PABX, per Paragraph 1.2(c) above).

ISDN

3.2 An important development in 1990 is the introduction, by both BT and Mercury, of *Integrated Systems Digital Networks,* which in effect makes the entire telephone network digital - it will therefore be possible to send voice, data, fax from a single desktop computer system, over the telecommunication link.

3.3 A subscriber to ISDN can contact any other user along *two* independent high speed digital channels. Both channels are accessed by a single standarised wall socket. This feature means that two independent but simultaneous calls can be made along these channels. This means that, for example, one channel can be used to transmit data and a voice conversation can be held over the other. Thus an architect could send building plans along one from a terminal and speak via a handset along the other.

3.4 Another feature of ISDN is Calling Line Identification (CLI). This transmits the caller's phone number to the phone or terminal of the recipient of the call. Thus for example a business receiving a call from a customer could use a call management system which automatically retrieves information files relating to the customer from its database.

3.5 Other advantages of ISDN are that computer networks can be extended to small branch offices and a number of services can be sent over the link at one time.

Telex

3.6 Telex is a service which enables users to transmit and receive printed messages over a telephone line. Users have to be telex subscribers, with their own telex equipment and code number, in order to send or receive messages. The telex service started in the 1930s, and from the mid-1970s it developed significantly as an international message transmission system. As a communication system, it has certain disadvantages:

(a) data transmission speeds are very slow compared with other methods of telecommunication, such as leased telephone lines or teletex;

(b) only a restricted set of characters can be used in messages.

3.7 However, the great strength of telex is the number of telex users, around 100,000 in the UK and two million worldwide in 1988. Advances in telex technology have made it possible for a telex user to connect word processors and microcomputers to the telex system via an inexpensive message switch (itself a microcomputer). A user's message switch can also:

(a) store a large number of commonly-used telex addresses;
(b) store messages for transmission at a predetermined time;
(c) re-dial numbers automatically if the addressee's line is busy or hard-to-obtain;
(d) send the same message to a large number of users.

3.8 Telex, in spite of earlier predictions to the contrary, therefore continues to be an important communication facility for businesses. BT and Mercury are investing in a digital telex network. Telex is likely to be superseded by fax machines. 1984 sales of telex and fax machines in Europe were equal. By 1989, however, sales of telex machines were unchanged whereas sales of fax had increased 15 times. Fax machines were adopted by smaller businesses, expanding the market.

Teletex

3.9 Teletex should not be confused with teletext. Teletex was established in 1980, and first marketed in the UK by British Telecom in 1985. It was intended to replace telex, and compares favourably with telex because:

(a) data transmission speeds are 40 to 45 times faster than with telex;
(b) a full set of characters can be used in messages, a facility which ordinary telex lacks;
(c) transmission costs are lower than with telex.

3.10 Other features of Teletex are that:

(a) British Telecom has developed a 'gateway' that allows the Teletex system to link with the ordinary telex system;

(b) the Teletex system in the customer's premises will consist of a 'box' plugged into telephone links or Packet Switch Stream (PSS) which is BT's public data network. Up to 8 Teletex screens can be provided for one office user. The 'box' converts messages prepared on the user's word processors or microcomputers into Teletex signals.

Facsimile (Fax)

3.11 Facsimile transmission or fax involves the transmission by data link of *exact duplicate copies* of documents. The original is fed into the fax machine, which 'reads' it, converts it into electronic form so it can be transmitted over the telephone. It is printed by the recipient's fax machine. *PC fax* systems do not even require the document to be input in *hard copy* form to the sender's fax machine. The computer communicates directly with the receiving fax machine.

3.12 It was thought that facsimile might be beneficial to the legal profession in particular, because speed in sending documents (with signatures) - albeit 'photocopies' - might have many practical advantages in reducing the time needed to complete contracts or settle cases etc. However, the service appears to be gaining much more widespread appeal, and the use of Fax is growing rapidly. It is not, however, a *low-cost* alternative to the post.

Electronic mail (e-mail)

3.13 The term 'electronic mail' is used to describe various systems of sending data or messages electronically via the telephone network or other data network and via a central computer, without the need to post letters - ie pieces of paper - or despatch documents by courier. It therefore has the advantages of:

(a) speed (transmission, being electronic, is almost instantaneous);
(b) economy (no need for stamps etc);
(c) security (access can be restricted by the use of passwords, although a commited hacker might breach access controls).

3.14 One form of electronic mail is a system of sending 'letters' and information over a tele-communications network, whereby the information is 'posted' by the sender to a central computer which allocates disk storage as a 'mailbox' for each user. The information is subsequently 'collected' by the receiver from the mailbox. In other words, the receiver does not receive the information when it is sent, but collects it later at a time to suit his or her convenience.

British Telecom's e-mail service is known as Telecom Gold.

(a) The sender prepares his information on a microcomputer and transmits the message via the telephone network to a central 'mailbox'. This is a part of a large BT computer's information store, which is assigned to the Telecom Gold subscriber.

(b) The subscriber picks up any message in his mailbox using another microcomputer and his telephone.

The system therefore works much like the traditional postal mailbox, except that the 'letters' are in an electronic form and the boxes are opened via the telephone.

Teletext

3.15 There are a number of Teletext systems in the UK. The most widely received are provided by the BBC (Ceefax) and the independent television companies (Oracle). Users must have a television set with a teletext facility; otherwise they pay no fee for use of the service.

The information is broadcast on pages over the air, dealing with items such as weather reports, news, sports reports, subtitles for certain television programmes, cooking hints and other items of general interest. Oracle allows some information to be provided as advertising at a low cost to the advertiser.

Information is transmitted in between the sending of each frame of normal television transmission.

Viewdata/Videotex

3.16 Viewdata is the 'generic term applied to systems which provide information through a telephone network to a television or terminal screen' (CIMA *Computing Terminology*).

3.17 The most important feature of viewdata, that makes it different from teletext, is that it is *interactive* – in other words, a viewdata customer can transmit information through the viewdata network as well as receive it.

In the UK the viewdata service provided by British Telecom is called *Prestel*. In the Prestel service most of the information is paid for by organisations that wish to provide the information. The Prestel service is provided over the telephone system, and so throughout the time he is connected to it, the user must pay for the 'telephone call', at normal call rates. In addition, the user must pay a fee for consulting most pages of information (but not index pages and some other pages). This fee is paid to British Telecom, which then passes it on, less commission, to the information provider.

3.18 *Viewdata electronic mail (VEM)*. Viewdata systems, such as Prestel in the UK, have a much larger database than teletext systems such as Oracle and Ceefax. The information is stored in a network of computers, with each computer serving a local area of customers but also capable of transmitting data to another computer in the network and so to customers in other areas.

3.19 Another potentially important facility of a viewdata system is a 'gateway' whereby data on a private customer's own computer files can be transmitted to a viewdata customer via the viewdata network. The sender of the message must key in the recipient's viewdata address number. The data is despatched and the recipient (if his screen is switched on) receives a message on his screen informing him to switch to the viewdata channel to obtain the data. (Alternatively, the data is stored locally until the recipient is switched on and ready to receive the displayed message.) A security measure can be introduced for confidential information, whereby the recipient can only obtain the message by keying in a password.

3.20 Note that although both teletext and viewdata are carried to tv screen, teletext is *broadcast*, whereas viewdata arrives over the telecommunications network.

Electronic data interchange (EDI)

3.21 Electronic data interchange is a form of computer-to-computer data interchange, and so another form of electronic mail. The general concept of having one computer talk directly to another might seem straightforward enough in principle, but in practice there are three major difficulties.

(a) Each business wants to produce documents (and hold records on file) to its own individual requirements and structure. Thus a computer of X Ltd could not transmit data to a computer of Y Ltd because the records/data transmitted would not be in a format or structure to suit Y Ltd.

(b) Different makes of computer cannot easily 'talk' to each other. The problem of compatibility between different makes of computer is a serious one, and some form of interface between the computers has to be devised to enable data interchange to take place.

(c) Businesses may work to differing time schedules, especially when they are engaged in international trade - eg a computer in London and a computer in San Francisco will probably work to differing time schedules, and so if a London company's computer wants to send a message to a computer in San Francisco, the San Francisco computer might not be switched on or otherwise able to receive the message.

3.22 A way of ensuring that electronic communication is possible is by having an agreed format for these electronic documents so that they can be recognised by all parties to the transaction. A standard which is widely adopted in the UK and Europe is *Edifact* (Electronic data interchange for administration, commerce and transport).

3.23 Joining an EDI network (there are several) is quite expensive. Many smaller companies are encouraged to do so by their suppliers and/or customers. Many of Marks and Spenser's suppliers have been converted to EDI. Alternatively one or two low cost services are offered, such as Ethosfax offered by INS for small companies dealing with the UK National Health Service. However, it is possible that these services could be challenged by the Public Data Network provided by the telecommunications companies.

3.24 Successful *implementation* of EDI depends on:

(a) deciding which categories of information are to be sent or received;
(b) adapting internal systems, so that they match up with the EDI translation software;
(c) changeover.

3.25 The advantages of EDI extend to purely *internal* uses, too

(a) If an organisation is decentralised, EDI can expedite internal billing.
(b) If an organisation's paperwork is intricate and complex, EDI can speed it up.
(c) EDI can be used to create files of historical information.

3.26 EDI has not yet been developed for office documentation, but the International Standards Organisation (ISO) has defined an Office Document Architecture (ODA) for transmissions of this nature. It is supported by the EEC, and works with UNIX.

All three of these problems have to be overcome for electronic data interchange to work between different companies and different types of computer.

Electronic Funds Transfer (EFT)

3.27 Electronic Funds Transfer describes a system whereby a computer user can use his computer system to transfer funds – eg make payments to a supplier, or pay salaries into employees' bank accounts, or transfer funds from one bank account to another account (eg deposit account to current account), by sending electronic data to his bank.

3.28 Since businesses keep most of their cash in bank accounts, electronic funds transfer must involve the banks themselves.

(a) A system for the electronic transfer of funds internationally between banks themselves is known as SWIFT (the Society for Worldwide Interbank Financial Telecommunications). If X Ltd in the UK wishes to make a payment to a company in, say, West Germany, and if his UK bank and the West German company's bank are members of the SWIFT network (all the UK clearing banks are members), the settlement between the banks themselves can be made through the SWIFT system. (Each bank holds accounts with 'correspondent' banks in other countries, and those accounts are used to settle such payments, but the *authorisation* to transfer the funds is given via the SWIFT system).

(b) Interbank settlements by the clearing banks within the UK are also made by electronic funds transfer, using the CHAPS system (Clearing House Automated Payments System). Many large companies now pay the salaries of employees by providing computer data to their bank, using the BACS (Bankers' Automated Clearing House) or BACSTEL service. Originally, the banks could only process magnetic tapes sent by employers, but with the BACSTEL service, they can now process salary data sent by telecommunications link, and in addition will accept floppy disks or magnetic tape cassettes from customers. It has been estimated that 'switching to BACs can save 90% on transaction charges'. *(Management Accounting*, July 1989)

Value Added Network Services (VANS)

3.29 VANS is a collective term for the range of computer services provided by external organisations, which are used in conjunction with the telephone network or another (private) communications network. The term 'value added network services' derives from the idea that by combining a computer system with a communications network, the service is able to provide something extra (ie an added value) to the user, greater than the sum of its individual component parts. Examples of VANS are:

(a) electronic mail (the added value here being the facility to hold messages in an electronic mailbox);

(b) services that provide financial information to subscribers, eg on share prices, foreign exchange rates and interest rates;

(c) bibliographic database systems (ie in libraries of computerised information);

(d) videotex/viewdata services such as Prestel. The most significant type of VAN is currently the provision of access to information databases (on-line information retrieval systems, eg on commodity prices, share prices, money market interest rates, foreign exchange rates, company information etc);

(e) electronic data interchange.

4. DOCUMENT IMAGE PROCESSING (DIP)

4.1 *Document image processing* is an electronic form of filing. In a DIP system, a document is passed through a *scanner*, translated into digital form and a *digitised image* is then stored on a storage device (perhaps an *optical disk*). (This can then be retrieved at will and shown on a computer screen. The image of the document can include handwriting etc.)

4.2 Some DIP systems not only store the electronic image of a document, but allow the stored documents to be used in other office systems. It might be possible to display, on the VDU, both the scanned document, and keyed-in text commentary.

The advantages are:

(a) reduced space needed for files;
(b) the same file can be viewed by different users simultaneously;
(c) files cannot be 'lost' as the original image is on disk.

An example of a DIP system is Philips' Megadoc.

4.3 As an indication of the power of DIP systems, one manufacturer (Canon) has indicated that one optical disk could contain 60,000 pages of A4 (that is over 100 copies of this text!)

4.4 The main cost savings of using DIP over paper are in storage and retrieval, as the time taken to hunt for a file is eliminated. In order for these savings to be achieved, documents must be scanned as soon as they are received by the mail room, for computer usage.

4.5 Applications of DIP include:

(a) electronic data interchange;

(b) desktop publishing by enabling photographs, for example, or other images to be stored;

(c) management of accounting transactions - all the documentation relating to an accounting transaction can be referenced to the ledger record: an entry in the sales ledger for example could be accompanied by *images* of all the related paperwork.

4.6 A possible disadvantage of DIP is that a lot more information is stored than is strictly necessary. So, organisations installing a DIP system should bear in mind the following.

(a) The *importance* (or criticality) of the documents, if their loss would be a major disaster.

(b) How often documents are *accessed*. If a document or file is greatly in demand, document imaging might be a useful technology.

(c) The *volume* of documents in an issue: small volumes of documents probably do not justify the expense of a DIP system. Large volumes, in saved storage space, almost certainly do.

(d) The *uses* to which a document is put. If a document is altered (eg a design), it might help to have one 'master' copy so that all can refer to it.

Exercise

Imagine that you are a consultant advising a regional chain of supermarkets which has 15 branches spread over three counties. All head office functions are performed on a single site and there is little computing at present. Describe five areas where, taking a broad view of the opportunities available, the introduction of IT might bring benefit to the business.

Solution

(a) *Payroll*. The company is likely to employ a wide range of temporary and permanent staff. A payroll system might be useful in calculating the different pay entitlements, bonuses if any, tax and national insurance levels, for both hourly paid and salaried employees.

(b) *Accounts*. The company could computerise its accounts-production systems. This has the advantage of enhancing the provision of management information in the company, as the information could be fed directly into a spreadsheet or other decision-support package. Reports could be produced at regular periods indicating key performance ratios.

(c) *Checkout sales*. Many products have a preprinted bar code for direct input into a computer. It is thus possible to keep an accurate up-to-date record of sales as they occur, updating the stock system at the same time. Moreover, this would mean that the service to customers is speeded up. The sales statistics generated could be used at head office to see which products were selling well and whether special promotions had been successful.

(d) *Stock*. A stock control system is a logical extension of the sales processing system. The information from the sales system could be fed directly to the stock system, so that the sale and the stock movement were recorded at the same time. This means that a much better idea of demand patterns can be recorded, and as a consequence, the company might be able to release warehousing or storage space in each store.

(e) *Purchasing*. This system might also enable the calculation of stock reorder levels, with the automatic generation of a purchase order. If electronic data interchange is adopted, direct computer contacts might be established with a supplier's sales system, avoiding the need for masses of paperwork.

---

5. OFFICE AUTOMATION AND ITS EFFECT ON BUSINESS

5.1 Many of these systems presuppose an integrated office environment, in which word processed documents, for example, can be shared between computers, e-mail can be sent to and from, computers can be used for informal communications (or conferencing, 'bulletin boards').

5.2 Office automation requires top management guidance because it changes the ways companies are run.

5.3 However, it is arguable that technology has been oversold at the expense of human factors. An office may be inefficiently run for managerial not technological reasons.

5.4 Office automation has an enormous effect on business, in a variety of ways.

(a) The processing of routine data can be done in bigger volumes, at greater speed and with greater accuracy than with non-automated, manual systems.

(b) There might be less paper in the office (but not necessarily so) with more data-processing done by keyboard. Data transmission is likely to shift from moving paper to moving data electronically. Files are more likely to be magnetic files or microform files rather than paper files.

(c) Office staff will be affected by computerisation. The behavioural or 'human' aspects of installing a computer system is discussed later, but broadly speaking:

(i) office staff must show a greater computer awareness, especially in areas of the office where computerisation is most likely to occur first - ie the accounts department;

(ii) staff must learn new habits, such as the care of floppy disks and VDU screens, how to use keyboards, and remembering to make back-up copies of files for data security purposes;

(iii) managers may have to learn to work at a 'work-station', as if they don't they will be less skilled than their staff.

(d) The nature and quality of management information will change.

(i) Managers are likely to have access to more information - eg from a database. Information is also likely to be more accurate, reliable and up-to-date. The range of *management reports* is likely to be wider and their content more comprehensive.

(ii) Planning activities should be more thorough, with the use of models (eg spreadsheets for budgeting) and sensitivity analysis.

(iii) Information for control should be more readily available. For example, a computerised sales ledger system should provide prompt reminder letters for late payers, and might incorporate other credit control routines. Stock systems, especially for companies with stocks distributed around several different warehouses, should provide better stock control.

(iv) Decision-making by managers can be helped by decision support systems.

(e) The organisation structure might change.

(i) Stand-alone microcomputers give local office managers a means of setting up a good local management information system, and localised data processing. Multi-user systems and distributed data processing systems also put more data processing and information processing 'power' into the local office, giving local managers access to centrally-held databases and programs. Office automation can therefore encourage a tendency towards decentralisation of authority within an organisation.

(ii) On the other hand, multi-user systems and distributed data processing systems help head office to keep in touch with what is going on in local offices. Head office can therefore readily monitor and control the activities of individual departments, and retain a co-ordinating influence. It can therefore be possible for a head office to retain a co-ordinating (centralising) role, and to manage an expanding organisation with reasonable efficiency. Arguably, mega-mergers between large companies are only possible with the computerisation of management information systems.

(f) Office automation commits an organisation to continual change. The pace of technological change is rapid, and computer systems - both hardware and software - are likely to be superseded after a few years by something even better. Computer maintenance engineers are anyway often unwilling to enter into maintenance contracts for hardware which is more than a few years old, and so organisations are forced to consider a policy of regular replacement of hardware systems.

(g) Office automation, in some organisations, results in better *customer service*. When an organisation receives large numbers of telephone enquiries from customers, the staff who take the calls should be able to provide a prompt and helpful service if they have on-line access to the organisation's data files.

Telecommuting

5.5 Consider the following facts.

(a) Office space is expensive (eg some central London office rents cost over £50 per square foot).

(b) Many people feel that time spent commuting between home and office is time wasted.

(c) For practical purposes, information distributed electronically takes no longer to travel a hundred miles than a hundred feet.

Telecommuting is a term that describes a solution to facts (a) and (b) by applying fact (c).

5.6 It is now quite possible technically for employees of many descriptions to work from home. A microcomputer sited at home enables a user to handle data just as if he were in the office, using spreadsheet and word processing packages. Links to the office provide a means of transmitting information and receiving new data. Links are provided by means of a modem at each end of the telephone line. The modem, or modulator-demodulator, converts the digital signals used by the computer to analogue signals for transmission along the telephone line; at the other end they are reconverted by the second modem. A network enables communication with the office by e-mail. Sophisticated e-mail systems allow whole documents (eg reports) to be sent as attachments to memos.

5.7 Advantages of telecommuting are the savings of office space and the elimination of travelling time. A disadvantage is the loss of face-to-face contact, which can be very important in meetings and negotiations and is not fully compensated for by mail or by phone calls. A means of overcoming this is teleconferencing, as described earlier in this chapter.

6: THE ELECTRONIC OFFICE

The application of information technology

5.8 One sector where developments in IT have been harnessed to make a significant difference to the way in which business is done is the banking industry. *Automated Teller Machines* (ATMs) can now be found outside almost every branch of all the major High Street banks and building societies in the UK. They can also be found at remote locations such as airports, supermarkets and university campuses. A more recent development is *Electronic Funds Transfer at Point Of Sale* (EFTPOS). The customer comes into contact with this not at his or her bank, but in retail stores.

ATMs

5.9 Individual services available from ATMs depend on how sophisticated the banks wish these to be. As a minimum customers can withdraw cash and obtain a balance of account notification. Cash withdrawals are subject to a periodic (usually weekly) maximum; data to ensure this is not exceeded is stored on a track on the magnetic strip and updated at each transaction. This, combined with an on-line link to the central computer to check that funds are available, validates a withdrawal. The balance of account will be either current or as at the previous day's close of business, depending on whether the bank utilises real-time or batch processing of ATM transactions.

5.10 Further services which banks may elect to provide to customers via the ATM network include deposit-taking, ordering of statements, cheque book requests and bill payments. Deposits are made using a standard envelope issued by the ATM, with a receipt being issued for the purported value of the deposit, and are checked later by bank tellers. Ordering of statements and cheque books simply flags a request to be acted on by staff during banking hours and bill payments require the setting up in advance of a number of specific payees with appropriate account details. They then operate in a similar way to other deposits.

5.11 Banks commonly market other banking products through their ATMs; these may ask a customer to request details of loans, mortgages, assistance with travel arrangements, insurance and other services. This is an example of the use of IT for competitive advantage.

5.12 An ATM combines several input and output devices. A card reading device reads the magnetic strip on the back of the card, and a numeric keypad allows the customer to input his Personal Identification Number (PIN). This ensures security; if an incorrect PIN is entered more than twice, the card will be retained by the machine and recovered by bank staff. There are also a number of special arrow keys sited next to the screen - these allow the customer to select specific options in response to prompts from the system.

5.13 The screen provides input and output details - it allows the customer to check his input by reproducing keystrokes (except for the PIN number!) and provides output, for example a balance may be displayed. Where hard copy output is required eg written confirmation of a withdrawal, acknowledgement of a deposit or a 'mini-statement', this is produced on a small 'transaction slip' from a printer inside the machine.

5.14 In addition to these devices, an ATM incorporates a number of other electromechanical devices, including a receipts slot for 'posting' deposit envelopes, an automatic drawer which contains unused deposit envelopes and which only opens when the 'deposit' option is selected, and a note counter to ensure customers receive the requested amount of cash.

EFTPOS

5.15 EFTPOS (Electronic Funds Transfer at Point of Sale) aims to handle, electronically, the high volume, low value transactions which make up the bulk of the payments by number which banks currently have to handle and process in paper form. EFTPOS systems integrate the retailer's POS system, which might consist of bar-code scanning or involve a sophisticated computerised cash register, with an electronic payment system. By this means stock control, retailing and receipt of funds can be fully automated.

5.16 EFTPOS is already changing the way banks and their customers (both retailers and personal customers) carry out the receipt or making of payments for everyday transactions.

5.17 The plastic cards used in EFTPOS transactions are known as *debit cards*. This is because payment is debited to the customer's bank account, usually within two or three days of the transaction taking place. It is important that the clear distinction between credit cards and debit cards is understood. A debit card functions as an electronic cheque book providing access to the holder's current account, and allowing instant electronic authorisation of the transaction by the paying bank. A credit card provides a means of charging purchases to the cardholder's credit card account, on which credit is provided by the card issuer.

5.18 The key steps of a typical payment by debit card at the retailer's terminal are as follows.

(a) Cardholder's card swiped through terminal.

(b) Data captured: sort code, account number, expiry date, card number.

(c) Amount of purchase keyed in.

(d) Data, together with retailer's identification, coded and transmitted to central electronic funds transfer switch, run by Nexus.

(e) Central switch forwards electronic message to cardholder's bank computer system for authorisation.

(f) Bank decodes message, checks account balance and returns coded approval (or decline), logging item against cardholder's account.

(g) Central switch forwards message to retailer's terminal.

(h) Cardholder and cashier advised of approval and advice slip printed for signature.

(i) Customer signs advice slip as identification and transaction completed.

(j) Settlement occurs two or three days later when the respective banks' accounts with the Bank of England are debited and credited.

6: THE ELECTRONIC OFFICE

6. CONCLUSION

6.1 Office automation is made possible by the convergence of microcomputing and communications technology. It is likely to lead to greater flexibility in the way in which data is held and distributed.

6.2 Many office automation projects involve the creation and processing of documents (eg word processing) or the automation of commercial documentation (eg EDI).

TEST YOUR KNOWLEDGE

The numbers in brackets refer to paragraphs of this chapter

Explain the following terms.

1   ISDN. (3.2)

2   Electronic mail. (3.10–3.11)

3   Facsimile. (3.8)

4   Viewdata. (3.13–3.14)

5   Electronic data interchange. (3.18–3.26)

6   EFT. (3.28)

7   DIP (4.1)

Now try question 8 at the end of the text

PART B
APPLICATION
OF SYSTEMS

Chapter 7

THE STRUCTURE OF BUSINESS SYSTEMS

This chapter covers the following topics.

1. Introduction
2. The finance function
3. Production systems
4. The marketing function
5. Personnel systems

---

1. INTRODUCTION

1.1 For your examination, you will be required to have an understanding of the structure of systems commonly found in business, and the types of computer system that are available for these business applications.

1.2 Computer systems can be categorised into two types.

    (a) *Application-specific systems.* These are systems for a particular business application, such as for sales ledger processing, purchase ledger processing, stock control, production control and so on;

    (b) *General purpose systems.* These are systems which have a purpose which is more general, and so a general purpose system can be adapted to carry out a variety of different specific applications. Examples of general purpose systems are:

        (i)   word processing systems;
        (ii)   spreadsheets;
        (iii) database systems.

1.3 The software for both application-specific systems and general purpose systems can be designed and developed 'in-house' by a company, or they can be purchased 'off-the-shelf' as software packages, from software companies or their agents.

In this chapter we shall look at application-specific systems. In the following chapter, we shall go on to look at general purpose systems, and the features of off-the-shelf software packages for these systems.

7: THE STRUCTURE OF BUSINESS SYSTEMS

1.4 The major business computer application areas are:

    (a) finance;
    (b) production and purchasing;
    (c) marketing;
    (d) personnel.

1.5 Accounts systems for very large companies have 'traditionally' been put on to a mainframe computer, and it has been small and medium-sized companies that have used off-the-shelf application software and microcomputers for their computerised accounting systems. However, there is now a range of off-the-shelf accounting software for multi-use microcomputer systems, aimed specifically at large organisations.

2. THE FINANCE FUNCTION

> *Tutorial note.* Accounting systems are a primary implementation of IT. Paragraphs 2.1 to 2.7 describe a typical finance department of a large company, for those students not familiar with that environment.

2.1 In *UK companies*, the head of the accounting management structure is usually the finance director. The finance (or financial) director has a seat on the board of directors and is responsible for routine accounting matters and also for broad financial policy matters.

2.2 The management structure varies from company to company, but in many larger companies the finance director has a 'number two' below him, called the Financial Controller. The responsibilities of the Financial Controller might include:

    (a) routine accounting;
    (b) cost and management accounting;
    (c) providing accounting reports for other departments;
    (d) cashiers' duties and cash control.

2.3 Some companies employ a Treasurer, who might be equal in 'rank' to the Financial Controller, and responsible for:

    (a) raising funds - borrowing;
    (b) investing surplus funds on the money markets or other investment markets;
    (c) cash flow control.

2.4 Some companies have made junior accountants subordinate to line managers, so that the line managers can instruct their own accountants about what reports they want to receive. In other words, some of the cost and management accounting function might be taken outside the accounting department.

2.5 Some smaller companies make the accounts department responsible for data processing, on the grounds that most DP work in the company is for accounting applications.

2.6 An organisation chart of the accounts department might be as follows:

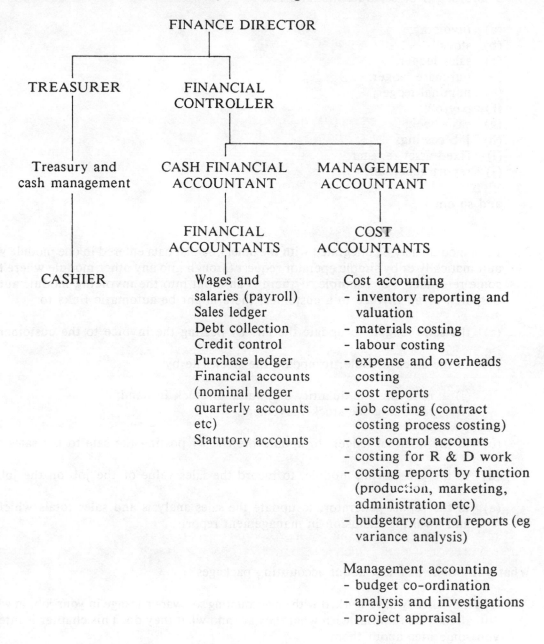

FINANCE DIRECTOR

TREASURER   FINANCIAL CONTROLLER

Treasury and cash management   CASH FINANCIAL ACCOUNTANT   MANAGEMENT ACCOUNTANT

FINANCIAL ACCOUNTANTS   COST ACCOUNTANTS

CASHIER

Wages and salaries (payroll)
Sales ledger
Debt collection
Credit control
Purchase ledger
Financial accounts (nominal ledger quarterly accounts etc)
Statutory accounts

Cost accounting
- inventory reporting and valuation
- materials costing
- labour costing
- expense and overheads costing
- cost reports
- job costing (contract costing process costing)
- cost control accounts
- costing for R & D work
- costing reports by function (production, marketing, administration etc)
- budgetary control reports (eg variance analysis)

Management accounting
- budget co-ordination
- analysis and investigations
- project appraisal

2.7 The financial accounts work is divided up into section, with a supervisor responsible for each section (eg for credit control, payroll, purchase ledger, sales ledger etc). Similarly, management accounting work is divided up, with a number of cost accountants are supervisors of sections responsible for keeping cost records of different items (eg materials, labour, overheads; or production, R&D, marketing etc) and a management accountant. Some companies that spend large amounts on capital projects might have a section assigned exclusively to capital project appraisal (payback appraisal, DCF appraisal, sensitivity analysis, the capital budget).

2.8 Accounting packages are probably the most widely-used sort of 'off-the-shelf' package in business. A package may consist of a suite of program modules, and the computer user can use a single module for a specific application, or a number of modules in a more integrated system.

There might be separate modules for:

(a) invoicing;
(b) stock;
(c) sales ledger;
(d) purchase ledger;
(e) nominal ledger;
(f) payroll;
(g) cash book;
(h) job costing;
(i) fixed asset register;
(j) report generator;

and so on.

2.9 Each module may be integrated with the others, so that data entered in one module will be passed automatically or by simple operator request through into any other module where the data is of some relevance. For example, if there is an input into the invoicing module authorising the despatch of an invoice to a customer, there might be automatic links to:

(a) the sales ledger, to update the file by posting the invoice to the customer's account;

(b) to the stock module, to update the stock file by:

(i)   reducing the quantity and value of stock in hand;
(ii) recording the stock movement;

(c) to the nominal ledger, to update the file by posting the sale to the sales account;

(d) to the job costing module, to record the sales value of the job on the job cost file;

(e) to the report generator, to update the sales analysis and sales totals which are on file and awaiting inclusion in management reports.

What you ought to know about accounting packages

2.10 You may already have worked with an accounting software package in your job, in which case you will already be familiar with what they are and what they do. This chapter is intended to give you some idea about them.

The approach we shall take here is to look at an example. The 'module' that will be described is a system for sales ledger accounting.

Sales ledger

2.11 A sales ledger package will be required to:

(a) keep the sales ledger up to date;

(b) produce certain output (eg statements, sales analysis reports, responses to file interrogations etc). The output might be produced daily (eg day book listings), monthly (eg statements), quarterly (eg sales analysis reports) or periodically (eg responses to file interrogations, or customer name and address lists printed on adhesive labels for despatching circulars or price lists).

2.12 We will assume that invoices are produced by the package, although with some accounting systems there is a separate invoicing module, and output from this module would then be input as transaction data to the sales ledger module. (If the sales ledger system doesn not include invoicing, inputs to the system would include data about invoices, rather than data about sales transactions.)

2.13 The sales ledger system will require a microcomputer with a hard disk or floppy disk drive, one or more printers (with each printer loaded with a different type of stationery), and one or more keyboard-and-screen terminals.

2.14 The data processed by the system can be thought about in terms of:

(a) what data should be held on the sales ledger file?
(b) what output is required, and how frequently?
(c) what input data is needed?

2.15 The input data that is needed must be sufficient to allow the user to keep the sales ledger file up-to-date and, together with the data on this file, be capable of producing the desired output. In other words, there must be a logical connection between input, file data, processing and output.

2.16 A suggested list of what the file data, output and input should be is as follows:

(a) *Sales ledger file*. Individual records on file for each customer account.

(i) *Standing data for each file record*

(1) Customer account number
(2) Customer name
(3) Address
(4) Credit limit
(5) Account sales analysis code
(6) Account type (open item or balance forward)*

* Where the number of invoices each month is small, and the customer usually pays promptly, the customer's account may be processed by the balance forward method. With this method, there is no attempt to identify individual invoice debts; instead, the customer's balance is maintained in total:

Balance b/f
Add new invoice amounts
Less payments received
Equals
Balance c/f.

The only check on the customer is that he does not exceed his total credit limit. In contrast, the open item method identifies specific invoices, and credits individual payments against specific invoices. Late payments of individual invoices can be identified and chased up. The customer's outstanding balance is the sum of the unpaid open items.

(ii) *Variable data relating to transactions for each file record*

(1) Transaction date
(2) Transaction description
(3) Transaction code
(4) Debits
(5) Credits
(6) Balance

(b) *Output*

(i) *Day book listing*. A list of all transactions posted each day. This provides an audit trail. Batch and control totals will be included in the listing.

(ii) *Invoices*.

(iii) *Statements*. End of month statements for customers.

(iv) *Aged debtors list*. Probably produced monthly.

(v) *Sales analysis reports*. These will analyse sales according to the sales analysis codes on the sales ledger file.

(vi) *Debtors reminder letters*. Letters can be produced automatically to chase late payers when the due date for payment goes by without payment having been received.

(vii) *Customer lists* (or perhaps a selective list). The list might be printed on to adhesive labels, for sending out customer letters or circulars etc.

(viii) *Responses to enquiries*, perhaps output on to a VDU screen rather than as printed copy.

(ix) *Output on to disk file for other modules* - eg to the stock control module and the nominal ledger module, if these are also used by the organisation.

(c) *Input data*

(i) *Amendments*

(1) Amendments to customer details, eg change of address, change of credit limit etc
(2) Insertion of new customers
(3) Deletion of old 'non-active' customers

(ii) *Transaction data relating to*

(1) Sales transactions, for invoicing
(2) Customer payments
(3) Credit notes
(4) Adjustments (debit or credit items)

2.17 Different parts of the module will be operated with differing frequencies:

(a) the input data might be daily, with daily production of invoices and a day book listing;

(b) monthly production of an aged debtors list, reminder letters and statements; and sales reports for management;

(c) daily or weekly output of data on disk files to other modules in the accounts system;

(d) on-demand response to file enquiries - eg to deal with customer queries;

(e) periodic production of customer lists.

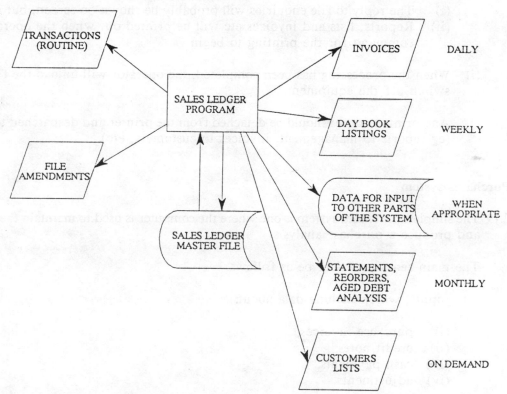

Operations with the sales ledger module

2.18 If the sales ledger system is run on a microcomputer, the following operations would be performed by the accountant.

(a) Check to make sure that the correct stationery is loaded in the printer (eg pre-printed invoice stationery, self-adhesive address label stationery, plain stationery etc).

(b) Insert the floppy disk containing the program into the disk drive and read the program into the computer's memory.

(c) Insert the floppy disk containing the sales ledger file and any other stored data into the disk drive.

(d) Key in the password and identity codes to gain access to the data.

(e) A menu will probably appear on the screen, offering a choice of the kind of processing required. The operator will select the required kind of processing from the menu (eg file enquiry).

(f) The program should be user-friendly, and display a series of prompts on the screen, including formatted screen layouts to help with data input. The user will respond to the prompts, keying in input data and commands, and pressing control keys (whichever is appropriate).

(g) Whenever it is appropriate, the program will display a customer's account on screen. The operator might then key in new transaction data, and there will be a new debit or credit entry into the account, and a new balance displayed.

(h) The required output will be produced.

    (i) The reply to file enquiries will probably be shown on screen, but not printed out.
    (ii) Reports, lists and invoices etc will be printed out when the operator keys in the command for the printing to begin.

(i) When the processing has been completed, the operator will unload the floppy disks and switch off the equipment.

(j) Any printed output should be detached from the printer and despatched to its destination (eg reports to management, invoices to customers, etc).

Purchases system

2.19 The simplest purchases system is one where the computer is used to maintain the purchase ledger and produce a purchase analysis.

The main features would be as follows.

(a) Inputs, which include data about:

    (i) purchase invoices;
    (ii) credit notes;
    (iii) cash payments;
    (iv) adjustments.

(b) Outputs, which include:

    (i) lists of transactions posted - produced every time the system is run;

    (ii) an analysis of expenditure for nominal ledger purposes. This may be produced every time the system is run or at the end of each month;

    (iii) list of creditors balances together with a reconciliation between the total balance brought forward, the transactions for the month and the total balance carried forward;

      (iv) copies of creditors' accounts. This may show merely the balance b/f, current transactions and the balance c/f. If complete details of all unsettled items are given, the ledger is known as an *open-ended ledger*. (This is similar to the open item or balance forward methods with a sales ledger system).

      (v) Any purchase ledger system can be used to produce details of payments to be made. For example:

         (1) remittance advices (usually a copy of the ledger account);
         (2) cheques;
         (3) credit transfer listings.

      (vi) Other special reports may be produced for:

         (1) costing purposes;
         (2) updating records about fixed assets;
         (3) comparisons with budget.

  (c) Files used. The main file in such a system is the purchase ledger. There will be a record on file for each supplier account. The fields in each record will include:

      (i)   account number;

      (ii)   name;

      (iii) address;

      (iv) credit details;

      (v)   bank details (eg method of payment);

      (vi) cash discount details, if appropriate;

      (vii) details of transactions. This may include just current transactions or, in an open ended system, all unsettled ones;

      (viii) balance outstanding.

2.20 The purchase ledger module can be integrated with other modules of the accounting system. For example, if it were linked to the stock control module the original input might be the goods received details. The computer would update stock records, match GRNs against invoices, post invoice details and produce accruals information, (ie unmatched GRNs). Purchase orders would be generated on the basis of predetermined minimum stock levels, and details of orders awaiting delivery from particular suppliers could be held on the purchase ledger file.

2.21 The purchases module in a software package called *Masterpiece 2* contains quality control facilities, so that competitive tenders can be constructed for *price, reliabilty* and *quality*.

7: THE STRUCTURE OF BUSINESS SYSTEMS

Stock control systems

2.22 Stock control systems or modules vary widely. The simplest types involve just updating a stock file from movement records. In a manufacturing company it is necessary to distinguish between different categories of stocks (eg raw materials, work-in-progress, finished goods, consumable stores etc) and appropriate internal movement documents will be required. In on-line (real-time) systems it would be possible to give customers up-to-date information on stock availability. A good stock control system should reduce working capital that would otherwise be tied up in stocks. The main features of a simpler stock control system are as follows.

(a) Inputs, which would include data about:

    (i) goods received notes;
    (ii) issues to production (ie raw materials to WIP);
    (iii) production to finished goods store;
    (iv) despatch notes;
    (v) adjustments.

(b) Outputs, which would include:

    (i) details of stock movements - produced every time the system is run. Summary movements listings may also be produced less frequently as management reports;

    (ii) stock balances produced as required, eg weekly;

    (iii) stock valuation lists - produced at the end of each accounting period;

(c) Files used. The main file is the stock ledger. There would be a record on file for each stock item, and record fields might include:

    (i) stock number;
    (ii) description;
    (iii) standard cost (if appropriate);
    (iv) quantity in stock.

If summary movements schedules are produced it will also be necessary to maintain the appropriate details on file.

2.23 The stock control module is often linked to the purchase and/or sales modules, and other inputs/outputs would then be necessary.

(a) Additional inputs might be:

    (i) changes in re-order levels, quantities etc;
    (ii) orders placed with suppliers (if orders are not computer-generated);
    (iii) customers orders - so that finished goods can be allocated;
    (iv) notification of despatch to customers.

(b) Additional outputs might be:

    (i) purchase orders or re-order schedules;
    (ii) overdue purchase orders;
    (iii) production requirements;
    (iv) unmatched customers' orders over a predetermined age.

Inputs from the sales ledger or purchase ledger modules would be on magnetic disk or tape, and outputs to those modules would also be on tape or disk.

2.24 Another important role common to many stock control systems is the identification of slow moving items. A print-out will be obtained of all materials and products whose turnover has failed to reach a predetermined level over a specified time.

2.25 Finally, it is worth mentioning that it is normal for the results of physical stock counts to be matched against the stock file so that a list of differences can be printed out. This should be done as often as necessary to enable wastage, pilferage etc to be identified and to allow the stock files to be corrected.

Payroll systems

2.26 A simple payroll module would be mainly concerned with the production of a weekly wages payroll. Salary systems are similar to those encountered for wages, the principal difference being that it is usual for the monthly salary to be generated by the computer from details held on the master file and, therefore, (with the exception of overtime, bonuses etc) there is no need for any transaction input. The main features of a simple wages system are:

(a) inputs, which include:

   (i) clock cards or time sheets (sometimes both are used). Details of overtime worked will normally be shown on these documents;

   (ii) amount of bonus or appropriate details if the bonus is calculated by the computer.

(b) outputs, which include:

   (i) payslips;

   (ii) payroll (this is often a copy of the payslips);

   (iii) payroll analysis, including analysis of deductions (tax, national insurance etc) and details for costing purposes;

   (iv) coin analysis, cheques, credit transfer forms, as appropriate;

   (v) in some cases, a magnetic tape, cassette or floppy disk with payment details, for despatch to the bank and payment through the BACS system;

(c) files used. The master file will hold two types of data in respect of each employee:

   (i) standing data, eg rates of pay, details of deductions (tax code etc), personal details;

   (ii) transaction data, eg gross pay to date, tax to date, pension contributions etc.

2.27 With the nominal ledger module a large amount of the data will be presented to it from the other modules in the integrated system. Another important source of input is the journal voucher (for year-end audit adjustments and so forth).

2.28 As the general ledger deals with so many different types of accounts, and is used to produce a number of reports, the coding system must be sufficiently sophisticated to allow for this analysis.

Outputs from the system would include:

(a) final accounts (profit and loss account, balance sheet) with prior-period and/or budget comparisons;

(b) technical reports, to ensure that the system has been working properly eg:

    (i) transaction listings for indivdual accounts;
    (ii) audit trails;
    (iii) trial balance, listing the balance on every account;

(c) management reports, of various kinds.

If a company employs job-costing than this too can be integrated with the other systems providing the coding system is adequately flexible.

General features of accounts packages

2.29 When choosing an accounting package, the data user should look at several features of the package, to decide whether they suit the user's needs. The factors to consider include the following.

(a) The degree of integration between the various modules (eg debtors, creditors, stock, fixed assets, job control, nominal ledger).

(b) Whether the system can handle the data volumes and master file sizes that the user will have.

(c) Whether the fixed field length for account codes is long enough.

(d) Whether the program allows more than one reference number to be recorded for a single transaction - eg reference numbers for:

    (i) invoice number;
    (ii) order number; and
    (iii) job number.

(e) How are the accounts organised? In *Masterpiece 2.* an accounting system from Computer Associates 'each account can point to, or point from any other group of accounts' as well as 'being able to split the 24 character account code into sub-sections for company, department, cost centre and analysis group.' (*Accountancy*, March 1990).

(f) Is it possible to link *revenue* from a product to its *cost of sales* to establish a product gross profit?

(g) Data ranges. What range of prices can the system cope with (eg from 1 penny to £10,000,000.00?) What are the maximum limits on any value, and are these suitable - eg is a maximum value of £9,999,999.99 suitable?

(h) How does the system deal with *foreign currency values* and exchange rates?

(i) Does system provide for several operating units (eg subsidiary companies) and multi-currency, multi-company consolidation?

(j) Can it be linked to a spreadsheet package? or a modelling facility?

(k) What standard reports are produced by the system and how are they formatted? Are these reports sufficient for management's information needs? Can the user design his/her own reports to add to the standard reports available (eg using a 4GL)?

(l) How user-friendly is the system?

   (i) Are the menus it uses clear?

   (ii) Are the screen layouts formatted clearly and easy to read. Do they display at the same time all the data the user wants for a particular transaction or query?

       (1) Are the screen formats for *data input* clear, prompting the operator what to do next, and designed in such a way as to limit the likelihood of an input error?

       (2) Are the on-screen displays in response to *file queries* clear and easy to read?

   (iii) What is the quality of graphics offered (3-D)?

(m) How speedy is the system in operation?

(n) What security features does the package offer, to prevent unauthorised access? Are these features adequate? The package should provide *multiple layers* of authorisation. (Some files may be open to all staff; others will be available for everybody to read but can be updated only by certain staff; and some will need to be restricted completely to certain groups);

(o) Is the system documentation for the computer user well written and easy to understand? Are the operating manuals well indexed for easy reference?

(p) Does the system have a multi-user facility?

(q) Will it work on a local area network system?

(r) Does the package provide adequate audit trails?

Exercise

Imagine that you are the IT manager in a manufacturing company. The production director had asked whether, when the new order processing and inventory control system is implemented, he can have the following: commodity picking lists, despatch notes, stock replenishment reports and sales analyses. What is the purpose of each of these reports?

Solution

(a) *The commodity picking list* would be produced after the processing of a customer's order to assist despatch staff in the selection of those product lines which comprise the customer's order.

(b) *Despatch notes* would be sent with the goods on the delivery run in order to provide the customer with a written record of the goods being delivered to him.

(c) The *stock replenishment report* would be the result of stock lines reaching or falling below a pre-determined re-order level. The report would be used as the basis for purchase requisitions which the purchasing department would then use to place official orders with the company's approved suppliers in order to see that the company's stocks are replenished.

(d) *Sales analysis*. This could be used for a variety of purposes such as monitoring the performance of sales representatives against budget, assisting production control staff in planning production needs and enabling marketing staff to direct the company's advertising campaigns in the most effective way.

Good accounting software: ICAE&W guidelines

2.30 In July 1986, the ICAE&W issued an Information Technology Statement No 2 on Good Accounting Software, which sets out to give clear guidance about the qualities which contribute to well-designed accounting software, whether designed in-house or purchased externally as a package.

2.31 The Statement gives the following suggestions.

(a) The user should determine what his requirements are first of all: good software must be able to meet those requirements.

(b) The status, reputation and expertise of software developers and suppliers should be considered. In the case of packaged software which is already on the market, the number of current users should be established, and some of these users should be asked whether they find the package satisfactory.

(c) The software

    (i) must be able to perform the requisite accounting functions, ie the functions that

        (1) are claimed for it
        (2) are required by statute
        (3) constitute good accounting practice
        (4) provide sufficient information to allow the user to comply with disclosure requirements (eg of SSAPs);

    (ii) must be reliable and so help to ensure the completeness, accuracy and integrity of the accounting records and processes;

    These features must help users to maintain:

        (1) full accounting records;
        (2) accounting controls;
        (3) security and continuity of processing.

    (iii) must be properly supported and maintained by the software supplier or developer;

(d) ideally the software should be:

    (i) easy to use (eg with interactive processing and good user documentation);

    (ii) efficient - ie as quick in operation as is consistent with adequate programmed control routines and the need to produce routine accounting reports;

    (iii) flexible in operation and easy to expand and upgrade.

2.32 The Statement goes on to say that in order for good accounting software to be effective in practice, there must also be:

(a) good installation procedures and
(b) proper training for staff in using the software.

3. PRODUCTION SYSTEMS

3.1 The function of the production director is to provide to the marketing department an agreed volume of products within an agreed delivery plan and at a pre-planned cost and level of quality, and also to achieve a planned return on assets employed.

3.2 Production systems involve:

(a) the organisation and operation of the manufacturing department and assembly department;

(b) the provision of a production engineering capability to plan manufacturing methods, use of tools, design of machine tools, assembly fixtures etc;

(c) the provision of a purchasing activity capable of buying the raw material, components, tools and equipment necessary for efficient high quality minimum cost manufacture;

(d) the provision of a quality control department with the capability of ensuring adequate quality commensurate with cost, by inspection at various stages of manufacture and assembly and 'bench testing' of final products;

(e) the provision of a production control department with the capability of translating customer orders and stockists' requirements into orders in the factory. The problems of economic machine loading and provision of customer and stockists' requirements is one of the most complex in modern factory management. Most large companies now handle this complicated data processing activity with the help of computers and a possible system is illustrated below;

(f) the efficiency of the company's facilities, plant, buildings, tools etc. by establishing and controlling a maintenance department;

(g) the provision of economic and efficient storage of consumable goods, raw materials and components for further fabrication, with records capable of ensuring that quantities held in stock are within the predetermined budgets.

3.3 You should notice that *manufacture* is only one aspect, although an important one, of the overall production function.

3.4 Production management information systems provide information to help with the planning and control of production. One application which is frequently computerised is production planning, ie the provision of a production plan to meet the requirements of customers and stockists. The diagram on the next page shows the stages which might be found in a computer system designed to meet this objective.

3.5 Computer systems are being used in a number of contexts in advanced manufacturing environments.

3.6 *Just-in-time* systems are used to monitor, in detail, the flow of stock and components through the system, to minimise inventory levels.

3.7 *Material requirements planning* systems are used to plan backwards, as it were, from expected output, to materials and subassemblies required, taking into account purchase delivery and production lead times.

3.8 *Computer aided design* is the use of advanced computer graphics (described in Chapter 8) in product design. In particular this reduces the amount of time needed to be spent on technical drawing.

3.9 *Computer integrated manufacture* is the integration of a number of manufacturing systems so that stock control etc are integrated with process control and design.

4. THE MARKETING FUNCTION

4.1 Marketing is not simply the task of selling goods which are produced or services which are offered; if is a means of trying to ensure beforehand that the goods produced or services offered conform with what potential customers want and will buy. Selling is only one aspect of the marketing process. Marketing is concerned with events before the act of selling (eg research and product development, product quality) and after the act of selling (eg after-sales service).

4.2 The principal functions of marketing management might be listed as marketing research, advertising and sales promotion, public relations, selling, servicing and methods of payment and credit.

4.3 The organisation of marketing management is fairly standard across industry. Marketing directors will usually report directly to the chief executive or managing director. Reporting to the marketing director himself there may be a sales manager, a merchandising manager (responsible for advertising and public relations) a market research manager and a service manager.

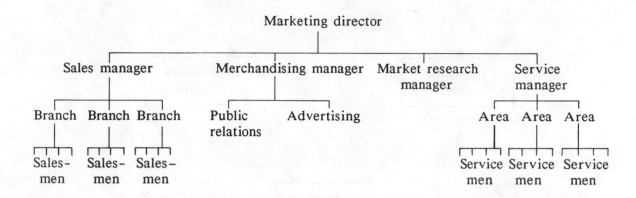

4.4 Many of the data processing needs of the marketing function are suitable for computerised methods. Typical data requirements within the department would include:

(a) data for market research, including the results of surveys, questionnaires etc, needed to determine marketing strategy;

(b) data relating to the success or failure of advertising. You may yourself have been asked where you heard of a product or service which you have ordered;

(c) data relating to sales and distribution. This may include:

(i) customer orders and enquiries;
(ii) sales made by each salesman and commission earned;
(iii) sales per outlet, per geographical area, per product, per product group;
(iv) comparisons with budget;

(d) data relating to after-sales service and warranty work.

4.5 A typical use of computer systems in marketing and market research would be a customer database. Details of customers would be accessed on a variety of different criteria.

5. PERSONNEL SYSTEMS

5.1 The personnel manager is in most large organisations a senior official reporting directly to the managing director. His primary function is to recommend to the chief executive the personnel management policies, practices and procedures needed to ensure satisfactory relationships between employees and management.

5.2 More detailed functions of the personnel manager include:

(a) responsibility for the adequacy and competitiveness of the company's wages and salaries structure (and therefore also for staff grading);

(b) responsibility for training, particularly management skills;

(c) responsibility for relations with trade unions and for negotiating and administering industrial agreements;

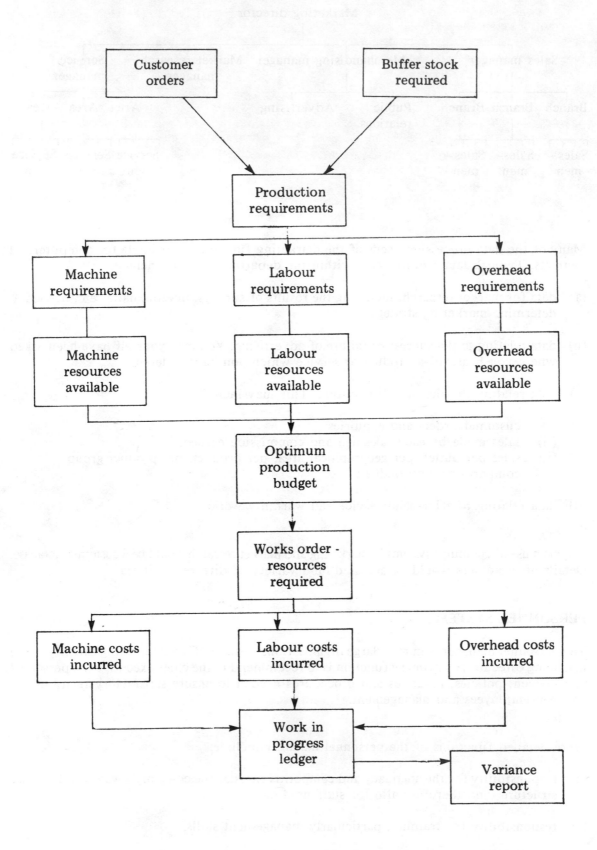

Production budget

(d) maintaining the company's retirement and pension plans, and supervising this and other employment benefits;

(e) maintenance of personnel statistics and records. This is an area which particularly lends itself to computerisation.

5.3 Some of the data kept by a personnel department will overlap with the data used in the payroll system. For example, the personnel department is likely to maintain a file on each employee showing rate of pay, tax code etc. However, a fuller employee database may also be maintained with applications beyond the payroll system, for example:

(a) manpower planning and allocation, based on staff qualifications, disclosed in the database;
(b) for each employee, maintaining a record of career progress, training and experience, etc;
(c) selection of appropriate staff for further training and/or promotion;
(d) preparing statistics on sickness, injuries and absenteeism.

6. CONCLUSION

6.1 This chapter has described some of the possible applications of computer technology in an organisation.

6.2 Computer systems can also be used to enhance communication between these different functions (eg sales order processing with production scheduling) thus, it is hoped, enhancing efficiency.

TEST YOUR KNOWLEDGE
The numbers in brackets refer to paragraphs of this chapter

1 What inputs would you expect to see in a typical computerised purchases system? (2.19)

2 What files would you expect to be used in a typical computerised sales system? (2.16)

3 What *additional* reports would you expect to see in a typical computerised stock system if it were linked to the sales and purchase systems? (2.23)

4 What outputs would you expect to see in a typical computerised payroll system? (2.26)

5 What features should you look for in an accounting software package? (2.29)

6 List the responsibilities of a typical production director. (3.1, 3.2)

7 Give examples of the data which might be required within a marketing department. (4.4)

8 Give examples of the uses to which an employee database might be put. (5.3)

Now try questions 9 and 10 at the end of the text

Chapter 8

REVISION CHAPTER: GENERAL PURPOSE PACKAGES

This chapter covers the following topics.

1. Word processing (WP)
2. Computer graphics
3. Desktop publishing
4. Spreadsheets
5. Database software packages

---

1. WORD PROCESSING (WP)

1.1 Definitions of word processing are as follows.

(a) 'The processing of text information. Typically, word processing software may be used for the production of standard letters and for the drafting and redrafting of documents.'
(CIMA)

(b) 'Word processing uses a computer system to assist with the tasks of editing and production of typed letters and documents, including the addition of stored text (eg for personalised circulars)'
(British Computer Society)

1.2 Word processing enables the person preparing the text:

(a) to check the input visually on the VDU screen as it is being keyed in, and to correct errors immediately (some spelling checks can be built into the word processing software, as a sort of data validation check);

(b) to check printed text and correct errors easily and neatly, so that instead of having to erase typing mistakes with a typewriter eraser, the WP user can quickly key in the corrections and print a fresh corrected version of the text;

(c) to make amendments to the original text.

(i) If the contents of the text are discussed and as a result of these discussions, changes are agreed, the changes can be made quickly and simply. (Contracts under negotiation can be amended in this way, for example.)

(ii)   Text can be held on file and subsequently updated. For example, a company might hold its rules and procedures books, or its price lists etc, on a WP file and update them just before they are to be reprinted. Updating can be done quickly and with a low error rate;

(d)   To merge text with with other text already held on file (eg common text for standard letters). The facility to merge some keyed-in text with 'standing' text on file enables the WP user to produce personalised standard letters quickly and with few keying-in errors.

Word processing hardware and software

1.3   Word processors are essentially microcomputers with a word processing software package although some WP systems were implemented on mainframes. When they first arrived on the market several years ago they appeared as *dedicated* systems with only one function, word processing. However, most people acquire a WP package for use on a general purpose microcomputer.

1.4   Different word processors have been developed with different design philosophies as to which type of user interface is most appropriate.

(a)   Some word processors use, predominantly a system of *commands* whereby the operator remembers a number of keystrokes (or consults a list of commands as a *'help'* facility in memory) and uses them appropriately.

(b)   Some word processors use a *menu system*, whereby, at the top or bottom of the screen, a number of options are listed. Some WP packages operate several menus.

(c)   Finally, some WPs employ a WIMP interface (eg using an icon of a pair of scissors for 'cut and paste' editing).

1.5   The WYSIWYG (What You See Is What You Get) facility is another helpful feature for users who wish to see on screen exactly the format and typeface they will get on paper. Thus italics etc. would actually appear on screen rather than as a visible or invisible code; a whole page of text might be readable on screen without 'panning' about.

Document creation

1.6   When saved on to backing store, a word processed letter, for example, is a file of data, like any other file. So, creating a document means giving it a name and setting it up as a file. In some word processors, setting up a document may also involve filling in a formatted screen giving basic details about the document (eg originator, destination, date).

1.7   The word processor screen is first of all given all the characteristics of a sheet of paper. The operator is able to specify the *width* and *length* of the area (s)he wishes the text to cover on the page, taking into account desired margins when the text is printed on to paper. If the text area is larger than the screen can accommodate, the operator has the facility, rather like a movie cameraman, to scroll up and down or to pan from side to side in order to view and edit a page.

8: REVISION CHAPTER: GENERAL PURPOSE PACKAGES

Editing

1.8 Once the text in its basic form has been keyed in, the editing facilities of the software come into their own. The functions of *erasure, correction, insertion* that used to have to be done by hand in updating or reorganising printed material are all available on screen with the word processor. Text can be *moved* or *duplicated*, for example. Moreover, text can be *justified* automatically within preset margins.

1.9 Single characters, words, lines or specified blocks of text can be removed from the screen, to be erased, replaced, or moved elsewhere. Keying-in can be set to *type over* existing text - the electronic equivalent of correction fluid - or to *insert* text immediately to the left of the cursor. Repeated errors or items for updating can be found, and corrected automatically if desired, using a 'search' and 'replace' function eg 'search for TYPEWRITER ... replace with WORD PROCESSOR'. The 'search for' facility is also useful for moving quickly to required points in the text.

1.10 Layout can be altered with equal ease. Blocks of text can also be indicated and moved from their original position to a specified point in the document in a few simple moves. Other valuable aids in producing documents include the following.

(a) *Page headers* keyed in only *once* appear at the top of each page.

(b) *Trailers* such as page numbers will be printed automatically.

(c) *A spell-checker* program checks a specified word, page or file against its own dictionary and calls attention to any word it cannot recognise: the operator then has the choice of ignoring the word (if it is unfamiliar to the machine, but correctly spelt), adding it to the dictionary (if it is unfamiliar, correctly spelt and much used), or correcting the error (by substituting a word offered by the machine from its dictionaries, or by typing afresh).

(d) *Typescript variations,* for emphasis, appearance etc. These are entered as controls in the text, or selected from a menu, as instructions to a printer, and may or may not actually appear on screen as they will on paper. Variations include underlining, italics, emboldening and different type sizes and type faces.

1.11 *Calculation.* Most software packages contain basic calculator facilities, including automatic totalling of columns and rows of figures. The calculator program may also be used to provide checking and correction of paragraph numbering, cross-references and indexing: a code is entered with each number, and the calculator can then be asked to check and match sequences.

1.12 *Form design and graphics.* Associated software packages are increasingly added to basic word processing to increase the flexibility and application of the available hardware. Graphics facilities enable lines to be drawn on screen, directed by cursor movement from the keyboard or by means of a 'mouse', areas to be shaded, points to be plotted etc. and even the application of colour in advanced graphics systems. For users of word processors, perhaps the most useful application of a graphics-related program is in the design of forms and documents of camera-ready quality for bulk printing and use. Once a graphic format has been designed to the user's satisfaction, it can be 'downloaded' or overlaid onto a separate text file (with the form headings, document contents etc) which has been appropriately laid out: the two are printed together to create the finished document.

1.13 *Communications*. Any computer running a particular software package should be able to communicate with other computers running the same or 'compatible' software: they may be close enough to be linked by a cable, or by telephone using a modem (acoustic coupler or direct connect modem - see the chapter on data transmission.) This means that documents or disk files can be sent or 'read across' from one terminal to another, with complete confidence that the text will be sent and received correctly. Some WPs accept data from databases, spreadsheets, graphics packages.

1.14 *Macros*. A macro is an automated sequence of commands that can be executed with a single keystroke. If a text editing function is repeated over many pages, it can be automated and executed easily.

1.15 We have seen how the capabilities of word processing packages enable text editing and manipulation, and also the production of eg mailing lists, price lists, standard letters, 'tailor-made' forms and reports, repetitive or standard documents eg legal contracts, merging files etc.

Such facilities are obviously most useful to secretaries and typists, writers and publishers, especially where typing tasks are repetitive, text needs frequent correction and updating, and storage on paper is bulky.

Mail merge is where the typist need only enter names and addresses, and a proforma letter, for a number of standard letters to be printed.

1.16 The advantages of word processing for producing text are:

(a) the ability to produce personalised letters of a standard type;
(b) the ability to amend, correct or update text on screen easily;
(c) a low error rate in the text;
(d) speed of keying in text, and corrections;
(e) lower text production costs as a result of (c) and (d);
(f) easy formatting of text;
(g) *quality* is improved;
(h) *security* may be enhanced.

1.17 The widespread use of WP by businesses might suggest that there are few, if any, disadvantages to word processing. There are two points, however, that are worth noting.

(a) WP operators might suffer physical injury (eg eye strain, repetitive strain injury) from continually looking at a VDU screen or using a WP keyboard. (Using a typewriter requires other hand movements than simply keying in text (eg repositioning paper etc).

(b) There can be some vexing delays and inactive periods for the WP operators.

(i) When a WP operator is correcting or editing a lengthy text, there may be a considerable waiting time, with some WP systems or packages, between keying in a command to call up a certain page of text, and the page eventually appearing on the screen.

(ii) In some WP systems, when the printer is producing printed output, the operator cannot be doing other work (ie inserting new text on another job) because the printer 'ties up' the word processor.

However, these are problems related to stand-alone micros of limited power rather than WP in principle.

2. COMPUTER GRAPHICS

2.1 Another use of computers is the production of information in the form of pictures, diagrams or graphs.

'Computer graphics is the representation of information by a computer in graphical form, the display being either as charts or diagrams in hard copy or as animation on a VDU.'

(British Computer Society's *Glossary of Computing Terms*)

Graphics software

2.2 Graphics software comes in a variety of forms and may provide any of the following facilities (in ascending order of 'sophistication' or complexity):

(a) the facility to interpret and represent data in a simple graphical form;
(b) the facility to interpret and represent data in an enhanced graphical form;
(c) presentation graphics;
(d) free-form graphics.

Basic interpretation of data in graph form

2.3 Some programs with a graphics facility allow the user to display data in a simple graphical form, as:

(a) line graphs (eg a time series graph, showing sales and profits over a period of time);

(b) bar charts;

(c) pie charts;

(d) XY graphs, ie scattergraphs which plot the value of one item against the corresponding value of a second item, for a number of pairs of data;

(e) maps (in two or three dimensions);

(f) time series charts;

(g) architectural drawings;

(h) organisation charts.

2.4 Most graphics programs are menu-driven, allowing the computer user to select the type of graph that is required. The numerical data must be input or produced by other parts of the program's operations. The software then produces the graphical data automatically on screen - eg pie charts are segmented in the right proportions and bar charts accurately divided into component parts.

8: REVISION CHAPTER: GENERAL PURPOSE PACKAGES

Presentation graphics

2.5 Programs for presentation graphics are programs which allow the user to build up a series of graphical displays or images which can be used for presentation. With additional hardware, this type of software can be used to produce 35mm slides for an on-screen slideshow or storyboard (which can be synchronised with a sound track). The VCN Concorde software package is an example: this includes a library of over 200 icons, symbols and images for inclusion in graphical presentations.

Graphics hardware: CPU, input and output equipment

2.6. All graphics packages accept commands from the standard keyboard terminal 'but detailed positional editing and drawing benefit from specialist input devices such as the light pen, joystick, mouse and digitisers'. (*Which PC?* Oct/Nov 1986)

A powerful processor chip and colour monitor are essential for implementation of an advanced graphics package.

2.7 For a computer to be able to produce graphics, it must have the appropriate CPU hardware. With microcomputer systems, a *graphics card* can be inserted into the microcomputer (there are monochrome graphics cards and colour graphics cards). This hardware will then be used with suitable software to produce graphics. With IBM PC systems, for example, a Hercules Graphics Card (produced by Hercules Computer Technology) can be inserted into the IBM PC and used with graphics-based word processor software, such as Microsoft's Word 3 package.

How computers make graphics on a VDU screen

2.8 Graphics, like letters and numbers, can be displayed on a VDU screen by lighting up tiny dots called pixels (which stands for picture elements). The quality of the graphics (whether high or low resolution) depends on the size of the individual pixels. A program can instruct the VDU screen to light up a pixel on any x and y co-ordinate, and this is how computer graphics are formed on a screen.

(a) *Line graphics* are created on screen by specifying two points on the screen and instructing the computer to light up all the pixels between them. In this way, several lines can be created to build up the full line drawing.

(b) *Animated graphics* create a moving effect by creating a whole series of 'frames'. By deleting one frame and replacing it with the next in very quick succession, the impression of movement is given.

(c) *3-D graphics* give the illusion of a three-dimensional object. One way of doing this is to create a 'wire frame drawing' in which all the lines which make up the picture are shown even if they would be hidden if the object were really solid; eg:

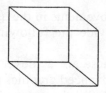

149

(d) *CAD* stands for computer aided design, which is the use of computer graphics to help professional designers in industry in their design of new products (eg motor cars).

Hard copy output of graphics

2.9 Graphics software packages will incorporate the facility for displaying charts or diagrams on a *VDU screen*, and pictures can also be animated - you have only to think about all the home computer games you have seen or played with to get an idea of animated graphics!

2.10 A graphics software package will be of limited value if the images it produces can only be displayed on a VDU screen. There ought to be a way of producing the image either:

(a) on paper; or
(b) on photographic film.

2.11 *Dot matrix printers* can be used to print graphics, using the pins on the print head to build up a picture in dots. Higher quality graphics are available from the newer dot matrix printers with 24 pins on the print head (instead of the 9 pins which are on many printers). These printers can print in monochrome (black on white paper) but colour options are available for them (even though not many graphics software packages currently support colour printing options).

2.12 *Laser printers* can produce graphics output more quickly and to a better quality than dot matrix printers. Not every make of printer is compatible with a particular graphics software package, because not all printers obey the same set of commands and so one of the most important considerations in buying a printer for graphics is whether it is compatible with the graphics software.

2.13 *Plotters.* Graphics plotters are output devices which actually draw on paper or transparencies, using pens held in a mechanical arm. Unlike dot matrix printers, they can draw unbroken straight lines, and so are particularly useful for computer-aided design work (eg engineering design). Because they work by moving pens over the paper, they can be very slow output devices, which often makes graph plotters unsuitable for normal office applications (eg producing a graphical presentation for a management report). As with printers, compatibility between the graphics software and the make of graph plotter is essential.

2.14 *Photographic output.* Graphs on a VDU screen can be photographed, but the quality of picture that this produces is variable. A fairly recent development is a special item of hardware, the Polaroid Palette, which can be used to make 35mm slides from graphics screens (thus taking data from the graphics program itself rather than from the image on the screen).

Improvements in the quality of computer graphics

2.15 There have been some significant improvements in the quality of colour display graphics fairly recently. Some graphics packages provide the following facilities.

(a) The use of different *colours*. These are achieved either by specifying, from a fairly limited selection on offer, or, in advanced graphics packages from mixing or matching the desired colours from a palette. ArtWorks paint offers in theory 16 million colours.

(b) *Multi-level masking*. This facility enables images to be superimposed on each other, with the image behind still visible.

(c) *Colour cycling*. Colours can be animated to suggest movement such as water flowing through a pipe.

(d) *Video feed*. Some packages will enable picture fed from a video to be displayed on screen, with computer graphics at the same time.

(e) The stages of image creation can be saved and replayed *as a sequence*.

(f) Images can be drawn, freehand, using a mouse. Alternatively, some packages offer stencils to help you draw. A 'rubberband' feature might be presented, which means that circles or ovals can be pulled to the required shape.

(g) A package might be able to generate, automatically, three dimensional graphs, with shading.

The choice of graphics software package

2.16 The choice of graphics software package will depend largely on what sort of graphics the user wants to produce. However, relevant factors in the choice should be:

(a) Will the package provide exactly what the user needs?

(b) How user-friendly is the package? Does it use menus or on-screen prompts?

(c) How much memory does the package need? Graphics packages often need a great deal of CPU store in order to perform reasonably.

(d) Does the user want to create graphs or charts using data from other files? If so, the graphics software must be compatible with the software that produces the file data.

(e) Does the package need a *colour* graphics card in the CPU or not?

(f) Does the package provide enhanced graphics (ie better-quality resolution of images)? If so, does the user have hardware that can display and print out enhanced graphics (eg a high resolution VDU screen)?

The user will probably want a package that allows him or her to mix drawings and graphs with word processor text.

Summary: graphics

2.17 Computer graphics can help in the production of management reports and forecasts, and for creating graphics for making presentations. Engineering design is another obvious business use for graphics, since design diagrams/drawings can be displayed and amended via a VDU screen.

Even so, the use of computer graphics in business is not as extensive as the use of word processing, software packages and accounting packages, although it is likely that graphics will be used more extensively as time goes by.

8: REVISION CHAPTER: GENERAL PURPOSE PACKAGES

3. DESKTOP PUBLISHING (DTP)

3.1 *Desktop publishing* is the use of office computers to implement computerised typesetting and composition systems. A desktop publishing package has at its root a word processing package, but it is more sophisticated than a work processing package. A WP package produces high quality text, suitable for letters and some reports. However, if the text so produced is to be embellished with, for example, graphs, diagrams, photographs or tables, the text will require further (manual) manipulation and making-up prior to publication. A DTP package allows pages to be made up on screen and printed in the required format. The need for a messy cut-and-paste exercise is avoided and the package will produce pages of the type found in books, magazines or newspapers. It is used to produce output which is well finished, professional and above all well designed. It is really a form of electronic publishing. Earlier in this chapter we discussed word processing. It is likely that, with time, the two types of software will move closer as WP becomes more sophisticated.

3.2 These capabilities mean that organisations wishing to produce a wide range of documents no longer require outside typesetters, make-up studios and printers. Annual reports, sales catalogues, marketing brochures, reviews of the business, newsletters, press releases and other documents for which a high quality finish is required can be produced in-house without any necessity for specialist facilities or staff. The only equipment required is a PC and a laser printer. DTP packages are becoming increasingly user friendly, so that any operator can learn how to use a package without difficulty. The lead time necessitated for sending documents to external printers is eliminated and documents can be produced to extremely tight deadlines.

3.3 Desktop publishing software packages vary in complexity.

(a) Some are suitable for the general micro user producing an occasional document.

(b) Others are appropriate for 'full-time DTP departments, producing brochures, company reports and advertisements, with sophisticated photography and artwork for output on professional typesetting printers'. *(Which Computer?* February 1990)

(c) DTP systems pull *graphics* and *text* together from other programs. However, with one or two exceptions, DTP programs are not good programs with which to *create* text or graphics.

3.4 The finished page can be made to resemble any newspaper, magazine or brochure page, with boxes, ruled lines and frames delineating or emphasising areas of text. Text can be spread right across the page, or in two or more columns; it can be wrapped round diagrams or presented in blocks.

3.5 DTP's main function is that it enables the page, both graphics and text, to be seen as the 'artwork' image for editing and production. WYSIWYG, and the use of a mouse, are obvious necessities. A space for a picture can be moved around the page, like 'cut and paste' artwork. This cuts out the intermediate stage in publishing or sending material to a phototypesetter to make up pages for printing.

3.6 DTP systems need:

(a) high-quality graphics software;
(b) the use of a mouse, for ease of relocating text and pictures around a page;
(c) high quality output (on to laser printer).

They should also offer WYSIWYG ie what appears on the VDU screen should approach, in terms of visual quality as well as final output, the page that is being made up.

3.7 An organisation can use DTP in a number of ways, eg:

(a) design of management reports with use of figures and graphics to make complex data easy to grasp;

(b) design of external documentation, for example

    (i) press releases;
    (ii) mailshots;
    (iii) advertisements;
    (iv) annual report;

(c) in-house magazine;

(d) design of an organisation's standard documentation (eg order forms etc).

3.8 DTP software should:

(a) as far as possible, be easy to use;

(b) be well-documented (publishing and printing are full of technical terms);

(c) give WYSIWYG editing;

(d) support Postscript for output (Postscript is software which enables users to work with a variety of printers 'such as a monochrome laser for checking layout and content, and an imagesetter or typesetter for final copy' *(Which Computer?* February 1990));

(e) be able to import text from a wide variety of WP and graphics software;

(f) feature some (elementary) text-editing;

(g) support colour output;

(h) provide standardised style sheets, for typeface and layout, which can save time in determining the look of a document;

(i) provide WIMP, or Windows, Icons, Mouse, Pull-down menus. This is a user-friendly set of facilities allowing the user to:

    (i) pan and zoom around the page on screen;
    (ii) select functions by means of indicating the relevant pictorial symbol;
    (iii) move the cursor around the screen using a mouse rather than arrow keys;
    (iv) scroll through menus and sub-menus without losing sight of what is on screen;

(j) be able to work with a document scanner for input of photographs etc.

3.9 It is important that the user does not get carried away with the features of DTP for its own sake. This kind of package can become addictive and an end in itself, rather than a means to an end. Discipline is required; many organisations experience a flurry of beautifully designed but relatively unimportant memos and notices after the acquisition of DTP. Similarly users must be aware of what constitutes good design. The positioning of illustrations, the size of headlines, the choice of fonts and the overall 'feel' of the made-up page can have a large effect on how the finished product is received. The 'cropping' of photographs to emphasise important subjects is a technique commonly used in newspaper publishing and can be adopted in DTP.

3.10 What hardware is required for DTP? Most organisations have PCs and many have laser printers – these are all that is necessary. A scanner is useful if diagrams are to be imported rather than created,although some package offer a range of predesigned diagrams - maps, forms of transport, buildings, computers, starbursts and an endless array of line drawings which can be adapted or embellished.

3.11 DTP is likely to need a powerful computer to run it, as it uses up lots of memory. A computer running an 80386 chip might be necessary.

4. SPREADSHEETS

4.1 A spreadsheet is defined in the CIMA's Computing Terminology as 'the term commonly used to describe many of the modelling packages available for *microcomputers*, being loosely derived from the likeness to a 'spreadsheet of paper' divided into rows and columns.'

4.2 It can be used to build a model, in which data is presented in these rows and columns, and it is up to the model builder to determine what data or information should be presented in it, how it should be presented and how the data should be manipulated by the spreadsheet program. A model represents in mathematical terms the relationships between the significant variables in a business situation.

Uses of spreadsheets

4.3 The uses of spreadsheets are really only limited by your imagination, and by the number of 'rows and columns' in the spreadsheet, but some of the more common accounting applications are:

(a) balance sheets;
(b) cash flow analysis/forecasting;
(c) job cost estimates;
(d) market share analysis and planning;
(e) profit projections;
(f) profit statements;
(g) project budgeting and control;
(h) sales projections and records;
(i) tax estimation.

Since spreadsheets can be used to build a wide variety of models, spreadsheet packages are 'general purpose' software packages, as distinct from software packages which are designed for specific applications (eg a sales ledger package).

4.4 What all these have in common is that they all involve data processing with:

(a) numerical data;
(b) repetitive, time-consuming calculations;
(c) a logical processing structure.

You may have noticed that the spreadsheet models listed above contain examples of information at strategic (eg (d) and (e)), tactical (eg (g) and (h)) and operational level (b). Spreadsheets are therefore a vital component of information systems at *all* levels.

4.5 The great value of spreadsheets, however, derives from their simple format of rows and columns of data, and the ability of the data users to have direct access themselves to their spreadsheet model via their own personal microcomputer.

For example, an accountant can construct a cash flow model with a spreadsheet package on the microcomputer in his or her office: (s)he can create the model, input the data, manipulate the data and read or print the output direct. He or she will also have fairly instant access to the model whenever it is needed, in just the time it takes to load the model into his or her microcomputer. Spreadsheets therefore help to bring computerised data processing more within the everyday reach of data users.

The appearance of a spreadsheet

4.6 When a 'blank' spreadsheet is loaded into a computer, the VDU monitor will show lines of empty rows and columns. The rows are usually numbered 1, 2, 3 . . . etc and the columns lettered A, B C . . . etc. Typically, it will look like this:

```
        :   A  :   B  :   C  :   D
1:          [        ]
2:
3:
4:
5:
```

Each 'box' in the table - eg column A row 1, column A row 2, column B row 1 etc - is referred to as a *cell*.

4.7 The screen will not be able to show all the columns and rows. Lotus 1-2-3 v2 contains 230 columns and 8192 rows, and the spreadsheet will 'scroll' in any direction when the computer user operates the cursor keys on the keyboard, to find the rows and columns that the user wishes to look at on the screen.

4.8 If the user wishes to look at two different parts of a spreadsheet on the screen at the same time, there is a command in all spreadsheet packages which enables the user to 'split' the screen. It is usually called a *window* command, and enables two separate parts of a large spreadsheet to be viewed at the same time on the screen.

4.9 A spreadsheet, then, consists of a large number of cells, each identified by a reference such as A4, D16, AA20 etc. (AA20 is immediately to the right of Z20 and left of AB20.) The screen cursor will highlight any particular cell - in the example above, it is placed over cell B1. At the bottom of the screen, the spreadsheet program will give you such information as:

(a) the reference of the cell where the cursor lies;

(b) the width of the column where the cursor lies (you can alter column widths to suit yourself, up to about 100 characters, without changing the total number of columns available on the spreadsheet);

(c) the contents of the cell where the cursor lies, if there is anything there.

4.10 The contents of any cell can be one of the following.

(a) *Text*. A cell so designated contains words or numerical data (eg a date) that cannot be used in computations.

(b) *Values*. A value is a number that can be used in a calculation.

(c) *Formulae*. A formula refers to other cells in the spreadsheet, and performs some sort of computation with them. For example, if cell C1 contains the formula +A1-B1 this means that the contents of cell B1 should be subtracted from the contents of cell A1.

(d) *Macros*. These are automated commands (see below).

How is a spreadsheet used?

4.11 The idea behind a spreadsheet is that the model builder should construct a model, in rows and columns format, by:

(a) identifying what data goes into each row and column, by inserting text - eg column headings and row identifications;

(b) specifying how the numerical data in the model should be derived. Numerical data might be:

(i) inserted into the model via keyboard input; or

(ii) calculated from other data in the model by means of a formula specified within the model itself. The model builder must insert these formulae into the spreadsheet model when it is first constructed; or

(iii) occasionally, obtained from data on a disk file from another computer application program or module.

4.12 Spreadsheets are versatile tools. Different spreadsheets will offer different facilities, but some of the more basic ones which should feature in all spreadsheet programs are as follows. Many commands appear in a menu bar across the screen, perhaps at the top, with a submenu bar beneath the main menu bar.

8: REVISION CHAPTER: GENERAL PURPOSE PACKAGES

(a) *Print commands.* You should be able to print the contents of the spreadsheet in total or in part, with or without the spreadsheet row and column labels. In this example, it should be possible to print out the finalised balance sheet.

(b) *File commands.* You should be able to *save* the balance sheet as a file of data on your disk. Other file commands allow you to *combine* data from another spreadsheet model into your current one.

(c) *Cell editing facilities.* The program should allow alteration of anything shown on the spreadsheet. This is particularly useful for 'what if?' calculations. For instance, in our simple example, you might want to know what net current assets would be if taxation was £1m instead of £0.8m. Using the edit facility (on Lotus 123 provided by depressing the F2 key) you just have to change the taxation figure, then ask the computer to recalculate the entire spreadsheet on the basis of the new figures. This 'what if' manipulation of data is probably the most important facility in a spreadsheet package, and we shall return to it again later.

(d) *Facilities to rearrange the worksheet.*

  (i) *Insert* a column or row at a desired spot. For example, you might wish to split 'debtors' into 'trade' and 'other'. The insert command facilitates this, and the formulae in the spreadsheet are adjusted automatically.

  (ii) *Move* or *copy* a cell, row or column (or block of cells) elsewhere.

  (iii) *Delete* a cell, row or column.

(e) *Format.* This command controls the way in which headings and data are shown, for example by altering column widths, 'justifying' text and numbers (to indent or have a right-hand justification, etc), changing the number of decimal places displayed etc. You can format a *range* of cells or, if you wish, the whole spreadsheet.

(f) *Copy* a formula or cells. For example, suppose you wanted to have a cumulative total of a list of numbers, as follows:

	A	:	B	:	C	:
1:						
2:	9		9			
3:	10		19			
4:	14		33			
5:	3		36			
6:	86		122			
7:	9		131			
etc						

The numbers in the A column are data. The cumulative numbers in the B column are calculated from the formulae A2; B2 + A3; B3 + A4; B4 + A5 etc. Clearly it would take a long time to input all these formulae individually, and so to save time it is possible to input + B2 + A3 in the B3 cell, and then *replicate* the formula down the column, and the computer will input all the others automatically. It is usually possible to replicate downwards or sideways throughout the spreadsheet.

(g) *Graphics facility.* It will usually be possible to convert tabulated data in a spreadsheet into a bar chart or graphical format, eg

ASSETS

Fixed assets	55%
Stocks	23%
Debtors	20%
Cash	2%

Bar charts or graphs can be printed out if required.

(h) *Database facility.* A spreadsheet package will often provide a facility for sorting data (alphabetically or numerically).

(i) Some spreadsheets offer a *search and replace* facility to highlight and alter individual formulae.

(j) *Macros.* Many spreadsheet commands are provided as *options* in a menu. Some procedures require a number of commands to be executed. This is often time consuming. For example, if you wish to 'print' some or all of your spreadsheet, you will first execute the print command. You may then see a menu which asks you to specify for example:

● what range of the spreadsheet you wish to print;

● what print 'options' you wish to use. This will lead to a submenu, which will ask you to specify the length of the pages you are using in the printer, what you wish the size of the margins to be and so forth.

Several commands must be executed before the spreadsheet is printed, and you will have to repeat them each time you wish to print your spreadsheet. Many spreadsheets provide a *macro* facility. This allows the user to automate a sequence of commands, executing them with the depression of two keys.

(k) Some spreadsheets offer a 'protect' facility to ensure that the contents of a specified range of cells cannot be tampered with.

An example of a spreadsheet model: cash flow projection

4.13 If you have never used a spreadsheet yourself, it will probably be helpful to look at an example, which illustrates the advantage of being able to ask 'what if?' questions and so manipulate the data to obtain extra management information.

4.14 The accountant of a small company wishes to computerise his cash flow projections using a spreadsheet package. The cash flow projection is to provide a monthly cash flow analysis over a 5 year period. The following data is relevant.

(a) Initial cash held by company on 1 January 19X1 is expected to be £15,000.

(b) Sales in January are expected to be £25,000, and a growth rate of 2% per month in sales is predicted throughout the forecast period.

(c) The company buys stock one month in advance and pays in cash.

(d) On average, payment is received from customers as follows:

   (i) 60% one month in arrears;

   (ii) 40% two months in arrears.

   All sales are on credit. There are no bad debts.

(e) The cost of sales is 65% of sales value. Overhead costs (cash expenses) are expected to be £6,500 per month, rising by 5% at the start of each new calendar year.

(f) Purchases of capital equipment and payments of tax, interest charges and dividends must also be provided for within the model. The interest rate on bank overdrafts is expected to be 1% per month.

4.15 The accountant might decide to label the spreadsheet rows and columns as follows:

	A		B	C	D	E	F
1:			19X1				
2:			Jan	Feb	March	April	May
3:			£	£	£	£	£
4:	Sales						
5:	Cash receipts						
6:	One months in arrears						
7:	Two months in arrears						
8:	Three months in arrears						
9:	Total receipts						
10:							
11:	Cash payments						
12:	Stock						
13:	Overheads						
14:	Interest						
15:	Tax						
16:	Dividends						
17:	Capital purchases						
18:	Total payments						
19:							
20:	Cash receipts less payments						
21:	Balance b/f						
22:	Balance c/f						

4.16 The formulae required can be constructed in a variety of ways. One way would be to insert some 'constant' values into cells of the spreadsheet, eg.

	Column A	B
Row		
23:	Sales growth factor per month	1.02
24:	Interest rate per month	0.01
25:	Debts paid within 1 month	0.6
26:	Debts paid within 2 months	0.4
27:	Debts paid within 3 months	0
28:	Bad debts	0
29:	Cost of sales as proportion of sales	0.65

Alternatively, these values could be specified in the formulae in the spreadsheet.

4.17 Examples of constructing formulae for the spreadsheet are as follows. Note that multiplication is achieved by using an asterisk.

(a) The formulae for sales in February 19X1, in this example, would be (+B4*B23), in March 19X1 (C4*B23), in April 19X1 (D4*B23) etc. Replication of the formula could be used to save input time.

(b) The formula for cash receipts in April 19X1 would be:
E6 = +D4*B25
E7 = +C4*B26
E8 = +B4*B27
E9 = +E6 + E7 + E8

(c) Cash payments for stock would be expressed as the cost of sales in the previous month; for February 19X1, this would be:

C12 = +B4*B29

(d) Total cash payments in May 19X1 would be the sum of cells F12 to F17, ie

F18 = @ SUM (F12..F17)

and so on.

4.18 Input data would include the opening cash balance on 1 January 19X1, dividend and tax payments, capital purchases, sales in January 19X1, the constant values (in our example in column B, rows 23 to 29) and the other data needed to establish cash receipts and payments in the first month or so of the forecast period (eg receipts in January 19X1 will depend on sales in November and December 19X0, which the simplified model shown here has not provided for).

With this input data, and the spreadsheet formulae, a full cash flow projection for the five year period can be produced and, if required, printed out.

8: REVISION CHAPTER: GENERAL PURPOSE PACKAGES

Using spreadsheet models: sensitivity analysis

4.19 Whenever a forecast or budget is made, management should consider asking *'what if?' questions*, and so carry out a form of sensitivity analysis.

For example:

(a) what if the cost of sales is 68% of sales, not 65%?

(b) what if payment from debtors is:

1 month in arrears	40%
2 months in arrears	50%
3 months in arrears	10%?

(c) what if sales growth is only 1% per month?

4.20 Using the spreadsheet model, the answers to these questions, and others like them, can be obtained simply and quickly, using the editing facility in the program.

(a) To test the consequences of the cost of sales being 68% instead of 65%, the only change needed would be to alter the value in cell B29 in our example from 0.65 to 0.68, and to run the model again to produce amended output.

(b) To test the consequences of slower payments by debtors, it would merely be necessary to alter the contents of cells B25, B26 and B27 in our example from 0.6, 0.4 and 0 to 0.4, 0.5 and 0.1 respectively, and then to run the model again.

(c) Similarly, the consequences for cash flow of slower sales growth of only 1% per month can be tested by altering the value of Cell B23 in our example from 1.02 to 1.01.

4.21 A great number of such 'what if' questions can be asked and answered quickly, eg what if sales growth per month is nil, ½%, 1%, 1½%, 2½% or minus 1% etc? The information obtained should provide management with a better understanding of what the cash flow position in the future might be, and what factors are critical to ensuring that the cash position remains reasonable - eg it might be found that the cost of sales must remain less than 67% of sales value, or that sales growth of at least 1½% per month is essential to achieve a satisfactory cash position, etc.

Three-dimensional spreadsheets

4.22 One of the problems with using spreadsheets for financial modelling is that spreadsheets work only in two dimensions (columns and rows). Combining information in three dimensions is difficult. For example, you may wish to produce financial statements for a number of companies in a group, as well as the consolidated results for the group as a whole, analysed over a number of months. In a normal two-dimensional spreadsheet you would have, say, the months across the top as columns, and the income and expenditure information down the side as rows. If there is more than one company involved you have to repeat this two-dimensional design *separately* for each company.

4.23 Lotus 123 version 3, released in 1989, has a facility that permits working in *three* dimensions, as 256 *sheets* can be held in memory at one time. A filing cabinet is perhaps a good analogy, as the user can flip between different sheets stacked in front or behind each other. Cells in one sheet refer to cells in another sheet. So, in our example, the top sheet would be the consolidated results, and the lower sheets the constituent companies or regions.

	A	B	C	D
1	UK NORTH	February	January	
2	SALES (£'000)	1000	800	
3				

	A	B	C	D
1	UK SOUTH	February	January	
2	SALES (£'000)	1000	750	
3				

	A	B	C	D
1	ALL UK	February	January	
2	SALES (£'000)	2000	1550	
3				
4				

READY

Three dimensional spreadsheet

Exercise

You are preparing a spreadsheet which will be used to display your company's balance sheet. You have inserted headings in the 'A' column as follows, starting on line 5 and ending on line 17.

Fixed assets (cost)
Fixed assets (accumulated depreciation)
Fixed assets (net book value)
Stock
Debtors
Cash
Current assets

Overdraft
Creditors
Taxation
Current liabilities
Net current assets
Total assets less current liabilities

Assuming that you are using a two-column format, what formulae might you insert in cells C7, C11, C16 and C17?

Solution

```
C7  = + B5 - B6
C11 = @ sum (B8...B10)
C16 = +C11 - C16
C17 = +C7 + C16
```

---

5. DATABASE SOFTWARE PACKAGES

5.1 The possibility for many organisations to contract and use a database system has been considerably enhanced by the availability of database software packages. Users of the software package can insert their own data into a database file framework that the package contains, and then use the database. Special database programming languages are used to operate a database system.

5.2 There are three broad categories of database software package.

(a) Flat file database.
(b) Multiple file database.
(c) Relational database.

5.3 Some databases combine *programmability* to flat file or relational data handling. Programmability means that the database user, by learning how to program in a *database language*, can structure the data files and reports to suit his or her exact requirements.

Flat file database packages

5.4 The most basic and simple type of database, a *flat file database*, consists of a single file of individual records, with a limited number of fields and records. This type of database can be used to sort and arrange the records into order, and respond to interrogations by selecting records from the file, but only according to a limited set of criteria. At this simplest level, a database might be described as an automated card-index system.

Flat file database software can incorporate fairly sophisticated features such as multi-level indexing and multi-level sorting of data.

An example of a flat file database is Reflex. The simple database provided with Lotus 123 v2 is also a flat file database.

Inverted files

5.5 Inverted files can be used in a computer system to enable a computer to find records with specified 'attributes' more quickly than it could if inverted files were not provided. This facility is sometimes provided with flat file systems. Inverted files might be explained most easily with an example.

5.6 Suppose that a company has a customer file with the following records:

KEY	ATTRIBUTES				
Customer Number	Customer Name	Address	Area Code	Business Category	Credit Rating
0001	A Ltd	XX	2	A	1
0002	B plc	XX	3	A	1
0003	C & Co	XX	3	B	2
0004	D plc	XX	1	A	1
0005	E Ltd	XX	1	B	1
0006	F Ltd	XX	2	B	2
0007	G Ltd	XX	1	A	2
0008	H & I	XX	2	A	2
0009	J Ltd	XX	3	A	2
0010	K plc	XX	3	B	1
0011	L Ltd	XX	1	A	1
0012	M Ltd	XX	2	B	2

5.7 *Customer number* is the key field. In this example, a *secondary index* is maintained for the attributes of *area code* and *business category*. Inverted lists are lists of records grouped according to an (indexed) attribute value first, and key field/identifier data as a secondary item. In our example, we can produce two inverted lists.

Area Code			Business Category		
1	0004	D plc	A	0001	A Ltd
	0005	E Ltd		0002	B plc
	0007	G Ltd		0004	D plc
	0011	L Ltd		0007	G Ltd
				0008	H & I
2	0001	A Ltd		0009	J Ltd
	0006	F Ltd		0011	L Ltd
	0008	H & I			
	0012	M Ltd	B	0003	C & Co
				0005	E Ltd
3	0002	B plc		0006	F Ltd
	0003	C & Co		0010	K plc
	0009	J Ltd		0012	M Ltd
	0010	K plc			

The inverted lists together will form an *inverted file*. This is achieved by the attributes *area code*, and *business category*.

Multiple file databases

5.8 *Multiple file databases* are a bit more sophisticated, and consist of two or more separate files which can be accessed, if required, at the same time. For example, if there is a file for customers' details and a file for supplier details, the database user can access both files to find all companies, say, which are based in Scotland.

5.9 As an example, an equipment supplier might have a main database containing names and addresses of customers. Other databases might include details of:

    (a) customer purchases and

    (b) equipment maintenance and servicing details, etc.

It would be a waste of disk storage space to include the customers' names and addresses in each database, and so a 'link' is made between the various items of related data within all the files. Here, for example, a link could be provided between the customer's name and address on the main database, and his purchase details and maintenance details on the other database.

5.10   A core feature of a sophisticated multiple file database is the ability to link two or more *files* together through at least one common field. This means, for example, that if a database user were looking at an invoice, he or she could display information from the customer file and the product file, and update both files, in the same operation. With a flat file database, the user would be limited to one file at a time.

5.11   Multiple file database packages offer the following advantages.

    (a) Reducing the duplication of information on file. For example, a customer's name can be put on one file and a short ID (cross reference) to it can be used on other files.

    (b) Memory allocation is therefore more economical.

    (c) Data access times are also fast.

    (d) Giving users greater flexibility in organising and manipulating data.

'Relational' databases and multiple file databases

5.12   'The term *relational database* is, unfortunately, more of a marketing ploy than a technical description, especially in the microcomputer world' *PC Business World*, 4/4/1989.

It can be argued that many 'relational' database software packages are in fact sophisticated multiple file databases. The fact that *files* can be related to each other, and data accessed in a variety of ways, does not imply *true* relationality.

General features of a database software package

5.13   The database software is software that sees to the administration and use of the database files, providing a bridge between the data files and the user's application programs. All databases use up a great deal of memory and processing power.

5.14   All database software packages ought to have certain basic features. The recent trend in database software has been away from the 'traditional' complex software to user-friendliness.

    (a) Older DBMS included:

        (i)   *data description language* (DDL) to define, logically, the database structure;
        (ii) a *data manipulation language* (DML) to enable data to be accessed, stored etc.

        DDLs and DMLs were similar to a programming language (ie not user-friendly).

(b) For interrogating the files, a database should allow the user to construct queries (or interrogations), either singly or chained together. This is referred to as a *query language*. In relational database systems this has replaced DML. IBM's SQL is a sort of 'standard'.

(c) The database must be capable of being restructured and reorganised without losing data. For example, the database management software will automatically re-index records on file according to changes that are made.

(d) The package should allow the user to print out information eg on to address labels or in reports.

(e) The package may support a graphic user interface.

(f) Report writers enable users to design their output.

(g) Security features are invaluable if data is to be shared.

The features of database packages therefore include the facility to write program instructions for data storage, retrieval and reporting, normally using a programming language* that comes with the database software.

5.15 Different database packages have other features which vary from package to package.

(a) Some packages limit the number and size of the fields that are permitted on the file - eg an address field might be limited to, say, 40 characters. Other programs allow much more flexibility in the number of fields, and also variable length fields.

(b) Some packages limit the number of allowable key fields - ie fields which are used to speed up sorting and searching.

(c) Some packages offer a facility which enables the data user to update the data files in batches.

(d) Packages vary in the way they handle and store data, and the degree of control the user has in retrieving information.

(e) Some packages enable a database file to be accessible from several terminals.

(f) For data security, some packages offer a system of passwords for restricted access to the files or to specific records or fields.

(g) Some packages allow the user to define his own menus and help screens.

Query languages

5.16 It was mentioned earlier that a database can be interrogated by a *query language*. This section examines query languages in a little more detail.

5.17 A query language is a formalised method of constructing queries in a database system. Basically a query language provides the ways in which you ask a database for data.

5.18   Some query languages can be used to change the contents of a database.

5.19   A simple query is given below. You are interrogating a database of customer information, and you wish to discover which customers in the database owe you £2,000 or more. You want a list in alphabetical order.

'List all customers who owe £2,000 or more.'

5.20   However, in fact the queries need to be formulated more precisely. Our query might be formulated instead as:

FIND (ACCOUNTS, CUSTOMER-NAME) WHERE (ACCOUNT-BALANCE >= £2,000)

Here we are specifying the data to be interrogated. We are trying to find out the customers, who are held in the relation ACCOUNTS and who owe £2,000 or more.   The relation ACCOUNTS refers to the two-dimensional table(s) where the data is held. There might be two or more tables if linked by the relation ACCOUNTS.

5.21   The most widely-used query language is IBM's SQL, which has the basic structure:

SELECT (ie what data items you are looking for)
FROM (the relation involved in the query)
WHERE (the condition that must be satisfied).

The example above might be written as

SELECT   CUSTOMER-NAME, BRANCH-NAME
FROM   ACCOUNTS
WHERE   ACCOUNT BALANCE >= £2,000

5.22   A variety of logical functions (including ANDs, NOTs and ORs) and operations (eg averages, maxima, minima, ordering in specified sequence) can be performed.

5.23   Some menu systems have been devised so that the query could be presented as a list of questions.

Other ways of interrogating data

5.24   A software pckage like DBASE 3+ uses a menu system. You would

(a)   select the RETRIEVE RECORDS menu;
(b)   then select the DISPLAY command;
(c)   then select the BUILD A SEARCH CONDITION option.

You would then specify the parameters for the query.

6. CONCLUSION

6.1 Word processing is the computerised creation, editing and storage of text.

6.2 Computer graphics packages are for the computerised creation storage and manipulation of images.

6.3 Desk-top publishing software is used to design the layout and appearance of a document.

6.4 A spreadsheet is a software application which allows you to define a problem logically in terms of text, data and formulae, and then lets the computer bear the brunt of complicated or tedious calculations. It can be used wherever the problem can be set out in logical stages (not just accounting).

6.5 A database is a file or set of files where records are stored in such a way that they do not depend on the applications which use them.

TEST YOUR KNOWLEDGE
The numbers in brackets refer to paragraphs of this chapter

1   Define word processing. (1.1)

2   What is WYSIWYG? (1.6)

3   What are the advantages of word processing over traditional forms of preparing office correspondence and literature? (1.25)

4   What are computer graphics? (2.1)

5   Define spreadsheet. (4.1)

6   What is a cell? (4.6) What does it contain? (4.10)

7   What types of data processing are suitable for spreadsheet analysis? (4.3, 4.4)

8   List as many spreadsheet features as you can. (4.12)

9   When might a three-dimensional spreadsheet be useful? (4.22)

10   What features would you expect a database software package to contain? (5.14, 5.15)

Now try question 11 at the end of the text

PART C

ANALYSIS OF SYSTEMS

Chapter 9

MANAGING SYSTEMS DEVELOPMENT

This chapter covers the following topics.

1. The information strategy
2. Projects
3. Project management: the steering committee
4. Project management: the project manager
5. Planning: project management and control
6. Project evaluation
7. End-user computing
8. The human factors
9. Operating systems options

---

1. THE INFORMATION STRATEGY

1.1 In previous chapters, three types of management decision were identified: strategic, management and operational, dealing, by and large, with long-term planning, control of operations and detailed transaction activity.

1.2 The potential strategic importance of information systems for organisational effectiveness was also mentioned. Information systems can provide competitive advantage to an organisation. A number of trends in the management context of IT are outlined below.

Integration of hardware technologies

1.3 The term information technology itself, as you will recall, refers to the convergence of computer and telecommunications technologies. In the past, these would have been quite separate *management* responsibilities.

   (a) Computer applications, limited to bulk volume transaction processing, would be managed by the data processing department.

   (b) An organisation's telecommunications needs might be managed by a general administration manager.

   (c) The purchase of office equipment (eg typewriters, photocopiers) would have been managed by yet another department.

1.4 However, the advent of cheap personal computers and the increasing prevalence of networking have eroded any *technological* reason for these managerial demarcations: decisions taken in one area affect decisions taken elsewhere. Some degree of co-ordination is therefore required.

9: MANAGING SYSTEMS DEVELOPMENT

1.5 *Information technology costs.* While the costs of individual items of hardware have been reduced, organisations are spending more on Information Technology. It has been estimated that in 1989 the average DP department with five or more members had a budget of over £2.7m. Much of that expenditure (£0.912m) is devoted to staff. (These statistics have been taken from a survey conducted by Price Waterhouse, quoted in the *Guardian* 10 May 1990.) Moreover, many companies have suffered financial loss due to computer security breaches.

The role of end users

1.6 More day-to-day decisions relating to information systems are being taken by user departments (eg buy a new PC, develop a new spreadsheet application). The report quoted above estimated that in 1990 users would account for 25% of IT spending. User departments now take more responsibility for applications and systems development.

1.7 The information systems of an organisation therefore seem to merit the same sort of management attention as, say, the production function or the sales and marketing function all of which are recognised to have a key role.

1.8 Organisations have responded to these trends in a number of ways:

(a) developing overall *strategies* for information systems (similar in concept to sales strategies etc);

(b) raising the level of *IT staff*, sometimes to the extent of appointing IT directors;

(c) setting up *information centres* to aid users develop their own applications;

(d) setting *standards* for hardware and software acquisition;

(e) increasing resources devoted to *information systems security*.

1.9 A strategy is a statement of long-term objectives and goals. Before an organisation develops such a strategy, an analysis must be made of the importance of information technology and information systems in its current activities. Information technology can be said to function in four different ways in an organisation:

(a) as a *support activity* (eg providing ad hoc responses to queries) which is useful but not critical to organisational success;

(b) as a *factory activity* 'where information systems are crucial to current operations and their management but not at the heart of the company's strategic development';

(c) as a *turnround activity* in which IT is seen as crucial to a firm's business development, and is used to open up new opportunities (eg information technology acquired to enhance flexibility of marketing and production of consumer goods);

(d) as a *strategic activity*, where, without IT, the firm could not function at all (eg many financial services companies *depend* on computers, telecommunications and databases, just like a manufacturing company depends on raw materials).

(from Earl: Management Strategies for Information Technology.)

1.10 An information strategy for an organisation can be said to cover three areas.

(a) *Information Systems strategy*

This has been defined as the 'long-term directional plan...seen to be business-led, demand-oriented and concerned to exploit IT either to support business strategies or create new strategic options.'

An IS strategy therefore deals with the integration of an organisation's information requirements and information systems planning with its long-term overall goals (customer service etc).

(b) *Information Technology strategy*

This leads on, as it were from the IS strategy above, in that it deals with the technologies of:

(i) computing;
(ii) communications;
(iii) data;
(iv) application systems.

This provides a framework for the analysis and design of the technological infrastructure of an organisation. For example, this might involve guidelines for makes of computers purchased (limited to IBM for example) and so forth.

(c) *The Information Management strategy*

This refers to the basic approach an organisation has to the management of its information systems, including:

(i) planning IS developments;
(ii) organisational environment of IS
(iii) control (eg cost control);
(iv) technology (eg systems development methodologies).

1.11 The strategy will therefore affect all an organisation's information systems and information technology activities. Not only should IT be considered as seriously as sales, production and so forth, but the IT strategy should be developed in conjunction with the strategy of the business.

2. PROJECTS

2.1 Whilst the strategy gives the overall direction of IT developments in an organisation, detailed *implementation* of the strategy can be managed in a number of different ways:

(a) Larger-scale systems need a firm management grasp, and the means by which their introduction is controlled is known as *project management*. The analysis and design of a new system is given the same management effort of planning and controlling as, for example, a new product launch, or production process.

(b) *End-user computing* is one means by which some systems can be acquired and/or developed.

2.2 The importance of good management of projects cannot be exaggerated as it is often the case that;

(a) new systems do not arrive on time;

(b) new systems often cost a lot more than was budgeted;

(c) new systems do not meet user requirements;

(d) any one or combination of (a), (b), (c) above leads to wasted time, money and effort.

3. PROJECT MANAGEMENT: THE STEERING COMMITTEE

3.1 The introduction of a new system is likely to involve a great deal of time and effort, both from data processing professionals (eg systems analysts, programmers) and user staff.

3.2 If the organisation introduces new computer systems regularly, it might set up a *steering committee* whose tasks would be:

(a) to approve (or reject) projects whose total budgeted cost is below a certain level and so within their authorisation limit; and

(b) to recommend projects to the board of directors or the Information Director for acceptance when their cost is high enough to require approval at board level.

A steering committee might also be set up for a 'one-off' computer project.

3.3 The steering committee might include:

(a) the information director, or a senior DP staff member;

(b) an accountant for technical financial advice relating to costs and benefits;

(c) senior user management.

3.4 The steering committee's responsibilities are likely to include the following.

(a) Under the guidance of the information director, *implementing overall objectives* and policies for the organisation's data processing activities. For example, objectives might be to reduce staffing and administrative costs, to improve management forecasting, to provide more decision support for management, to improve accounting procedures or to provide a better service for customers or clients.

(b) Under the guidance of the information director, to *establish company guidelines* within the framework of the IT strategy for the development of computer based processing and management information systems.

(c) To set up feasibility *study groups* to investigate and report on existing data processing systems and to make recommendations for their improvement or for a new system development.

(d) The co-ordination and control of the work of the study group(s) and project development groups, in respect of *development time, cost and technical quality* of the investigations, thus aiming to overcome the problems outlined in 2.2 above.

(e) The evaluation of the feasibility study reports and system specifications. The steering committee must be satisfied that each new system has been properly *justified*.

(f) *Monitoring and controlling* individual development projects.

(g) Ensuring that projects' *benefits* (financial or otherwise) outweigh their costs.

(h) Possibly, giving *approval to new projects*, at the feasibility study and system specification stages.

(i) Possibly, to *authorise capital expenditure* on new hardware or software.

(j) To monitor and review each new system after *implementation* to check whether the system has met its objectives.

(k) In an organisation which has a *continuing programme* of new DP projects, the steering committee will assist in the:

   (i) assessment of the contribution of each project to the long term corporate objectives of the organisation;

   (ii) ranking of projects in order of priority and assigning resources to the most important projects first;

   (iii) taking of decisions to defer projects when insufficient resources are available.

4. PROJECT MANAGEMENT: THE PROJECT MANAGER

4.1 A project is limited by a number of factors, often in conflict with each other:

(a) *quality* of the system required, in terms of basic system requirements;

(b) the *resources*, in terms of staff recruitment, work scheduling and technology;

(c) *time*, both to complete the project, and in terms of the opportunity cost of time spent on this project which could be spent on others;

(d) *costs*, which are monitored and controlled, in accordance with the budget set for the project.

4.2 It is with these aims in mind that management of the project must be conducted. A *project manager* is usually responsible for:

(a) *planning* and work scheduling;

(b) establishment of feedback procedures to aid the *control* and *monitoring* of the project (timeliness, keeping to budget, quality control etc);

(c) ensuring that the different members of staff working on different segments of the project *communicate* with each other, and with the project manager;

(d) *quality control* over work done, perhaps enforced through the use of systems development standards;

(e) *reporting* to the steering committee and/or the IT director on a regular basis as part of the control procedure, as to how the project is progressing in terms of the four factors mentioned above.

4.3 The job of the project manager varies from organisation to organisation. In some circumstances the project manager will have a strategic role, in terms of a broad analysis of the project's rationale in the context of the organisation's information systems strategy. In others, the project manager's role might be simply to manage a project with precisely defined objectives.

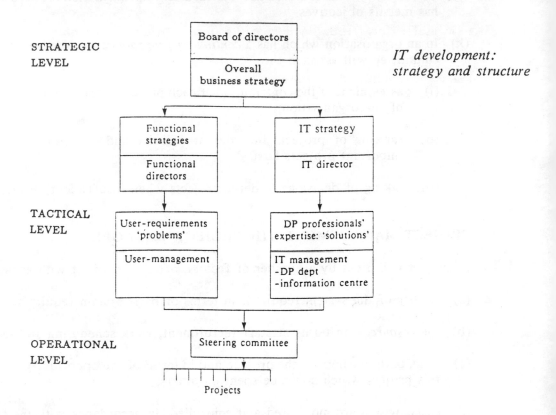

5. PLANNING: PROJECT MANAGEMENT AND CONTROL

5.1 As the development and implementation of a computer project may take a considerable length of time (eg 18 months from initial decision to operational running for a medium-sized installation) a proper plan and time schedule for the various activities must be drawn up.

Project management involves

(a) the *estimation* of project resources in terms of time cost and staff;
(b) planning;
(c) control and monitoring.

In devising the plan all known facts about the organisation, the staffing problems, the accommodation, the computer manufacturer/software house, etc must be taken into account and analysed precisely. Aids to planning which may be used include *network analysis* and/or the preparation of *Gantt charts. Project management software* is now available.

9: MANAGING SYSTEMS DEVELOPMENT

Network analysis (critical path analysis)

5.2 Network analysis is used to program and monitor the progress of a project so that the project is completed in the minimum time and on schedule. It pinpoints the parts of the project which are 'critical', ie those parts which, if delayed beyond the allotted time, would delay the completion of the project as a whole. The technique can also be used to assist in allocating resources such as labour and equipment, and so basically, the method is concerned with 'the deployment of available resources for the completion of a complex task'. (PG Moore 'Basic Operational Research').

5.3 It is useful for scheduling and controlling projects where many *separate tasks* (which collectively make up the whole project) can either happen simultaneously or must follow one after another such that it is difficult to establish the relationships between all the separate tasks. The technique can be applied to any purposeful chain of events involving the use of time, labour and physical resources. With computer projects, it is likely to be a very useful project planning and control technique where

(a) the project is a big one; and
(b) the project includes system design work and programming work, because the system is being tailor-made.

5.4 Network analysis is operated in various forms under a number of titles which include critical path analysis (CPA) or critical path method (CPM). In case you have not learned network analysis before, a brief explanation is given here.

5.5 A project is analysed into *activities* which are particular *tasks* within the overall project. These activities are listed and their sequence is then presented in the form of a pictorial 'flow diagram' or network diagram. An activity within a network can be represented by an arrowed line.

Events mark the point in time when an activity is started or completed. Events are represented by circles. 'Dummy' activities may be included in order to show properly the logical sequence of activities and events.

5.6 An outline network diagram showing many of the principal activities involved in a computer project is illustrated on the next page. (The activity times are not standard.) In this diagram, it is assumed that the computer system is being designed and programmed by an 'in-house' DP department's systems analysts and programmers. The critical path in this example consists of activities AHJKLO.

5.7 The critical path is the '*bottleneck route*'. Only by finding ways to shorten jobs along the critical path can the overall project time be reduced. Remember that:

(a) the time required to perform non-critical jobs is irrelevant in terms of affecting the total project times. This means that the costly practice of '*crashing' the time* taken on non-critical jobs to complete them more quickly is an unnecessary waste of expense, and yet it can happen all too easily in practice;

Computer project: CPA diagram

Times in weeks

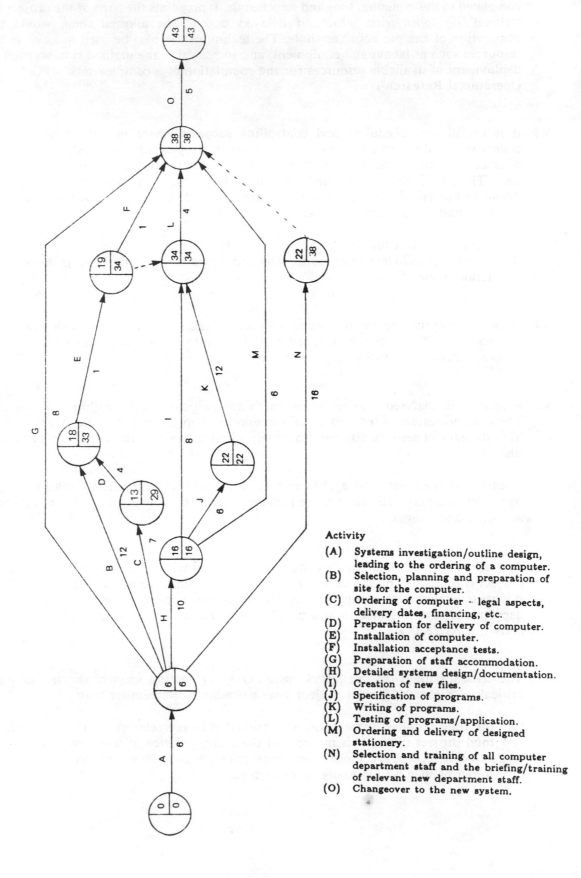

Activity

(A) Systems investigation/outline design, leading to the ordering of a computer.
(B) Selection, planning and preparation of site for the computer.
(C) Ordering of computer – legal aspects, delivery dates, financing, etc.
(D) Preparation for delivery of computer.
(E) Installation of computer.
(F) Installation acceptance tests.
(G) Preparation of staff accommodation.
(H) Detailed systems design/documentation.
(I) Creation of new files.
(J) Specification of programs.
(K) Writing of programs.
(L) Testing of programs/application.
(M) Ordering and delivery of designed stationery.
(N) Selection and training of all computer department staff and the briefing/training of relevant new department staff.
(O) Changeover to the new system.

(b) if some means is found to reduce the time required to complete activities along the critical path, the total project time would be shortened;

(c) if the completion time for any activity on the critical path slips, the completion date for the total project will slip back too.

For example, it may be possible at extra expense to cut the project time by assigning extra labour or equipment to various jobs on the critical path.

(d) PERT can also help save costs. For example, if staff numbers are limited, it may be appropriate to delay some activities, if this is possible, whilst others are undertaken, PERT indicates the ease with which this can be achieved.

During the computer project some activities will inevitably fall behind schedule. A continuous monitoring and updating, possibly on a weekly basis, is necessary so that either corrective action may be taken or the completion date adjusted in good time to warn management.

Gantt charts

5.8 Sometimes referred to as 'horizontal bar charts', Gantt charts may be used to plan the time scale for a project and to estimate the amount of resources required. In its simpler form the Gantt chart is used to show the time to be taken for each activity, which commences at the appropriate stage in the project plan. As the activity is achieved the 'bar' is shaded in and by using a data 'cursor' it is easy to see if the time scale is being adhered to.

5.9 A Gantt chart, illustrating some of the hardware-related activities involved in systems development and implementation is shown below:

As at end of week 10

Activity	Weeks
	1 2 3 4 5 6 7 8 9 10 11 12 13 14 15 16
1. Order computer/arrange finance etc	
2. Agree delivery dates	
3. Select site	
4. Plan and prepare site	
5. Prepare for delivery	
6. Install computer	
7. Engineers acceptance tests	
8. Operational tests	
9. Plan & prepare perm- anent staff work areas and accommodation	

At the end of the tenth week activity 9 is running behind schedule and more resources may have to be allocated to this activity if the staff accommodation is to be ready in time for the changeover to the new system. Activity 4 had not been completed on time, and this has resulted in some disruption to the computer installation (activity 6), which may mean further delays in the commencement of activities 7 and 8.

5.10 One of the main problems with this type of Gantt chart is that it does not reflect the interrelationship between the various activities in the project as does a network diagram. However, a combination of Gantt charts and network analysis might be used for project planning and resource allocation.

Project management software

5.11 Project management software exists which automates these techniques, and will contain computerised equivalents of Gantt charts and Network analysis. Examples of project management software packages are MacProjectII, Hoskyns Project Management Workbench.

5.12 The assumption behind all project management software is that a project is broken down into tasks, the basic unit to which resources are allocated. Resources are time, money, personnel and equipment usage.

5.13 Some packages enable a number of different projects to be tracked at the same time, so that the effect of resources allocation to one project on other projects can be estimated.

5.14 'Resources' may be held on a central database. A typical software package might offer four options as to *how* they are to be allocated (the first three being determined by the software):.

    (a)   as soon as possible;
    (b)   as late as possible;
    (c)   averaged; or
    (d)   assigned manually.

5.15 Some software will enable the project plan to be rearranged in response to *actual* outcomes.

6.   PROJECT EVALUATION

6.1 It has been noted that one of the features of project management is that it is monitored and controlled, and that regular reports are often sent to senior management.

6.2 Once the system has been introduced into the user department two types of assessment can be made.

    (a)   Does the system fulfil the requirements it was supposed to satisfy?
    (b)   Was the project managed successfully?

6.3 While question (a) measures the overall success of the project (and is discussed further in the chapter on systems installation), a review of the management of the project itself will cover the following areas.

(a) Were there any major problems in meeting deadlines?

(b) Were there any serious management problems?

(c) Were there any serious cost overruns?

(d) Were the problems encountered the result of:

(i) poor planning (in which case they could have been foreseen);
(ii) factors beyond anybody's control?

(e) What lessons are there for future projects?

(f) Are the organisation's systems development standards appropriate?

7. END-USER COMPUTING

7.1 In the past, especially with large mainframe systems, an organisation's data processing capacity was controlled centrally. A data processing department would produce reports from data submitted to it, and would be responsible for any upgrades or developments to the system. If a user wished, for example, to be given a new report it would be up to the data processing department to write applications software and be responsible for implementation. This specialisation was inevitable: even the construction of logically simple applications required a degree of specialist knowledge which most users could never possess. Similarly, it was not possible for users to have easy access to program or data files for experimentation.

7.2 However, recent developments in software (eg report generators, fourth generation languages, described in the chapter on program development) and hardware technology have breached the ramparts of the isolated data processing department. The microcomputer is a familiar feature of office life. Users who are quite happy, for example, to interrogate databases, design spreadsheet applications, or use relatively simple command languages in financial and other modelling packages, may now wish to extend their computing expertise. End-user computing therefore is the process by which users design applications and perform other computing tasks which were previously the prerogative of data processing professionals.

7.3 *End-user computing* has been defined as:

'the direct, hands-on use of computers by users - not indirect use through systems professionals on the data processing staff. End-users include executives, managers, professional staff, secretaries, office workers, salespeople and others'.
(Sprague and McNurlin: Information Systems Management in Practice)

Accounts staff *designing* and *using* spreadsheet models is an example of end-user computing.

7.4 End-user computing has been fuelled by the introduction of personal computers to user departments, user-friendly software, and greater awareness of computers and what they can do. Another factor in its growth is the *applications backlog*. Most DP departments do not have the resources to cope with all the demands for new applications pressed on them.

7.5 The uses of computers by end-users include:

(a) accounting, calculating (spreadsheets);
(b) writing (word processing);
(c) search and retrieval of information (interrogating a database);
(d) communications (computer networks, electronic mail);
(e) presentation of information (graphics);
(f) planning, scheduling and monitoring (project management);
(g) personal organisation (electronic diary facilities);
(h) routine transaction processing;
(i) learning and education (computer based training);
(j) end-user programming (developing new programs);
(k) decision support.

7.6 There are a number of management issues related to end-user computing.

(a) Should responsibility for the development of applications rest with user departments or the DP department?

(b) How does the organisation avoid the development of similar applications in different departments thus duplicating programming effort?

(c) How is security maintained if access to the system is easy to obtain?

7.7 An approach to dealing with these problems is the *information centre*, which provides guidance to users, whilst maintaining a certain degree of control and standardisation.

The information centre approach

7.8 An information centre is a small unit of staff with a good technical awareness of computer systems, whose task is to provide a support function to computer users within the organisation. The information centre staff would act as a go-between or bridge between computer users and the organisation's DP department, or external hardware and software suppliers.

7.9 They are particularly useful in organisations which use distributed processing systems or microcomputers quite heavily, and so have many 'non-technical' people in charge of hardware, files and software scattered throughout the organisation.

The role of the information centre

7.10 The key functions of the information centre are set out below.

(a) To provide users of existing programs and software packages with technical support and training.

(b) To encourage users who wish to develop their own applications and to provide them with technical assistance (eg training in the use of 4GLs) so that the programs are *well-written* and *well-documented*.

(c) To ensure that applications developed are replicated by others in the organisation, where this would be of benefit to the organisation.

(d) To ensure that the data used in these disparate applications is properly controlled and is consistent.

(e) To encourage users to conform to any hardware, software or programming standards that the organisation might use, eg

  (i) to make sure that all the microcomputers purchased by the organisation are compatible, and so could be moved around from department to department if necessary; or

  (ii) to make sure that if the organisation uses spreadsheets in various departments, the same package (Lotus, or Supercalc etc) is used in every department.

(f) To keep a look out for new technical developments.

7.11 All this is intended to get applications in operation which would otherwise take significantly longer to develop; or perhaps would not be developed at all.

7.12 The information centre will also increase the security of an organisation's systems by educating the users about security. Data security is generally improved, for example, where users have available simple utility programs which ease the creation of backup files.

Technical support

7.13 The centre's staff will also be able to give advice to end-user staff about:

(a) any problems with using the computer itself, eg using certain operating system commands or facilities, or setting up new files and sub-files;

(b) the specific capabilities of a particular software package, eg how to use a word processing package to produce print in double columns on a page, or how (as in the production of this text) to 'draw' boxes round various items of print;

(c) using access software to gain access to the processing capabilities of a mainframe computer from a 'local' office microcomputer in the same network.

(d) Information centre staff will be able to give help with the use of important software aids such as:

  (i) report writers;
  (ii) query languages;
  (iii) fourth generation languages (application generators).

7.14 The centre's services should be readily available to end-users, and the centre's staff should try to keep a 'high profile' with end-user departments. The centre's services could be provided by means of:

(a) a telephone 'hot-line', with a number for end-users to call whenever they have difficulties. This hot-line should always be manned;

(b) a 'drop-in' advice centre, so that end-users could call in at the Centre's office without having to make an appointment.

7.15 Information centres have been well received since they offer significant benefits to both the organisation and the users within the organisation.

8. THE HUMAN FACTORS

8.1 Management should be aware of the effect of a new system on the people who will use it. Resistance to a new system can develop, both during the design phase (of a tailor-made system) and the implementation phase of the project, and resistance of this kind will be damaging. For example, to design an efficient system, the analyst needs the co-operation of the user department's staff. They can supply the essential details that the analyst needs, and they can judge whether the system an analyst proposes will 'work' in practice and resolve all the problems it is intended to. Without user department co-operation, participation and enthusiasm for the new system, the analyst will face an uphill struggle.

8.2 The human problems with systems design can fall into several different categories.

(a) *Job security and status.* Employees might think that the new system will put them out of a job, because the computer will perform routines that are currently done manually, and so reduce the need for human intervention. An office staff of, say, 10 people might be reduced to 8 say, and the threat of being out of work would unsettle the entire office staff.

Even when there is no threat of losing a job, a new system might make some staff, experienced in the existing system, feel that all their experience will be worthless when the new system goes live, and so they will lose 'status' within the office.

In some cases, the resistance to a new system might stem from a fear that it will result in a loss of status for the *department* concerned. For example, the management of the department concerned might believe that a computer system will give 'control' over information gathering and dissemination to another group in the organisation. Dysfunctional behaviour might therefore find expression in:

(i) interdepartmental squabbling about access to information;
(ii) a tendency to disregard the new sources of information, and to stick to old methods of collecting information instead.

(b) *Career prospects.* In some instances, managers and staff might think that a new system will damage their career prospects by reducing the opportunities for promotion. When the effect of a system is to reduce the requirement for staff in middle management and supervisory grades, this could well be true. On the other hand, today's successful manager should be able to adapt to information technology, and to develop a career means having to be flexible, accepting change rather than resisting it.

(c) *Social change in the office.* New systems might disrupt the established 'social system' or 'team spirit' in the office. Individuals who are used to working together might be separated into different groups, and individuals used to working on their own might be expected to join a group. Office staff used to moving around and mixing with other people in the course of their work might be faced with the prospect of having to work much more in isolation at a keyboard, unable to move around the office as much. Where possible, new systems should be designed so as to leave the 'social fabric' of the workplace undamaged. Group attitudes to change should then be positive rather than negative.

(d) *Bewilderment.* It is easy for individuals to be confused and bewildered by change. The systems analyst must explain the new system fully, clearing up doubts, inviting and answering questions, etc from a very early stage in systems investigation onwards through the design stages to eventual implementation.

(e) *Fear of depersonalisation.* Staff may be afraid that the computer will 'take over' and they will be reduced to being operators chained to the machine, losing the ability to introduce the 'human touch' to the work they do.

Suspicion or fear of a new system is likely to result in resentment and possibly resistance from user department staff.

8.3 Dysfunctional behaviour might manifest itself in the antagonism of operating staff towards data processing specialists who are employed to design and introduce a computer system. It might take the form of:

(a) an unwillingness to explain the details of the current system, or to suggest weaknesses in it that the new system might eradicate. Since DP staff need information from and participation by the operating staff to develop an efficient system, any such antagonism would impair the system design;

(b) a reluctance to be taught the new system;

(c) a reluctance to help with introducing the new system.

8.4 A new system will reveal weaknesses in the previous system, and so another fear of computerisation is that it will show up exactly how poor and inefficient previous methods of information gathering and information use had been. If individuals feel that they are put under pressure by the revelation of any such deficiencies, they might try to find fault with the new system too. When fault-finding is not constructive - ie not aimed at improving the system - it will be dysfunctional in its consequences.

8.5 In extreme cases, dysfunctional behaviour might take a more drastic, aggressive form. Individuals might show a marked reluctance to learn how to handle the new equipment, they might be deliberately slow keying in data, or they might even damage the equipment in minor acts of vandalism.

Overcoming the human problems

8.6 To overcome the human problems with systems design and implementation, management and DP systems analysts must recognise them, and do what they can to resolve them.

(a) Employees should be kept fully informed about plans to install the new system, how events are progressing and how the new system will affect what people do.

(b) It should be explained to staff that 'change is for the better' with the reasons why this is so.

(c) User department employees should be encouraged to participate fully in the design of the system, when the system is a tailor-made one.

    (i) Their suggestions about problems with the existing system should be fully discussed.

    (ii) The systems analyst's ideas for a new system should be discussed with them, and their views considered.

    (iii) Their suggestions for features in the new system should be welcomed.

Participation should be genuine.

(d) Staff should be informed that they will be spared boring, mundane work because of the possibility of automating such work and so will be able to take on more interesting, demanding and challenging work.

(e) Employees should be told that they will be able to learn new skills which will make them more attractive candidates either for internal promotion or on the external labour market. For example, experience with using databases or spreadsheet models could greatly enhance an office worker's experience.

(f) A training programme for staff should be *planned* in advance of the new systems being introduced. If there *are* to be job losses, or a redeployment of staff, these should be arranged in full consultation with the people concerned.

(g) Careful attention should be given to:

    (i) the design of work organisation;

    (ii) the developments or preservation of 'social work groups' - the new technology and systems should not leave individuals feeling cut off from their fellow workers;

    (iii) the inter-relationship between jobs and responsibilities in the new system.

(h) Change should be planned. Reductions in jobs should be foreseen, and redundancies can be avoided if plans are made well in advance (eg staff can be moved to other job vacancies in the organisation). Training (and retraining) of staff should be organised.

(i) A member of the staff should be appointed as the office expert or 'guru' in the system, to whom other members of staff can go to ask for help or advice. When the software is bought as an off-the-shelf package, this office expert should be made the person who contacts the software supplier about any problems with the system.

(j) *Management and the systems.* When systems are designed in-house, the systems analyst should:

    (i) introduce changes gradually, giving time for personnel to accept the changes before their implementation;

(ii)   build up a *good personal relationship* with all the people he or she has to work with. To do this he or she must listen sympathetically to their ideas, and encourage constructive thoughts and suggestions;

(iii)   persuade management to give sound guarantees for the future, as regards job retraining, redundancy payments etc;

(iv)   work towards getting employees to accept change as a matter of course. Frequent changes (resulting from new technology, diversification etc) become more acceptable;

(v)   be willing to listen to criticisms of the system he or she is designing, and do something to meet them.

(k)   The system should not be introduced in a rush. Users of the system should be given time to become familiar with it. Implementation by means of 'parallel running' might be advisable.

(l)   Confidence between the systems analyst and operational staff should be built up over time.

(m)   The systems analyst should have the full and clearly expressed support of senior management for what he is trying to do. There should be no danger that his authority could be undermined.

8.7   In some cases, it is managers (especially middle managers) who provide the most opposition to IT as it threatens their status as managers. Shoshana Zuboff has argued (in her book: In the Age of the Smart Machine) that information technology requires that workers have the same sort of expertise as would have been required by managers, and that managers feel threatened from below by this sharing of their exclusive knowledge.

8.8   On the other hand the status of middle management is also threatened from 'above' by the fact that, with EISs, senior management can go directly down to operational level for information with speed and ease.

8.9   In summary, the ability of both the systems analyst and user department management and staff to handle interpersonal relationships is probably the most critical factor in overcoming resistance to new systems and dysfunctional behaviour.

9   OPERATING SYSTEMS OPTIONS

9.1   Until recently many computer users have not given a great deal of thought to their operating system. Purchasers of mainframes and microcomputers are supplied with a proprietary system by the hardware manufacturer and that is usually the end of the story. IBM users have OS/VS, ICL users have VME and each machine will only run on its own system. At the microcomputer end of computing, where all micros are IBM compatible, MS-DOS is the standard OS.

9.2   Over the last year or two, the market has changed and this change is set to continue. Mainframe and mini users are talking of Unix and microcomputer users, instead of accepting MS-DOS, are asking for OS/2 or Windows NT. Suddenly, there is consumer choice in an area where users have traditionally had to use what they were given.

9: MANAGING SYSTEMS DEVELOPMENT

Unix

9.3 The Unix operating system was developed by AT&T in 1969 as a multi-tasking OS (non-proprietary) that could be portable to different computer architectures. It is an example of an *open system*. It first gained popularity in universities, where many computer science students needed to be able to work at the same time, but was seen as lacking in user-friendliness and uneconomic by commercial suppliers and users. However, its popularity among those who used it ensured that it survived and by the 1980s it had been developed far enough for commercial users to take an interest in it.

9.4 The current version of Unix is SVR4. Software companies are now starting to make applications available for a wide range of systems. Unix works equally well in a network environment as in a multi-user system. Particular areas where Unix has already demonstrated its capabilities are communications, where the ability to accommodate PC operating systems in the Unix environment supports the use of electronic mail, and engineering, where Unix's capabilities are suited to driving high-resolution graphics systems.

9.5 Just at the moment when Unix looks set to become the standard choice for mainframes and minis, the OS which has been the natural choice at micro level is under threat from two new systems.

OS/2

9.6 OS/2 was developed jointly by IBM and Microsoft to replace the latter's MS-DOS. Microsoft have now ended their involvement with the project and so IBM have released version 2 alone. Microsoft have followed a different route, developing the Windows GUI.

9.7 The feature of OS/2 which is likely to be most popular is its multitasking capability (hence a recent series of advertisements in the national press depicting an elephant performing a variety of circus tricks). The user can switch between computer applications without being forced to follow long exit procedures from one and logon procedures to the other.

9.8 Like Windows, OS/2 offers a graphical-based interface rather than MS-DOS's text-based approach. Graphical interfaces can be tailored to meet the needs of the organisation, and standard icons can be replaced with graphics created by the user or imported from any of a number of packages now on the market which offer a wide range of alternatives.

Windows

9.9 Windows was developed as a front-end addition to the MS-DOS operating system. The latest version is Windows 3.1. During 1992, Microsoft are expected to launch Windows NT, a complete operating system in its own right. This will place it in direct competition with OS/2. (Users of Apple Macintosh computers have worked with GUIs for some years already - their OS is called System 7.) Windows offers a full graphical user interface, simplifying DOS commands, so that the user, instead of having to memorise commands to type in after the 'C prompt', can either pull down menus and select commands from them or 'point' to icons to make selections.

9.10 Windows provides a comprehensive working environment, managing programs specifically written for it (Wordperfect for Windows, 1-2-3 for Windows etc) and those which were written for DOS (Wordperfect, Lotus 1-2-3 etc). This should mean that it becomes easier for beginners to learn how to use PCs, as all applications will look and 'feel' the same.

9.11 GUIs are discussed further in the chapter on systems design.

10. CONCLUSION

10.1 An information strategy is necessary as an organisation's information is crucial to its success.

10.2 Individual applications are developed in the context of the strategy.

10.3 Projects must be controlled and monitored to ensure they achieve what is required of them.

TEST YOUR KNOWLEDGE
The numbers in brackets refer to paragraphs of this chapter

1   Why do some organisations develop an information strategy? (1.3-1.8)

2   What is the role of a project manager? (4.1-4.3)

3   Describe critical path analysis (5.2-5.7), and Gantt charts (5.8-5.9)

4   What will be the subject of a project evaluation review? (6.3)

5   What is end-user computing? (7.3)

6   What is the role of the information centre? (7.10)

Now try question 12 at the end of the text

Chapter 10

THE STAGES IN A SYSTEMS DEVELOPMENT PROJECT

This chapter covers the following topics.

1.   The systems development life cycle
2.   An introduction to methodologies
3.   SSADM (Structured Systems Analysis and Design Methodology)

---

1.   THE SYSTEMS DEVELOPMENT LIFE CYCLE

1.1   In the early days of computing, systems were developed in a fairly haphazard fashion.

(a)   Systems were developed in a piecemeal, one-off fashion, automating current procedures rather than as part of a planned strategy.

(b)   The development of systems was not properly planned.

The consequences were poorly designed systems which cost too much to make and which were not suited to users' needs.

1.2   The National Computing Centre in the 1960s developed a more disciplined approach to systems development, which could be applied almost anywhere. This was called the *systems development life cycle*. It contained the following stages.

(1)   *Feasibility study*. Those conducting the study take a brief look at the present system and identify alternative solutions, one of which is recommended to management on the basis of its costs and benefits. A formal report is the result of the study which may include stages 2 and 3 below in some circumstances.

(2)   *Systems investigation*. This is a thorough fact-finding exercise, using a number of methods to investigate current systems requirements and problems, volumes of data processed and so forth. This *may* be conducted, substantially, during the feasibility study.

(3)   *Systems analysis*. Once facts about the present system have been obtained, the present system is analysed in terms of its problems, working methods, bottlenecks, inefficiencies and so forth. Again, substantial analysis work may be conducted during the feasibility study.

(4)   *Systems design*. The design is broadly based on that suggested during the feasibility study, but will go into considerable detail on inputs, outputs, files, security and so forth. The main documentation produced here is the *system specification*.

(5) *Implementation*. This stage includes the writing of computer programs, testing and, eventually, changeover to the new system.

(6) *Review and maintenance*. Maintenance involved keeping the system up to date, and the system would be subject to review to see that it conformed to the requirements identified in the feasibility study.

You should note that this is only a *model* of the development life cycle. The feasibility study in particular will vary from project to project.

1.3 A stage perhaps missing from this analysis is *identification of a problem*, once the system is up and running. If we add this in, we are faced with a genuine cycle of development as outlined below.

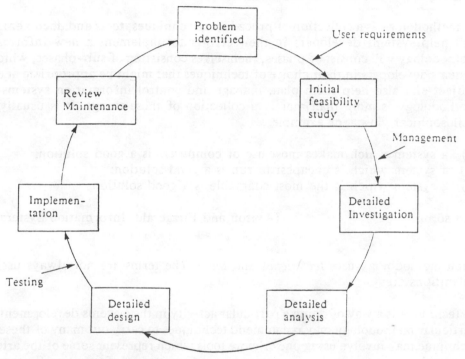

1.4 There are a number of problems with this approach.

(a) While it is efficient at automating operational areas such as payroll and sales ledger, it is less good at identifying the requirements for management information systems, at strategic level.

(b) It often results in the mere automation of manual systems rather than a new design concept.

(c) Partly as a consequence of (b) above, the systems design is inflexible, and does not take into account the fact that business processes change over time.

(d) Users fail to see the repercussions of their decisions regarding their requirements until late into the project when these are hard to change.

(e) The necessary documentation is oriented towards the programmer rather than the user, which makes it difficult for users to understand the system.

1.5 However, the systems development life cycle is still a valuable approach for charting systems development. Later chapters will examine some of the stages of the cycle in more detail.

2. AN INTRODUCTION TO METHODOLOGIES

2.1 The systems development life cycle above was an example of a systems development *methodology*. It may be helpful to begin with a definition of this term.

Methodology

2.2 A systems development methodology can be defined as follows.

'A methodology is a collection of procedures, techniques, tools and documentation aids which will help systems developers in their efforts to implement a new information system. A methodology will consist of phases, themselves consisting of sub-phases, which will guide the systems developers in their choice of techniques that might be appropriate at each stage of the project and also help them plan, manage and control information systems projects. But a methodology is more than merely a collection of these things. It is usually based on some philosophical view...for example:

(a) a system which makes most use of computers is a good solution;
(b) a system which is cheapest to run is a good solution;
(c) a system which is the most adaptable is a good solution;

and so on.' (Avison and Fitzgerald: Information Systems Development)

2.3 Each methodology uses *techniques* and *tools*. The terms are not always used precisely, but definitions are:

'A technique is a way of doing a particular activity in the systems development process and any particular methodology may recommend techniques to carry out many of these activities. Each technique may involve using one or more tools which represent some of the artefacts that might be used.' (Avison and Fitzgerald: Information Systems Development)

2.4 The *systems development life cycle* is a methodology, according to the above definitions:

(a) it is split into discrete phases;
(b) it makes extensive use of documentation;
(c) it is standardised and can be applied in many circumstances;
(d) it uses techniques and tools (eg questionnaires);
(e) there is an implied *philosophy* (ie that computerisation is a good way of dealing with clerical problems, and that perhaps the purpose of computerisation is the automation of clerical procedures).

2.5 Recently there has been a trend towards the logical design of a system before any physical implementation issues are addressed. Moreover, users, who are not computer professionals, can have a greater say in how a system is developed. The assumption is that the *data* flows in an organisation are likely to be more stable than the actual *processes* by which these flows are implemented. In principle, the same logical design could be implemented in a number of different ways.

2.6   There are a variety of other methodologies. Here are some examples.

(a)   SSADM (Structured Systems Analysis and Design Methodology), which is described below.

(b)   STRADIS (Structured Analysis and Design of Information Systems).

    (i)   Initial study
    (ii)   Detailed study
    (iii)   Defining and designing alternative solutions
    (iv)   Physical design (of chosen alternative).

(c)   Business systems planning

    (i)   Requirements are identified
    (ii)   Requirements are defined
    (iii)   General system design
    (iv)   Detailed system design
    (v)   System development and testing
    (vi)   Installation
    (vii)   Operation

(d)   JSP (Jackson structured programming)

    (i)   Definition of real-world entities (entity action).

    (ii)   Expresion of entity actions in chronological order (entity structure).

    (iii)   Creation of model which simulates entity structure and which is suitable for computerisation (initial model).

    (iv)   Design of outputs for certain combinations of circumstances (function step).

    (v)   Specification of time constraints (system timing).

3.   SSADM (STRUCTURED SYSTEMS ANALYSIS AND DESIGN METHODOLOGY)

3.1   There are a number of methodologies based around the principles of structured analysis, including those developed by Yourdon and de Marco. SSADM proper was developed by Learmonth and Burchett Management Systems in conjunction with the UK government's Central Computer and Telecommunications Agency.

3.2   SSADM:

(a)   describes how a system is to developed;

(b)   reduces development into phases: each phase is reduced into stages, and each stage contains a number of steps which contains tasks, inputs and outputs;

(c) is self-checking, and can be tailored to a number of applications.

3.3 The structure of a systems development project using SSADM is outlined below. You might like to compare this with the stages of the systems life cycle described earlier; remember that one is a *model* and the other is a *methodology*.

SSADM (with feasibility study)

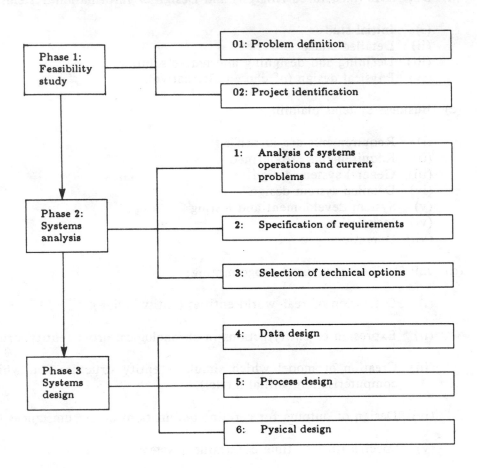

3.4 *Phase 1: Feasibility Study*
This phase, although not mandatory in many SSADM projects, examines the 'case' for undertaking a particular project in terms of its technical feasibility and the cost/benefit implications.

In short this phase involves a limited investigation and analysis of the problem, the current system and alternatives, so that management can make a decision whether or not to commit resources of time, money hardware and expertise to the later stages of the project (ie *analysis* and *design*).

This phase is divided into two *stages*.

(a) *Problem definition*. A problem (ie some deficiency in the system as it is now running, or an anticipated future deficiency) is identified. It is then analysed in more detail.

(b) *Project identification.* At this stage a series of options are identified for solving, or at least coping with the problems defined. Each potential project identified will have an outline specification and will be costed.

The results of this stage are formalised into a *feasibility study report,* which should also contain costings for the next phase.

3.5 *Phase 2: Systems analysis*
This contains the following stages.

(a) *Analysis of systems operations and current problems.* This is to ensure that the current system is properly documented, for both its physical processes, and its *data flows.* A list of 'current problems' is made.

Some or all of these tasks may have been carried out as part of a feasibility study.

(b) *Specification of requirements.* Here, what *users* actually required are laid down in detail. In informal systems development, users may not be sure of what they need exactly, or the instructions may be unclear. Here, the aim is to the matters down there exactly.

(c) *Selection of technical options.* At this stage users, having defined their requirements choose the means by which they would like the system to be implemented. Some of these 'technical' options (eg type of computer) may have been outlined in brief in the feasibility study phase.

3.6 *Phase 3: System Design*
From the requirements laid down earlier the system is designed, both logically and physically.

(a) *Data design.* This might involve 'entity' analysis as discussed earlier.
(b) *Process design.* Involves stating exactly which processes are to produce which outputs.
(c) *Physical design.* In this stage:

    (i)   program specifications are made for all transactions;
    (ii) testing and implementation are planned; and
    (iii) operating instructions are designed.

Exercise

The logical system design and physical system design are both important stages in systems development. Distinguish between them by describing the major tasks accomplished within each.

Solution

Logical design is that part of the process which determines *what* the system is supposed to do, and physical design is concerned with determining *how* those objectives are to be achieved. The major tasks performed in each stage might be as follows.

Logical design

(a) Ensure that agreement has been reached on requirements.
(b) Define scope of system.
(c) Detail aspects of old system which are to be retained.
(d) Detail aspects of old system which are to be amended.
(e) Detail aspects of new system definition requiring designing.
(f) Analyse data requirements of new system.
(g) Produce data structures.
(h) Identify user requirements for access to data.

Physical design

(a) Determine contents and organisation of files.
(b) Determine form, nature and content of systems inputs and outputs.
(c) Identify most appropriate processing method.

---

4. CONCLUSION

4.1 A methodology is a way of organising the design and documentation of a system.

4.2 Many methodologies were developed to assist non-experts. However *no* methodology instructs the developer 'on how to distinguish the relevant from the peripheral ... how to conceptualise the intrinsic nature of the problem ...[or] generate ideas which can be built into designs.
(Downs, Clare, Coe: SSADM Application and Context).

Methodologies concentrate routine mechanistic work in the hands of non-experts, but cannot in themselves create 'good' systems.

4.3 Most methodologies specify the logical design of the system before its physical implementation (ie what the system should achieve, as opposed to how it should do so).

TEST YOUR KNOWLEDGE
The numbers in brackets refer to paragraphs of this chapter

1   What are the stages of the systems development life cycle? (1.2)

2   What is a methodology? (2.2)

3   List the stages of SSADM. (3.3)

4   Why do we distinguish between logical and physical design? (2.5)

Now try question 13 at the end of the text

Chapter 11

THE FEASIBILITY STUDY

This chapter covers the following topics.

1. What is a feasibility study?
2. Feasibility study stage 1: problem definition
3. Feasibility study stage 2: project identification
4. The cost/benefit analysis
5. Dealing with manufacturers and suppliers
6. The feasibility study report

Tutorial notes

(a) The techniques noted here are described in more detail later in the text.
(b) DFD is the abbreviation for data flow diagram.

---

1. WHAT IS A FEASIBILITY STUDY?

1.1 In the last chapter, we saw that the feasibility study is the first stage of systems development in the *systems development life cycle*. It also constitutes the first phase of SSADM.

1.2 It was also mentioned that some of the work performed at the feasibility study stage may be similar to work performed later on in the development of the project. This is because some of the information necessary to decide whether to go ahead with a project or trying to define a problem is common to both tasks.

1.3 Amongst factors which may be considered as part of the feasibility study which might also feature in a later stage in the systems development are:

(a) some investigation and analysis work;
(b) some cost/benefit analysis;
(c) identification of user requirements, at least in outline.

In your study, therefore, bear in mind that there is some overlap between the various stages.

1.4 One of the reasons for having a feasibility study is that new systems can:

(a) cost a great deal to develop;

(b) be very disruptive during development and implementation in terms of the opportunity cost of management time;

(c) have far reaching consequences in a way an organisation conducts its business or is structured.

1.5 A feasibility study, as its name suggests, is a formal study to decide what type of system can be developed which meets the needs of the organisation. Practice will vary between different organisations. In SSADM, the feasibility study is an optional stage.

The feasibility study group

1.6 A feasibility study team should be appointed to carry out the study (although individuals might be given the task in the case of smaller projects). Membership of the feasibility study team will probably be limited to a few top-calibre individuals, including:

(a) managers from the 'user' departments;
(b) individuals with technical knowledge of computer systems, such as a **DP manager** or chief systems analyst.

1.7 There are a number of important points to consider in connection with the members of the group.

(a) One person should not attempt to carry out the feasibility study on his own.

(b) Members of the team should be drawn from the departments affected by the project.

(c) At least one person must have a detailed knowledge of computers and systems design (in a small concern it may be necessary to bring in a systems analyst from outside, or to rely on an accountant as the 'computer expert').

(d) At least one person should have a detailed knowledge of the organisation and in particular of the workings and staff of the departments affected. Managers with direct knowledge of how the current system operates can contribute enormously to the study. They will know what the information needs of the system are, and whether any proposed new system (eg an off-the-shelf software package) will do everything that is wanted. They are also likely to be in a position to recognise improvements that can be made in the current system, which a new system might be able to offer.

(e) It is possible to hire consultants to carry out the feasibility study, but their lack of knowledge about the organisation may adversely affect the usefulness of their proposals.

(f) Before selecting the members of the study group, the steering committee must ensure that they possess suitable personal qualities, eg the ability to be objectively critical.

(g) All members of the study group should ideally have undergone some form of training in data processing techniques and systems design. They should also be encouraged to read as widely as possible and take an active interest in current innovations.

1.8 With larger projects it may well be worthwhile for a small firm to employ a good systems analyst (possibly through a computer staff agency or a firm of DP consultants) and then appoint a management team to work with him. Manufacturers of hardware may agree to carry out feasibility studies (with obvious risks as regards the recommendation) and there are also software houses, computer bureaux, and consultants who undertake such work.

Feasibility study: terms of reference

1.9 The terms of reference for a feasibility study group must be set out by the steering committee, the information director or the board of directors, and might consist of the following items.

(a) To investigate and report on an existing system, its procedures and costs.
(b) To define the systems requirements.
(c) To establish whether these requirements are being met by the existing system.
(d) To establish whether these requirements could be met by a new system.
(e) To specify performance criteria (systems objectives) for the system.
(f) To recommend the most suitable system to meet the systems objectives.
(g) To prepare a detailed cost budget for the proposed system, within a set limit.
(h) To prepare a draft plan for implementation within a set timescale.
(i) To establish whether the hoped-for benefits could be realised.
(j) To establish a detailed design, implementation and operating budget.
(k) Date by which the study group must report back to the steering committee.
(l) Which operational managers should be approached for information.

2. FEASIBILITY STUDY STAGE 1: PROBLEM DEFINITION

2.1 This stage contains a number of steps which can be listed as follows. Much of the work done at this stage will be a result of the terms of reference established earlier.

(a) The *feasibility study* must be planned within the *base constraints* of time and manpower.

(b) The terms of reference will indicate the main areas of concern that the study is to address. (In SSADM these are listed in an initial *problems/requirements* list.)

(c) These problems identified and broadly defined user requirements lead to further documentation.

(d) A data flow diagram (DFD) is prepared to give an overview of the system. An overall structure of the processes and the data flows behind them are established. The main *entities* are defined.

(e) This further work will mean, perhaps, that more problems have been identified.

2.2 This stage should finally result in the production of a set of documents which *define the problem*. These have been indicated above and can include:

(a) data flow diagrams representing, in overview (ie level-1 DFDs):

(i)   the current physical flows of data in the organisation (documents);
(ii) the activities underlying them (data flows);

(b) the current entity model;

(c) the problems/requirements list established from the terms of reference and after consultation with users.

These are reviewed to ensure they are of sufficient standard to be used as input to the next stage. They should give a definition of inputs and outputs and identify existing problems. They may also be included as part of the feasibility study report. (They are described in more detail in the chapter on systems analysis.)

2.3 The remit of a feasibility study may be narrow or quite wide. (In SSADM, the process is controlled by the requirement to produce formal documentation.) The feasibility study team must engage in a substantial effort of fact finding. These facts may include matters relevant to the project which are not necessarily of a data processing nature.

2.4 The problems/requirements list can cover, inter alia, the following areas.

(a) the data input to the current system;
(b) the nature of the output information (contents, timing etc);
(c) methods of processing;
(d) the expected growth of the organisation and so future volumes of processing;
(e) the systems control in operation;
(f) staffing arrangements and organisational structure;
(g) the operational costs of the system;
(h) type of system (batch, on-line);
(i) response times;
(j) current organisational problems.

In some circumstances the 'problem' (eg the necessity for a real-time as opposed to a batch processed application) may be quite exact.

3. FEASIBILITY STUDY STAGE 2: PROJECT IDENTIFICATION

3.1 This stage involves both suggesting a number of options for a new system, evaluating them and recommending one for adoption. It concludes with a final feasibility study report.

3.2 More formally, the aim is to create a series of system options to tackle the problem defined in the first stage. The number will vary depending on the complexity of the problem, or the size of the application, but is typically between three and six.

3.3 The principal inputs to this phase will be the final outputs from the first stage as outlined in Paragraph 2.2 of this chapter.

3.4 The main tasks to be carried out are as follows.

(a) Create the base constraints in terms of expenditure, implementation and design time, and system requirements, which any system should satisfy, in terms of:

(i)   operations (eg faster processing, larger volumes, greater security, greater accuracy, better quality, real-time as opposed to other forms of processing);

(ii)   information output (quality, frequency, presentation, eg GUIs, database for managers, EIS facilities);

(iii)   volume of processing;

(iv)   general system requirements (eg accuracy, security and controls, audit trail, flexibility, adaptability);

(v)   compatibility/integration with existing systems.

(b)   Create *outlines of project options*, describing, in brief, each option.

(c)   Assess the impact each proposal has on the work of the relevant user department and/or the organisation as a whole.

(d)   Review these proposals with users, who should indicate those options they favour for further analysis.

3.5   The favoured options are expanded in *outline project specifications*. These include detailed diagrams of data flows, processes and as importantly a *cost/benefit* analysis of *each* project (see below). Outline project specifications provide a high level description of the project, and include a project plan and hardware considerations. These are then evaluated with users and one chosen.

System justification

3.6   A new system should not be *recommended* unless it can be *justified*. The justification for a new system would have to come from:

(a)   an evaluation of the costs and benefits of the proposed system; and/or

(b)   other performance criteria.

Exercise

You are chairing a feasibility study group assembled to examine whether your company's existing system can be upgraded to meet the needs of the business, which has grown rapidly. Give a brief summary of the contents of your report to the Board.

Solution

Your report might be structured as follows:

(a)   introduction, including executive summary and terms of reference;

(b)   description of existing system (and its faults);

(c)   system requirements;

(d) proposed system, including alternatives, recommended equipment, details of each application (input, output, files, processing method) software, maintenance and staffing requirements;

(e) costs and benefits;

(f) timetable and implementation plans; and

(g) recommendation as to preferred option.

---

4. THE COST/BENEFIT ANALYSIS

The costs of a proposed system

4.1 Cost-benefit analysis of information systems is complicated by the fact that many of the system cost elements are poorly defined (particularly for development projects) and that benefits can often be highly qualitative and subjective in nature.

4.2 In general the best cost estimates will be obtained for 'turnkey' systems bought in toto from an outside vendor who provides a cost quotation against a specification. Less concrete cost estimates are generally found with development projects where the work is performed by the organisation's own employees.

4.3 The costs of a new system will include:

(a) *Equipment costs* (capital costs/leasing costs) of:

    (i) computer and peripherals;
    (ii) ancillary equipment;
    (iii) the initial system supplies (disks, tapes, paper etc);

(b) *Installation costs:*

    (i) new building (if necessary);
    (ii) the computer room (wiring, air-conditioning etc);

(c) *Development costs* (software/consultancy work or systems analysis and programming/changeover costs);

(d) *Personnel costs:*

    (i) staff training;
    (ii) staff recruitment/relocation;
    (iii) staff salaries and pensions;
    (iv) redundancy payments;
    (v) overheads;

(e) *Operating costs:*

    (i)   consumable materials (tapes, disks, stationery etc);
    (ii)   maintenance;
    (iii) accommodation costs;
    (iv) heating/power/insurance/telephone;
    (v)   standby arrangements.

4.4   A distinction can be made between capital costs and revenue costs, which may be 'one-off' costs in the first year or regular annual costs.

4.5   The distinction between capital costs and revenue costs is important because:

(a)   to establish the *cash* outflows arising from the system, the costs/benefit analysis of a system ought to be based on cash flows and DCF;

(b)   the annual charge against profits. One-off revenue items will be charged in full against the first year's profits, capital items will be depreciated and revenue items will be a regular annual cost.

Capital cost items	'One-off' revenue cost items	Regular annual costs

1 Hardware purchase costs	1 System development costs
	  - consultancy fees, if any
	  - systems analysts' and programmers' salaries
	  - costs of testing the system (staff costs, consumable items used etc)
	  - costs of converting the files for the new system (possibly involving bureau costs; otherwise staff costs etc)
		1 Operating staff salaries/wages

2 Working capital (supplies of paper, disks etc)		2 Data transmission costs (eg line rentals)
3 Purchase of accommodation (if needed)		3 Consumable materials
4 Installation costs (new desks etc)		4 Power
		5 Extra rental costs (for accommodation or hardware) if any
	2 Redundancy payments (if any)	6 Hardware maintenance costs
		7 Costs of software system support
	3 Staff recruitment fees (if any)	8 Cost of standby arrangements
	4 Initial staff training	9 Other variable overhead costs (perhaps difficult to quantify)
		10 Regular staff training

11: THE FEASIBILITY STUDY

The benefits of a proposed system

4.6 The benefits from a proposed new system must also be evaluated. These ought to consist of:

(a) savings because the old system will no longer be operated. The savings should include:

   (i) savings in staff costs;
   (ii) savings in other operating costs, such as consumable materials;

(b) extra savings or revenue benefits because of the improvements or enhancements that the new system should bring - eg

   (i) possibly more sales revenue and so additional contribution;

   (ii) better stock control (with a new stock control system) and so fewer stock losses from obsolescence and deterioration;

   (iii) further savings in staff time, resulting perhaps in reduced future staff growth;

(c) possibly, some 'one-off' revenue benefits from the sale of equipment which the existing system uses, but which will no longer be required. Second-hand computer equipment does not have a high value, however! It is also possible that the new system will use *less office space*, and so there will be benefits from selling or renting the spare accommodation.

4.7 Some benefits might be *intangible*, or impossible to give a money value to. These might include:

(a) greater customer satisfaction, arising from a more prompt service (eg because of a computerised sales and delivery service);

(b) improved staff morale from working with a 'better' system;

(c) better 'decision-making' is hard to quantify, but may result from better MIS, DSS or EIS.

DCF

4.8 Because a project will have an operational life of several years, the comparison of the costs and benefits of the proposed system should ideally be made using discounted cash flow (DCF) analysis, with perhaps payback being taken into account as well.

4.9 This is because many of the costs of the project will occur early on during the development and installation of the project, before any benefits are earned eg:

(a) hardware purchase costs;

(b) software purchase costs, or the costs of developing the system with an 'in-house' team of systems analysts and programmers;

(c) costs of initial training for staff.

When the system goes live, there will be running costs as well. The benefits of the system will hopefully exceed the running costs, to give net annual benefits.

11: THE FEASIBILITY STUDY

4.10 DCF analysis provides an evaluation technique which allows managers to assess whether the 'front-end' costs of buying or developing the project are worth the expected net benefits that will eventually follow on. DCF recognises that there is a 'time value' or interest cost and risk cost to investing money, so that the expected benefits from a project should not only pay back the costs, but should also yield a satisfactory return.

(a) £1 is now worth more than £1 in a year's time, because £1 now could be used to earn interest by the end of year 1. Similarly, £1 at the end of year 1 is worth more than £1 at the end of year 2, for the same reason. Money has a lesser and lesser value, the further from 'now' that it will be earned or paid.

(b) With DCF, this time value on money is allowed for by converting cash flows in future years to a smaller, present value, equivalent.

(c) A DCF evaluation of a proposed computer project might be as follows.

Project: new network system for administration department

Development and hardware purchase costs (all incurred over a short time period)	£150,000
Operating costs of new system, expressed as cash outflows per annum	£55,000
Annual savings from new system, expressed as cash inflow	£115,000
Annual net savings (net cash inflows)	£60,000

Expected system life	4 years
Required return on investment	15% pa

Year	Cost/Savings	Discount factor at 15%	Present value at 15%
	£		*£*
0	(150,000)	1.00	(150,000)
1	60,000	0.87	52,200
2	60,000	0.76	45,600
3	60,000	0.66	39,600
4	60,000	0.57	34,200
		Net present value of the project	21,600

(d) In this example, the present value of the expected benefits of the project exceed the present value of its costs, all discounted at 15% pa, and so the project is financially justifiable because it would be expected to earn a yield greater than the minimum target return of 15%. Payback of the development costs and hardware costs of £150,000 would occur after $2\frac{1}{2}$ years.

Buy or lease computer hardware?

4.11 An organisation may have the choice between buying or leasing a computer.

(a) The *cash flow* advantage of leasing, is that there is no high initial capital outlay.

If a lease is arranged with a finance company, the equipment can normally be retained on the expiry of the lease for a nominal rent, or sold by the user, with the proceeds of the sale then shared with the finance company. If the lease is with a brokerage company, the brokerage company will normally take possession of the equipment on expiry of the lease, for re-letting (if not obsolete) to another user.

When deciding whether to buy a computer the organisation should establish its purchase cost, expected disposal proceeds and writing down allowances (ie capital allowances for tax purposes). Discounted cash flow techniques (DCF) may be used to arrive at a realistic assessment of the cost of the computer in terms of net present value, for comparison against leasing costs (net of tax).

(b) Yet another option which is occasionally favoured by some organisations is handing over the operation of their computer system to a computer bureau.

Other performance criteria

4.12 The justification for a new system might not be purely economic, and there are non-economic benefits which might persuade an organisation to introduce the system, even when its costs are high in relation to the tangible, quantifiable money benefits.

The non-economic benefits which might justify the development of a new system ought to be measurable performance objectives, so that the system can be evaluated according to whether its costs justify the achievement of those objectives.

Some of these performance criteria are listed as measures of effectiveness in paragraph 46.

Hardware and software

4.13 The feasibility study must reach some conclusions about the hardware and software requirements for the system.

(a) The basic question regarding software is whether the system should be designed and the programs written 'in-house' by the DP department or externally by a software house, or whether the requirements can be met by a supplier's ready-made application package. Buying a package has many advantages, and for small businesses, it is the only practical option.

A feasibility study should be carried out even when the organisation wishes to purchase a software package from a supplier.

Systems requirements can only be established from an investigation of the current system, and there is every possibility that the organisation buying a package will ask the supplier to make a few adjustments to the software to fit in with its individual operating characteristics.

(b) The questions regarding hardware are:

(i) what equipment is needed to handle the software?
(ii) should the equipment be bought, rented or leased, or should the operation of the system be put into the hands of a computer bureau?

Tailor-made or off-the-shelf software?

4.14 The advantages of using an 'off-the-shelf' package as opposed to designing a system from scratch are as follows.

(a)   It should have been written by software specialists and so should be of a high quality.

(b)   A successful package will be continually updated by the software manufacturer, and so the version that a customer buys should be up-to-date.

(c)   Other users will have used the package already, and a well-established package should be error-free and well-suited to the general needs of users.

(d)   Good packages are well-documented, with easy-to-follow user manuals. Good documentation is a key feature of successful software development.

(e)   The computer user does not need to employ his own specialist staff to develop, write and test 'in-house' programs, which could *take time* to produce and would be *costly*.

(f)   Some packages can be tailored to the user's specific needs.

(g)   Tailor-made 'customised' software, on the other hand

   (i)   will take time to write;
   (ii)   will cost a lot more; and
   (iii) will be untried, and so will need thorough testing and might still contain undiscovered errors even after the tests have been carried out.

(h)   An *in-house* tailor-made development is only feasible for large organisations with their own DP department.

4.15 The disadvantages of application packages are as follows.

(a)   The computer user gets a standardised solution to a data processing task. A standard solution may not be well-suited to the individual user's particular needs.

(b)   The user is *dependent* on the supplier for maintenance of the package - ie updating the package, providing assistance in the event of problems for the user or even program errors cropping up.

Add-ons and programming tools

4.16 Two other ways of trying to give a computer user more flexibility with packages, and systems which are more tailor-made, are:

(a)   the sale of 'add-ons' to a basic package, which the user can buy if they suit his particular needs;

(b)   the provision of programming tools, such as fourth generation languages, with a package, which allows a computer user to write his own amendments to the package software (without having to be a programming expert).

11: THE FEASIBILITY STUDY

Hardware

4.17 In general terms, the choice of computer hardware will depend on the following factors.

(a) The ease with which the computer configuration fits in with the user's requirements (eg direct access facilities, hard-copy output in given quantities).

(b) The power of the CPU must be sufficient for current and foreseeable requirements.

(c) Reliability. There should be a low expected 'break-down' rate. There should be back-up facilities, and in the case of a microcomputer, this might mean being able to resort temporarily back to a manual system when the computer is down.

(d) Simplicity. Simple systems are probably best for small organisations.

(e) Ease of 'communication' between the hardware and the user. The system (hardware and software) should be able to communicate well with the user. Software is referred to as 'user-friendly' or 'user-unfriendly' but similar considerations apply to hardware (eg not all terminals are of standard screen size; the number and accessibility of terminals might also have a bearing on how well the user is able to put data into the computer or extract information).

(f) Flexibility - the hardware should be able to meet new requirements as they emerge. More powerful CPUs tend to be more flexible.

(g) Security. Keeping out 'hackers' and other unauthorised users is easier with more powerful systems, although security can be a major problem for any computer system.

(h) Cost.

(i) Whether the choice of hardware will help with a smooth changeover from the old to the new system.

(j) Networking capacity, if a micro has been purchased.

5. DEALING WITH MANUFACTURERS AND SUPPLIERS

5.1 A computer user might buy hardware direct from a manufacturer, but is more likely to buy it through an intermediate supplier. Similarly, software packages might be bought direct from the software house that wrote it, but are more likely to be bought through an intermediate supplier. However, no matter whether the user deals with the manufacturer or a supplier, he ought to give careful attention to what deals he makes. The supplier, after all, will be needed to provide support in case the user has any trouble with the system or package he buys.

General points

5.2 The points to bear in mind have been referred to already in various parts of this text, but it is worth drawing them together now.

(a) How well established is the supplier's company? Has it been trading long? In the computer industry, it is quite common for small firms of suppliers or software houses to set up in business and then go into liquidation soon after. A firm with a reasonably long history of trading would be more likely to have some financial stability.

(b) Do the supplier's staff appear to have a good knowledge of the application to which the software relates? For example, a firm that sells accounts software packages ought to have support staff who know something about accounts as well as computers. Otherwise a customer would find it hard to discuss with the supplier any operational teething troubles he might be having with the package.

(c) Can the supplier introduce the customer to any other users of the hardware or software package who would be willing to demonstrate it and recommend it?

The purchase arrangement

5.3 The purchase deal is not just a matter of cost. The supplier might provide 'extras' as part of the purchase package, but just how many extras he is willing to provide will depend to a large extent on how far he is 'squeezed' on price.

(a) *Cost*. Cost is obviously an important factor. By shopping around, a customer might be able to negotiate quite a large discount on the price from a supplier.

(b) *Utility software, software tools*. A hardware supplier should supply a range of utility software and software tools with the hardware. It might be worth checking what these are, and whether they vary between different suppliers.

(c) *Warranty*. All hardware comes with a warranty, but the warranty period might vary from just a few months to well over a year. One year is quite a common warranty period. As part of the warranty cover, there will be arrangements for maintenance in the event of a breakdown. The terms of the maintenance support can be important:

   (i) They will specify how quickly the supplier promises to have a repair engineer out to visit the customer.

   (ii) If the hardware has to be taken away for repair, the supplier *might* promise to provide back-up - eg a standby computer, or a replacement microcomputer to stand in for the one being repaired.

(d) *Maintenance*. The customer might want a maintenance contract after the warranty period expires. Will the supplier sign a maintenance contract? If so, what would the contract cost the customer, and what would be the other terms?

(e) *Software support*. In a similar way to hardware maintenance, a software supplier should be prepared to offer software support to the customer, in case the customer runs into difficulties (eg accidentally wipes out the contents of an important file). The supplier should give the customer a 'hot-line' to telephone in case of difficulty, and if necessary, send out a specialist to the customer's premises to help to resolve the problem. Software support, like hardware maintenance support, might be 'free' for a short time, and then be provided at a cost.

(f) *Training*. Another element in the purchase deal could be training of the customer's staff. There might be an agreement by the supplier to provide training for a specified number of the customer's employees (probably on the supplier's own premises unless the customer is buying a mainframe or a large software system) for a specified period of time.

   (i) How many will be trained?
   (ii) How long will they be trained for? are negotiable points.

(g) *Tailor-made amendments to software packages*. The customer might be able to persuade a software house or supplier to write some tailor-made amendments to an off-the-shelf package, to make the package suit the customer's requirements better. The customer might be able to persuade the supplier to write the amendments (and test them) free; however, the supplier might only agree to write amendments for a fee.

(h) *Keeping the package up-to-date*. New improved versions of popular software packages are frequently brought on to the market. Occasionally, errors in existing packages are discovered and corrected. The purchase deal for a software package should specify what arrangements there will be, if any, for the software supplier to provide the customer with any amendments or enhancements to the software as they occur.

5.4 Once the outline project specifications are prepared, these are presented to users who, with the assistance of technical staff will evaluate each option and make a final choice. This stage is much more intensive than when the original options were first examined. All the systems specified in the project specifications are feasible and it is simply a matter of weighing up the advantages and disadvantages of each.

You should note than one option may be to carry on with the existing system as it is, with no development option being chosen. If the feasibility study has been quite a lengthy one, circumstances beyond the control of the study teams may render any systems development inappropriate. For example, interest rates may rise increasing the organisations cost of capital, and in this context the cost/benefit analysis might render the system uneconomic.

Checklist for an application package

5.5 There is a long check-list of points to consider when choosing a suitable package, if that is the final recommendation of the feasibility study.

(a) Does the package fit the user's particular requirements?

  (i)   Does it produce all the reports that are wanted?
  (ii)   Can it handle the anticipated volume of data on file?
  (iii) What data validation routines does it contain, and are these adequate?
  (iv)   Does it exclude some processing that the user wants? (If so, are these omissions serious?)

(b) Does the package come with useful 'add-on' facilities? (For example, a nominal ledger package might be sold with the add-on of a report generation facility, to interrogate key accounts on the nominal ledger file so that simple management accounts could be produced).

(c) If the package requires substantial changes to the user's organisation, the package might be rejected as unacceptable. The package should ideally be suited to the user and the user might rightly object to having to adjust his organisation to the dictates of the software;

(d) Are the processing times fast enough? If response times to enquiries, for example, are fairly slow, the user might consider the package unacceptable because of the time wastage.

(e) Is there full and clear documentation for the user? User manuals can be full of jargon and hard for a non-technical person to understand. They shouldn't be.

(f) Can the supplier/dealer demonstrate the package, perhaps in the offices of an existing user of the package?

(g)   Is the package easy to use? Is the software 'user friendly' with menus and clear on-screen prompts for the keyboard operator? Some microcomputer packages are more user friendly than others. If a system operates in 'command mode', for example, the operator must know which commands to key in, and when. A user-friendly package will provide prompts and will be menu-driven, giving the operator a clear choice of what to do next. Some packages also provide extensive on-screen 'help' facilities for when the operator runs into difficulties and doesn't know what to do next.

(h)   What controls are included in the package (eg passwords, data validation checks, spelling checks, standard accounting controls and reconciliations, an audit trail facility etc)?

(i)   How will the package be kept up-to-date? (eg what if a fault is discovered in the program by the software manufacturer? In an accounting package, what if the rate of VAT alters? etc).

(j)   Can the package be modified by the user - eg allowing the user to insert amendments to the format of reports or screen displays etc? Or will the software supplier agree to write a few tailor-made amendments to the software?

(k)   How many other users have bought the package, and how long has it been on the market? New packages might offer enhanced facilities, whereas well-established (but regularly updated) packages are more likely to be error-free.

(l)   Will the package run on the user's computer? Will additional peripheral equipment have to be bought - eg does the package need a hard disk file, when the computer user only has floppy disk drives with his micro?

(m)   What support and 'maintenance' service will the software supplier provide, in the event that the user has difficulty with the package?

(n)   *Comparative* costs of different packages should be a low priority. Off-the-shelf packages are fairly cheap on the whole, and a company should really buy what it needs for efficient operations rather than the least-cost package available. The savings in purchase price would not be worth the trouble caused by trying to use an unsuitable package for a business application.

(o)   However, the package must not cost "so much" that the costs are greater than the benefits of having it.

6.   THE FEASIBILITY STUDY REPORT

6.1   This is the final step of the feasibility study phase. A number of projects were mooted. A few favoured ones were examined and specified in more detail, and a choice made after evaluation. The results of these deliberations are included in a feasibility study report. This should contain the following points.

---

1   PROBLEM DEFINITION

This will contain material from the Problem Definition stage, as outlined in Paragraph 2.2.

2   OUTLINE PROJECT SPECIFICATIONS

These are summaries of the detailed project specifications prepared for a number of project options.

3   REASONS FOR SELECTION OF PREFERRED PROJECT OPTION

This may include cost/benefit analyses, or any of the non-economic criteria noted above.

4   SPECIFICATION OF SELECTED PROJECT OPTION

This will include:

(a)   outline DFDs and processes of the new system;
(b)   a description of the entity model;
(c)   an updated problems/requirements list;
(d)   a brief description of the system's physical implementation.

---

7.   CONCLUSION

7.1   A feasibility study is carried out to define a systems problem and to identify a number of possible solutions to it.

7.2   Some investigation and analysis will take place, but less than in later stages.

7.3   Users are consulted as to which of the systems options suggested as solutions to the problem are acceptable.

TEST YOUR KNOWLEDGE

The numbers in brackets refer to paragraphs of this chapter

1   What are the reasons for having a feasibility study? (1.4)

2   List some probable items in a feasibility study term of reference. (1.9)

3   What documents in SSADM are likely to be produced at the problem definition stage? (2.2)

4   What type of factor will influence the creation of options for system development. (3.4(a))

5   What type of costs will be incurred in the construction of a new system? (4.3) How can these be classified? (4.4)

6   Describe a means of comparing system costs and benefits. (4.8–4.10)

7   What are the advantages and disadvantages of choosing an application package as opposed to developing a system in-house? (4.14–4.15)

8   Detail the subject matter of a purchase agreement with a supplier. (5.2)

9   What are the contents of a feasibility study report? (6.1)

Now try questions 14 and 15 at the end of the text

Chapter 12

COMPUTER BUREAUX AND SOFTWARE HOUSES

This chapter covers the following topics.

1. The shortage of DP resources
2. Computer bureaux
3. Software houses
4. Consultancy firms
5. Turnkey operations
6. Computer manufacturers
7. Timesharing
8. Other DP resources

---

1. THE SHORTAGE OF DP RESOURCES

1.1 Many organisations do not employ specialist DP staff because they cannot justify the costs of full time systems analysts and programmers. Other organisations might employ some specialist DP staff but not enough for all their system design and implementation requirements. In some cases, organisations will not possess the equipment to do their own computerised DP work.

1.2 If an organisation does not wish (or cannot afford) to have its own in-house computer, or requires technical information, or needs expert advice on systems development without employing its own computer-experienced staff, it may prefer to use external data processing resources. This might involve buying application packages from a supplier, but also a range of other resources and services which we shall look at in this chapter.

1.3 In many organisations there is an applications backlog. New systems do not get built because staff are patching up old ones.

2. COMPUTER BUREAUX

2.1 Computer bureaux are organisations which provide DP facilities to their clients.

The types of computer bureaux include:

(a) independent companies formed to provide specialist computing services;

(b) computer manufacturers with bureaux and increasingly, 'Value Added Network Services' (VANS) These provide services such as insurance quotations to brokers or holiday reservation systems to travel agents;

214

(c) computer users (eg universities) with spare capacity who hire out computer time when it is not required for their own purposes. This type of 'bureau' is now much less common than it was some years ago.

The falling cost of computers has led to a decline in the demand for traditional batch processing. Instead there is a growing market in providing sophisticated networks and related services which most large computer manufacturers such as ICL and IBM now provide.

2.2 The range of services offered by computer bureaux is considerable, with some offering a complete service while others specialise in particular areas. The services offered include:

(a) *data preparation:* transcribing data from source documents into a machine readable form (eg on to magnetic tape/disks etc), including the services offered for file conversion on system implementation;

(b) *hiring computer time:* the bureaux will process the clients' data on its own computer. The client may be responsible for providing the programs, but many bureaux offer application packages (eg for payroll);

(c) *do-it-yourself:* the bureaux will provide the computer but the client will provide operators, programs etc. This type of service may be provided by computer users with spare capacity in off-peak periods;

(d) *consultancy:* the bureaux will provide advice and assistance in connection with feasibility studies, system design, equipment evaluation, staff training etc;

(e) *software:* the bureau will design, write, test and provide software for a particular application; or may design and/or adapt application packages;

(f) *time-sharing/remote job entry (RJE):* the client uses his own terminal(s) (linked by a data transmission method) to process data on the bureau computer. As business data processing usually involves large volumes of data input/output, the terminals must be powerful and fast enough to deal with the data efficiently. In the past, time sharing tended to be used for computation-oriented applications (eg financial analysis, technical work etc), but with the development of powerful terminals (eg mini-computers or micro-computers in their own right) and the improvement in data transmission systems, time sharing is a useful facility that can be used to increase in-house computing power. Time sharing is considered in more detail below;

(g) *turnkey operation:* where the bureau undertakes the client's conversion to a computer system. For example, a computer bureau may be engaged to carry out the feasibility study, order the computer hardware from a supplier and supervise its installation, do all the systems design work, write (or adapt) application programs and test the programs and the system. When the system is complete in every detail and working perfectly it is handed over to the client. All he has to do is 'turn the key' to commence using the system.

(h) *a system integration service.* This is described later.

2.3 These services might usefully be grouped under three headings:

(a) *batch services:* a bureau accepts a batch (or batches) of input documents from a client, processes it (or them) and returns the printed outputs to the client. A widespread batch service is payroll preparation. The client sends data about the work done by each employee in the week or month. The bureau will also hold standing data for each employee. The bureau will process the data and produce wages/salary slips, a wages analysis and any other information the client needs. The client will receive the output within a stipulated turn-round time so that wages processing is not delayed;

(b) *time-sharing services*;

(c) *systems support services*; ie the range of other services listed above.

Only large bureaux offer the entire range of support services.

Bureaux and system integration

2.4 Bureaux might provide a data transmission service which can integrate one organisation's computer system with another's, and allow them to process data interactively. For example:

(a) the Tradanet computer system is a system linking food manufacturers and food retailers, allowing them to exchange orders, confirmations and invoices etc. The technical task of linking one company's computer system to another company's system is done by a bureau;

(b) similarly, a bureau is used in a system linking motor car manufacturers to component suppliers, translating purchase orders from a manufacturer's computer system into a form that a supplier's computer can understand and act on.

Reasons for and against computer bureaux

2.5 Having outlined the services that are offered by computer bureaux it might be apparent why some are successful and why some businesses continue to use them. The reasons may be summarised:

(a) to obtain experience of computerised data processing. A company that is considering acquiring a computer may find it extremely beneficial to use a bureau because:

(i) it can evaluate the type of computer it is interested in;
(ii) it can test and develop its programs prior to the delivery of its own computer;
(iii) its staff will become familiar with the requirements of a computer system.

(b) cost. Many companies cannot justify the installation of an in-house mainframe computer on cost-benefit grounds and the use of a bureau does not require a high capital outlay. However, with the enormous increase in the number of relatively cheap mini-computers and micro-computers available, this reason is becoming much less common;

(c) to cope with peak loads. Some computer users find it convenient to employ a bureau to cope with peak loads arising, for example, from seasonal variations in sales;

(d) to provide a standby computer. A bureau's computer may be used in the event of a breakdown of an in-house machine;

(e) to enable the data processing to be done by people who have the expertise. System integration services are a good example of this;

(f) to obtain advice on all aspects of systems development and operation;

(g) to enable the client to obtain the use of up-to-date computer technology;

(h) to deal with a 'one-off' application.

2.6 The principal disadvantages of using a computer bureau are:

(a) loss of control over the time taken to process data and in particular the inability to reschedule work should input delays occur;

(b) problems which may be encountered in the transfer of data to and from the bureau;

(c) the problems of dealing with error corrections;

(d) the bureau may close down leaving the customer without any data processing facilities for a period of time;

(e) a loss of control over an important area of business. Many potential users will not employ a bureau's services because they feel that they will lose control, and furthermore, feel that it is bad security to allow confidential information to be under the control of an outsider. Their fears are normally groundless; the bureau will certainly not try to run the business and its security may well be considerably better than that of its customers;

(f) the standards of service and the provision of adequate documentation control may not be entirely satisfactory.

Choosing a bureau

2.7 A list of bureaux can be obtained from the telephone *Yellow Pages*, the *Computing Services Association*, the *Computer Users Year Book* or *Which Computer*. An organisation will wish to draw up a shortlist of bureaux to approach, and the initial considerations in making a choice for the shortlist would be:

(a) *location:* a near location would be helpful if the customer wants a batch service. Data and output can be delivered more quickly and it is easier for the bureau's personnel to meet with the customer's personnel;

(b) *expertise:* no bureau is an expert in everything. A customer might want the bureau to adapt its standard software packages to his own particular requirements, and the bureau might not have the programming expertise to do this. Enquiries, ideally to existing users of the bureau, might establish where the bureau's expertise lies;

(c) *costs:* a customer will be influenced by the relative charges of the bureau. Bureaux do not have a price cartel, and charges can vary substantially. Charge rates are normally based on a charge per 'computing unit' which customers cannot readily understand, and so a potential customer would have to ask a bureau to supply specimen charges for a 'trial run' of input data to assess the likely costs. Large bureaux with large computers may benefit from economies of scale and be cheaper than smaller bureaux or conceivably in-house systems. In all circumstances, it is essential to establish costs precisely *before* starting to use a particular bureau.

2.8 Having established a short-list of bureaux, the final decision will depend on location, expertise and costs, and perhaps also on:

(a) the size, experience and financial stability of the bureau;

(b) the turn-round time promised by the bureau for a batch service;

(c) contractual details (eg length of contract, whether the bureau would make an initial charge for set-up or program writing, whether terminals for a time sharing service must be hired from the bureau);

(d) what back-up facilities are available in the event of a bureau's computer breaking down (especially important for a payroll service, for example);

(e) what are the bureau's security arrangements and system for controlling and protecting a client's data?

Working with a computer bureau

2.9 Even if the bureau does most or all of the data processing for a client firm, a small data processing department should be set up by the firm to liaise with the bureau and to ensure that adequate systems controls are maintained. These will include controls over:

(a) the physical movement of data to and from the bureau (eg methods of transporting magnetic tapes or disks);

(b) data transmission;

(c) accuracy and completeness of processing;

(d) resubmission of rejected data;

(e) correct distribution of output.

3. SOFTWARE HOUSES

3.1 Software houses do not normally provide a range of data processing facilities in the same way as computer bureaux but concentrate instead on the provision of 'software services'. These services include feasibility studies, systems analysis and design, development of operating systems software, provision of application program packages, application programming, specialist systems advice, and so on. For example, a software house might be employed to write a computerised system for the clearing banks, or the London Stock Exchange etc.

3.2 A software house may offer a wide range of services or may become successful by specialising in a particular area, so becoming an expert in that area. At present there is considerable interest in the development of software for small business systems (those using minicomputers and microcomputers) and it is only in the last few years that effective packages for these systems have become available. The UK is still a substantial force in software development and British companies are exporting software packages (and software writers) to other countries.

3.3 Many of the considerations dealt with above, in the paragraphs on computer bureaux, will of course apply to software houses. Remember that their services are not cheap, and the client company must be quite certain how much it will be charged and what the end product will be.

4. CONSULTANCY FIRMS

4.1 Some consultancy firms work at a fairly high level, giving advice to management on the general approach to solving problems and on the types of systems to use. Others specialise in giving more particular systems advice, carrying out feasibility studies and recommending computer manufacturers/software houses that will supply the right system.

A recent entrant to the range of consultancy firms uses a computer data base containing details of most of the UK computer systems currently available. After carrying out a feasibility study an appropriate system is recommended. This apparently impartial advisory service is offered free to the client, the consultancy firm claiming commission from the manufacturer only if a sale is made.

As always, whenever a consultancy firm is used, the terms of the contract should be agreed at the outset.

5. TURNKEY OPERATIONS

5.1 A turnkey operation is one in which a software firm or consultancy firm will supply a customer with a full ready-to-use system - ie hardware plus software, and perhaps also master files that have already been set up. Involvement by the user is minimal until the system has been delivered and installed, so that the system is fully operational when the user takes over. All the user has to do is switch on ('turn a key') and the system is operational.

5.2 Turnkey systems simplify the task of buying a computer and buying software to go with it. The user simply has to state his operational requirements, and then leaves it to the software firm to deliver an operational system that meets his requirements.

6. COMPUTER MANUFACTURERS

6.1 Computer manufacturers or designated suppliers will provide the equipment necessary for a system. They will also provide, under a maintenance contract, engineers who will deal with any routine servicing and with any breakdown of the equipment. In addition they will supply the operating systems software and very often application programs. Indeed, they may undertake to 'tailor' the application programs to fit into the client's system. On supplying the equipment and software, the manufacturer will normally offer a training course for the client's staff, the cost of which may be included in the total price, or may be charged separately.

6.2 It might be possible to get quite good cash 'deals' from manufacturers and suppliers and to insist on amendments to the standard contracts, for example, to alter any clauses in the contract which require the payment of the total price in advance of installation, or which exclude various liabilities. However, the lower the price that a customer squeezes out of the supplier, the less the supplier is likely to be willing to offer support services, such as a reasonable period of warranty for the purchased hardware.

7. TIMESHARING

7.1 Where the use of a computer is required but its cost cannot be justified, or finance cannot be raised, or its use would be infrequent, then it might be appropriate to buy the use of computer time from another organisation. Timesharing facilities may be provided by a computer bureau or a company with spare processing capacity, and there will be many individual customers of the time-sharing computer with each customer using separate files and separate programs. Timesharing machines are large computers, and so multi-programming is another feature, with many users operating their programs simultaneously.

7.2 A large number of users (say 150) can 'timeshare' on a computer; but because (as in any multi-access system) queuing techniques are used, specific areas of the CPU are allocated to different users. The CPU is large enough to cope with all users, so that *each user feels that he has the undivided attention of the computer*. Naturally, multi-access or timesharing systems depend on a sophisticated operating system and a large amount of backing store. As there are so many different users, good file and program security is essential to ensure privacy of information (there is a limit to the security measures which can be adopted and few systems, if any, can claim to be totally secure).

7.3 The cost of timesharing is normally calculated on the basis of the elements which make up the processing facility that is being provided. These elements are:

(a) connect time - during which the user is on-line to the computer;

(b) CPU time - the actual time the CPU is used (each user is allocated a *time-slice* for processing;

(c) storage cost - charged at characters per period;

(d) terminal cost - dependent upon the application;

(e) data transmission cost - the hire (or purchase) of modems; charges for the use of the telephone line.

7.4 Timesharing is particularly suited to applications which require a fair amount of CPU time and little input/output time; for example, scientific work. This is mentioned in the CIMA's Computing Terminology definition of timesharing as:

'The availability of a computer to more than one user, traditionally used to describe the facilities available on a dial-up basis to a centralised mainframe computer . . . . Whilst the advent of the minicomputer has somewhat reduced the need, time sharing has been particularly valuable in academic and program development environments.'

8. OTHER DP RESOURCES

8.1 The computer user (or prospective computer user) may obtain additional help, advice or information from various other sources. He may, for example:

(a) hire staff on a temporary basis from a computer personnel agency;

(b) obtain access to business and technical information stored on large data banks;

(c) attend training courses (run by the NCC, manufacturers, professional bodies etc);

(d) study text books and computer journals to keep abreast of technological developments.

Whatever the problem, he should be able to find someone competent to give advice.

8.2 One way of coping with the applications backlog is end-user computing. The use of fourth generation systems, prototyping and so forth enables users to play a greater part in application development.

Exercise

Attempt a quick answer to the following question.

An organisation which regularly develops its own computer systems, employing its own in-house DP staff, is suffering from a shortage of systems development staff, and work on projects is being held up.

Identify *five* possible courses of action which may be taken to overcome the shortage of systems development staff and thus permit the more rapid development and implementation of new systems.

Solution

Five possible courses of action are:

(a) use the services of a computer bureau or DP consultant to do systems design work;

(b) purchase a software package for some systems;

(c) use of bureau to take on the operation of some systems, based on software packages already used by the bureau;

(d) consider whether any systems can be developed in phases, so that the initial phase can be designed and implemented more quickly than if the whole system were to be designed and implemented in one go;

(e) hire more full time systems development staff, or part-time 'contract' staff.

---

9. CONCLUSION

9.1 The computer bureau industry has suffered a decline in recent years, for two reasons:

(a) the rapid growth in the use of the office microcomputer;
(b) the falling cost of computer hardware, including mainframes.

9.2 It is very difficult nowadays for a bureau to survive by offering a timesharing service. Not enough customers are interested. The ways that bureaux are surviving are:

(a) by taking an increasing share of the declining market, as weaker competitors pull out; and

(b) by offering a wide variety of services, including the supply of software systems for customers to use themselves 'in house'.

9.3 The main shortages relate nowadays not to hardware, but to programming and application development time.

TEST YOUR KNOWLEDGE
The numbers in brackets refer to paragraphs of this chapter

1   What is a computer bureau? (2.1)

2   What services might a bureau offer? (2.2)

3   What factors should influence the choice of a bureau? (2.7, 2.8)

4   What services might be offered by a software house? (3.1-3.3)

5   What is a turnkey operation? (5.1)

Now try question 16 at the end of the text

Chapter 13

SYSTEMS INVESTIGATION

This chapter covers the following topics.

1. Introduction to systems analysis and design
2. Investigating the current system
3. Fact finding techniques
4. Concluding the investigation

---

1. INTRODUCTION TO SYSTEMS ANALYSIS AND DESIGN

1.1 Not every systems development project will commence with a feasibility study in the manner described in the previous chapter. Some systems may be too small to warrant it. In some cases there might be little point in evaluating alternative options if, realistically, there are none. Alternatively, the type of feasibility study carried out may be less formal than suggested.

1.2 Systems analysis and design are heavily documented in any methodology. You should remember most approaches to systems design these days:

(a) focus on the information needs and requirements of users as a justification for processing methods and techniques;

(b) work on a top-down philosophy from the general to the specific;

(c) leave physical implementation until last.

1.3 Methodologies like SSADM document the analysis and design phase extensively. Each stage requires a number of documents to be provided, as a sign that it has been completed, and to ensure that the outputs from one stage are used as inputs to the next. That being said, some methodologies may be too elaborate from some systems development, so users may adapt them to their own particular needs.

2. INVESTIGATING THE CURRENT SYSTEM

2.1 At this stage the system as it is currently operated must be investigated. The aim is to produce a description of the data flows (in DFDs) and the logical data structures (entity models). Entity models were described in the chapter on databases. DFDs (data flow diagrams) are described in the chapter on systems design.

2.2 Some of the issues which the team may wish to investigate have been discussed already. However, at this phase, when the team is trying to discover the details of a system with which they are generally quite unfamiliar, they will be interested in all sorts of facts about the organisation. After all, the organisational context of the system will affect its operation. Consequently, fact-finding can cover a broad area, as below.

(a) *Plans and objectives*

    (i)   Does the department have clear plans and objectives?
    (ii)   Are these consistent with the plans and objectives of the whole organisation?
    (iii) Is there a clear understanding of the department's plans and objectives?
    (iv) Are they realistic and achievable?
    (v)   What matters would be relevant in deciding whether they could be improved?

(b) *Organisation structure*

    (i)   Establish an organisation chart for the department.
    (ii)   Is the organisation structure a good (efficient) one?
    (iii) Are responsibilities clearly delegated and defined?
    (iv) Are there overlapping or duplicated functions?
    (v)   Should any work be transferred to or from the department?
    (vi) Is the work load efficiently shared between staff?
    (vii) Is there good co-operation and communication between various staff?
    (viii) Do staff understand the formal organisation structure?
    (ix) Can the organisation structure be improved?

(c) *Policies, systems, procedures*

    (i)   What documents are used in the current system?
    (ii)   What data is collected, filed and processed and when? How is it used?
    (iii) How has the department established its current policies? Are these written down?
    (iv) Are they formally reviewed?
    (v)   Are the department's policies consistent with its objectives?
    (vi) Are the policies understood by staff, or even communicated to staff?
    (vii) How does management ensure that policies are adhered to?
    (viii) What are the specific policies of the department?
    (ix) Are the department's systems meeting all the current requirements of the department?
    (x)   Can improvements be made in the system - eg in processing time or in paper handling?
    (xi) Are the procedures of the department fully documented in procedure manuals?
    (xii) Are there adequate control procedures?
    (xiii) What is the condition of the department's record files (is there a backlog)?
    (xiv) Do the department's procedures and records conform to legal requirements?
    (xv) Are there any unnecessary records that can be got rid of?
    (xvi) Are there any procedures that require further study with a view to improvement?

(d) *Personnel*

    (i)   How are staff recruited?
    (ii)   Are working conditions satisfactory?
    (iii) Are staff used to their full potential?
    (iv) Are there adequate systems and procedures for job specifications and appraisals?
    (v)   Are there adequate systems for staff development and training?

(vi)   What is the rate of staff turnover, absenteeism, transfer requests?

(vii) What proportion of the work done is skilled?

(viii) What proportion of skilled or clerical work is done by supervisors and managers?

(e) *Equipment and the office*

(i)   What is the general condition of office equipment?

(ii)   Is the equipment located in a convenient place? Is it used to full advantage?

(iii)   How are file records stored?

(iv)   Is the layout of the office efficient?

(f) *Operations and control*

(i)   What are the operations of the department, in detail?

(ii)   What methods exist for expediting work?

(iii)   What controls exist? Are they adequate?

(iv)   What exceptional cases are dealt with, and how are they dealt with?

(v)   Are management reports adequate, clear and prompt?

(vi)   Can any operations be eliminated or improved?

(vii) Are there any bottlenecks in operations, and if so, what can be done to ease them?

(viii) Is there scope for mechanisation/computerisation?

(ix)   How is productivity measured?

(x)   Are there standards for various aspects of work?

(xi)   Does management exercise a scheme of budgetary control?

(xii) Is the quality of work adequate? Could quality be improved?

(xiii) What is needed to improve efficiency?

2.3 As you will appreciate from this list, there are many items about which facts ought to be obtained, and so the systems investigators should begin by drafting a check list of points before they start asking questions.

3.   FACT FINDING TECHNIQUES

3.1 Three broad techniques are used in fact finding:

(a) interviews;

(b) questionnaires;

(c) observation and inspection of records: fact recording.

The facts obtained from the investigation must be fully recorded.

Interviews

3.2 Interviews with members of staff are undoubtedly the most effective method of fact finding. There are some helpful guidelines for conducting a fact-finding interview. The interviewer must be able to adapt his approach to suit the individual interviewee, rather than follow a standard routine and should be fully prepared for the interview, he should:

(a) inform employees *before* the interview that a systems investigation is taking place, and its purpose explained;

(b) ask questions at the level appropriate to the employee's position within the organisation;

(c) not be too formal ('question and answer'), but should encourage the interviewee to offer opinions and suggestions;

(d) not jump to conclusions or confuse opinions with facts;

(e) not propound his own opinions in the interview.

(f) refrain from making 'off the record' comments during the course of the interview, eg about what he is going to recommend.

(g) conclude the interview by a resume of its main points (so that the interviewee can confirm that the interviewer has obtained what he should have done).

Questionnaires

3.3 The use of questionnaires may be useful whenever a limited amount of information is required from a large number of individuals, or where the organisation is decentralised with many 'separate entity' locations. Questionnaires may be used in advance of an interview to save the analyst's and employee's time, but it should be remembered that:

(a) employees ought to be informed before receiving the questionnaire that a systems investigation is to take place, and its purpose explained;

(b) questions must be designed to obtain *exactly* the information necessary for the study;

(c) busy employees may consider it a waste of time to answer page after page of questions, and may be unwilling to do so, or may put the questionnaire in the 'pending' tray for a rainy day.

3.4 If a questionnaire is necessary, for example to establish the function of all employees within the organisation, the interviewer/analyst may design a form that enables the individual to list his duties under various headings. The form should be designed with the specific organisation in mind and an example (not exhaustive) is shown on the next page.

3.5 Whenever possible, questionnaires should:

(a) not contain too many questions;

(b) be organised in a logical sequence;

(c) include an occasional question the answer to which corroborates the answers to previous questions;

(d) ideally, be designed so that each question can be answered by either 'yes' or 'no' or a 'tick' rather than sentences or paragraphs;

13: SYSTEMS INVESTIGATION

CHAMBERS LIMITED

EMPLOYEES JOB DESCRIPTION - QUESTIONNAIRE

Employees:

Surname: _____ Location: _____

Other names: _____ Department: _____

Job title: _____ Form completion (date): _____

As you are all aware an analysis of company procedures and routines is being carried out. To help the systems investigation we would be very grateful to receive information as regards the details of your job. Please return the completed form to your manager by 31 October 19X1.

A. What are your main duties? Please describe each function and estimate the time taken per week.

No.	JOB DESCRIPTION	Hours worked
1		
2		
3		
4		
	Total hours worked per week	

B. What documents do you use in connection with each job? Please list all forms and reports, outlining their use and principal contents, and referencing each to the job detailed in A above. Attach a copy of each document to the completed questionnaire.

Document No: _____ Document title: _____

Job No: _____ Document function: _____

Principal contents

1	_____	6	_____	11	_____
2	_____	7	_____	12	_____
3	_____	8	_____	13	_____
4	_____	9	_____	14	_____
5	_____	10	_____	15	_____

Document No: _____ Document title: _____

Job No: _____ Document function: _____

etc

C. What books/ledgers/equipment/machinery do you use for each job? Please list under the appropriate job number.

Job No.	Books/Equipment used	
1	1 _____	4 _____
	2 _____	5 _____
	3 _____	6 _____
2	1 _____	4 _____
	2 _____	5 _____
5	2 _____	5 _____
	3 _____	6 _____

(e) be tested independently before being issued to the actual individuals. The test answers should enable the systems analyst to establish the effectiveness of his questions and help determine the level of subsequent interviews and observations;

(f) take into account the sensitivity of individuals in respect of their job security, change of job definition etc.

3.6 It must be stressed that questionnaires, by themselves, are an inadequate means of fact finding, and should usually be followed up by an interview or observation.

Observation

3.7 Once the analyst has some understanding of the methods and procedures used in the organisation, he should be able to verify his findings and clarify any problems areas by an observation of operations. Observation is a useful way of cross-checking with the facts obtained by interview or questionnaire. Different methods of recording facts ought to produce the same information, but it is not inconceivable that staff do their work in one way, whilst management believe they do something different.

Document investigation: document description form

3.8 The systems analyst must investigate the *documents* that are used in the system for:

(a) data capture/data collection - ie input;
(b) output.

3.9 One way of recording facts about document usage is the *document description form*. This is simply a standard form which the analyst can use to describe a document. For example:

DOCUMENT DESCRIPTION FORM

TITLE OF DOCUMENT . . . .
DOCUMENT NUMBER . . . .
ORIGINATING DEPT . . . . NO OF COPIES . . . .
FILLED IN BY . . . .
COPIES SENT TO . . . .
REMARKS

DATA ITEM DESCRIPTION	MAXIMUM ITEMS PER DOCUMENT	SIZE/ PICTURE	ENTERED BY	REMARKS

PREPARED BY (SYSTEMS ANALYST)	DATE	PROJECT

Notes

(a) *Data item description*. This column lists all the items on the document. For example, a sales order form will include name of customer, address of customer (invoice address, delivery address), date of order, items ordered, quantity per item ordered, signature of customer etc. The maximum number of times each item appears on the document is shown in the next column.

(b) *Size/picture*. This indicates the size of the data item (which might be a fixed length or variable length item). In the case of variable length items, the maximum size might be indicated on the form. 'Picture' means the format of the item, in terms of alphabetic, numeric or other characters, eg:

> A(15)   means 15 alphabetic characters
> 9999   means 4 numeric characters
> ANN   means a letter followed by two numbers
> 9(6)   means 6 numeric characters

(c) *Entered by*. This indicates the person (or machine) responsible for entering the data item on the document.

(d) *'Remarks'* leaves space for the system analyst to make any further notes - eg where the data comes from (eg price or discount allowed on a sales invoice, whether the size of the data item is the maximum size of a variable length item or a fixed length item, whether the completed document is checked and authorised by a supervisor etc).

Exercise

You are an analyst working on the transfer of sales ledger procedures to computerised operation. Under what headings might you group the questions you wish to ask staff in fact finding interviews?

Solution

You might wish to group your questions as follows.

(a) Staff and organisation.
(b) Customer base/profile.
(c) Inputs.
(d) Outputs.
(e) Processing.
(f) Credit control.
(g) Environment.

---

4. CONCLUDING THE INVESTIGATION

4.1 The results of these investigations are recorded. The DFDs produced in the feasibility study may be expanded here. Also recorded are *function descriptions*. These are simply the main processes which operate on data and transform it. (*Function* is sometimes used synonymously with *process*.)

4.2 The project team will investigate and record the entity model. You will remember from the chapter on databases some of the techniques by which this is achieved:

(a) discover and describe the entities in the systems (or, alternatively, extend and check the descriptions already produced during the feasibility study);

(b) create a data dictionary;

(c) normalise the data (also referred to as relational data analysis);

(d) check this analysis against the data flow diagrams.

4.3 A *problems/requirements list* is defined. Again, this may have been carried out during the feasibility study, but it is likely to be expanded as the system is investigated in more detail. To recap, problems could be encountered over:

(a) data input;
(b) poor controls;
(c) volumes higher than the system can cope with;
(d) poor user interface;
(e) slow response times;
(f) inflexibility in processing;
(g) system outputs are too inflexible/unwieldy for more advanced MIS applications (eg DSS, EIS).

4.4 *Requirements* can in fact be solutions to the problems identified in the current system, but could also imply a completely new way of doing things, (eg replacing batch by on-line processing, providing direct input to data from transaction processing systems to spreadsheet models).

5. CONCLUSION

5.1 At the end of systems investigation, some of which may have been carried out during the feasibility study, documentation produced will include:

(a) current physical DFDs detailing document flows;
(b) elementary function descriptions (ie the basic processes that transform data);
(c) a logical data structure (entity model) of the current system;
(d) the problems/requirements list.

5.2 Thus a detailed picture of the current system is built up.

TEST YOUR KNOWLEDGE

The numbers in brackets refer to paragraphs of this chapter

1 What issues might be addressed in a fact finding exercise? (2.2)

2 Draw up guidelines for a successful interview. (3.2)

3 What are the desirable features of a questionnaire? (3.5)

4 What in summary, are the contents of a list of problems and requirements? (4.3)

Now try question 17 at the end of the text

Chapter 14

SYSTEMS ANALYSIS

This chapter covers the following topics.

1. Systems analysis and the systems analyst
2. Data modelling and data flow diagrams (DFDs)
3. Entity models
4. Entity life histories
5. System flowcharts

---

1. SYSTEMS ANALYSIS AND THE SYSTEMS ANALYST

1.1 *Systems analysis* is 'the methodical study of a system, its current and future required objectives and procedures in order to form a basis for systems design.' (CIMA) In other words, systems analysis is the detailed look at a current system and what a new system will be required to do, and systems analysis leads on to systems design, which is the development of a new system that will meet these future requirements.

1.2 Systems analysis may be carried out by a *systems analyst*. This might be a person employed in the organisation's DP department, or he might be an external consultant.

1.3 A systems analyst is 'the person responsible for the analysis of a business system to assess its suitability for computer application. He may also design the necessary computer system.' (British Computer Society).

1.4 To design and develop a larger system may require a number of systems analysts and programmers, and so a project team might have to be formed (a computer consultancy or bureau may provide one). The chief analyst, preferably the one who was also responsible for the feasibility study, will have individuals with differing backgrounds and experience (technical and business) working in his team.

1.5 Systems analysis might be done in two stages, depending on the size of the project.

(a) The first stage is carried out during the feasibility study. The feasibility study team must go into some detail about the current system and what the requirements for a new system should be, and this means having to do systems analysis work. For large computer projects, the feasibility study team should therefore ideally include a systems analyst, either an employee in the organisation's DP department, or an external consultant hired to lend his expertise.

(b) If the feasibility study report recommends a new project, and the recommendation is accepted, the second stage in the systems analysis work might be an even closer 'in-depth' analysis of the system, which will then lead straight into systems design work.

1.6 These two stages in systems analysis would only differ in the amount of detail they go into, and so the length of time they might take. The two stages could be combined into one, and all the systems analysis work could be done during the feasibility study.

System design

1.7 When designing the new system the development team must consider:

(a) output requirements and formats;
(b) file design;
(c) input requirements and formats;
(d) coding design;
(e) procedure design (including system controls);
(f) the hardware to be used;
(g) costs and benefits:
(h) documentation of the system.

Design tools and techniques

1.8 When systems analysts and programmers set about the task of designing and developing a new system, they will use a number of tools and techniques to help them. Some techniques are helpful with creating the broad outline design of the system; others are used for the more detailed work of program or file design.

2. DATA MODELLING AND DATA FLOW DIAGRAMS (DFDs)

2.1 A data processing system is created to take input data, process it, and produce output. A starting point for system design work is to establish what data processing is needed, ie what the input data should be, where it comes from, what data is filed, and where, how data is processed, what output is produced and where the output goes.

The term 'data modelling' is sometimes used to describe the technique of looking at a system from a data handling perspective, and analysing:

(a) what data is needed?
(b) why is it needed?
(c) what is the data used for?
(d) who uses the data?
(e) where does the data originate and how?

2.2 The answers to these questions, once obtained, should then lead on to other, more detailed design issues, such as:

    (a)   when is the data needed, and how frequently?
    (b)   when does the source data originate?
    (c)   how should the data be processed?
    (d)   where should the data be filed?
    (e)   how should the data be maintained and updated, and who should be responsible for this?
    (f)   who should be allowed access to file data?

The answers to these questions should help the systems analyst to design the outline of a system that meets the user's needs, and the 'technical' issues of whether to use micros or a mainframe, a network or stand-alone computers, a database or separate files etc, should only then be resolved.

Data flow analysis

2.3   One useful way of recording the ways in which data is processed, without bothering with the equipment used, is a *data flow diagram*. The production of a data flow diagram is often the first step in a structured systems analysis, because it provides a basic understanding of how the system works.

2.4   Data flow analysis is a broadly applicable design tool, which may be used for manual as well as computerised systems. A great advantage of using this technique is that it may be applied to existing systems so that they can provide a model of current operations, and indicate any gaps in the logic or flow of data.

The description of what is being done, or should be done, does not in any way imply that a specific technology ought to be used, and so it is a method for understanding how a system works without forcing computerisation upon it.

2.5   When a systems analyst first looks at a system, to find out how the data is processed (or should be processed) in the system, he might not want to bother with what equipment is currently used for the processing. All he wants to do is to sort out what data is used, who uses it, and where it is stored. The problem of *designing* a new system for the data processing, and of deciding what equipment and computers should do it, will come later.

2.6   The symbols which might be used in a data flow diagram are as follows.

    (a)   DATA SOURCE
           DATA DESTINATION

        People or groups who are sources of data or 'destinations' for data - ie who receive data or output information.

(b) **DATA STORES**

Identifying number
of data store

	Name of data store

Data stores – eg transaction records, data files, reports, documents etc. A data store is a point which holds data, and receives a data flow. Data stores are not restricted as to their form, and might be held in a computer's CPU memory, or in the form of various magnetic media, or in the form of documents in a filing cabinet, or on microfiche etc.

(c) **DATA FLOWS**

A data flow represents the movement or transfer of data from one point in the system to another. This may involve a document transfer or it may simply involve a notification that some event has occurred without any detailed information being passed. Multiple data flows may also exist. When a data flow occurs a copy of the data transferred may also be retained at the transmitting point.

A data flow could be 'physically' anything – eg in a letter, by telephone, by Fax, between computers, a verbal statement etc.

(d) **PHYSICAL FLOWS**

Occasionally it may be necessary to detail the flow of goods or objects.

(e) **DATA PROCESSES**

Identifying
number of
process

Data processes – ie processing actions carried out from a data store, and to produce a data store.

The processes could be manual, mechanised or automated/computerised.

A data process will use or alter the data in some way. An example of a process which simply uses the data would be an output operation, where the data held by the system is unchanged and it is merely made available in a different form, eg printed out. A process which alters the data would be a mathematical computation or a process such as sorting in which the arrangement of the data is altered. Systems widely vary in the amount of data processing which they perform. Some systems are dominated by the amount of data movement which they provide, whilst others are intensively concerned much more with transforming the data into a more useful form.

2.7 An example might help to illustrate what a data flow diagram records. The example used here is a sales, despatch and warehousing system.

2.8 A level-0 DFD shows the inputs and outputs to the system and makes the *system boundary* perfectly clear.

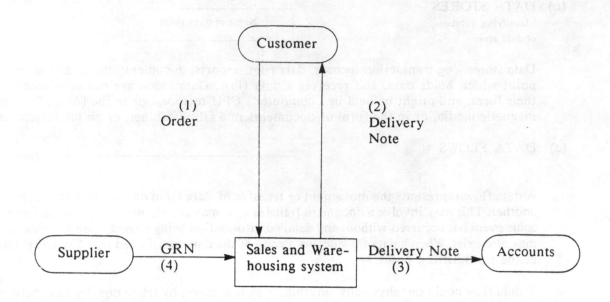

(1) Document: customer order form
     Data: amount (and value) of goods ordered

(2) Document: delivery note (top copy)
     Data: amount (and value) of goods despatched

(3) Document: delivery note (bottom copy)
     Data: as per (2)

(4) Document: goods received note
     Data: amount (and value) of goods received.

2.9 A level-1 DFD which details the data flows between the subsystems in the system might appear as follows.

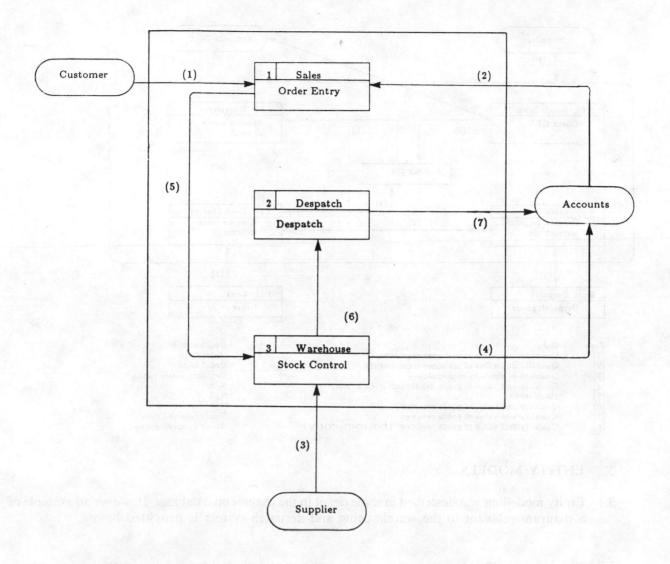

Flow Data		Document
(1)	Customer order details	Customer order
(2)	Credit limit authorisation	Authorisation list
(3)	Quantity and value of goods received	GRN - top copy
(4)	Quantity and value of goods received	GRN - bottom copy
(5)	Customer order details	Requisition
(6)	Quantity and value of goods despatched	Instruction
(7)	Quantity and value of goods despatched	Despatch note

2.10 A separate DFD (level-2) would be prepared for each of the sales, despatch and warehouse subsystems, eg:

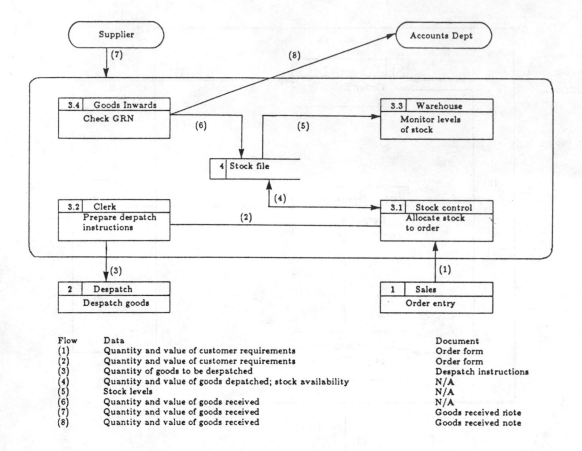

Flow	Data	Document
(1)	Quantity and value of customer requirements	Order form
(2)	Quantity and value of customer requirements	Order form
(3)	Quantity of goods to be despatched	Despatch instructions
(4)	Quantity and value of goods depatched; stock availability	N/A
(5)	Stock levels	N/A
(6)	Quantity and value of goods received	N/A
(7)	Quantity and value of goods received	Goods received note
(8)	Quantity and value of goods received	Goods received note

3. ENTITY MODELS

3.1 Entity modelling was described in some detail in the chapter on databases. However an example of a diagram relevant to the warehousing and despatch system is provided below.

3.2 This indicates that a single customer may make many orders; that a single order form can contain several order lines; that each line on the order form can only detail one product but one product can appear on several lines of the order.

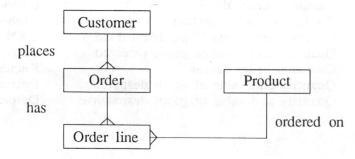

3.3 In some cases, a correlation will be made between the entities and the various data stores containing data about the entities, for example

Entity

| 2 | Credit limit file |
| 3 | Address list |

Customer

4. ENTITY LIFE HISTORIES

4.1 An entity life history is a diagram of the processes that happen to an entity. For example, a customer order forms part of a number of processes, and is affected by a number of different events.

4.2 The following diagram relates to opening a customer account.

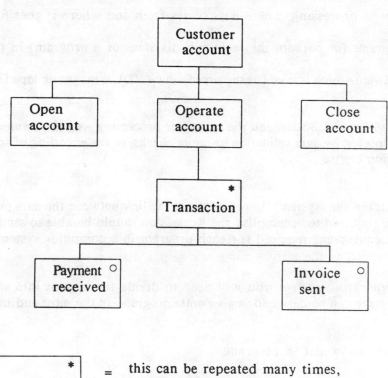

Note:

	*

= this can be repeated many times, as there might be many transactions

	o

= a transaction will either be a payment received, or an invoice

5. SYSTEM FLOWCHARTS

5.1 A computer run flowchart or system flowchart provides a high level description of the major elements of a system. Where a conceptual model, such as a data flow diagram, presents a rather general description of the system's functions, the purpose of the run flowchart is to define these functions and their inter-relationships more accurately and with a bit more technical detail.

5.2 The run flowchart is often used to specify in outline the procedures or sub-routines which are to be used by the system.

For a computer system, a computer run flowchart will show:

(a)   the input data and input data files;

(b)   all transaction files, master files and reference files;

(c)   the output;

(d)   the flow of processing; where data comes from and where it goes to, if filed;

(e)   the programs (or perhaps the main sub-divisions of a program) in the system;

(f)   the hardware which is used for the processing - VDUs, magnetic tape files, magnetic disk files, etc;

(g)   any activities which surround the computer processing - eg the immediate correction of errors reported by data validation program checks, or the encoding of source data at a data conversion centre.

5.3 In other words the run (system) flowchart shows the link between the data processing itself and the hardware required to accomplish the work. You should be able to study a flowchart and envisage the equipment required for each program in a computer system.

5.4 In a *batch processing system*, you will need to divide the system into separate processing stages. Each stage can be designed as a separate program. In the most rudimentary system you would find:

(a)   a data vet or validation program;

(b)   a sort program, ie 'sort records to key field order' which is:

    (i)   optional if the master file is on disk, or any other direct access storage medium;
    (ii)   compulsory if the master file is on magnetic tape and the transaction data have not been pre-sorted (manually) to master file order;

(c)   a master file update program: in this 'all purpose' program, the main processing might be done all at once. Master file cumulative data would be brought up to date, and all processing for output would also be done. Print instructions might also be included in the program so that output reports are produced for the user.

5.5 It is likely, however, that a batch processing system will require a few more stages of processing, ie a few more programs. For example, if there are two master files, there could be two master file update programs (and possibly two sort programs).

5.6 Print instructions might be separated into an individual program, where the volume of printing required is large (and therefore time-consuming). If different output is required at different times, separate programs will be necessary. For example, if two reports ar required as output, say a daily report (A) and a monthly report (B), a separate, additional program might be run once each month to produce report B. Report A and Report B would not be produced by the same program since this would involve the unnecessary production of Report B every day. Alternatively, the same program might offer the computer user the option of printing certain reports or not.

Example: system flowchart

5.7 Comforter Ltd maintains its financial records on a computer system with key-to-tape input data preparation and magnetic tape storage. The Finance Director is responsible for computer operations but not for general office management, property administration or legal and secretarial matters.

You are required to:

(a) list the master files which must be maintained in connection with the processing of accounting data in order to generate accounting reports;

(b) present a systems flowchart suitable for the batch processing of fixed asset records by Comforter Ltd;

(c) suggest what advantages you think that Comforter Ltd might gain by introducing disk storage in its accounting systems in place of magnetic tape.

Solution

5.8 Using the approach previously described a solution could be formulated as follows:

(a) Purpose of the system: to generate accounting reports - ie:

   (i) profit and loss account;

   (ii) balance sheet;

   (iii) cash flows (or budgets) or funds flow statements;

   (iv) variance analysis reports, or other measures of performance within a management control system;

   (v) analysis of return on investment.

   Other reports could be listed.

(b) Type of system required: the question states that key-to-tape data preparation and magnetic tape files are used; therefore a batch processing system is in operation. The replacement of magnetic tape with disks will not alter the system to an on-line process unless the key-to-tape preparation method is also replaced by remote direct-input terminals.

5.9 Output consists of the reports listed in (a) above. Input will consist of transactions affecting those reports - ie:

(a) fixed assets purchased and sold (including data about their type and the provision for depreciation to be made each year);

(b) stock purchased and used;

(c) labour hours worked in each department and their cost;

(d) other expense items;

(e) bad debts written off;

(f) cash received and paid.

Other items of input might be added.

5.10 Master files will consist of:

(a) fixed assets register;
(b) customers' master file;
(c) creditors' master file;
(d) payroll file;
(e) treasury file (for cash);
(f) stock file;
(g) nominal ledger for recording actual expenses, standard costs, variances etc.

Separate master files might be kept for each profit centre or investment centre in the company.

5.11 The processing of fixed asset records will involve:

(a) the addition of new purchases to the fixed assets master file, with each purchase given a unique identification code. Input details would include purchase cost, fixed asset category and depreciation category;

(b) the deletion of fixed assets sold. The sale price may be included so that a profit or loss on sale could be transferred to the nominal ledger system;

(c) revaluations of fixed assets;

(d) output from the fixed assets system may be a magnetic tape and will be used as input to the nominal ledger system. Information will include depreciation for the period, and for balance sheet purposes, assets at gross book value and accumulated depreciation to date. Profit or loss on the sale of assets might also be included.

(a)   Additions, disposals and revaluations   (b)   Listing

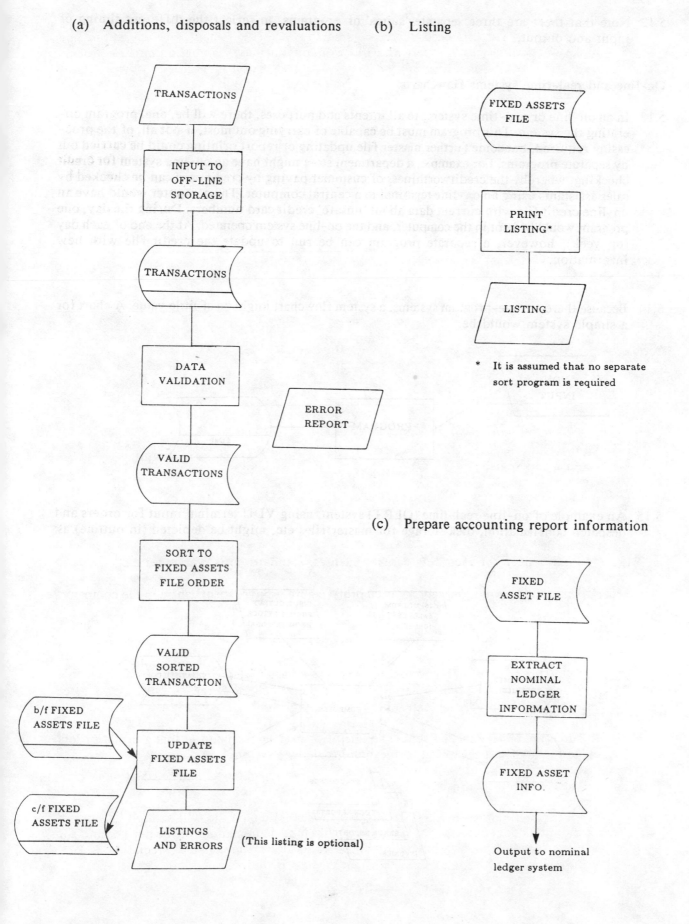

TRANSACTIONS

INPUT TO
OFF-LINE
STORAGE

TRANSACTIONS

DATA
VALIDATION

ERROR
REPORT

VALID
TRANSACTIONS

SORT TO
FIXED ASSETS
FILE ORDER

VALID
SORTED
TRANSACTION

b/f FIXED
ASSETS FILE

UPDATE
FIXED ASSETS
FILE

c/f FIXED
ASSETS FILE

LISTINGS
AND ERRORS   (This listing is optional)

FIXED ASSETS
FILE

PRINT
LISTING*

LISTING

*   It is assumed that no separate
    sort program is required

(c)   Prepare accounting report information

FIXED
ASSET FILE

EXTRACT
NOMINAL
LEDGER
INFORMATION

FIXED ASSET
INFO.

Output to nominal
ledger system

243

5.12 Note that there are three separate 'suites' of programs, to reflect the different timing of input and output.

On-line and real-time systems flowcharts

5.13 In an on-line or real-time system, to all intents and purposes, there will be 'one' program operating the system. This program must be capable of carrying out most, if not all, of the processing required, but some further master file updating or report printing could be carried out by separate programs. For example, a department store might have an on-line system for credit checking, whereby the creditworthiness of customer paying by credit card can be checked by sales assistants using an on-line terminal to a central computer. The computer would have an on-line credit file with current data about 'unsafe' credit card numbers. During the day, one program would be kept in the computer, and the on-line system operated. At the end of each day (or week), however, a separate program can be run to update the credit file with new information.

5.14 Because there are one-program systems, a system flowchart might be of little value. A chart for a simple system would be:

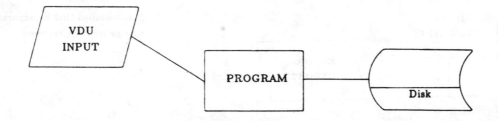

5.15 An example of on-line real-time (OLRT) system, using VDU terminal input for orders and despatch confirmation, disk storage for master files etc, might be depicted (in outline) as:

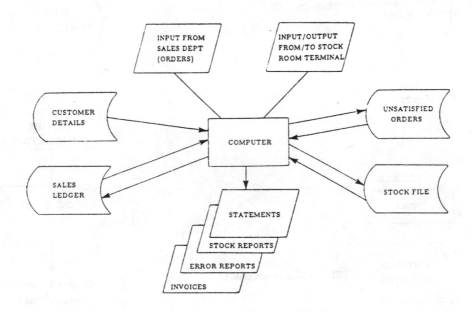

Deciding what files and programs are needed

5.16 Drawing system flowcharts can take some getting used to. As general guidelines, you might find the following hints useful.

(a) Identify the source data. What is it and how will it be processed?

(b) What output is needed, and in what form? (eg printed output, VDU screen output, output on to file).

(c) What master files or reference files might be needed? Unless an examination question tells you what the files are to be, you are likely to have some freedom of choice in deciding for yourself what master files or reference files might be needed.

(d) Is the system an on-line system? If so, the master files must be on disk. Any reference files ought to be on disk, because *direct* access of this file will almost certainly be needed.

(e) Does the processing vary or is it the same every time? For example, is there routine daily processing for daily output, and then a monthly processing operation to produce monthly management reports? If so, draw separate flowcharts for each different variation of processing – eg a flowchart for daily operations and another flowchart for monthly operations.

6. CONCLUSION

6.1 In this chapter we have considered some widely used analysis techniques. The work done using those techniques can be used in the next stage of systems development, the detailed design work. Data flow diagrams and run flowcharts provide an outline design on which to build.

TEST YOUR KNOWLEDGE
The numbers in brackets refer to paragraphs of this chapter

1 Define systems analysis. (1.1)

2 What is data modelling? (2.1)

3 What is data flow analysis? (2.3, 2.4)

Now try question 18 at the end of the text

PART D

DESIGN AND IMPLEMENTATION
OF SYSTEMS

Chapter 15

SYSTEMS DESIGN

This chapter covers the following topics.

1. Input, output and file design: introduction
2. Output design
3. Input design
4. Document design
5. Code design
6. Screen design and dialogue design
7. File design

---

1. INPUT, OUTPUT AND FILE DESIGN: INTRODUCTION

1.1 The techniques used to design a computer system, once the outline system design has been prepared, are likely to vary between systems.

(a) Where a system uses application-specific files, the design of the system will involve:

    (i)   deciding what data will be held on each file, as cumulative or standing data;

    (ii) what the contents of the data input ought to be;

    (iii) what the form and content of the system outputs ought to be.

    This work involves file design, code design, input design, VDU screen and dialogue design, and output design (eg the design of output documents).

(b) When a system uses a database, the design of the system will focus more specifically on how the database files should be structured.

1.2 In this chapter, we shall now consider design issues for a system with application-specific files, although most of these issues are relevant to database systems too.

1.3 The design sequence might be:

(a) outputs (results);
(b) inputs (data);
(c) files;
(d) procedures (program and programs).

15: SYSTEMS DESIGN

2. OUTPUT DESIGN

2.1 The specification of what output the user wants from a system dictates both the requirements for input and files in the system, since the data input or held on file must be sufficient to provide the output. (An output 'system', as a sub-system of a DP system, must inter-relate with input, processing and files. This is a theoretical point, but it ought to draw your attention to the relevance of systems theory.)

2.2 Output design will cover three separately identifiable types of results:

(a) *external results* - ie results that will be sent out to people outside the user's organisation. These include invoices and purchase orders etc.

(b) *internal results* - ie results that will be distributed within the organisation. These include management reports, error reports and audit listings etc.;

(c) *internal system results* - ie information relating to the operations of the system itself, such as system operating statistics and control totals and reports.

2.3 The design of output will cover the following aspects.

(a) *Identification of output*. All output report documents and VDU screen displays etc must be clearly specified and uniquely identified.

(b) *Content and format*. Obviously, this is a fundamental part of output design work, and it is dealt with more fully later.

(c) *Frequency of production*. The frequency with which the output will be produced must be specified, including whether there might be a requirement for *urgency* in its production. Response times for keyboard interrogations should be specified. Reports might be routinely produced (every week, month, year etc.) or produced only on demand.

(d) Where appropriate, the *conditions giving rise to the production of output* should be specified - ie what needs to happen for a particular report or item to be produced as output?

(e) The *volume* of expected output must also be specified. When output volumes are very large, and a mainframe computer is being used, the systems analyst will probably opt for high-speed printer output. When output volumes are low and a hard-copy of the output is required, the systems analyst might choose to use a low-speed printer, perhaps situated at a remote location from the mainframe computer.

(f) The *sequence* in which output is produced must be specified. (This is another aspect of form design, even when output is not produced in hard copy but is displayed instead on a screen.)

(g) The *output medium* must be specified (eg screen, line printer, daisy wheel printer, graph plotter etc). Also the number of copies might have to be considered. Output which will be used as input to another program or module will need a magnetic file medium, such as disk.

The choice of output medium will have regard to:

(i)   whether a hard copy is required;
(ii) what quality the output should be, whether hard copy or VDU display.

2.4 The costs and benefits of output information would be considered. The user might be asking for information that would be too costly to produce in view of the benefits obtainable from it. Questions that the systems designer might consider in designing the output are:

(a) is the user asking for too much information?

(b) can two or more required outputs be combined into a single multi-use output?

(c) is the output required as frequently as specified, or can the frequency be reduced?

(d) should output be produced automatically, or only on demand (thus reducing output regularity and so output volume)?

(e) does the response time in a random access interactive system have to be so short, or can it be longer (by a matter of seconds, minutes or even hours/days)?

(f) should the user be allowed some control over the format and sequence of output, or should format and sequence be rigidly designed?

The answers to these questions cannot be decided by the systems analyst alone, but he or she should discuss these matters with the user.

Example: output design

2.5 In a department store, there are fifty cash desks where customers pay for their goods. The department store has a POS computer system, with each cash desk terminal linked to a central computer. A stock master file includes details of selling prices for each stock item, and quantities held in stock for each item.

Required: list the possible contents of a printed output report:

(a) for each customer;
(b) daily, for management.

Solution

2.6 The customer's output 'report' is his or her receipt. This will give:

(a) the name of the store;
(b) its VAT number;
(c) date of transaction;
(d) a list of each item purchased, and its price;
(e) the total price for all the customer's purchases;
(f) possibly, method of payment;
(g) if payment is in cash, amount of cash paid and change given.

2.7 The output for a daily management report might include:

(a) a list of the total quantities and value of sales for each stock item;
(b) total sales for the day, possibly analysed by department or cash desk;
(c) a list of stock items for re-ordering (and quantities already on order);
(d) possibly, a current list of quantities of each item still held in stock.

3. INPUT DESIGN

3.1 The design of input is most important because in most computer systems, data is first of all collected in human-sensible form and must be 'converted' into computer input (eg keyboard input). People are thus very much involved in providing the data that the computer system will use, and in input design the systems analyst must balance the requirements of the system with the personal capabilities of its users.

Input design is closely bound up with data collection and data capture.

3.2 There are a number of different considerations for input design. These are as follows:

(a) Which input data will become 'standing' or 'static' master file data and which input will be regular transaction data? There should be no unnecessary re-input of data - for example, if standing file data includes

(customer name)	Harold Heights Ltd
(customer address)	Standen Still Road
	Stuck-on-Tweed
(customer code number)	123455

it should only be necessary to input the unique customer code number with any transaction data for the customer. Transaction records should not contain name and address.

(b) What *volumes* of input are expected? Large volumes of input are more likely to lend themselves to a batch processing system rather than a random access interactive processing system.

(c) What will be the *frequency* of input? Infrequent transaction data might suggest a random access system from keyboard terminals.

With batched input, however, the frequency of input must be considered, eg:

(i) how often must input data be used to keep the master file up-to-date with standing data - ie how often should *file maintenance* be carried out?

(ii) how often must transaction data be input - daily? weekly? monthly? etc.

(d) In what *sequence* should batched data be input? For example, data for file maintenance ought to be input in batches before transaction data, to ensure that the standing data on the master file is up-to-date before the transaction data is processed.

(e) *Where* will data be collected or captured for input? Where will it be converted into machine-sensible form? In general, it is preferable to capture data as soon as possible and to keep to a minimum the transcription of data from one 'source' document to other document before input.

(f) For computer systems, what should be the *input medium?* Is the need for accuracy very important (eg are inaccuracies costly or unacceptable?) and so should there be *verification* of input?

(g) How extensive should *data validation* (data vet) checks be?

(h) *What data* should be input? and in *what form?* Form design and code design are important aspects of input design as well as output design.

Data preparation control

3.3 In addition to input design, the systems analyst should also give some consideration to data preparation control, ie the transcription of data from source documents for input to the computer. Depending on the system, data preparation work may be done by data preparation staff at a computer centre; alternatively, data might be keyed in by staff in the user department. Data preparation design work must try to ensure that:

(a) all the data that should be input is received and fed into the system;

(b) all the data is processed through the system (apart from any errors which are rejected, and which must also be accounted for).

Data preparation also includes any required *verification* of data.

3.4 Data preparation control in a batch processing system is achieved by means of batch control - ie batching incoming documents. Batching offers several advantages:

(a) it helps in the allocation of work between data preparation staff - ie individual staff can be given a certain number of identifiable batches of input to prepare, and their accuracy and speed etc, can be monitored;

(b) locating errors is simplified, because exception reports from the computer program notifying error conditions and rejected input can show which batch the incorrect entry belongs to;

(c) each batch can be controlled individually;

(d) an incorrect batch can be removed individually, so that the remaining input can be processed without difficulty.

3.5 To help with batch control, the systems analyst should give some thought to:

(a) whether batches should be an exact size (ie contain an exact number of input records) or whether a batch 'header' control record should identify the number (and perhaps the value) or records in the batch;

(b) how data preparation management should be notified of what batches to expect (eg can batches be received at regular intervals from the clerical staff preparing the original input forms, and can a list be provided of the batch numbers sent?)

3.6 Batch control assists with the 'manual' control of input data. Control totals on batch header records can also be compared with control totals of records processed by the computer, so that a check can be carried out within a program that all the submitted data has been processed or can be accounted for by rejection reports.

3.7 Quick response (interactive) computer systems are unsuitable for a centralised data preparation section, and data handling is reduced because the user inputs data directly via an on-line remote terminals. The user is then fully responsible for input control.

4. DOCUMENT DESIGN

4.1 In designing a system, an analyst may have to design a large number of different forms or documents for input data and for output. It is possible that you will be required to design documents in your examination and although documents (form) design is largely a matter of common sense and experience, you should not forget the purpose of the document, nor the few simple points discussed below. It is very easy to forget the obvious and to abandon common sense, unless you make yourself specifically aware of what you should be doing.

4.2 The purpose served by a form is to ensure the effective transmission of necessary information. A good form will allow the required information to be obtained, transmitted, interpreted, filed and retrieved at minimum total cost. It must be remembered that the total cost of a form is not only the printing and paper costs but also the handling costs. The latter may be significantly increased by bad design.

4.3 Before attempting to design a document the analyst must ask himself whether it is really necessary. He must ensure that there is no other form either existing or proposed, which serves, or can be made to serve, the same purpose. To help with analysing the documents, the analyst should prepare a document analysis form for each document in the existing system and for each document required in the new system.

4.4 The document analysis form for input documents is similar to a document description form (used to record facts about documents used in the 'old' system during systems investigation) and will include:

    (a) *identification* - form title and number;
    (b) *purpose* of the document;
    (c) *origination* of documents - place and means of origination.
    (d) *contents* of the document;
    (e) *sequence* of the data;
    (f) *volume* of use - maximum, minimum, average, seasonal fluctuations etc;
    (g) *frequency* of preparation, at present and in the foreseeable future;
    (h) *files* affected by the input - transaction and master files. The analyst must also consider the files used and should prepare a file analysis form to identify purpose, content, layout and volume of records. The organisation and content of files may affect the *format* of the input document.

4.5 The output document analysis form is similar and may include:

(a) *identification* - form title and number;

(b) *distribution* of output documents specifying who receives each document and his job title and responsibilities, the information used from the report, where the document is filed and for how long, or whether it is quickly thrown away;

(c) *frequency* of production - daily, weekly, monthly etc;

(d) *contents* of the documents;

(e) *sequence* of the data;

(f) *volume* of production - maximum, minimum, average, expected growth etc;

(g) *format* of the document - needs of the user, possibility of using pre-printed forms etc.

4.6 In designing a form there are a number of decisions to be made. These can be split into five areas:

(a) content;
(b) lay-out;
(c) make-up;
(d) printing;
(e) paper.

From the examination point of view the first two areas are the most important.

Content of forms

4.7 Generally, the content of a form will be determined by the system to which it belongs. There are, however, some items which appear on most forms:

(a) title;
(b) serial number;
(c) date;
(d) narrative, ie instructions, subsidiary headings etc;
(e) units, eg hours, £'s, tons;
(f) signature (perhaps with authorisation);
(g) distribution of copies (eg copy 1 - accounts; copy 2 - stores; copy 3 - production control etc).

4.8 The title of a form should be descriptive and easy to remember. The narrative, ie the headings or instructions relating to spaces where entries are required, must also be given careful consideration. The words used must be matched to the educational and technical level of both the originator and the interpreter. Different types of entry headings include:

(a) instruction, eg 'write your name in this space';
(b) question, eg 'what is your name?';
(c) title, eg 'name'.

Lay-out of forms

4.9 Points to consider include:

(a) direction of paper;

(b) position of title;

(c) position of reference numbers. These should normally be placed near a corner so that the document can be easily identified in a file;

(d) position of entry headings. These should always be near the space to which they relate. NB. Never leave an entry without a heading;

(e) entry sequence. Entries should always follow a logical sequence. This is particularly important when the forms will be completed by several different people;

(f) boxing items, to make reading the form or filling it in easier.

4.10 The document may contain 'heading' information which is common to a number of repeated items ('variable' information). For example on a sales invoice customer name, address, account number and invoice number is common 'heading' information whereas the itemisation of product details such as quantity, description, code number, price, etc is variable information, with several products likely to be listed on a single invoice.

Make-up, printing and paper

4.11 Considerations in this area will include:

(a) make-up:

(i) size of the form (for handling, filing etc; and to contain all information, perhaps on a sheet of standard document size such as A5 or A4);

(ii) colour (*colour coding* for ease of identification);

(b) printing:

(i) number of document required (multi-part sets, perhaps with some minor differences on separate copies); possible use of continuous stationery;

(ii) filing requirements (position of serial number/identification name or code on the form;

(iii) typeface (for easy reading and to stress important data);

(c) paper quality and thickness (eg how easily might a thin paper form be damaged, and how long will it be kept?)

Qualities of a good form/source document

4.12 A good form is one which is designed so that information can be easily:

(a) *obtained*: the layout of the form and instructions on how to fill it in should be clear to the user. As much information as possible should be pre-printed to avoid error and reduce the work-load. The form must be easy to use. Turnround documents might be a possibility;

(b) *transmitted*: the form must be capable where necessary of easy handling and transmission (eg it may need to be sent by post, and should therefore fit into a standard size envelope);

(c) *interpreted*: the layout of information on the form must be in a clear, logical sequence so that it can be readily understood. A good title will help, and colour coding might also clarify its use. The use of different typefaces (or block capital letters) should be considered.

(d) *filed*: the size of filing cabinets or trays should be considered for forms used as a hard copy standing file;

(e) *retrieved*: the problems of easy retrieval of a form from file should also be considered. In a hard copy file, the position of the serial number, or the identification (key field) of the record may be very important. Filing on microfilm may be possible.

4.13 Further features of good source documents are as follows:

(a) they should contain all the data required (which is not available on file from other sources of input) but not excessive, unnecessary data;

(b) the document should have a clear title (and perhaps a code or identity number);

(c) where appropriate, unique serial numbers for documents should be used (eg invoices);

(d) related items should be grouped together on the form;

(e) the items should be arranged in a logical sequence, to suit the needs of the user;

(f) some consideration should be given to the needs of the person keying in the data (eg the VDU operator) in designing the layout/arrangement of data on the form;

(g) where appropriate, clear instructions should be given on the form about the input data required;

(h) the document should have one use as an input document, ie it should not be used more than once to input data to different programs or systems.

4.14 Printing forms costs money and wastage (eg by spending unnecessarily on form size, quality, number of copies in a set etc) should be avoided. It is also important to remember that data should only be gathered if the cost of capturing it is justified by its value. Hidden costs may include the cost of writing the source documents, and the cost of data preparation and filing in a computer system.

4.15 In computer systems the source documents may have to be transcribed into a machine readable medium (eg encoded on to disk) but don't forget that they may have other functions than merely data capture for computer processing. For example, a sales invoice has to function as a sales invoice and so its contents may contain data which is not required for processing. The layout of the invoice must:

(a) a clear indication of which data is to be transcribed into machine readable medium, for example by shading parts of the document, or by entering the data in a particular section of the document, or by using chemically coated (carbon backed) documents for duplication.

(b) make sure that the data required is entered on the invoice in keying-in sequence (eg from left to right, top to bottom of the sheet).

5. CODE DESIGN

5.1 Linked with document and file design is the problem of code design. The purpose of a code is to identify. In commercial organisations codes are often used because they can identify items more concisely and precisely than written descriptions. Coding:

(a) can save data capture and preparation time, and it certainly facilitates processing, in both computer and non-computerised systems;

(b) in computer systems, saves internal storage space during processing and backing storage space. (Remember that in computer usage, codes can be re-converted into what they stand for by reference to standing data on a master file or reference file).

5.2 Occasionally, codes will be used for reasons of security. (The title 'Project S95' will not help a rival to establish the kind of research an organisation is carrying out).

Classifications and codes

5.3 The CIMA Management Accounting Official Terminology defines *classification* as 'the arrangement of items in logical groups, having regard to their nature (subjective classification) or the purpose to be fulfilled (objective classification).' Coding is defined as 'a system of symbols designed to be applied to a classified set of items, to give a brief accurate reference, facilitating entry, collation and analysis.'

Classifications are therefore groupings and individual items can be classified according to the grouping to which they belong. Coding is a system for identifying in a shortened symbolised form the grouping that a particular item belongs to.

Designing a coding system

5.4 The code used will to some extent vary with the types of item to be coded. The different types of code in common use are discussed below, but there are some general points which should be borne in mind before a coding system is introduced. These include:

(a) a code must be easy to use and to communicate;

(b) any coding system must allow for expansion;

(c) if there is a conflict between the ease of using a code by the people involved in a system and its manipulation by a computer, the human interest should dominate;

(d) the code should be flexible so that small changes in item classification can be incorporated without major changes to the coding system itself;

(e) the coding system must provide a unique reference code for key items such as customer account number, supplier account number, stock code number or employee number;

(f) it should provide a comprehensive system, whereby every recorded item can be suitably coded;

(g) the coding system should be brief, to save clerical time in writing out codes and to save storage space in computer memory and on computer files. At the same time codes must be long enough to allow for the suitable coding of all items;

(h) the likelihood of errors going undetected should be minimised. For unique reference codes, *check digits* should be used;

(i) there should be no duplication of the same code for different items in the same category;

(j) there should be a readily available index or reference book of codes;

(k) existing codes should be reviewed regularly and out-of-date codes removed;

(l) it is preferable in most cases that all codes should be of the same length. There are exceptions however, where different length codes are used for reasons of logical construction (eg hierarchical codes) or to reflect operational requirements (eg the STD telephone exchange codes, whose differing lengths were partly dictated by the nature of the telecommunications switching system);

(m) code numbers should be issued from a single, central point. Different people should not be allowed to add new codes to the existing list independently.

5.5 Various coding systems (or combinations of them) may be used when designing codes. The systems include the following.

(a) *Sequence codes* in which no attempt is made to classify the item to be coded. It is simply given the next available number in a rising sequence. New items can only be inserted at the end of the list thus the codes for similar items may be very different.

   For example:
   1   =   saucepans
   2   =   kettles
   3   =   pianos
   4   =   dusters

   Sequence codes are rarely used when a large number of items are involved, except for document numbering (eg invoice numbers).

(b) *Block codes* provide a different sequence for each different group of items. For example for a particular firm, customers may be divided up according to area:

South East   code numbers 10,000–19,999
South West   code numbers 20,000–29,999
Wales   code numbers 30,000–39,999

The coding of customer accounts is then sequential within each block.

(c) *Significant digit codes* incorporate some digit(s) which is (are) part of the description of the item being coded. An example is:

5000   Electric light bulbs
5025   25 watt
5040   40 watt
5060   60 watt
5100   100 watt
etc.

(d) *Hierarchical codes* are allocated on the basis of a tree structure where the inter-relationship between the items is of the paramount importance. A well known example is the Universal Decimal Code used by most libraries. For example:

5   Business
5 2   Finance
5 2 1   Cost accounting
5 2 1.4   Standard costing
5 2 1.4 7   Variance analysis
5 2 1.4 7 3 Fixed overhead variances.

(e) *Faceted codes* in which different features of the item are represented by the code. For example in a clothing store there might be a code based on the following facets:

Garment type	Customer type	Colour	Size	Style

If SU stood for suit, M for man and B for blue, a garment could be given the code SU M B 40 17. Similarly ND F W 14 23 could stand for a woman's white nightdress size 14, style 23. One of the great advantages of this system is that the type of item can be recognised from the code.

Faceted codes may be entirely numeric. For example, a large international company may allocate code numbers for each sales representative on the basis that:

Digit 1   Continent (eg America – 1, Europe – 2)
Digits 2/3   Country (eg England – 06)
Digit 4   Area (eg North – 3)
Digits 5/6   Representative's name – (eg Mr J Walker – 14)

The code number may be expressed as 2/06/3/14.

5.6 The use of *check digits* to provide a validation check for key items codes is described elsewhere.

6. SCREEN DESIGN AND DIALOGUE DESIGN

6.1 VDU screen display may be used for both input and output.

Displays which contain a great volume of data are often virtually useless since people cannot readily identify the important information. Whenever displays are being designed it is vital to consider their purpose and present the information so that the users can quickly see and understand it.

Screen design

6.2 The VDU is used as both an input and an output device in many systems, and the systems designer has the job of designing the layout of the data on the screen.

Keyboard/screen dialogue: cursor, menus, commands, help facility etc.

6.3 The design of the *keyboard* reflects the way in which the user communicates with the machine to direct its operating processes and to provide and manipulate the contents of its memory. The *screen* is the means by which the computer communicates with the user, giving him a visual reference for his activities, asking for decisions, instructions or information, offering prompts and warnings. The important thing about VDU and keyboard is therefore the capacity for 'feedback' between user and computer that they provide, allowing the system to be highly flexible, interactive and conversational.'

The way the keyboard is used, and what you would expect to see on the screen, will therefore depend on the particular strategy for 'screen dialogue' that the software adopts.

6.4 This dialogue between computer operator and computer might be a central feature of the running of a program, and the term *conversational mode* describes a method of operation in which the operator appears to be carrying on a continual interactive dialogue with the computer, receiving immediate replies to input messages.

6.5 *The cursor.* You know exactly where your next character will be if you enter data on a page by hand or typewriter, and in the same way the cursor (an arrow, line or 'blob') shows you on screen the point in your text that will be affected (written on, deleted, moved etc.) by your keyboard entries. It is basically a 'marker' of where the computer's 'attention' is at any given moment. It can be moved about the screen by:

(a) joystick;
(b) direction keys on the keyboard;
(c) mouse.

6.6 Broadly speaking, there are three ways of using a keyboard with VDU to input data.

(a) By selecting options from a menu. A menu is a display of a series of options, and the operator selects which option he or she wants by keying in an appropriate letter or number, (or perhaps by moving the cursor to the required option and then selecting the option by clicking the button on a mouse).

(b) Using commands. Command codes or instructions are keyed in, to indicate to the program what it should do with the data that follows; and then the data is keyed in, which the program processes.

(c) A graphic user interface (eg WIMP).

6.7 *Menu selection.* A menu is a list of items to choose from. A VDU screen might list a number of different options, from which the computer user must choose what he or she wants to do next.

6.8 For example, a main menu for purchase and sales ledger functions might include:

A - DEFINE CODES ETC.   B - SET UP STANDING ORDERS ETC.
C - PURCHASE LEDGER ENTRIES   D - SALES LEDGER ENTRIES
E - SUPPLIER DETAILS   F - CLIENT DETAILS
                                      etc.

By selecting D, the operator will be specifying that he or she wants to do some processing of sales ledger entries. When D has been keyed in, *another* menu may be displayed, calling for the operator to narrow down still further the specification of what he or she wants to do next. A menu-system is thus a hierarchical list of options.

Command codes

6.9 An alternative or supplement to menu selection, is the keyboard entry of *coded controls* and typed *commands* to tell the computer what processing is to be done. Individual keys, or a combination of keys, can be used to enter the controls and commands. This type of operation involves a more obvious 'dialogue', with a 'message' style of response between user and computer. For skilled operators it is a quicker form of dialogue than a menu system.

Form filling and formatted screens

6.10 The main part of the screen area, of course, will be the 'page' on which you will be entering data or text. In a standard word processing system, there is a 'blank page' available for document creation and manipulation. It is also possible to have the screen landscaped for specific user requirements. For spreadsheets, accounting applications and data files, there are suitable pre-formatted structures, into which items of data can simply be inserted. Relevant data fields may be set up and data entered automatically or by cursor movement, within a displayed skeleton of the standard document or file. Formatting includes

(a) different colours for different screen areas;
(b) reverse video (where colours in a selected area are the reverse of the rest of it);
(c) flashing items.

Software strategy for the computer user: WIMP

6.11 The way the screen is divided and landscaped and the way the keyboard is used are all part of the general strategy used in the design of software (ie programs) to integrate different ways of using available screen and keyboard space in an efficient and user-friendly manner to accomplish required tasks.

6.12 A useful mnemonic for one common strategy is **WIMP**. WIMP was designed to make microcomputers more user-friendly' to people without experience of using computers, and who might have difficulty in using a keyboard, or who might be resistant to the idea of becoming a computer user.

WIMP involves the use of two design ideas and two operating methods.

(a) *Windows*. This basically means that the screen can be divided into sections, 'windows' of flexible size which can be opened and closed. This enables two or more documents to be viewed and edited together, and sections of one to be inserted into another. This is particularly useful for standard documents (see the chapter on Word Processing Software Packages) and spreadsheets, which are too large for the VDU screen (see the chapter on Spreadsheets).

There are two main sorts of windows: 'directory' windows, which display the contents of a 'folder' on a disk, and 'application' windows, in which a part of the program which is being run is displayed.

(b) *Icons*. An icon is an image of an object used to represent an abstract idea or process. In software design, icons may be used instead of numbers, letters or words to identify and describe the various functions available for selection, or files to access. A common icon is a waste paper bin to indicate the deletion of a document.

Microsoft Windows, and the graphic user interface operated on the Apple Macintosh computer, tries to make the system user-friendly by employing WIMP systems. Here are some examples of icons.

(i)   The Trash is used to throw away material that you no longer need.

(ii)   This signifies a file.

(iii)   This icon is used to indicate programs which control your connection to a network.

(iv)   This indicates a command to enable you to turn on or suppress the 'beep' sound of the computer.

The icons chosen are used, instead of commands, in a number of contexts eg:

(i)   system configuration (eg activating a mouse);

(ii)   file management (eg displaying, graphically, the contents of directories or subdirectories);

(iii)   keyboard design (eg selecting a palette of colours).

(c) *Mouse.* A *mouse* is a small device which sits on the desk, and is plugged into the basic module of the micro, or into the keyboard. Underneath the mouse is a hard ball. The mouse is rolled by hand across the desk top, and as the mouse moves around on the desktop a pointer (cursor) on the VDU screen mimics its movements. A mouse can be used to pick out the appropriate icon (or other option), to mark out the area of a new window, mark the beginning and end of a block for deletion/insertion etc. It also has a button to execute the current command.

(d) *Pull-down menu*

   (i)   An initial menu (or 'menu-bar') will be shown across the top of the VDU screen.

   (ii) Using the mouse to move the pointer to the required item in the menu, the pointer 'pulls down' a subsidiary menu - somewhat similar to pulling down a window blind in the room of a house. The pointer and mouse can then be used to select the required item on the pulled-down menu.

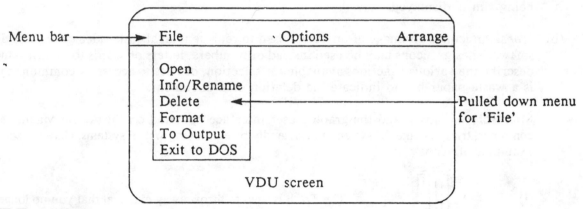

WIMP systems

6.13 A WIMP *system* refers to a software system which allows the computer user to organise his other software and data in such a way that he can access programs and data files using icons, mouse and pointer, and where appropriate displaying data on screen in windows.

WIMP strategy is a feature of Apple Macintosh computers, and all software written for Apple Macintosh machines can be worked with a mouse. There are leading WIMP systems for IBM-compatible micros.

(a) Windows (manufactured by Microsoft);
(b) GEM (manufactured by Digital Research);
(c) X/Windows (for UNIX);
(d) Presentation manager (for OS/2).

6.14 As an example of using GEM, for instance:

(a) the microcomputer user would access the GEM file, and start operating in the GEM system;

(b) a series of icons will be displayed on the VDU screen (possibly in two windows). Each icon represents a file, or a program directory, an individual program or a data file. Using the mouse to move a pointer to the required icon, and clicking the mouse when the pointer is positioned over the icon, the computer will either:

(i)   call up the required file or program;

(ii)   call up another series of icons to select from.

It is also possible to select several icons at the same time (eg an icon for a spreadsheet program and an icon for an associated worksheet file of data).

6.15   WIMP is not used on all microcomputers, and you might readily see where variations from the WIMP strategy occur. All the same operations could be performed by other means - using cursor control keys instead of the mouse, entering commands via codes or alphanumeric menu selection etc. The WIMP strategy has several advantages, however.

(a)   Icon selection is very easy to use, and less taxing for the user's memory than codes.

(b)   The mouse/pointer->icon system means that the keyboard is not actually used for controls. This avoids confusion over keys which have different meanings in different modes etc. and means that typing speed is no longer a constraint. (It may, however, be more convenient during the typing of documents to have the necessary controls also at the typist's fingertips.)

(c)   Although there are other ways of gaining fast access to secondary documents, for the purposes of 'cut and paste' merging bits of text together, the window system is really the only way of viewing both files simultaneously, for easier operation and greater accuracy. It also provides a convenient alternative to 'panning' around data 'documents' covering large areas eg spreadsheets.

Graphic user interfaces (GUI)

6.16   WIMP is an example of a trend towards *user-friendliness* and ease of use for computer operators, many of whom are not computer professionals. WIMP is a 'graphic user interface' in that dialogue is conducted through images rather than typed text.

6.17   It looks as if *graphic user interfaces* are to become the principal means with which humans communicate with machines. In addition to the WIMP features outlined above, many GUIs may display 'dialogue boxes, buttons, sliders, check boxes, and a plethora of other graphical widgets that let you tell the computer what to do and how to do it'. (*Byte* July 1989)

6.18   GUIs differ in the way they are integrated into the computer system as a whole. Some GUIs are completely integrated with the *operating system*. (See Chapter 8.) For example, when you switch on an Apple Macintosh, the machine on which the use of GUIs was pioneered, the GUI appears automatically. On the other hand, on many systems running Microsoft Windows or Unix, the GUI must be specifically chosen.

6.19   All GUIs however are made of three components.

(a)   A *windowing system* enables the construction of the windows, menus and dialogue boxes which appear on screen, and it controls how the user moves between different windows.

(b)   An *imaging model* defines how type faces, fonts and graphics actually appear on screen.

(c) An *application program interface* enables the programmer to specify which windows, scroll bars and icons appear on screen at a particular time.

6.20 There have been a number of legal problems arising from the use of GUIs. As they are very popular, many GUIs are functionally quite similar. Apple Computers has instituted legal actions in the US to ensure that the 'look and feel' of its GUI is kept sufficiently distinct from its competitors and is subject to the laws of copyright.

6.21 Some GUIs allow flexibility in the use of icons. The user can arrange icons into a hierarchy, combining several processing operations into one.

Dialogue design

6.22 When an on-line system involves interactive screen dialogue between the user and the VDU, dialogue design/screen design is obviously very important.

The screen dialogue should have the following features.

(a) Clear prompts should be given to the user about what information the computer wants next.

(b) It should give clear instructions to the user if the user wishes:

(i) to go to a different page of screen data;
(ii) to go to the next data item (eg 'PRESS SPACE BAR TO CONTINUE');
(iii) to quit the program (eg '(ESC) = QUIT').

6.23 The input required should be kept as short and simple as possible; for example:

(a) if the computer wants a straight yes or no answer from the user, the screen dialogue should

(i) state the question clearly, and
(ii) tell the user to key in Y for yes or N for no;

(b) menu selection should be used if possible, to allow the non-technical user to tell the computer what sort of data processing he or she wants to do next.

Exercise

What considerations would you take into account in designing a screen dialogue for:

(a) a senior manager who uses a system occasionally to make enquiries; and
(b) a sales order clerk who enters orders regularly onto the order processing system?

Solution

(a)   Senior managers are not regular computer users, so the screen dialogue must be user-friendly and easy to learn. An on-line help facility should be available. A menu system should be offered.

(b)   The clerk will be an experienced user who must input a high volume of data quickly. Suitable formatting of input screens is important; these might be laid out in the same way as a typical order form. Input fields would be highlighted. Data validation checks should provide prompt error messages.

---

7.   FILE DESIGN

7.1   A systems analyst must also design the transaction files, reference files, master files or database files used in a system.

7.2   In designing master files, the considerations of the systems analyst will include the following:

(a)   is there a requirement for random access of the file by the user? Random access would call for a direct access file medium - ie magnetic disk;

(b)   is there a requirement for a quick response time? If so direct access and magnetic disk would be called for;

(c)   what data or information the files should contain;

(d)   how the files will be used for processing transaction data;

(e)   what facilities should be available for file interrogation?

(f)   how will the files be maintained?

(g)   how large will the files be, and what capacity for file growth in the future should be built into the system?

7.3   If there is a choice of file medium (essentially, a choice between magnetic tape and magnetic disk, or a choice between exchangeable disk, Winchester disk, or floppy disk), the factors governing the decision would be:

(a)   the speed of moving data between the backing storage medium and the computer's internal memory;

(b)   the way in which records must be ordered for access (eg must there be indexing for direct access?);

(c) the volume of data:

    (i) allowing enough room on the file for both the current volumes and expected *future expansion* (eg floppy disks might be unable to hold all the data conveniently, perhaps for a database system, and so a file with a larger capacity, such as a Winchester disk, would be chosen);

    (ii) the expected '*hit rate*' – ie the ratio of the number of transaction records in a typical updating run to the number of master file records. As described in the chapter on external storage, the expected hit rate can affect the choice of file medium.

7.4 The systems analyst must provide facilities to insert new records on to the file and to amend or delete existing records. Adequate space must be allowed in the file for newly-inserted records. There might also be a requirement to *interrogate* the file, which might involve random access from a remote terminal.

8. CONCLUSION

8.1 In this chapter, we have concentrated on aspects of system design. In the next chapters, we shall go on to look at further aspects of design, programming and data security and controls. However, there is quite a large gap between reading about system design and actually doing it. For your examination, you may be required to do some simple and sketchy system design work, and so in a later chapter, one or two examples of systems design problems will be discussed, to help you to sort out your own approach to them.

TEST YOUR KNOWLEDGE
The numbers in brackets refer to paragraphs of this chapter

1 List the various aspects of output design. (2.3)

2 What considerations should apply to input design? (3.2)

3 What are the qualities of a good form or source document? (4.12)

4 What factors should be considered with code design? (5.1)

5 List various aspects of screen design (6.1-6.13) and dialogue design. (6.17)

Now try questions 19 and 20 at the end of the text

Chapter 16

PROGRAM DEVELOPMENT

This chapter covers the following topics.

1. Programming languages
2. Application program development
3. Fourth generation systems
4. Prototyping
5. The program algorithm
6. Structured programming
7. Decision tables
8. Decision trees
9. Program flowcharts
10. Structured narratives
11. Computer-aided software engineering (CASE)

---

1. PROGRAMMING LANGUAGES

1.1 For your examination, you need to know the principles of programming, although you are not required to be able to *write* programs yourself.

1.2 What you should know are:

(a) the stages in software development;

(b) how to define the logic of a simple program, perhaps in the form of a decision table or flowchart;

(c) something about programming languages.

1.3 To recap from your earlier studies of programming languages, the following paragraphs provide a brief reminder of the different generations of computer language.

Low level languages

1.4 The key features of low level languages are summarised below.

(a) A program must be in a computer's *machine code* before the computer will do anything with it.

(b) Programs are usually written in a *programming language*, as they are more easily understood by humans in this form.

(c) A program written in a programming language is the *source program*.

(d) A source program is translated into machine code by a specialised translation program. The translated program (in machine code) is the *object program*.

(e) *Assembly languages*, developed from machine code, are easier to use than machine code because they are in symbolic form and use mnemonics.

(f) Machine code and assembly languages are known collectively as *low-level languages*.

High level languages

1.5 The key features of high level languages are summarised below.

(a) *High level languages* were developed to overcome the machine dependency of low level languages.

(b) There is no clear visible relationship between a high level language program and the corresponding program in machine code.

(c) High level language programs are usually shorter than lower level language source programs.

(d) Examples of high level languages are BASIC, COBOL, FORTRAN and C.

(e) High level language programs are translated into machine code using *compilers* or *interpreters*.

Fourth generation languages

1.6 Fourth generation languages were developed to help programmes do their programming more easily.

2. APPLICATION PROGRAM DEVELOPMENT

2.1 The principal stages in the preparation of a fully tested application program, written in a high level language (or assembler language) are as follows. It is assumed that the source program will be written in a language that must be compiled (or assembled) into machine language rather than interpreted.

(a) *The preparation of program specification for every program in the system.* This details the inputs, processing and outputs required. (In SSADM, this is performed as part of stage 6: physical design.)

(b) Understanding the requirements outlined in the program specification and constructing an *algorithm*, that is, an analysis of the problem and the means to its solution. The *logic* of the program must be properly formulated and the programmer may use the techniques of

    (i) structured programming;
    (ii) modular programming;
    (iii) constructing decision tables or decision trees;

(iv)   computer procedure (program) flowcharting;

(v)   structured English.

(c)   Writing (*coding*) the logical steps which have been established in stage (b) on to program *coding sheets*, using an appropriate programming language. The program that is written is called a source program.

(d)   Checking of the logic and coding of the prepared source program (if possible this is done by another programmer), and correcting errors that are found. The process of detecting errors in a program and getting rid of them is called *debugging*. The programmer might use debugging programs as a programming tool to help with this task.

(e)   Preparing the coded instructions into a machine-sensible form. When using an interactive language, the programmer himself may key in the instructions on a VDU keyboard terminal, with 'text editor' software aiding the program construction.

(f)   *Compiling (assembling)* the source program.

(i)   identifies errors of logic, syntax and construction;

(ii)   produces a listing of both the source and object programs;

(iii)   writes the object program on to backing store.

(g)   Correcting any errors etc in the program and recompiling (reassembling) if necessary.

(h)   *Testing* the program by means of properly designed test data. If possible, the test pack should be prepared by the systems analyst (not the programmer) and will consist of input and standing file data designed to test the logic and operation of the program as rigorously as possible.

It should test that 'normal' data will be processed 'normally' and that erroneous data will be identified and dealt with appropriately.

As well as using designed test data, actual 'live' data may be used for testing the program which will be done in two stages:

(i)   a desk check - passing the data through the flowchart and the coded program instructions, a very lengthy and painstaking process;

(ii)   on the computer, to test the operation of the object program.

(i)   Correcting the program to remove all errors (ie more debugging), and recompiling (reassembling) it to produce a new object program. The process of testing and correction must continue until the programmer is satisfied that all is correct.

(j)   Integrating each fully tested application program or module into the system as a whole. This will have been taken into account at the design stage, but now the systems analyst must ensure that all programs are properly integrated. The system testing may reveal further programming errors which must be corrected.

(k)   Documenting the application program to provide a record of its method of construction, flowcharts, coding sheets, test data, test results etc.

(l)   Introducing the program or system into 'live' operations.

2.2   It may be useful (particularly in answering examination questions) to illustrate the main stages involved in preparing a fully tested application program by means of a flowchart.

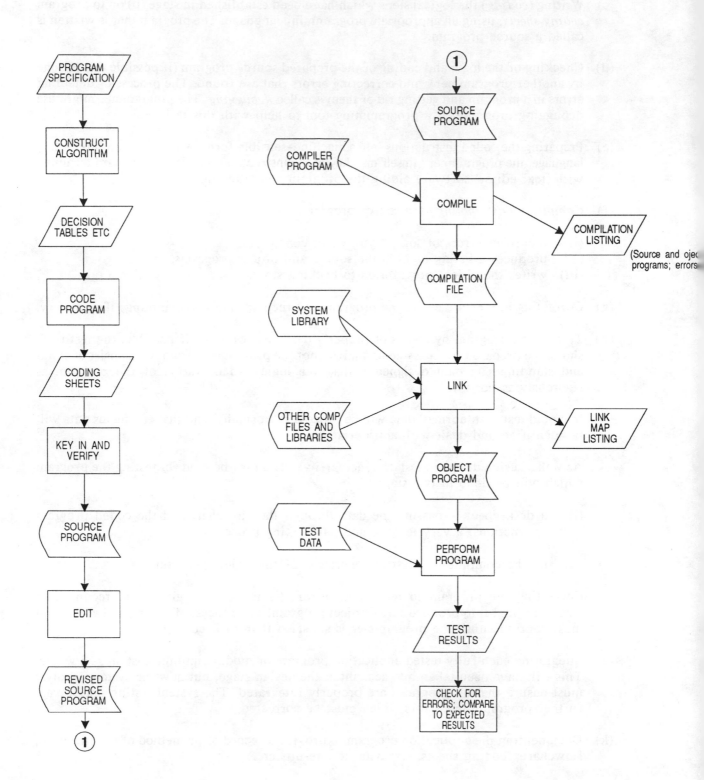

3.   FOURTH GENERATION SYSTEMS

3.1   A 4GL (fourth generation language) is software which enables the result of processing to be specified by the programmer or user, and then takes over the task of doing the basic procedural coding. It might form part of a *fourth generation system*. The basic aim is to speed up application development.

Most fourth generation systems use a mixture of text and graphics, often a WIMP interface. A fourth generation system should:

(a)   be easy to learn and use;
(b)   contain on-line 'help' facility for users;
(c)   be useable *interactively;*
(d)   be 'fault' tolerant (ie any mistakes in data entry could be dealt with easily);
(e)   document design work.

Application generators

3.2   An application generator is a type of 4GL used to create complete applications programs. The user describes what needs to be done and the data and files which are to be used. The applications generator then translates this description into a program.

The basis for this process is the recognition that many of the functions such as data input, sorting, searching, file management, report writing and the like are quite similar in operation even when these program segments are found in quite different applications programs. The objective is to use a number of standardised program segments to provide these common functions.

This is analogous to the use of interchangeable parts in manufacturing which helped stimulate the industrial revolution. Programs no longer need to be entirely custom made since the appropriate use of common modules may significantly reduce the cost and time involved in creating programs.

3.3   The usefulness of application generators lies in their ability to provide much of the program quickly and relatively easily. The major drawback to using these systems results from their inability to cover all possible program requirements. As a consequence application generators are used in two modes.

(a)   They may be used to provide relatively simple programs in a finished form, this would be appropriate for non-programmers with undemanding requirements.

(b)   As programs become more complex or use less common analytical methods the program generators become less useful. In these cases the generators provide common segments while a programmer then adds the specialised program segments. This combination of man and machine takes advantage of the relative abilities of each to provide a finished system.

3.4   Application generators can be used by non-programmers to develop their own program though some experience or training in programming generally aids the creation process and also allows the user to add in any specialised program segments when needed. Application generators are useful but limited tools.

Report generators

3.5 An example of a tool which is particularly useful for microcomputer users is a *report generator*. This is 'a program which gives the non-specialist user a capability of producing reports from one or more files, through easily constructed statements'. Many microcomputer software packages (eg for database systems or accounting systems) include a report generator which can be used by non-technical people. The value of a report generator is that it enables microcomputer users to extract information from their files - eg in a database or spreadsheet package - in the form of tabulated reports which can be presented to management.

4. PROTOTYPING

4.1 Traditional theories of systems development emphasise the structured approach which addresses logical design issues before committing resources to physical design. In this way, it is hoped that user requirements can be satisfied *before* physical design is commenced. However, the time factor inherent in performing logical design work on a large system leads inevitably to delays. This, together with shortages in resources, adds to the applications backlog and increases user dissatisfaction with systems when they do arrive.

4.2 Problems widely encountered in systems design often arise because end-users, although they may be involved in the development process, do not operate on the same 'wavelength' as analysts and programmers. Users may not know exactly what they do want from a system, and may express their requirements inaccurately. As noted earlier, end-users may, while contributing to a development project, be resistant to the changes which such a project necessarily entails. The development specialists may see development as linear, discouraging feedback to earlier stages of the process.

4.3 The timescale of a typical development project means that users' requirements at the end of the project are likely to be very different from their stated requirements at the start of it. This may be because their environment has actually changed or because their perception of it has changed. In either case they will be dissatisfied with the end product.

4.4 One way of ensuring full user involvement in and commitment to design is the technique of prototyping. Prototyping aids programmers by helping them to write application programs much more quickly and easily, and they involve little, if any, coding effort on the part of the programmer.

Using prototyping software, the programmer can write an application program quickly. (Much software production is repetitive, and this makes the development of prototyping software feasible.) He or she can then check with the data user whether the prototype program that has been designed appears to meet the user's needs, and if it doesn't it can be amended. Any number of 'prototype' programmes can be made for the user to sample, and it is only when the program does what the user wants that the final version of the program is ready.

4.5 R Vonk defines a prototype as 'a working model of (parts of) an information system, which emphasises specific aspects of that system'. Prototyping is further defined as 'an approach for establishing a systems requirements definition which is characterised by a high degree of iteration, by a very high degree of user participation in the development process, and by an extensive use of prototypes'.

4.6 Software prototyping therefore has the following features.

(a) The prototype is a *live, working* application which can perform actual work.

(b) It may eventually become the actual application, or it may be replaced by another.

(c) The prototype is used to test out assumptions about users' requirements and about systems design.

(d) It is created quickly.

(e) It is cheap to build.

(f) It is an *iterative* process. The first prototype is a very simple representation of the application. Systems designers or users discover through its use new requirements or features which are incorporated in the *second* version of the prototype etc.

4.7 Prototyping can be seen from this to be an interactive process. The process starts with the identification of the user's requirements. A prototype can then be prepared and presented to the user, who feeds back comments and any requests for additional features. The statement of requirements is then revised and a new prototype produced. The process is repeated until a version acceptable to all parties is produced. When the 'final version' is ready, the prototyping software will then code the program, which will then become the user's application program.

4.8 The advantages of prototyping are as follows.

(a) It makes it possible for programmers to present a 'mock-up' version of a program to a data user, to see how it works, before anyone has to commit substantial time and money to the project. The data user can judge the prototype before things have gone too far to be changed.

(b) It makes it more economical for data users to get 'custom built' application software, instead of having to buy off-the-shelf application packages which may or may not suit their particular needs properly.

(c) It makes efficient use of programmer time by helping programmers to develop programs more quickly. Prototyping may speed up the 'design' section of the systems development life-cycle.

(d) A prototype does not necessarily have to be written in the language of what it is prototyping (as an analogy, you can make a prototype car out of wood), and so prototyping is not only a tool, but a design technique.

4.9 There are some disadvantages with prototyping too.

(a) Many prototyping software tools assume that the data user is about to computerise an application for the first time. This may not be so: some data users might want to transfer an application from an 'old' program to an updated new one, and so transfer data from existing files on to files for the new program.

(b)   Many prototyping software tools produce programs that are tied to a particular make of hardware, or a particular database system, and cannot 'travel' from one system to another without further use of prototyping.

(c)   It is sometimes argued that prototyping tools are inefficient in the program codes they produce, so that programs are bigger and use up more computer memory than they would if they had been written by programmers without the aid of prototyping.

(d)   Some specialised program demands cannot be 'automated' and have to be hand-written. Not all prototyping tools allow programmers to insert hand-written codes into a program.

(e)   A serious criticism is that prototyping tools allow programmers to produce a bigger quantity of shoddy programs at a high speed.

(f)   Many prototyping tools do not produce suitable program documentation for the user.

4.10 Prototyping is often used with a 4GL to enable speedy development. Prototyping is less of a 'tool' but an approach to systems development. Prototyped output, for example, can be prepared by simply using a spreadsheet program to design a report.

5.   THE PROGRAM ALGORITHM

5.1 Just as we must define the problem for a whole system in order to develop a new system, so too must the development of a program or program module begin with the programmer defining the processing task. After all, if the programmer misunderstands what processing has to be done, or omits an item of processing, his or her program will be incorrect when it is written, and it will have to be re-written. It is therefore good sense to sort out the problem logically and carefully from the beginning.

5.2 This is sometimes referred to as constructing a program algorithm. An algorithm is a way of solving a problem in a certain number of steps. A programmer has to sort out the demands of a program specification, and to identify what steps need to be taken by the program so that it will achieve its purpose.

A simple example of an algorithm is shown below.

INVOICE AMOUNT = UNITS SOLD × PRICE PER UNIT × (100 - D)%

where D = customer's % discount

5.3 A program will often display one of three basic structures. Programs may contain *sequences*, *decisions* or loops.

5.4 In a *sequence:*

(a)   steps are executed one at a time;

(b)   steps are executed once;

(c)   the order in which the steps are executed is the same as the order in which they are written;

(d)   termination of the last step implies termination of the algorithm.

Example

1   Obtain listing of debtors and review
2   Write letters to debtors over 3 months old
3   Return listing.

5.5   In a *decision or selection construct*, the execution of an algorithm can be modified by writing the existence of certain conditions into the program. For example, it may be the case that there are *no* debtors over three months old. The set of instructions could be rewritten as:

1   Obtain listing of debtors and review
2   *If* there are debtors over 3 months old *then* write letters to them
3   Otherwise return listing.

5.6   In an *iteration, loop or repetition* construct, an action is repeated again and again until the desired number of repetitions is reached. The algorithm above does not mention the detailed examination of *each* record to find out if it represents a debt over three months old. If there are 100 records the algorithm *could* appear:

1   Obtain listing of debtors
2   Review debtor 1
3   If debtor 1 over 3 months old then write to debtor 1 otherwise
4   Review debtor 2
5   If debtor 2 over 3 months old then write to debtor 2 ... and so on.

5.7   Clearly, steps 3 and 5 are the same. Programs contain 'loop' instructions. The algorithm could be rewritten as:

1   Obtain listing of debtors
2   Look at debtor

repeat   if debtor over 3 months old write to debtor otherwise go to next debtor on list
until   the list is exhausted.

3   return listing.

5.8   A *routine* is a group of instructions that perform a certain procedure. A routine might be an entire program, or it might be a procedure that can be built into a larger program. For example, a standard routine might be to calculate the PAYE, National Insurance and pension deductions of employees, and a standard software routine can be supplied to do this. The routine can then be built into a computer user's larger payroll application program.

5.9 A subroutine is a small routine, which is part of a program. It is a set of instructions designed to carry out a well defined arithmetical or logical operation. Sub-routines are particularly useful when it is required to perform the same operation several times in a single program. The detailed instructions are laid down once and referred to using a branch instruction when needed again. After the sub-routine is completed, control is returned to the main program. The term is also used for operations which occur frequently in different programs, eg calculating square roots, PAYE etc.

5.10 The use of sub-routines is advantageous because:

(a) storage space is saved as there is no duplication of program instructions;

(b) programming time is reduced when using a sub-routine already tested and proved in another application;

(c) they can be employed in different programs or several times in one program without wastage of programming effort;

(d) they can be written by a programmer not involved in the main program;

(e) it is easier to locate faults in programs that are constructed on a modular basis and/or include sub-routines.

5.11 A sub-routine may be a set of program instructions written by the programmer and incorporated in his own coded instructions, or it may be a set of instructions written independently (by the manufacturer, another programmer, etc) and available for more than one application program and so held on file in a 'library' of sub-routines from which it can be borrowed by any program as required.

5.12 Computer manufacturers may include standard sub-routines in their sales package when they sell a computer to a buyer. Offering sub-routines in this way helps to made the sale package more attractive to the customer.

Housekeeping routines

5.13 *Housekeeping* is a term used to describe tasks that a computer carries out which are not *directly related to solving a program problem* and so which do not contribute directly towards achieving the objective or purpose of the program. The purpose of housekeeping, as the name might suggest, is to 'make things tidy' and housekeeping tasks include:

(a) optimising the efficiency of the use made of internal store, eg by clearing fields and indicators that are no longer needed;

(b) tidying up disk directories, which must be done from time to time.

Housekeeping might also be used to refer to the computer's tasks of handling input and output.

The parts of a program which instruct a computer to do housekeeping work are called *housekeeping routines*.

6. STRUCTURED PROGRAMMING

6.1 *Structured programming* is an approach to formalising a *program design*, shifting the emphasis away from good coding to good design and reflecting directly the structure of the problem. With a successful design, that can be tested before the program is written, the program instructions become very simple to write. Once written, such programs should be easy to follow, should contain few errors, and any errors that there are should be easier to find.

6.2 Structured programming has now become a preferred technique for most programmers, in preference to program flowcharts (which are described later). The problem with program flowcharts is that they tend to produce a badly structured design, by concentrating on decisions and branching instructions, and by discouraging the subdivision of programs into component parts or 'nests'.

6.3 With structured programming, the overall problem is sub-divided into parts, which are then sub-divided further and further until the small sub-divisions consist of logic which can be converted fairly readily into program code. Block diagrams are used to structure the problem into these sub-divisions or *modules*, which then provide the basis for program preparation and coding, without the need to construct flowcharts.

Formal definitions of structured programming are:

(a) 'a concept of programming encompassing 'top down' design philosophy and the use of specific program modules in which each module performs a defined and self-contained task thus making program maintenance an easier task.'

(CIMA Computing Terminology)

(b) 'an orderly approach to programming which emphasises breaking large and complex tasks into successively smaller sections. Sometimes referred to as *top down programming*.'

(British Computer Society)

A block diagram illustrating the modular structure of a program which reads records from a master file and a transaction file, and updates the master file, is shown on the following page.

6.4 Before describing decision tables and flowcharts, it will be useful to look at the sort of processing operations that can be done within a program.

(a) *Branching*. A computer will obey the program's instructions in sequence (when programs are written, each program instruction is numbered). If a program is required to follow certain instructions several times over, or if the sequence of instructions for some reason is broken, the computer can be made to go to another program instruction out of sequence and carry on processing from there. Moving to out-of-sequence instructions is achieved by means of a branch instruction in the program. Branching is the means by which repetition or iteration is achieved. There are two types of branch instruction:

(i) *conditional branching*: branching is dependent on some condition of the data determined by a comparison instruction - eg a check that 'if M = T then add M to A, otherwise add T to B' would involve a conditional branch instruction;

(ii) *unconditional branching*: the successive line of instructions is broken independently of any comparison instruction. Unconditional branches are sometimes necessary to write a program. For example, having finished processing one record, it is necessary to read the next record. The instructions to read the next record will involve an unconditional branch from the last instruction for processing the previous record to the 'read' instruction for the next record.

(b) *Arithmetic* calculations – eg add, subtract, divide and multiply.

(c) *Reading an input record*. A computer program must be told to read in an input record for processing.

(d) *Comparisons*. A program can compare two values, to establish whether one value is more than, less than or equal to another. For example, comparison checks are needed in a master file update program to match transaction records with master file records – ie to establish the *condition* of an item of data.

(e) *Output* of an item of information or data on to an output device – eg print out an item of data, or *write* a record on to a file;

(f) *Moving data*. Data can be copied from one place in the computer's internal store to another.

(g) *Giving an item of data a certain value.*

(h) Controlling instructions – these include:

   (i)   start and end instructions;
   (ii) instructions for allocation of store;
   (iii) checks for hardware errors; etc.

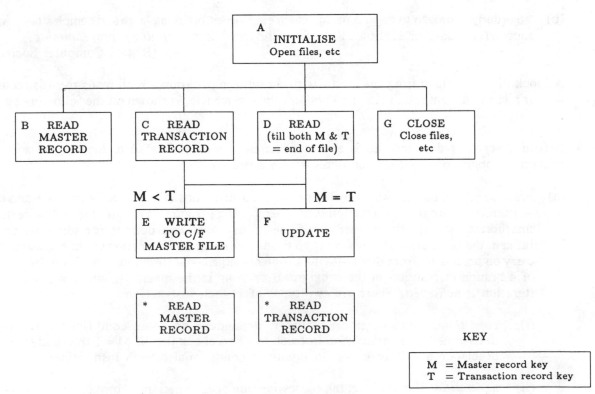

*Procedures already defined in the program at B & C.

6.5 A branch instruction makes it possible for a sequence of coded program instructions to be repeated, perhaps many times over, and this is essential to keep the length of programs down to a manageable size. The repetition of a sequence of program instructions is called a *loop*. The most obvious example of a loop in a program is the repetition of the program instructions to process each input record in turn.

A loop is defined therefore as a sequence of instructions that are executed repeatedly until a specified condition is satisfied, when the program will then go on to carry out another sequence of instructions.

6.6 When the logic of a computer program is defined, the most important types of processing are:

(a) arithmetical computations;
(b) comparisons;
(c) read (input) and write (output) instructions.

7. DECISION TABLES

7.1 Decision tables are used as a method of defining the logic of a process (ie the processing operations required) in a compact manner. They are more convenient to use than program flowcharts in situations where a large number of logical alternatives exist.

7.2 The basic format consists of four quadrants divided by intersecting double lines:

Condition stub	Condition entry
Action stub	Action entry

7.3 The purpose of the condition stub is to specify the values of the data that we wish to test for. The condition entry specifies what those values might be. Between them, the condition stub and condition entry show what values an item of data might have that the program should test for. (Establishing conditions will be done within a program by means of comparison checks.)

The condition entry quadrants are divided into columns, each column representing a distinct 'rule' or unique result of all the conditions. (Any immaterial condition is indicated by a '-' or blank in the appropriate condition entry box.) For example, if we consider the three conditions:

Is it raining?	Y	Y	Y	Y	N	N	N	N
Is it December?	Y	Y	N	N	Y	Y	N	N
Is it windy?	Y	N	Y	N	Y	N	Y	N

Y = Yes
N = No

There are eight separate rules. In this example the three conditions are totally independent, that is, the answer to one will not affect the answer to the others. In some tables the conditions are not totally independent and there will be less columns.

7.4 The action entry quadrant shows the action or actions that will be performed for each rule. The columns are marked with an 'X' opposite the actions(s) to be taken. In the computer program, instructions specify the action to take on a record, given the conditions established.

7.5 Continuing the above example, suppose that the actions are as follows. A person should never go to work if it is raining in December. If he does go to work, he should take an umbrella when it is raining and an overcoat when it is windy. Unless it is windy he must always take his hat when going to work. If it is windy in December he should switch on his central heating.

From this description we can isolate six actions:

Stay at home; Go to work; Take umbrella; Take overcoat; Take hat; Switch on central heating.

7.6 Consider the fifth rule in the table below. It is not raining but it is windy and it is December. The action entry will therefore show an X against 'Go to work', 'Take overcoat' and 'Switch on central heating':

Rule	1	2	3	4	5	6	7	8
Is it raining?	Y	Y	Y	Y	N	N	N	N
Is it December?	Y	Y	N	N	Y	Y	N	N
Is it windy?	Y	N	Y	N	Y	N	Y	N
Stay at home								
Go to work					X			
Take umbrella								
Take overcoat					X			
Take hat								
Switch on heating					X			

7.7 By considering each rule in turn the table can be completed:

Rule	1	2	3	4	5	6	7	8
Is it raining?	Y	Y	Y	Y	N	N	N	N
Is it December?	Y	Y	N	N	Y	Y	N	N
Is it windy?	Y	N	Y	N	Y	N	Y	N
Stay at home	X	X						
Go to work			X	X	X	X	X	
Take umbrella			X	X				
Take overcoat			X		X		X	
Take hat				X		X		X
Switch on heating	X				X			

7.8 When constructing a decision table from a narrative you must approach the problem methodically:

(a) list the conditions;

(b) list the actions;

(c) calculate the number of rules. This will be 2^n where n = number of conditions; draw up the required number of columns. If the conditions are not independent of each other, the number of columns can be less than 2^n.

(d) apply the *halving* rule:

(i) write in Y for half the rules and N for the other half, as answers to condition 1;

(ii) for condition 2, write in Y's and N's alternately, the number in each group being half the number of each group in condition 1;

(iii) continue halving for each condition;

(e) working down for each rule, enter 'X' against each appropriate action.

Extended entry/mixed entry decision tables

7.9 Decision tables of the type we have just examined are called 'limited entry' decision tables. In these, each condition is posed as a question requiring either a YES, NO or 'immaterial' answer and each action is either taken or not taken. In an *extended entry* decision table the condition and the action stubs are more general, the exact condition or action being specified in the entry quadrants.

A *mixed entry* table consists of both limited and extended entry lines within one table.

7.10 Extended entry and mixed entry decision tables are more compact when constructed, and are useful as a communication method (eg to show the analysed problem to management). However they are more difficult than limited entry decision tables to prepare and check for completeness.

Example: mixed entry decision table

7.11 Reservation requests for the flights of HDA (The Hi-jacker's Delight Airline) are dealt with according to the following rules:

(a) all flights contain both first and second class cabins;

(b) if a seat is available on the flight of the requested class allocate seat and output a ticket for that class;

(c) if not, where a first class passenger will accept a seat in the second class cabin and one is available, the seat is allocated and a second class ticket is output. Second class passengers are not offered a seat in the first class cabin;

(d) in cases where no seat is available to meet the request, output SORRY, NO SEAT message.

Construct a mixed entry decision table of the above procedure.

Solution

7.12 Decision table - HDA reservations

Request is for:	1st	1st	1st	1st	2nd	2nd
1st class seat available?	Y	N	N	N		
2nd class acceptable?		Y	Y	N		
2nd class seat available?		Y	N		Y	N
Allocate seat	1st	2nd			2nd	
Issue ticket	1st	2nd			2nd	
Output SORRY NO SEAT			X	X		X

The advantages of decision tables

7.13 The main advantages of using decision tables are that:

(a) it is possible to check that all combinations have been considered;
(b) they show a cause and effect relationship;
(c) it is easy to trace from actions to conditions (unlike in flowcharts);
(d) they are easy to understand and copy as they use a standardised format;
(e) alternatives can be grouped to facilitate analysis.

8. DECISION TREES

8.1 A decision tree is a design tool which aids in analysing the decisions that should be made within the processing and the sequence in which they occur.

It provides a graphic representation of the various choices or decisions which are available, the events which might occur and their consequences. A decision tree also describes the path or sequence of events and decisions which will lead a system to some final position or outcome.

8.2 At the most basic level a decision tree will describe an action to be taken if some condition is observed. As a consequence of this decision other events may occur and then lead on to further decisions.

8.3 For example, let's consider an order processing system. Whenever an order is received the system should first check to determine if payment has been received with the order, there are two possibilities - yes and no - which lead on to differing responses. If payment is included with the order, the system would then have to check on the availability of the items ordered. Here too there are two possibilities - the items can be in stock or not. If the items are in stock they would then be shipped or delivered to the customer. If the item is not in stock a record of the customer's order needs to be made so that the item will be despatched when stock becomes available. If the customer has not included payment with order a similar set of activities would be undertaken but they would be preceded by credit evaluations.

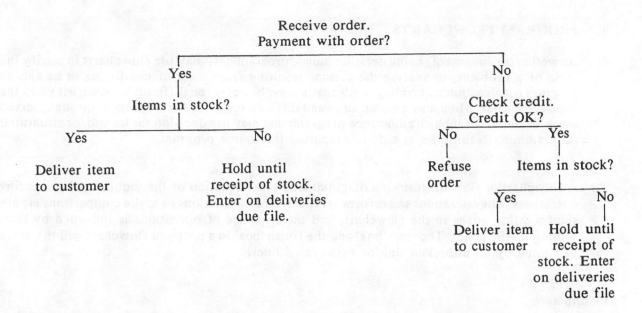

8.4   Many management decisions can be structured as decision trees where the selection of one choice leads on to others. In the discussion above the focus was upon imposing an order or structure upon the decision making process so that a computerised system could replicate the sequence of decision-event-decision as necessary. In many cases the likelihood of various responses or conditions can be predicted or is known. In the example used above, we may know from past experience that most orders are prepaid or for items held in stock. This information will be useful since it can be used to predict which systems functions may be most heavily used.

Exercise

Why are decision trees and decision tables impractical in certain situations?

Solution

Decision trees present logic flows as a succession of questions, each with clearly defined possible answers, where succeeding questions depend on the answers to previous questions. Since the questions and actions are often laid out end to end (to aid legibility) their use in large systems become difficult.

Decision tables present the same logic flows as decision trees, but here the questions are all laid out in a table, with the possible answers to each question listed against the question. Decision tables are comprehensive in concept, but since the number of table entries grows rapidly as the number of questions increases, their use is confined to small, often non-practical, examples.

9. PROGRAM FLOWCHARTS

9.1 As well as (or instead of) using decision tables, programmers may use flowcharts to clarify the logic of a problem, to analyse the actions resulting from a set of conditions or as aids to program construction and coding. Flowcharts may, however, be difficult to construct when the logic is complex. They may become large and difficult to follow (or trace back through) mixed levels of detail. In such circumstance programmers may use decision tables and/or structured programming techniques as aids to preparing the source program.

9.2 A flowchart or flow diagram is a diagrammatic representation of the sequence of processing operations. The operations to perform arithmetical computations or make comparisons etc are shown inside boxes in the flowchart, and the sequence of operations is indicated by lines joining up the boxes. The start 'box' and the finish 'box' in a program flowchart will therefore be joined by an unbroken link or network of lines.

Example

9.3 There are three types of customer, A, B and C. Type A receives a 10% discount on orders (12% for orders above £2,000 in value). Type B receives a 7% discount on orders (9% for orders above £2,000 in value). Type C receives a 5% discount on all orders regardless of value.

Draw the flowchart of a program which, for batches of order records, prints the discount for each order and calculates the total amount of discount allowed on all orders.

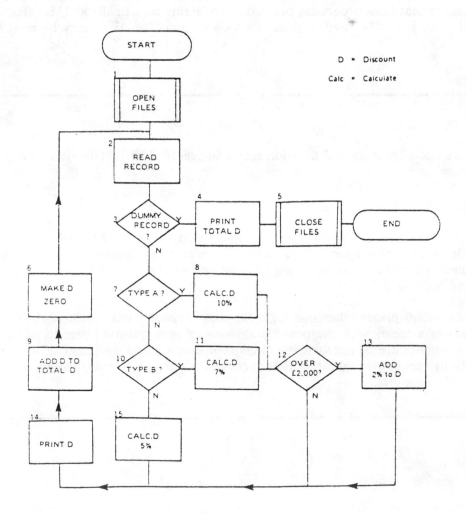

10. STRUCTURED NARRATIVES

10.1 A structured narrative is a design tool which describes the program tasks in a highly detailed narrative form. This method uses English as the language but severely limits the vocabulary and tries to follow the layout and logical operation of a computer program.

10.2 Because structured narratives appear to be fairly literal translations of programs they closely resemble the finished product. This tool is best suited for describing specific program activities or functions while the broader and more general concerns of system design are typically analysed by using data flow analysis, systems flowcharts and decision tables or trees.

10.3 There are several different kinds of structured English. What is important is that:

(a) it is more like spoken English than normal programming languages and so is easy for programmers and non-programmers to understand;

(b) it is much more *limited* than normal speech, as it has to follow a strict logical order;

(c) there is a *variety* of conventions for writing it.

10.4 Structured English uses *keywords* (eg IF, COMPUTE) which, by *some* conventions, are written in capitals and have a precise logical meaning in the context of the narrative. The logical order in which instructions are performed are sometimes expressed in *indentation*.

10.5 The data elements which are the subject of processing are, by *some* conventions, written in lower case and underlined. In other cases they are not. However, these named data elements are then taken from the set of files, data flows and elements specified in the data dictionary.

Sequence instruction

10.6 For example, the calculation of gross pay from hours worked and rate of pay could be written in structured English:

MULTIPLY hours worked by pay rate to get gross pay.

10.7 This type of instruction is known as a *sequence* instruction.

10.8 It is possible to aggregate sequence instructions. For example the computation of gross pay in a *program* not only involves simple calculation as in paragraph 4.6 above but includes:

(a) retrieving master records from a file for the employee reference, and the instruction would be:

GET MASTER RECORD;

(b) Counting records:

ADD 1 to <u>counter</u>

and so forth. The computation of gross pay may therefore involve several instructions. These could be grouped together in a *block*, named *compute gross pay*.

DO COMPUTE GROSS PAY.

Selection (decision logic)

10.9 Most computer programs offer a number of 'choices' and the consequent action taken depends on the choices being made. In structured English, a decision follows an

IF
THEN
ELSE
SO
structure

10.10 For example, a company offers discounts to trade customers only. How would this be expressed in structured English?

IF the <u>customer</u> is a <u>trade-customer</u>

THEN gives 10% discount

ELSE (customer is not trade customer)

SO no discount given.

10.11 Sometimes, decisions are more complicated. Assume that the company only offers 10% discounts to trade customers who have been customers for over one year, but other trade customers receive 5% discount.

IF the <u>customer</u> is a <u>trade customer</u>

IF <u>customer</u> is <u>customer over 1 year</u>

THEN 10% discount given
ELSE   5% discount given

ELSE (customer not a trade customer)

SO no discount given

10.12 On particular type of decision is a *case* statement. These might be used in types of structured English that are more like a programming language. Cases are a special type of decision structure to indicate mutually exclusive possibilities. A case structure is an alternative to the IF-THEN-ELSE-SO structure outlined above, which is satisfactory for making relatively simple decisions, but can become unwieldy when the decision becomes complex.

For example, we could have expressed the trade credit policy as follows.

IF <u>customer</u> a <u>trade customer</u>

    CASE <u>customer for more than one year</u>
            give 10% discount

    CASE <u>Customer for less than one year</u>
            give 5% discount
ENDIF

(*Note*. ENDIF ends the case statement.)

Repetition/loop

10.13 However, sometimes a block or set of instructions may need to be repeated until a final condition is reached. For example, assume we have called given a block the name *Block 1*. We wish this instruction to be executed until the number of records processed reaches 100. This requirement is a condition, which we can call *condition 1*.

In structured English, this can be written as:

    REPEAT
        block 1

    UNTIL
        condition 1

11. COMPUTER-AIDED SOFTWARE ENGINEERING (CASE)

11.1 In the mid 1980s, the increased power of PCs combined with reductions in the cost of computing meant that the possibility of using computers in software development became a reality. Systems analysis and design requires a methodology and a set of tools. The methodology sets out *how* the system will be developed and the tools are used to *do* the work. Traditional development techniques involved flowcharting templates, pen and paper and perhaps a typewriter.

11.2 Computer-aided software engineering utilises automated software tools in the system design and programming process. Two separate groups of tools have been developed for use in different stages of the development cycle. 'Upper' case tools are used to perform the overall design task and 'lower' case tools are used to generate programs. Recently, a number of companies have started to develop integrated toolsets which can be used throughout the systems development cycle. The term *programmer's workbench* is sometimes used to describe CASE tools.

Features of CASE toolkits

11.3 A typical toolkit offers:

(a) diagramming/drawing facilities;
(b) word processing;
(c) a fourth generation language; and, in some cases,
(d) project management software.

11.4 The diagramming facilities are used with a mouse, in a manner similar to most graphics packages. Toolkits come with a bank of predesigned symbols including those used in flowcharts and dataflow diagrams and, like graphics packages, allow on-screen editing.

11.5 The systems design process involves the output of text as well as drawings. Toolkits usually offer a simple word processing package to assist in the preparation of written material including narrative supporting diagrams, the system specification, and program specifications and any other reports produced.

11.6 Fourth generation languages and prototyping were discussed earlier in this chapter. CASE toolkits include prototyping tools and 4GLs. Product management software, covered in an earlier chapter, is also a feature of CASE toolkits. Typically, the user will be able to generate PERT charts, GANTT charts and tailored spreadsheets.

Advantages and disadvantages of CASE

11.7 Advantages of CASE include the following.

(a) The drudgery is taken out of document preparation and re-drawing of diagrams is made easier.

(b) Accuracy of diagrams is improved. Diagrammers can ensure consistency of terminology and maintain certain standards of documentation.

(c) Prototyping is made easier, as re-design can be effected very quickly.

(d) Blocks of code can be re-used. Many applications incorporate similar functions and processes; if pieces of software are retained in a library they can be used (or modified) as appropriate.

11.8 The main criticism of CASE is that many CASE toolkits support a particular development methodology. This means that organisations might not use CASE if they do not adopt a structured methodology. Thus Prokit Analyst supports STRADIS and Program Development Facility supports JSP.

12. CONCLUSION

12.1 Programs are prepared from the program specification.

12.2 The basic program constructs are sequence, decision and loop.

12.3 There are a variety of ways of designing program logic.

TEST YOUR KNOWLEDGE
The numbers in brackets refer to paragraphs of this chapter

1   Describe the stages of application program development. (2.1)

2   Describe some of the features of a fourth generation system. (3.1)

3   What is the value of application generators? (3.2)

4   What is prototyping? (4.1, 4.2)

5   What is an algorithm? (5.2)

6   List the three basic program constructs. (5.3)

7   List the advantages of sub-routines. (5.10)

8   Describe decision tables (7.1-7.7) decision trees (8.1) structured narratives (10.1)

Now try question 21 at the end of the text

Chapter 17

SYSTEMS INSTALLATION

This chapter covers the following topics.

1. The main stages in installation and implementation
2. Installing the hardware and software
3. User staff issues
4. System testing (system trials)
5. File conversion
6. Systems changeover
7. Systems evaluation (post-implementation review)
8. System maintenance

---

1. THE MAIN STAGES IN INSTALLATION AND IMPLEMENTATION

1.1 When the decision to go ahead with a computer system has been taken, the next steps are:

    (a) to order the hardware, if new hardware is required;

    (b) to order the software, or alternatively to design and program a tailor-made system in-house (as discussed in previous chapters);

    (c) to install the system.

1.2 The responsibility for the system installation will be given to the project manager, working in close coordination with the user department accepting the new system.

1.3 The main stages in the installation and implementation of a computer system are:

    (a) installing the hardware and software;
    (b) staff training;
    (c) testing;
    (d) master file creation (conversion of the files);
    (e) changeover;
    (f) review and system maintenance.

1.4 Items (a) to (e) in this list do not necessarily happen in a set chronological order, and some can be done at the same time – eg staff training and system testing can be part of the same operation. The requirements for installation also vary from system to system.

Ordering new hardware

1.5 While a checklist for the type of hardware required has already been described, an issue which is coming to increasing prominence in information systems management and design is that of *open systems* as opposed to *proprietary systems*.

1.6 In the early days of computing, in fact until the microcomputer revolution, it was common for manufacturers and suppliers of computers to try and 'lock in' their customers by making their products incompatible with those manufactured by competitors. For example, it was not practically possible to link up IBM and ICL equipment. Moreover, some manufacturers made it impossible for even some their *own* products to be connected in this way (eg in the past, a computer manufacturer's mainframe system could not be run with the same manufacturer's minicomputer system).

1.7 The microcomputer market changed all this, as competing manufacturers developed *clones*. In particular, the IBM PC became a 'standard' for others (eg COMPAQ) to copy.

1.8 The mini and mainframe markets did not develop this degree of competition.

1.9 However, the concept of *open systems*, whereby an industry-wide set of standards could be employed to enable machines made by different manufacturers to be connected, has become more widely accepted, partly as customers welcome a choice, and partly as it enables smaller manufacturers of computers to compete more effectively.

1.10 A chief feature of Open Systems is the concept of a common operating system. This is UNIX, developed by AT and T. Although there are several variants of it, it has been adopted as the operating system by a number of manufacturers. IBM, which as a company has historically demonstrated most commitment to proprietary systems, has demonstrated an interest in UNIX and open systems generally be co-founding the Open Software Foundation.

1.11 An organisation purchasing new hardware will need to consider the following.

(a) As part of its *strategy*, should it go for open systems or proprietary software. Open Systems might generate significant cost savings in the long run.

(b) However, if the organisation already has a substantial investment in proprietary systems, then an open systems strategy may not be financially feasible, if this means replacing a lot more of its equipment.

2. INSTALLING THE HARDWARE AND SOFTWARE

2.1 Installing a mainframe computer is a major operation that is carried out by the manufacturer/supplier. With a microcomputer on the other hand, the dealer may agree to install the computer for the customer, but he may not, and the customer may have to install the hardware himself. This should not be too difficult, provided that the manufacturer's instruction manuals are read carefully.

2.2 The office accommodation for microcomputers and peripheral equipment will also need a little bit of planning.

(a) Microcomputers can be used in any office environment, but they generate some heat when they operate (just like any other machine) and so it is inadvisable to put them in small, hot rooms.

(b) Large desks may be advisable, to accommodate a screen and keyboard and leave some free desk space for the office worker to use.

(c) There should be plenty of power sockets - enough to meet future needs as the system grows, not just immediate needs.

(d) If noisy printers (eg daisy wheels) are being purchased, it may be advisable to locate these in a separate room, to cut down the noise for office workers.

(e) There should be a telephone close to the computer, for communicating with the dealer or other organisation which provides system support and advice when the user runs into difficulties.

2.3 *Installing the software.* When the hardware has been installed, the software may then need installing too. To install the software, the computer user must follow the instructions in the user's manual. Installing software can be tedious and lengthy, taking perhaps an hour for a package.

2.4 If a microcomputer has a hard disk, there will be an initial software installation to load the operating system, such as MS-DOS. Thereafter, whenever the micro is switched on at the start of the day, the bootstrap program will automatically load up the OS.

Another feature of using micros with a hard disk is that software packages can be loaded on to a program file, and there is an initial registration process to register the package with the computer. When this has been done, the machine becomes the *licensed user* of the package, which cannot then be used on another machine. Computer software manufacturers are becoming more and more willing to sue organisations which copy software illegally or which make use of illegally copied software. In the UK, the British Federation Against Software Theft (FAST) conducts audits of companies to ensure no unauthorised copying has occurred. Many companies would rather submit to such an audit than undergo a court case.

2.5 *Back-up copies of disks.* When the computer is working, the user should learn how to make back-up copies of disks and make a working copy of each disk that is supplied. This will not be possible if the disk is copy-protected (and the user's manual will say which disks are copy-protected and which are not) but it will protect at least some of the data from accidental erasure.

2.6 *Insurance.* Insurance should be arranged against losses due to fire or theft. It is also possible to obtain insurance against accidental loss of data. If all the data on a hard disk were lost, for example, it could be a long job to re-enter all the lost data, but with insurance cover, the cost of the clerk to do the re-inputting would be paid for by the insurance.

2.7 If a *mainframe* computer installation is to be successful it must be carefully planned. The particular problems of planning the installation include:

(a) *the selection of the site,* whether in an existing or a new building. Factors in the choice of site are the need for:

    (i) adequate space for computer and peripherals, including servicing room;

    (ii) room for expansion;

    (iii) easy access for computer equipment and supplies (it should be unnecessary to knock holes in outside walls, as has happened, in order to gain access for equipment);

    (iv) nearness to principal user departments;

    (v) strength of flooring, (so the equipment does not fall to the floor below – as once happened in a skyscraper in New York);

    (vi) space available for a library, stationery store, data preparation department, programmers' offices etc.

(b) *the site preparation,* including the problems of:

    (i) air conditioning (temperature, humidity and dust);

    (ii) special electricity supplies;

    (iii) raised floor (or false ceiling) so that cables may pass from one piece of equipment to another;

    (iv) fire protection devices;

    (v) furnishings.

(Where minicomputers or microcomputers are to be used the amount of site preparation can be significantly reduced, as they take up little floor space and there is usually no need for air conditioning and special electricity supplies.)

(c) *arranging for standby equipment* to ensure continuity of processing in the event of power or computer failure. Such equipment may include rechargeable storage batteries, standby generators and standby computers.

(d) *planning for delivery.* The actual delivery of a computer can cause a considerable disruption and it is often desirable for it to take place at a weekend. With larger installations this is obviously not possible.

2.8 Once all the required rooms have been completed (or nearly so) and decorated and furnished, the equipment can be installed. This is the manufacturer's responsibility and his engineers will install it and carry out acceptance tests. Any further maintenance or repair of the equipment will normally be carried out by the manufacturer under a maintenance agreement.

2.9 In addition to the computer equipment, all the ancillary equipment (eg desks, trolleys etc) and the useable media (stationery, magnetic tapes, disks etc) must also be delivered and allocated to the appropriate work areas and stores.

2.10 Installing a distributed system or a network may lead to a number of other managerial problems.

(a) If hardware has to be installed at a number of different sites, then the activities of the installation engineers must be coordinated.

(b) If the telecommunications network is to be used as a data link then the necessary arrangements must be made with the link suppliers (leased lines etc).

(c) If a LAN is to be installed in an office, or linking two or three offices, considerable disruption may be caused as the extensive cabling required may necessitate the floors being taken up.

3. USER STAFF ISSUES

Selection of user staff

3.1 When choosing staff for the new system it is advisable, where possible, to appoint as many as possible from within the organisation. Staff responsible for the existing manual systems should if possible be transferred to the same modules of work in the computer system. The only exception to this rule would be when a member of staff is unable or unwilling to adapt to the new technology. This policy will help to maintain good staff relations and reduce suspicion of the 'new methods'. It is also helpful however, if some of the staff have had computer experience in other systems, particularly if the new system is a large one. Where an old *computer* system is being replaced, the initial problem of hostility may be less in evidence.

3.2 Naturally, the number of staff involved in a computer application will vary with the size of the installation. *Segregation of duties* (division of responsibilities) is an important feature of internal control in this area.

User training

3.3 Training is not simply an issue that can be left for clerical staff. As microcomputers are used more and more as management tools, training in information technology affects all levels in an organisation, from senior managers learning how to use an executive information system for example, to accounts clerks learning how to use a sales ledger system.

Why train senior managers?

3.4   Some commentators have argued that managers who are knowledgeable about computers and related technologies make wiser decisions in the following areas.

(a)   Allocation of resources to information systems (especially if the information system gives an organisation competitive advantage).

(b)   Planning for information systems.

(c)   Establishing an appropriate corporate culture for technological development.

(d)   The establishment of an informed skepticism when dealing with IT professionals means that managers won't be blinded by science, and will be able to communicate their needs more effectively.

(e)   Informed managers will have a better knowledge of the type of work their subordinates actually do.

3.5   Senior management can be 'trained' in a number of ways of varying degrees of formality:

(a)   completely informal, such as:

(i)   newspapers (most of the quality press run regular articles on IT and computing);

(ii)   through subordinates (getting subordinate members of staff to demonstrate the benefits of a new system);

(iii) individual demonstrations of computer systems for senior executives;

(b)   semiformal, such as:

(i)   executive briefings (eg presentation before or after board meetings, when resource-allocation decisions are taken);

(ii)   video-demonstrations (eg during lunch time);

(iii) short seminars, designed around an issue that is narrowly defined;

(c)   formal sessions such as day courses, probably necessary if managers are to learn how to use a particular system.

Training middle management

3.6   (a)   The type of training middle management receives is likely to be more structured and more tailored to the particular applications within their remit.

(b)   Middle management, whose status, it has been argued, is most under threat from IT in the long term, are responsible however, for the correct use of systems in an age of distributed processing and end-user computing.

(c)   Middle management are also responsible for implementing in detail the organisation's computer security policy.

(d)   Middle management need to have some basic understanding of the actual systems they are responsible for.

Staff

3.7   There is no point in training staff in a new system until the new system has been installed and is ready for testing. This is because what staff learn will be quickly forgotten unless they can reinforce their learning with continual practice. Training can be provided by:

(a)   reading the user's manuals;
(b)   training by computer, using *disk-based tutorials* provided by a software house;
(c)   attending courses that the dealer has agreed to provide;
(d)   attending courses on a leading software package (eg Lotus 123 or an operating system (such as MS-DOS) provided by third-party training establishments.

3.8   With large computer systems, extensive training of large numbers of staff will probably be necessary, and so additional training measures may include:

(a)   lectures on general or specific aspects of the system - possibly with the use of films, video, tape-recordings, slides, overhead projectors etc;

(b)   discussion meetings, possibly following on from lectures, which allow the staff to ask questions and sort out problems;

(c)   internal company magazines, to explain the new system in outline;

(d)   handbooks, detailing in precise terms the new documentation and procedures. Different handbooks for each function will often be prepared by different persons. For example:

(i)   Systems specifications - prepared by systems analysts.

(ii)   Software manuals - prepared by manufacturers/software houses.

(iii)   Program specifications - prepared by senior programmers.

(iv)   Computer operating instructions - prepared by programmers or the software supplier.

(v)   Data preparation instructions - prepared by systems analysts and the operations manager.

(vi)   Data control/library procedures - prepared by the systems analysts and the operations manager (with possible internal/external involvement).

(vii)   Clerical procedure manuals - prepared by systems analysts and user department representatives.

(e)   using trials/tests on the new system to give staff direct experience before the system 'goes live'.

3.9   Training will be the ultimate responsibility of the information director, if one exists or personnel department in cooperation with user and computer professionals. Some organisations, especially larger ones, have their own training departments.

3.10 The actual content of training courses will vary according to the seniority of the managers and staff being trained. At the Midland Bank, 'the course for directors, heads of department and other senior executives provides insights into the strategic role of information technology' (*Administrator* November 1989).

3.11 With senior management, the training involves the managerial and strategic aspects of IT. 'Managers don't need to know how computers work. They need to know how to define information, how to integrate systems – what computing does and can do for them.' (*Administrator* November 1989)

User documentation

3.12 At some stage before staff training takes place, the system must be fully documented for the computer user. User manuals or user documentation, are 'that part of the full documentation relating to a program, which gives the user information necessary for the successful running of the program (but does not include technical specification, program listing, flowcharts etc)'

(British Computer Society)

3.13 The user documentation is employed:

(a) to explain the system to the user;
(b) to help to train staff;
(c) to provide a point of reference should the user have some problems with the system in the future – eg an error condition or a screen message that he or she does not understand.

3.14 Explaining the system involves:

(a) specifying the input needed to the system, the format of input records, the content of each record field, the coding systems used etc. If the system uses keyboard input, the user documentation should also set out the VDU screen designs for input, the nature of any menus or other screen prompts, the nature of any interactive processing etc;

(b) explaining the nature of the processing method – eg on-line input and file enquiry;

(c) specifying the nature of the system's files and what they contain;

(d) explaining the system's outputs, eg reports and documents, including the meaning of any exception reports, where input data has been rejected as invalid;

(e) giving instructions about what to do in the event of a system failure;

(f) establishing the clerical procedures or other ancillary procedures that will have to be carried out.

3.15 User documentation is such an important necessity that good documentation is a key selling feature of successful off-the-shelf packages. The term 'software', in fact means both the program *and* its documentation.

3.16 When a system is developed in-house, the user documentation might be written by a systems analyst. However, it might be considered preferable for the user documentation to be written by a member of the user's department's staff, possibly a junior manager who has spent some time with the project development team, learning about the system.

Walkthroughs.

3.17 'Walkthroughs' are a technique used by those responsible for the design of some aspect of a system (eg analysts and programmers) to present their design to interested user groups. These presentations, which will require a high level of communication skills, are used both to introduce and explain the new systems to users and also to offer the users the opportunity of making constructive criticism of the proposed system, and suggestions for further amendments/ improvements before the final systems specification is agreed.

4. SYSTEM TESTING (SYSTEM TRIALS)

4.1 A system must be thoroughly tested before implementation, otherwise there is a danger that the new system will go live with faults that might prove costly.

4.2 The scope of tests and trials will vary with the size of the system.

(a) When a system is designed 'in-house' there should be *program tests* for each individual program in the system. There will then be testing of the 'interface' between individual programs in the system, in an overall *systems test*.

(b) The user department will want to carry out tests or trials on the system, whether it is designed in-house or bought from a software house. The initial trials ought to be carried out by management personnel, who know the current operational system extremely well and who also ideally know something about computers. The trials would be intended to sort out any major bugs or problems, using dummy data (ie invented data).

4.3 Various personnel will be involved in system tests.

(a) The DP manager will have overall responsibility for the DP department, and must ensure that the tests are planned and executed properly, and the system is fully documented.

(b) The systems analysts must check with their tests that the system achieves the objectives set for it, and do not contain any errors.

(c) Programmers must be on hand to debug any faults which the earlier program tests had not spotted.

(d) The computer operations manager will be in charge of data preparation work and operations in the computer room and report any faults or weaknesses to the DP manager and chief systems analyst.

(e) The user department managers must decide that the system has been tested to their satisfaction. They may choose to carry out acceptance tests to do this.

4.4 Test data should be constructed to test all conditions. For example, dummy data records should be input which are designed to test all the data validation routines and master file update error reports in the system. Unusual, but feasible, transactions could be tested, to see how the system handles them - eg several sales orders from the same customer in the same batch input, or two wage packets in the same week for the same employee.

4.5 The data used in trials will not be wanted when the system goes live, and so it does not matter whether bulk data for the trials comes from current transactions or from historical data. Many managers prefer to use historical data in trials, because it is then possible to check the output of the computer system against the output that the current manual system actually produced.

Acceptance testing

4.6 Acceptance testing is testing of a system by the user department, after the system has passed its systems test. The purposes of having trials conducted by the user department's managers are to:

(a) find software errors which exist but have not yet been detected;

(b) find out exactly what the demands of the new system are, and whether any major changes in operating procedures will be necessary.

4.7 Another aspect of the user department trials (or a subsequent stage of trials) might be to test the system with large volumes of data, and at the same time use the tests as an opportunity to train staff in the new system and the new procedures.

These 'bulk' tests on the system involve checks on:

(a) error correction procedures (ie user department routines);

(b) the inter-relationship between clerical and computer procedures;

(c) the timing of computer runs;

(d) the capacity of files, file handling, updating and amendment;

(e) systems controls, including auditing requirements;

(f) procedures for methods of data capture, preparation and input and the distribution of output;

(g) ancillary clerical procedures.

5. FILE CONVERSION

5.1 File conversion means converting existing master file records and reference file records on to a file suitable for the new system.

301

A system cannot become operational until master files for the new system have been created. For example:

(a) a sales ledger application package cannot be brought into use until the user has created a sales ledger file for existing customers for the new system;

(b) a database cannot be used until the database file has been created.

5.2 File conversion is a major part of the systems implementation. It is often an expensive part of the systems implementation because it usually means the conversion of existing manual file records into a medium used by the computer. This itself may involve the transcription of records, or parts of them, on to specially designed forms before they are keyed on to the appropriate computer medium.

5.3 File conversion can be tedious and time consuming. Because of the volume of data that must be copied on to the new files, the problem of input *errors* getting on to the master file is a serious one, in spite of data validation checks in the file conversion program.

Once the file has been created extensive checking for accuracy is essential, otherwise considerable problems may arise when the system becomes operational.

5.4 Where the file conversion is from manual records the manager or systems analyst in charge of planning the conversion must establish:

(a) the location of the data (and whether all the data for each record is on a single existing document or on a number of different forms);

(b) whether the existing forms are suitable for data capture;

(c) whether the data format and sequence is suitable for the computer system;

(d) whether the existing records are maintained centrally or not;

(e) whether each record is easily accessible;

(f) the volumes involved (how many records of each type are there?);

(g) whether the existing files are to be converted directly or amalgamated in some way.

5.5 Before starting to load live data about customers, suppliers or employees etc, management should check whether the system must be registered under the Data Protection Act.

5.6 If the system is already computerised on a system that the organisation now wishes to abandon, the difficulties of file conversion will usually be reduced and the answers to the above problems more easily established. Furthermore, when it comes to the actual transcription from the old files to the new computer files the use of a *special conversion program* will speed up the whole process.

5.7 The stages in file conversion from manual files to computer files are normally as follows:

(a) ensuring that the original record files are accurate and up to date;

(b) recording the old file data on specially designed input documents. This will usually be done by the user department personnel (with additional temporary staff if required) following detailed instructions laid down by the systems designer or software supplier. These instructions will include the procedures for allocating new code numbers (a coding system, including check digits if necessary, may have to be designed by this stage) and for checking the accuracy and completeness of the data selected and entered on the input documents (usually verification by another person and the establishment of control totals);

(c) transcribing the completed input documents on to the computer media. This may be done by user department staff keying in the data from terminals, or in large systems, by data preparation staff at the (mainframe) computer centre when proper verification techniques would be used;

(d) using special programs to read the transcribed data and produce the required files in the appropriate form. These programs would include *validation* checks on the input data. The contents of the file must then be printed out and completely checked back to the data input forms (or even the original file if possible);

(e) correcting any errors that this checking reveals.

5.8 The steps in file conversion may be summarised as follows:

(a) encode and verify data;
(b) validate data with computer software;
(c) investigate, correct and re-code all errors;
(d) produce listing of all accepted data and check this on a one-for-one basis with inputs;
(e) produce control reconciliations to reconcile data totals to existing system.

It is assumed here that the file data has to be encoded. When the changeover is from an old computer system to a new system, a special program can be written that will convert the old file records into a new file format, thus saving time and avoiding file conversion errors.

5.9 Other problems of file conversion which must be considered and planned by the systems analyst include the following.

(a) The possible provision of additional staff, or the use of a computer bureau, to cope with the file conversion and prevent bottlenecks.
'It may be worth considering hiring a third-party organisation to load the data for you. This method can be a quick and surprisingly economical solution, but these advantages must be offset against the fact that the 'imported' temporary staff will not be familiar with the data and errors must undoubtedly get through.'
(R Piper, *Micro Decision*, Sept 1986)

(b) The establishment of cut-off dates where live files are being converted (should the conversion be during slack times, for example, during holidays, weekends?).

(c) The decision as to whether files should be converted all at once, or whether the conversion should be file by file or record group by record group (with subsequent amalgamation).

Exercise

You have been asked to transfer 400 Sales Ledger manual record cards to a microcomputer based system using floppy disks. The program menu has a record create option.

Explain how you would set about this process, and the steps you would take to ensure that the task was completed successfully.

Each record consists of 600 characters. How long would you expect the file conversion procedure to take, once the data has been transferred on to data input forms?

Solution

The steps that should be taken are as follows.

(a) Check the manual records, and remove any dead accounts.

(b) Assign account codes to each record, ideally with codes that incorporate a check digit.

(c) If necessary transcribe the data from the card records on to documents which can be used for copying from, for data input.

(d) Add up the total number of accounts and the total value of account balances as control totals. This task might be done by the office supervisor.

(e) Select the record create option from the program menu and key the standing data/current data on to the new computer file. This should ideally be done at a quiet time, perhaps over a weekend.

(f) Input that is rejected by a data validation check should be re-keyed in correctly.

(g) A listing of the records put on to file should be printed out. This listing should be checked for errors, ideally by someone who did not do the keying in. Errors should be reported, and corrected data keyed in to amend the data on file.

(h) The program should produce control totals of the number of records put on to the file, and the total value of account balances. These control totals should be checked against the manually pre-listed control totals. Discrepancies should be investigated, and any errors or omissions put right.

(i) A security back-up copy of the new file should be made.

(j) The file and the new system should then be ready for use.

(k) Assuming direct keyboard entry of data and an average keyboard input speed of, say, 200 characters per minute, the actual data input time will be approximately

$$\frac{400 \times 600}{200} = 1,200 \text{ minutes, or 20 hours.}$$

Checks and error correction procedures might slow down the input process substantially, perhaps adding an extra five hours or so. Allowing time to make a back-up copy of the file (say ½ hour) the estimated file conversion time is 25½ man hours, say 30 man-hours.

---

6. SYSTEMS CHANGEOVER

6.1 Once the new system has been fully and satisfactorily tested the changeover can be made.

This may be:

(a) direct changeover;
(b) parallel running;
(c) pilot tests;
(d) 'phased' or 'staged' implementation.

Direct changeover

6.2 This is the method of changeover in which the old system is completely replaced by the new system in one move. This may be unavoidable where the two systems are substantially different, where the new system is a real-time system, or where extra staff to oversee parallel running are unobtainable. While this method is comparatively cheap it is risky (system or program corrections are difficult while the system has to remain operational) and management must have complete confidence in the new system. The new system should be introduced during slack periods and in large systems it may be introduced application by application, allowing several months between each stage to ensure that all problems are cleared up before the next stage becomes operational;

Parallel running

6.3 This is a form of changeover whereby the old and new systems are run in parallel for a period of time, both processing current data and enabling cross checking to be made. The CIMA's *Computing Terminology* defines parallel running as 'the processing of a function by means of a new computer system whilst continuing to maintain the old method such that the results from both systems can be compared prior to placing reliance on the new system.'

This method provides a degree of safety should there be problems with the new system. However, if there are differences between the two systems cross-checking may be difficult or impossible. Furthermore, there is a delay in the actual implementation of the new system, a possible indication of lack of confidence in the new system, and a need for more staff to cope with both systems running in parallel. This cautious approach, if adopted, should be properly planned, and the plan should include:

(a) a firm time limit on parallel running;
(b) details of which data should be cross-checked - all of it? - on a sample basis?
(c) instructions on how errors are to be dealt with - could they be errors in the old system?
(d) instructions on how to cope with major problems in the new system (it could be a new machine with unknown reliability and the old system is being used to provide standby facilities in the case of a breakdown).

Pilot operation

6.4 This is cheaper and easier to control than parallel running, and provides a greater degree of safety than does a direct changeover. There are two types of pilot operation:

(a) *retrospective parallel running* in which the new system operates on data already processed by the old system. The existing results are available for cross-checking and the system can be tested without the problems of staffing and disruption caused by parallel running. This is really a form of system testing;

(b) *restricted data running* in which a complete logical part of the whole system file is chosen and run as a unit on the new system. If that is shown to be working well the remaining parts are then transferred. Gradually the whole system can be transferred in this piecemeal fashion. Again, the planning should involve the setting of strict time limits for each phase and instructions on how problems are to be dealt with. It must be remembered that two systems have to be controlled and additional staff, as well as a longer period for implementation, may be required.

An example of a pilot operation would be when a nationwide organisation introduces a new system into one office at a time - eg Bristol first, Glasgow next, Manchester next, and so on.

'Phased' implementation

6.5 This is fact a form of parallel running, the difference being that instead of running two complete systems (old and new) in parallel in order to compare the results of live processing on the new system with those generated by the old, only a portion of the data is run in parallel, eg for one branch only.

The use of this method of implementation is best suited to very large projects and/or those where distinct parts of the system are geographically dispersed. Where this approach is adopted care must be taken to control any systems amendments incorporated in the later phases in order to ensure that the overall system remains totally compatible.

6.6 When deciding upon which method, or combination of methods, should be used for the changeover, management should consider:

(a) the co-ordination of the changeover - who is responsible? how is co-ordination to be achieved?

(b) the means of complete and accurate communication throughout the system during the changeover period;

(c) the method of controlling errors and the amount of system change or program modification that can be permitted;

(d) the people who are involved, how the change affects them, how they can be trained and get used to working the new system;

(e) the maintenance and operation methods of the new system (to allow for easy and effective modification;

(f) the method of monitoring and evaluating the results of the systems changeover.

6.7 The *duration* of the parallel run or pilot test can vary quite substantially between systems, with experts quoting anything from 2 weeks to 6 months. However, with tailor-made software purchased from a software house, it may be important to complete the changeover quickly, because the software house's 'bug fixing' warranty will normally expire 3 months after the date of purchase.

6.8 *Timing*. The new system should be installed and become operational at a time that is convenient to the user - eg when the workload is fairly light, and certainly not at a peak workload time in the year. An accounting system might be installed to coincide with the beginning of a new accounts year.

6.9 At the satisfactory conclusion of a parallel run or pilot operation, the system will go fully operational, benefitting from the lessons learned during the trials and the changeover.

7. SYSTEMS EVALUATION (POST-IMPLEMENTATION REVIEW)

7.1 The system should be reviewed periodically so that any unforeseen problems may be solved and to confirm that it is achieving and will continue to achieve the desired results. Indeed in most systems there is a constant need to maintain and improve applications and to keep up to date with technological advances and changing user requirements.

The system should have been designed with clear, specified objectives, and justification in terms of cost-benefit analysis or other performance criteria. Post-implementation review should establish whether the objectives and targeted performance criteria have been met, and if not, why not, and what should be done about it.

7.2 In appraising the operation of the new system immediately after the changeover, comparison should be made between actual and predicted performance. This will include (amongst other items) consideration of:

(a) throughput speed (time between input and output);
(b) use of computer storage (both internal and external);
(c) the number and type of errors/queries;
(d) the cost of processing (data capture, preparation, storage and output media, etc);
(e) timely production of information;
(f) work flow bottlenecks.

7.3 It should be the steering committee's or senior management's responsibility to ensure that post-implementation reviews are carried out, although the internal audit department may be required to do the work of carrying out the reviews.

The scope of performance reviews

7.4 Performance reviews will vary in content from organisation to organisation, but the matters which will probably be looked at are:

(a) the growth rates in file sizes and the number of transactions processed by the system. Trends should be analysed and projected to assess whether there are likely to be problems with lengthy processing time or an inefficient file structure due to the volume of processing;

(b) the clerical manpower needs for the system, and deciding whether they are more or less than estimated;

(c) the identification of any delays in processing and an assessment of the consequences of any such delays;

(d) an assessment of the efficiency of security procedures;

(e) a check of the error rates for input data. High error rates may indicate inefficient preparation of input documents, an inappropriate method of data capture or poor design of input media;

(f) determining whether any amendments to the system are needed;

(g) investigating external factors to decide whether any unforeseen circumstances have affected system performance;

(h) an examination of whether output from the computer is being used to good purpose - ie is it used? is it timely? does it go to the right people? etc;

(i) checking that the system documentation is adequate and comprehensive;

(j) carrying out a cost-benefit review of the system:

   (i)   have expected benefits been achieved or not?
   (ii) are any unplanned benefits apparent?
   (iii) are the costs of the system comparable with estimates?

(k) user's comments on the system - ie what its strengths and weaknesses are;

(l) operational running costs, examined to discover any inefficient programs or processes. This examination may reveal excessive costs for certain items although in total, costs may be acceptable;

(m) the preparation of a report of the review making appropriate recommendations, for submission to senior management (eg the steering committee).

Outputs from a computer system

7.5 The efficiency of the system can be assessed by looking at the outputs and the inputs of a computer system. With regard to outputs, the efficiency of a computer system would be enhanced in any of the following ways:

(a) More outputs of some value could be produced by the same input resources; for example:

(i) if the system could process more transactions;

(ii) if the system could produce more management information, eg sensitivity analysis in modelling packages or a graphical display of output etc;

(iii) if the system could make information available to more people who might need it (eg using file enquiry and databases).

(b) Outputs which have little or no value could be eliminated from the system, thus making savings in the cost of inputs. For example:

(i) if reports are produced too frequently, should they be produced less often?

(ii) if reports are distributed too widely, should the distribution list be shortened?

(iii) if reports are too bulky, can they be reduced in size, using the principle of reporting by exception? Shorter reports might also save management time.

(c) The timing and *frequency of outputs* could be better. Information should be available in good time for the information-user to be able to make good use of it. Reports that are issued late might lose their value. Computer systems could give managers immediate access to the information they require, by means of file enquiry or special software (such as databases or spreadsheet modelling packages).

7.6 It might be found that outputs are not as satisfactory as they should be, perhaps because:

(a) *access* to information from the system is limited, and could be improved with

(i) a database and/or
(ii) a multi-user or network system;

(b) *output volume* is restricted because of

(i) the method of data processing used, eg stand-alone microcomputer systems, might be slower and less efficient than multi-user systems; or

(ii) the type of equipment used. A system's capabilities might be limited by the restrictions of:

(1) the software's capabilities
(2) the size of the computer's main store
(3) the capacity of the computer's backing storage (eg hard disks or floppy disks)
(4) the number of printers linked to the computer
(5) the number of terminals.

Inputs and computer efficiency

7.7 The efficiency of a computer system could be improved if the same volume (and frequency) of output could be achieved with fewer input resources, and at less cost. Some of the ways in which this could be done have already been mentioned, eg:

(a) multi-user systems might be more efficient than stand-alone systems. Multi-user systems allow several operators to access the same files at the same time, so that if one person has a heavy work load and another is currently short of work, the person who has some free time can help his or her busy colleague - thus improving operator efficiency;

(b) microcomputer systems might be more efficient than batch processing with a mainframe computer;

(c) using computers and external storage media with bigger storage capacity;

(d) using better (eg more 'up-to-date') software.

7.8 A frequent complaint with many microcomputer systems is that 'waiting time' for the operator can be very long and tedious. For example, if an operator wants to call up a particular file, he or she might have to wait several minutes before the file becomes available. File enquiries can involve a lengthy wait too. Computer systems with better backing storage facilities can reduce this operator waiting time, and so be more efficient.

7.9 Management might also wish to consider whether the checks on input data are too extensive, or could be achieved at less cost.

(a) In traditional batch processing systems, it might be unnecessary to verify all input data (ie re-key all transactions before input); alternatively, it might be possible to reduce the amount of 'manual' or 'visual' checks on output.

(b) An alternative method of input might be chosen. For example, if an accounts system is switched to an integrated, modular computerised system (instead of stand-alone systems for sales ledger, purchase ledger, nominal ledger etc) a single transaction needs to be input only once, thus

(i) saving input time and effort; and
(ii) improving the accuracy and reliability of processing.

Computer systems efficiency audits: conclusion

7.10 Computer systems efficiency audits have not (yet) become standardised, but they are all concerned with improving outputs from the system and their use, or reducing the costs of system inputs. With falling costs of computer hardware and software, and technological advances (eg the emergence of network systems) there should often be scope for improvements in computer systems, which an audit ought to be able to identify.

8. SYSTEM MAINTENANCE

8.1 System maintenance involves:

(a) 'updating' the system, to adapt it to developments in the user's methods of operations or to 'environmental changes' as and when they occur (eg new legislation on the protection and privacy of data, such as the Data Protection Act 1984 in the UK, some years ago). New processing requirements, changing volumes of processing, new methods of organisation and operation etc, all make changes necessary. Systems can be amended to keep them functional;

(b) correcting errors as and when they are found;

(c) documentation of the system updates and corrections.

8.2 With large computer systems which are designed 'in-house' a systems analyst and a programmer in the DP department might be given the responsibility for system maintenance.

8.3 With purchased software packages, the software supplier might agree with a customer to provide details of any new versions of the software package as they are produced, and perhaps to agree terms for providing the new version to replace the old one that the customer is using.

The computer user should have a keen interest in using the same package as long as possible - after all, buying a new system would mean having to go through a feasibility study and installation of a new system all over again. To help to prolong the life of a system, updated versions of a software package might be essential - eg in the past, new versions of software have been developed to use hard disk instead of floppy disk files, so that users take advantage of hard disk technology for microcomputers that had emerged.

8.4 There is also likely to be an agreement between the supplier of software and the customer for the provision of a software support service. Software support involves providing experts in a system to give advice and help when a customer runs into difficulties operating the system. The help will initially be given by telephone, with a 'hot line' to call in case of difficulty. If a telephone call does not resolve the problem, the software expert will arrange to visit the customer's premises within a period of time (agreed in the contract between the software supplier and the customer).

8.5 A software support service must normally be paid for. When a software house writes a tailor-made system for a customer, there will be a warranty or guarantee period, perhaps three months, after which a contract for a continued software support service might be agreed between the customer and the software house.

8.6 The key features of system maintenance ought to be *flexibility* and *adaptability*, so that:

(a) the system, perhaps with minor modifications, can cope with changes in the computer user's procedures or volume of business;

(b) the computer user can benefit from advances in computer hardware technology without having to switch to another system altogether.

8.7 If applications exceed initial forecasts of computing resources all is not lost because it is possible to contend with increasing volumes and communication needs by enhancing the existing computer system on site, on a modular basis, by:

(a) increasing its internal storage capacity by additional storage modules;
(b) installing disks of greater capacity and higher speed;
(c) installing a more powerful processor;
(d) changing to faster printers; or
(e) installing additional terminals or network facilities, whichever suits the business needs best.

Stages in program maintenance

8.8 Some changes in a company's software are almost inevitable at some stage in a project's life. To ensure that maintenance is carried out efficiently, the principles of good programming practice should be applied. These include the following:

(a) Any change must be properly authorised by a manager in the user department (or someone even more senior, if necessary).

(b) The new program requirements must be specified in full and in writing. These specifications will be prepared by a systems analyst. A programmer should use these specifications to produce an amended version of the program.

(c) In developing a new program version, a programmer should keep working papers. He or she can refer back to these papers later to check in the event that:

(i) there is an error in the new program;
(ii) the user of the program asks for a further change in the program - eg for an extra bit of processing on input data, perhaps to produce an additional report.

(d) The new program version should be tested when it has been written. A programmer should prepare test data and establish whether the program will process the data according to the specifications given by the systems analyst.

(e) Provisions should be made for further program amendments in the future. One way of doing this is to leave space in the program instruction numbering sequence for new instructions to be inserted later. For example, instructions might be numbered 10,20,30,40 etc instead of 1,2,3,4.

(f) A record should be kept of all program errors that are found during 'live' processing and of the corrections that are made to the program.

(g) Each version of a program (eg versions that are produced with processing modifications or corrections to errors) should be separately identified, to avoid a mix-up about what version of a program should be used for 'live' operating.

Hardware maintenance

8.9 Computer hardware should be kept serviced and maintained too. Maintenance services are provided:

(a) by the computer manufacturers themselves (especially for mainframes but also for some micros); and

(b) by third-party maintenance companies.

8.10 Maintenance of hardware can be obtained:

(a) on a contract basis. Microcomputer hardware maintenance contracts are usually negotiated for one year;

(b) on an ad hoc basis - ie calling in a maintenance company whenever a fault occurs.

8.11 Contract customers will get a priority service from maintenance companies, and so if a computer user would suffer badly if a machine went down, he would be well advised to arrange a maintenance contract. Guaranteed 'response times' are commonly 8 hours or so, although a quicker service might be guaranteed at a higher contract price.

9. CONCLUSION

9.1 The main stages in systems installation are:

(a) installation of hardware and software;
(b) staff training;
(c) system testing;
(d) file conversion;
(e) systems changeover; and
(f) maintenance and review.

TEST YOUR KNOWLEDGE
The numbers in brackets refer to paragraphs of this chapter

1 What are the main stages in the installation/implementation of a new computer system, after the programs have been written or purchased? (1.3)

2 How might user department staff be trained to use a new system? (3.3-3.11)

3 What is acceptance testing? (4.6)

4 What is file conversion? What, typically, are the stages in file conversion for a new system? (5.4, 5.7-5.8)

5 Describe three methods of systems changeover from an old to a new system? (6.2-6.5)

6 What might be the scope of a systems performance review by the internal audit department? (7.4)

7 What does system maintenance involve? (8.1)

Now try questions 22 and 23 at the end of the text

Chapter 18

SYSTEMS DOCUMENTATION AND STANDARDS

This chapter covers the following topics.

1. Introduction
2. The systems specification
3. Program specifications
4. User documentation: the user manual
5. Data processing standards

---

1. INTRODUCTION

1.1 The thorough documentation of a system is essential for:

(a) system specification and design;
(b) training staff; and
(c) system maintenance.

A badly documented system will be poorly designed, badly used or badly maintained.

1.2 The most important items of documentation are probably the *system specification, program specification* and *user documentation.*

1.3 To help with the design and documentation of systems, certain Data Processing Standards have been established.

2. THE SYSTEMS SPECIFICATION

2.1 When a system development team has designed a new system it must be 'sold' to top management for final approval. The report on the new system must:

(a) assure management that the new system will satisfy the objectives which have been set for it;

(b) show that the system will be beneficial in financial terms and provide improved management information;

(c) show that the system is stable, flexible and capable of catering for any expected growth or developments.

2.2 The systems specification may be prepared initially in an outline form and then in more detail later when system design work is carried out.

2.3 The *systems specification* is the systems analyst's means of communicating with

(a) management (for final approval)

(b) programmers (to give details for program preparation)

(c) operations staff (to detail all operating procedures)

(d) user departments (to make them aware of the parts of the system for which they will be responsible) and

(e) the auditors (who need to satisfy themselves in respect of controls, safeguards etc)

2.4 The systems specification has four main uses:

(a) as a reference document for the systems analysts;

(b) as a document which can be studied by the management of the user department to check that the system analysts are designing a system that will do what they want it to;

(c) as a document that computer programmers can use as the starting point for writing a program. Within the system specification, there will be a detailed specification for each program in the system;

(d) as a document that a systems analyst or member of the user department can use as a starting point for writing the *user manual*.

2.5 The check list given below outlines the principal contents of a standard system specification.

SYSTEMS SPECIFICATION

Section A - | *Introductory information* |

(a) Title and responsibility:

    (i)   system name/date produced
    (ii)   produced by/for
    (iii) origination of amendments.

(b) Authorisation:

    (i)   statement of acceptance
    (ii)   signature of acceptor
    (iii) area of responsibility.

(c) Index

(d) Glossary of terms

315

(e) Time schedules:

    (i)   test with live data
    (ii) parallel/pilot running
    (iii) new system in operation
    (iv) linking in with other systems.

(f) Amendments index:

    (i)   amendments number/date/authority
    (ii) section/page
    (iii) description.

Section B - | *System objectives*

(a) Procedures covered
(b) Departments concerned
(c) Target measures of effectiveness
(d) Benefits (financial, staffing, information)
(e) Outputs (medium, description, volumes, use, reference to section F)
(f) Inputs (medium, description, volumes, source, reference to section G)
(g) Files (medium, description, volume, use, reference to section H)
(h) Controls (reference to section L)

Section C - | *Systems description*

(a) Clerical procedures:

    (i)   systems and clerical procedure flowcharts
    (ii) decision tables
    (iii) narrative.

(b) Data preparation/output distribution procedures

    (i)   clerical procedure flowcharts
    (ii) narrative.

(c) Computer procedures

    (i)   computer run flowcharts
    (ii) narrative
    (see also section J)

Section D - | *Changeover procedure*

(a) File conversion:

    (i)   methods of data collection
    (ii) codes required
    (iii) data preparation
    (iv) programs and runs required.

(b) Pilot running:

    (i) data to be used
    (ii) volumes
    (iii) processing period
    (iv) expected results.

(c) Parallel running:

    (i) volumes
    (ii) processing period
    (iii) check points.

(d) Direct changeover or pilot runs

    (i) changeover period
    (ii) extra staff/overtime.

Section E - | *Equipment* |

(a) Equipment specifications

    (i) type of computer
    (ii) peripheral and ancillary equipment.

(b) Computer utilisation

    (i) number and frequency of runs
    (ii) set up time
    (iii) estimated time per run
    (iv) end of run procedure times
    (v) total computer time per day/week/month.

(c) Ancillary equipment utilisation:

    (i) type of machine
    (ii) activity description/frequency/time
    (iii) total equipment time per day/week/month.

Section F - | *Output specification for each item of output* |

(a) Format planning chart

    (i) output name and reference
    (ii) system name and reference
    (iii) program name and reference
    (iv) number of print lines per day
    (v) maximum field sizes
    (vi) spacing requirements.

(b) Narrative

    (i)   medium (type of stationery, VDU etc)
    (ii)   distribution etc.

(c) Sample

Section G - | *Input specification: for each item of input* |

(a) Description

    (i)   identification
    (ii)   method of origination
    (iii) record details
    (iv) frequency.

(b) Samples

Section H - | *File specification* |

(a) All files

    (i)   medium
    (ii)   name
    (iii)   labels
    (iv)   size - records
    (v)   number of record types
    (vi)   sequence of records
    (vii) block size
    (viii) data fields in each record.

(b) Magnetic disk files

    (i)   details in 1 above
    (ii)   file organisation method
    (iii) storage access method
    (iv) block size/number of blocks
    (v)   number of back up files

(c) Magnetic tape files

    (i)   details in 1 above
    (ii)   packing details/volume
    (iii) number of tape reels
    (iv) frequency of use
    (v)   retention period.

Section I - | Test data |

(a) Input data (listings or layouts)
(b) Main files (layouts)
(c) Expected results (logic, arithmetic, layout).

Section J - | Program specification (one program specification for every individual program in the system) |

(a) Introduction

  (i) program name/number/purpose.

(b) Program description - ie the tasks to be carried out by the program. Program logic flowcharts might be included. Standard documentation might be used to record the program description. The items in the description will be:

  (i) detailed flowcharts/decision tables
  (ii) processing requirements
  (iii) maximum/minimum sizes.

(c) File formats and sizes, for every file used by the program.

(d) Validity and control total checks.

(e) Error conditions.

(f) End procedures

  (i) output of control totals, tables etc
  (ii) dumping requirements
  (iii) file closing
  (iv) operator messages.

(g) Dump and restart procedures.

(h) Schedule for program testing.

Section K - | System operating details |

(a) Computer operating instructions (for computer operators)
(b) User department instructions re inputs/outputs
(c) Control department instructions re error correction etc
(d) Further control details (administrative, systems development controls)

Section L - | Controls |

(a) Input and processing controls
(b) Audit trail

319

Section M - | Systems costs and benefits

This provides data for a further evaluation of the financial merits of the proposed system, in case the steering committee or board of directors wishes to re-assess the decision to go ahead with the project before the decision becomes irreversible.

3. PROGRAM SPECIFICATIONS

3.1 The program specifications are usually drawn up by the systems analyst (in Section J in our list of contents of the systems specification). A copy of each specification is then given to a programmer to write the specified program.

3.2 For each program in the system, an individual program specification will be prepared. It should include some or all of the following items, depending upon the type of system and the purpose of the program.

(a) Introduction, which includes the program name, number and purpose.

(b) Program description, ie the tasks to be carried out by the program. The program description will specify the processing requirements and may include algorithms, detailed flowcharts or decision tables, etc.

(c) File formats and sizes for every file used by the program.

(d) A list of validation checks to be included in the program.

(e) Other error conditions that should be tested.

(f) End procedures such as output of control totals, file dumping requirements, closing files and operator messages.

(g) A schedule for program testing.

4. USER DOCUMENTATION: THE USER MANUAL

4.1 At some stage before staff training takes place, the system must be fully documented for the computer user. User manuals or user documentation, are 'that part of the full documentation relating to a program, which gives the user information necessary for the successful running of the program (but does not include technical specification, program listing, flowcharts etc)'
(British Computer Society)

4.2 The user documentation is used:

(a) to explain the system to the user;
(b) to help to train staff;
(c) to provide a point of reference should the user have some problems with the system in the future - eg an error condition or a screen message that he or she does not understand.

4.3   The manual will explain the computer system in non-technical, general terms and give detailed information about the procedures required in the user department to operate the system.

4.4   Explaining the system involves:

(a)   specifying the input needed to the system, the format of input records, the content of each record field, the coding systems used etc. If the system uses keyboard input, the user documentation should also set out the VDU screen designs for input, the nature of any menus or other screen prompts, the nature of any interactive processing etc;

(b)   explaining the nature of the processing method - eg on-line input and file enquiry;

(c)   specifying the nature of the system's files and what they contain;

(d)   explaining the system's outputs, eg reports and documents, including the meaning of any exception reports, where input data has been rejected as invalid;

(e)   giving instructions about what to do in the event of a system failure;

(f)   establishing the clerical procedures or other ancillary procedures that will have to be carried out.

4.5   Information about some or all of the following would be included in the user manual, depending upon the type of system concerned.

(a)   Data collection procedures. How data should be collected and recorded on source documents. Codes to use for various items in a record.

(b)   Data input procedures, ie how the data should be input, and how regularly. If input is via keyboard and VDU, the user manual will explain the meaning of all the items that might be shown on the VDU screen (menus, icons etc) and what procedures should be carried out.

(c)   Error reports - what they mean and how errors should be corrected.

(d)   Data output - what it is and how it should be used.

(e)   Security measures, eg preventing unauthorised access to the terminals, using passwords, making backup copies of files, taking care of back-up files.

(f)   Who to consult in case of difficulty.

4.6   User documentation is such an important necessity that good documentation is a key selling feature of successful off-the-shelf packages. The term 'software', in fact means both the program *and* its documentation.

4.7   When a system is developed in-house, the user documentation might be written by a systems analyst. However, it might be considered preferable for the user documentation to be written by a member of the user's department's staff, possibly a junior manager who has spent some time with the project development team, learning about the system.

Exercise

What do you think the main features of a good standardised documentation system might be?

Solution

Features of a good standardised documentation might include:

(a) procedures for filing and referencing;

(b) procedures for amendments;

(c) comprehensive coverage for all users;

(d) simplicity, perhaps by using standard procedures in the system and a standard layout for documentation;

(e) the use of checklists for computer operators, data control staff etc, to act as procedural guidelines;

(f) clear instructions about error reports and corrective procedures.

---

5.   DATA PROCESSING STANDARDS

5.1 Data Processing Standards are standards for the development, procedures and documentation of computer systems. They have been developed by the National Computing Centre Ltd (NCC), the British Computer Society, IBM and other computer manufacturers, but some large organisations have developed their own in-house Standards.

Why are DP Standards needed?

5.2 The purpose of DP Standards is to minimise the likelihood of errors and misunderstandings in the development and operation of computer systems. More specifically, Standards are helpful in the following ways.

(a) Documentation of a system.
(b) Management control.
(c) Communication of information about the system.
(d) Continuity after staff changes.
(e) Aid to training.
(f) Aid to systems analysis and design work.

These are now discussed in detail.

(a) *Documentation of a computer system.* Documentation is needed for systems and program specifications, and also for operator instructions.

The existence of Standards for documentation:

(i)   establishes the need to document a system;

(ii)   provides a standard format for documenting the system, which helps to ensure that nothing is forgotten and left out of the specification;

(iii)   gives the people operating a system somewhere to look up and learn the system's operating requirements.

(b) *Management control*.

DP Standards should provide guidelines for managers to plan and control system development and then system operations.

(i)   Standards should suggest how the management meetings of the Steering Committee should be scheduled during systems development, and how projects should be costed.

(ii)   There should be performance standards, so that actual performance can be measured against what should be expected.

(iii)   There should be standard job specifications, indicating who ought to be responsible for what part of the system.

(c) *Communication of information about the system*.

Standard documentation provides a means whereby information about a system can be communicated, for example between programmers and systems analysts, and between the system developers and the users and operators of the system. Having Standards helps communication in two ways:

(i)   they state *what* information should be presented; and
(ii)   the *format* - ie how the information should be presented.

This should make the information about the system both complete and comprehensible.

(d) *Continuity after staff changes and an aid to training*.

People leave their jobs from time to time, or are absent for one reason or another. Unless a system is well-documented in a standard way, or has been designed according to standard procedures, it may be difficult for a person's stand-in or replacement to pick up the job where his predecessor left off.

Standards help people to learn a system. They are particularly helpful for DP staff moving from one job to another because they will have some familiarity with the format of documentation Standards. For example, if a computer operator moves from his job in A Ltd to a new job in the computer centre of B Ltd, he will be able to learn the ropes in his new job by referring to B Ltd's DP standards for computer operations. These Standards will be similar in format to the ones used in A Ltd, and so the operator will know how and where to look up procedures or information that he needs to know about.

(e) *An aid to system analysis and design work.*

Having Standards helps the systems analyst in his design work, so that:

(i) no aspect of system design is overlooked - ie. a check on completeness;

(ii) as an aid to thinking. Standards can help to steer a systems analyst's mind in the best direction when he is designing a system, eg. they can suggest controls to be built into the system.

(iii) the standard documentation also provides evidence that:

(1) systems development controls have been carried out; and
(2) the system incorporates sufficient procedural and processing controls.

A DP Standards manual

5.3 There should be a DP Standards manual in any organisation with its own DP department, and in software houses. Copies should be kept in every department that might need to use them. The contents and format of this manual might be as follows.

(a) *Introduction*

(i) Contents pages
(ii) A policy statement about the use of DP Standards within the organisation.

(b) *Management Standards*

(i) procedures for the approval of activities;

(1) approving the feasibility study;
(2) approving the system study and design;
(3) approving the system specification and program specifications;
(4) approving the purchasing of hardware (or software packages);
(5) amendments to a system or program;

(ii) procedures for the development of new systems: the role of the Steering Committee, the schedule of meetings, planning and the control of projects;

(iii) budgeting and costing procedures;

(iv) performance standards in computer operations;

(v) management reporting requirements.

(c) *Procedure Standards*

There should be standard procedures and methods of design, and so there will be:

(i) Systems analysis Standards, providing standards for system design, development, testing and implementation procedures, and for controls and security;

(ii) Programming Standards, providing standard methods of working, such as program structure, flowcharting, coding, testing and amendments;

(iii) Operating Standards, providing standard methods of work for the computer operators, such as:

    (1) handling each item of equipment;
    (2) recording breakdowns and what to do in the event of a breakdown;
    (3) filing and data security (eg. file library procedures and back-up files);
    (4) computer room security.

(d) *Documentation Standards*

There should be Standards for the way a system is documented, stating what information each item of documentation should contain and how the information should be recorded and presented in the documents. There should be standard documentation for:

(i) the systems specification;
(ii) program specification;
(iii) the user department's instruction manual;
(iv) the computer room operating manual.

(e) *Hardware*

There should be specifications for the CPU, peripheral equipment and all ancillary and auxilliary equipment.

Performance Standards

5.4 'Performance standards', as the name suggests, are documented standards of performance that ought to be achievable, against which actual standards can be compared for management control purposes.

They can be set for both equipment and staff, and they can be applied for:

(a) setting performance objectives for staff;
(b) controlling efficiency;
(c) controlling expenditure.

5.5 Examples of Performance Standards are:

(a) equipment

(i) time between breakdowns;
(ii) time taken to mend faults;
(iii) utilisation of available machine time.

(b) systems analysts and programmers

(i) pages of system specification produced per day;
(ii) number of lines of program coding written per day.

Systems Analysis Standards

5.6 Systems Analysis Standards provide guidelines for how a system should be designed, tested and implemented. You may be uncertain about what form these Standards might take.

There is a close connection between system design and system documentation, because the documents merely describe what has been designed, and so it might be helpful to look at two examples of design and documentation Standards:

(a)   standards for input;
(b)   Standards for output.

DP Standards for input

5.7 A systems analyst must specify his input design when he hands over to the programmers. A DP Standard for input would include the following standardised specifications:

(a)   an unambiguous *name* for the input record, and a name for the input file and the program or system;

(b)   a sample of the input documents, where the original input document must be translated into a computer input medium (tape, disk, punched card);

(c)   details of batching, for a batch processing system;

(d)   whether record lengths are fixed or variable;

(e)   whether the record format is always the same, or whether it is variable;

(f)   the record size (maximum);

(g)   the contents of each part or 'field' of a record, and the length of each field;

(h)   any value ranges for each field of data (eg. an item might be designed to have a code 1-4, and this must be specified);

(i)   any inter-relationships between fields;

(j)   a specification of the validation checks to be carried out by program;

(k)   the action to be taken by the computer when an error condition exists in an input record;

(l)   the manual procedure to be adopted for errors;

(m)   where the input data originates from.

DP Standards for output

5.8 In the program specification, a systems analyst must specify his output design for the programmers, as it is helpful to present this specification in a standarised format. The output medium might be hard copy (printer), visual display on a VDU screen, disk, magnetic tape or paper tape etc. It is convenient, perhaps, to concentrate here on hard copy output, but the same principles apply to all forms of output medium.

5.9   A DP Standard for output would include the following specifications:

(a)   a clear, unambiguous name for each output record, and a name for the output file and the program or computer system;

(b)   a sample of output layout;

(c)   a statement about whether the output should be on plain or pre-printed stationery;

(d)   areas on each sheet where printing may take place, and areas that must be left blank (eg. to allow for perforations or guillotining etc.)

(e)   for each output record;

(i)   the fields to be printed;
(ii)   whether each field is of fixed or variable length;
(iii) maximum length of each field (and the record);
(iv)   whether the record format is fixed or variable;
(v)   the format of each field (eg. all alphabetic, all numeric, mixed alpha-numeric etc.);
(vi)   the range of values permitted for each field (eg. A – Z excluding IOU; 001–999 (with non significant zeros), 1–999 etc);

(f)   the maximum permitted number of lines per report or per record (or permitted variations in the number of lines);

(g)   a sample of the print layout;

(h)   the work that the data processing department must do on the output (eg make a quick visual scan for obvious errors, despatch procedures etc.);

As with input specification, a DP Standard for output requires that the systems analyst should insert much of this information on to a standard record specification form.

Documentation Standards

5.10 Documentation is defined in the CIMA's *Computing Terminology* as 'a variety of technical and non-technical descriptions and diagrams relating to the use and operation of a computer system, such as User Manuals, Hardware and Operating Software Manuals, System Specifications and Program Documentation.'

5.11 DP Standards should ensure that all staff involved in the use of the computer system have proper instructions and that these have been fully documented.

This means that there must be:

(a)   operating instructions for each computer installation;

(b)   operating instructions for each program;

(c)   file library instructions, specifying how files should be labelled, safeguarded, issued, reconstructed (if necessary), etc;

(d)   data conversion instructions for the data preparation staff;

(e)   data control instructions for the control section;

(f)   user department instructions.

5.12 The main documents which ought to be prepared and standardised are:

(a)   the systems specification.

(b)   program specifications and other program documentation, which is 'the complete description of a program, usually including helpful notes, flowcharts, program listing*, test data and expected results'. (*ie the coded source program). (British Computer Society)

(c)   user manuals or user documentation;

(d)   operating software manuals. These are manuals that describe an operating system. If you have a microcomputer in your office, you will probably find an OS manual for MS-DOS or whatever OS the computer uses lying on a nearby shelf.

6.   CONCLUSION

6.1 Documentation Standards show:

(a)   what information about a computer system and its programs should be set out in writing; and
(b)   what form and format this information should take.

In other words, Documentation Standards provide a rigid guideline for documenting a system.

6.2 Data Processing Standards are established for procedures - ie how work should be done by DP staff, in designing, developing, testing and then operating and maintaining a DP system. Procedure Standards clarify what should be done and by whom, and limit the likelihood of errors.

TEST YOUR KNOWLEDGE

The numbers in brackets refer to paragraphs of this chapter

1 What are the purposes of a system specification? (2.3, 2.4)

2 What does a system specification contain? (2.5)

3 What is the purpose of a program specification? (3.1)

4 What does a program specification contain? (3.2)

5 What are the purposes of a user manual? (4.2)

6 What should a user manual contain? (4.5)

7 What are the purposes of DP Standards? (5.2)

8 Describe the contents and format of a typical DP Standards manual. (5.3)

9 What standardised specifications would normally be included in a DP Standard for input? (5.7)

10 What are the main documents that ought to be prepared in a standardised fashion? (5.12)

Now try question 24 at the end of this text

Chapter 19

SECURITY AND THE CONTROL ENVIRONMENT

<table>
<tr><td>

This chapter covers the following topics.

1. The need for security and controls
2. Evaluating system security
3. Staffing controls
4. Physical security
5. Back-up and standby facilities
6. Cost control
7. System development controls
8. The audit of computer systems
9. Small computer systems

</td></tr>
</table>

1. THE NEED FOR SECURITY AND CONTROLS

1.1 Security is 'the establishment and application of safeguards to protect data, software and computer hardware from accidental or malicious modification, destruction or disclosure.'

(British Computer Society)

1.2 The ICAEW's Information Technology Statement on Security and Confidentiality of Data (October 1985) summarises very well the need for security and confidentiality.

'Security of data requires procedures designed to ensure that computer facilities are available when required and that the integrity and confidentiality of stored data (including the requirements of the Data Protection Act 1984 as to personal data) can be maintained.'

1.3 Data is a valuable resource and must be kept secure.

(a) Organisations which lose computerised data, perhaps because of a hardware fault or a telecommunications fault, can suffer financial loss.

Computer users should do all they can to prevent the loss or corruption of data. The cost of repairing a hardware fault may be just a fraction of what it might cost to reinstate data that is lost because of a hardware fault or operator error.

The ICAEW's IT statement comments:

'Inaccurate, incomplete or false data may significantly affect turnover or profits, either directly (for example by making it impossible to keep track of outstanding debts) or indirectly (for example by requiring time to be devoted to recovering lost information rather than to the development of the business, or by causing management to make wrong decisions').

(b) Data about a company's operations which might be of interest to the company's competitors should not be allowed to fall into their hands. Confidential data which is being word-processed might be vulnerable to unauthorised access.

(c) There is a legal requirement in the UK to keep computerised *personal* data secure.

'Management will want to avoid the embarrassment, difficulties and damage to reputation that can occur if personal or other confidential data is lost or disclosed. In any event, the Data Protection Act 1984 incorporates a principle that computerised personal data be kept secure against accidental loss, destruction or inadvertent disclosure. While the Act only applies to personal data, it is probably not helpful for organisations to adopt differing standards for personal and other data, respectively, processed by the same systems.'

(d) If computerised data is not protected properly, there will be scope for computerised fraud.

Data controls

1.4 There is also a need for controls to ensure that data is:

(a) collected in full and with accuracy;
(b) generated at the appropriate times;
(c) kept up-to-date and accurate on file (ie there is a need for 'continuing data integrity');
(d) processed properly and accurately, to provide meaningful and useful output.

1.5 In other words, there is a need for controls over information so as to provide a good management information system. The ICAEW's IT Statement No 3 on Control and Management of Information (April 1987) comments:

'Information can only be reliable if the underlying data is also reliable. Reliable data can only be derived in the first instance from properly identified and responsible data providers. In order to remain reliable, such data must subsequently be processed and maintained in an adequately controlled environment.

Data processing, with a view to the production of useful management and accounting information, involves the implementation of controls over data collection and generation, continuing data integrity, access to data and the organisation of data on the computer files. Controls over producing, distributing and reporting information are also required.'

What can go wrong?

1.6 Errors might be accidental or deliberate. Data processing by computer creates extra problems for control because of its special characteristics, which are that:

(a) large volumes of data are concentrated into files that are physically very small - much smaller than a corresponding manual filing system would be to hold the same data;

(b) the processing capabilities of a computer are extensive, and enormous quantities of data are processed without human intervention, and so without humans knowing what is going on. This places great reliance on the accuracy of programs and of data on file;

(c) it is easy to lose data on file. Equipment can go wrong and malfunction, data files can become corrupt and store meaningless data, bits of information can get lost when files are copied, and data files are always susceptible to loss through theft, flood or fire in a way that manual files are not;

(d) unauthorised people can gain access to data on files, and read classified data or tamper with the data on file (eg. insert bogus data). This is a particular problem with on-line systems because access to a computer program and master file can be from any remote terminal. It is even possible for 'hackers' to use their home computers to gain access to the files and programs of other systems. A well-publicised problem in the past has been the ease with which some schoolboys in the USA have gained access to the Pentagon's top secret military data processing systems using their home computers;

(e) information on a computer file can be changed without leaving any physical trace of the change. In comparison, a change to a manual file would often involve leaving a trace - eg. crossing out data on a card file to insert new data etc.

1.7 It does not help matters that computers lack judgement, and errors in data processing by computer can go undetected when this would not be the case with manual data processing. For example, a payroll system might produce a salary cheque for an employee of £0.00 or for £1 million, and would not know that it had done something wrong. (This sort of problem can be overcome by building range checks/reasonableness checks into a program as a data validation routine.)

1.8 A further problem is that programmers are experts, and with careful planning, a dishonest programmer can tamper with a program to his own benefit. A case has been recorded, for example, of a programmer who arranged for all halfpennies in salaries to be paid into a bogus bank account which the programmer opened and from which he took the money. Several thousand halfpenny payments mounted up over time into substantial sums of money.

1.9 Accidental error can cause problems too. What is to stop a computer operator from using a file containing master file data as an output file in a different program? If this were done, the data on the master file would be wiped out. This is such an important source of potential error that controls to prevent this from happening should be built into any computer system.

1.10 Computer systems controls must be maintained regardless of the size of application or method of processing (batch or real time). If certain controls are difficult to establish in a microcomputer system (eg division of responsibilities), more emphasis has to be placed on other control areas (eg procedural and processing controls).

The risks to data

1.11 The risks to data are very well set out in the ICAEW's Information Technology Statement No 1, as follows:

'Errors

Human error
This is the risk with the highest incidence. Examples of human errors are entering incorrect transactions, failing to correct errors, using wrong data files during processing, and failing to carry out instructions in respect of security procedures.

Technical error
This is probably the second most common risk after human error. Technical error can involve malfunctioning of hardware, system software, application software or communications software. System software includes the operating system, file management software and database software. Hardware includes not only computers and disk drives but communication equipment, normal and emergency power supplies and air conditioning units.

Natural disasters
Fire, flooding, explosion, impact and lightning are examples of natural disasters, the possible consequences of which should be foreseen.

Deliberate actions
The scope for fraud needs particularly careful consideration if data is held on magnetic media, because such data is not immediately legible and it may therefore be difficult to obtain evidence of improper data amendment. Also, there is a wide variety of different methods by which such fraud can be committed.

Commercial espionage
When considering the value of data to competitors the organisation should consider how a particular item of data might complement other data which a competitor has obtained from publicly available sources.

Malicious damage
There are many cases of disaffected employees destroying data or software. Sabotage also falls under this heading.

Industrial action
The more concentrated the processing and storage of data the more vulnerable an organisation can be to industrial action.'

1.12 These risks are common to all data, in manual DP systems as well as computerised systems. With computers however, the risks are greater, because data is held on magnetic files, and cannot be seen or read by the human eye. It could easily go wrong, and no one would be able to spot the fault, except perhaps too late to correct it.

The dangers associated with information storage on a magnetic medium include:

(a) *Physical security*
Tapes or disks can be stolen or mislaid or damaged or destroyed by fire, flood or vandalism.

(b) *Environmental security*
Tapes and disks are susceptible to magnetic fields, dust and extremes of temperature and humidity. Although in modern mini- and microcomputer systems the problems of environment have been reduced, they are still quite important.

(c) *Loss of confidentiality*
Information stored in magnetic files may be accessed by unauthorised persons. This is a particular problem in larger systems with remote terminals, or in time sharing/computer bureau applications.

(d) *Processing the wrong file*
Since data is in magnetic form, and not visible, the wrong file could be read, or a file overwritten when its data is still needed.

(e) *Hardware or program corruption*
Hardware or software faults may damage or destroy the information on the files, as can updating a file with incomplete or inaccurate data.

1.13 Controls which can be implemented to counter the risks described above fall into two categories.

(a) *General controls* examined in this chapter, ensure that the computer *environment* is secure. They fall into two groups:

(i) administrative controls, which are designed to support the smooth continuing operation of systems; and

(ii) system development controls, which are designed to ensure that any new system does not present new risks to the environment.

(b) *Application controls*, examined in the next chapter, are *built in* to systems operations, and ensure that processed information is accurate, complete and valid.

19: SECURITY AND THE CONTROL ENVIRONMENT

2.   EVALUATING SYSTEM SECURITY

2.1 With so much more data being held in magnetic form, and much higher investment in IT, some organisations might embark on a security evaluation. This will identify:

(a) *threats* to an organisation's information systems ie potential dangers which, if realised, would destroy or alter the working of an information system;

(b) the *vulnerability* in an organisation's information system (ie its weak points).

These two issues combined can result in loss. (*Risk* is sometimes defined as a quantified assessment of *potential* loss). A further investigation may be made of *particular* information systems. For example, some information in some applications may be more 'sensitive' than others.

2.2 The importance of some attempt to quantify potential loss in financial terms is that this is a measure against which the cost of safeguards can be assessed.

2.3 V P Lane (in *Security of Computer Based Information Systems*) analyses four ways of coping with risks.

(a) Avoidance (eg modify a system so it is not vulnerable)
(b) Reduction (security measures reduce risk to an acceptable level).
(c) Nothing (as the risk is insignificant).
(d) Transfer (the financial consequences of the loss are transferred to an insurance company).

2.4 There are various ways of identifying and quantifying risks.

(a) *Courtney risk analysis* estimates the cost of the risk and its frequency, to come up with an 'annualised loss expectancy'.

(b) *Scenario analysis* is a technique whereby a number of possible loss-causing events are drawn up and circulated to the relevant functional managers who assess which are the most probable. Security measures are taken against any events which are thought likely to result in loss.

Developing a security policy

2.5 Information security is an important responsibility for all levels of management. A security *policy* is needed, not simply a collection of measures adopted ad hoc. Developing a security policy involves the following stages.

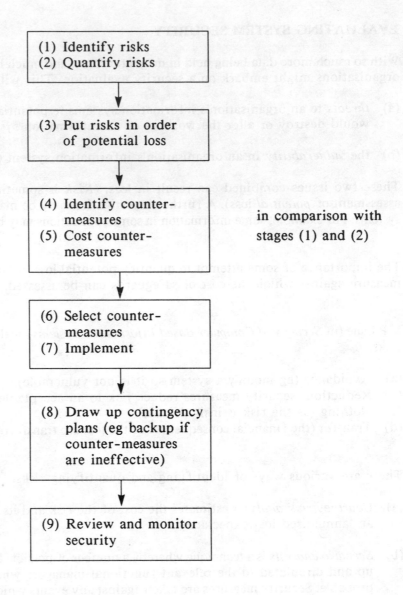

(1) Identify risks
(2) Quantify risks

(3) Put risks in order of potential loss

(4) Identify counter-measures
(5) Cost counter-measures

in comparison with stages (1) and (2)

(6) Select counter-measures
(7) Implement

(8) Draw up contingency plans (eg backup if counter-measures are ineffective)

(9) Review and monitor security

2.6 Security is the responsibility of all levels of management.

Organisation level	Responsibility	Examples
Top management	Organisational control environment	Initiate and approve contingency plan. Act on all incidents of known violation of management security policy (such as illegal and unethical transactions).
User management	Data integrity	Establish procedures (for example, segregation of duties or authorisation procedures). Strive to employ, train and develop competent and trustworthy personnel with clear lines of authority and responsibility
	Confidentiality and data integrity	Establish physical and access controls to assets and data. Establish and maintain check points and balances. Monitor compliance with controls through scheduled and unscheduled audits.
Data processing manager	Confidentiality, integrity and computer services	Ensure that hardware, software and computer operations meet security requirements
Personnel departments	Organisational control environment	Establish terms of employment and screening procedures consistent with company and department security aims

2.7 Controls cost money to develop and operate. Accuracy and security of data for example, are two aspects of control which should be improved by paying more to achieve them. In the design of a system, a balance must be struck between:

(a) the degree of control wanted; and

(b) the cost of achieving it.

2.8 When an organisation decides to buy a computer and an off-the-shelf application package, or if it decides to develop a tailor-made system, it is important to look at the controls that are wanted.

(a) If a software package is bought off-the-shelf, management must find out what controls the package offers.

(b) If an item of hardware is bought, management must check its reliability against breakdown or malfunction, and what provisions have to be made for maintenance and repair.

(c) If an organisation develops its own system 'in-house', or has a system tailor-made for it by a software house, its management will have to specify the controls that the system should contain.

Administrative controls

2.9 Some controls can be applied at relatively small cost, simply by introducing sensible administrative and organisational measures to reduce the risks to data, software or hardware. In the rest of this chapter, we shall look at what these administrative controls might be.

2.10 Administrative controls are controls over data and data security that are achieved by administrative measures. They should be applied:

(a) in the DP department, where an organisation is large enough to have one; and
(b) in the computer user's offices. With microcomputer systems, the computer user's administrative controls will include controls over handling the computer hardware, software and files.

2.11 They should include:

(a) controls over the selection of personnel and division of responsibility;
(b) physical security;
(c) back-up and standby facilities.
(d) cost control.

3. STAFFING CONTROLS

The selection of personnel

3.1 DP staff should be recruited with care. They should be honest and should have the qualities and/or experience to do their job well;

Sound personnel policies should be applied by both DP departments and user departments.

'Ultimately, security depends on people and sound personnel policies are implicit in data security. For example, references should always be taken up in connection with people recruited to handle and process sensitive data. Termination procedures, restricting their access to sensitive data, are required for employees about to leave an organisation; procedures are also required to identify disgruntled employees who are capable of disrupting computer systems. Management should also consider the possible effects of industrial action directed at computer processing and determine their attitude and reaction towards such events in the context of their commercial and personnel policies.' (ICAEW IT Statement No 1)

Division of responsibilities (segregation of duties)

3.2 Organisation controls are the controls that arise from having an organised structure of jobs in the DP department - ie. that work is divided between systems analysts, programmers and operating staff, and that operations jobs are divided between data control, data preparation and computer room operations etc. The functions of an organisation structure, as far as control is concerned, are:

(a) to assign the responsibility for certain tasks to specific jobs and individuals. A person in a given job has the responsibility for ensuring that certain controls are applied. Some jobs are specifically control jobs. These are the jobs of the data control clerks and, to a large extent, of the file librarian;

(b) to prevent deliberate error. It is easier for a person to commit fraud if he can input data, write programs and operate the computer all by himself. By dividing up the DP work, it is more difficult to commit fraud or tamper with data, except in collusion with others.

3.3 Organisation controls can be applied by creating a division of duties into at least three parts, between:

(a) data capture and the authorisation of data processing work. This will usually be the responsibility of staff in the 'user' department, and not a DP department job at all;

(b) computer operations work;

(c) systems analysis and programming work.

3.4 In other words:

(a) staff who are responsible for data capture and data entry should not be allowed to do any computer operations work or systems analysis and programming work;

(b) staff who are responsible for computer operations should not be allowed to do any data capture or systems analysis and programming work; and

(c) staff who are responsible for systems analysis and programming should not be allowed to do any data capture or computer operations work.

In addition, within the computer operations section, the computer operators should ideally not be given responsibilities for data control, nor should they be given responsibility for looking after the computer file library.

3.5 The most important points of control in a DP department and computer centre are:

(a) access to source documents should be restricted to data preparation and control staff;

(b) access to the computer should be restricted to operating staff;

(c) access to master files should be restricted to the librarian (or control clerk);

(d) computer operators and programmers must *not* originate live entries (eg amend input data if there are errors on the source document);

(e) control staff in a computer centre should have no other DP duties.

3.6 Achieving these organisational controls will be helped by drawing up an organisation chart and procedure manuals for the DP department, which set out clearly who does what, and what practices are forbidden. It is then the task of the DP manager to ensure that these procedures are obeyed.

3.7 Obviously, in the case of *microcomputer operations* these organisational controls do not apply. The same person who operates the computer also inputs data, and may even write his or her own programs for it. In these cases, however, it is still essential that the data being processed is not such as to have a bearing on the assets of the business. For example, if a microcomputer were to be used for a sales ledger system or payroll system, it is desirable that the person responsible for data input and operating the microcomputer should neither design the system nor write its programs, and there must also be suitable internal (and external) audit checks of the system.

3.8 DP staff should be properly trained in security and control measures and the need for them.

3.9 *Organisational controls in the user departments.* The ICAEW's Information Technology statement on security of data suggests that there are three types of management responsibility for the security of data, below top management level, in every organisation that uses computers. The three types of responsibility might all be held by a single manager, or responsibilities might be divided between different managers. The three types of responsibility are:

(a) *for data security management* - ie setting up and monitoring data security procedures which all departments will be expected to follow - eg locks on rooms or keyboards, password procedures, fire safety measures, security codes for access to buildings etc.

(b) *for the data itself.*

'Shared use of computing resources erodes physical security and, given the limitations of many operating systems, may provide easy opportunities for users to have access to data which management did not intend to be available to them. It is therefore necessary to identify some individual or department with primary responsibility for the security of each element of shared data.

Each element of data should therefore have a defined owner ....'

The responsibilities of a data owner include:

(i) keeping the data accurate and up-to-date;
(ii) deciding who should have access to the data;
(iii) developing security procedures in conjunction with the data security manager.

(c) *for using the data operationally* in such a way that the requirements for data security are met. This is a responsibility of all line managers who use computerised data in any way.

3.10 Another important control measure, with microcomputer systems in particular, should be the appointment of a system 'expert' in the office. This is a person who should be made responsible for learning as much technical detail about the office computer system as he or she can, so that the problems of other users of the system can first of all be referred to these office experts.

3.11 As an example of the value of having an office expert, a company using a number of stand-alone microcomputers had just installed a new micro with a hard disk. The operator, not being used to the new equipment, tried to copy the contents of the hard disk (which included the operating system) on to a back-up blank disk. Instead, he copied the blank disk on to the disk with all the data. Recovery procedures were possible, but if the company had relied on the hardware supplier to do the file restoration work, the new micro might have been out of action for three days or more, the time it would have taken the supplier to respond to the call for help and send assistance. Instead, the company's expert on the system was called in, and the file restoration accomplished within one or two hours. (Note: data does not disappear when a file is first deleted. Instead, the attributes of the file change so that it is possible to write over the data that is still on it. You 'loosen the chains that hold the file together'. This means that it is possible to change the file back to its original form and reinstate the data on the disk. However, the restoration work must be done properly and carefully - otherwise the data might really get lost.)

3.12 *Legal requirements*. In the UK, when a computer system holds 'personal data' it must officially register details of the data. This is a requirement of the *Data Protection Act*. There should be a person within the organisation who has the responsibility for:

(a) finding out what personal data is held on the organisation's computer system;
(b) ensuring that these details are registered with the office of the Data Protection Registrar;
(c) ensuring that the data that is held is kept accurate.

Any changes to the organisation's computer systems may result in a requirement to make a new registration under the Act.

4. PHYSICAL SECURITY

Physical security in the user's office

4.1 Guidelines for data security which should be applied within the office are as follows.

(a) Computer rooms should be locked when not in use. Only authorised personnel should have a key to get in.

(b) Fireproof cabinets should be used to store files, or lockable metal boxes for floppy disks. If files contain confidential data, they should be kept in a safe. Computer rooms should be equipped with fire alarms, fire extinguishers and sprinkler systems.

(c) Access to the data should be made difficult (ideally, impossible) for an unauthorised user. Programs which make use of passwords should be used. Computers with lockable keyboards are sometimes used. Computer terminals should be sited carefully, to minimise the risk of unauthorised use.

(d) The password systems should not be operated in a lax way. Passwords can be next to useless if the system is abused. Employees can be encouraged to change passwords every so often and never to 'lend' them to a colleague.

(e) Disks should not be left lying around an office. They can get lost or stolen. More likely still, they can get damaged, by spilling tea or coffee over them, or allowing the disks to gather dust, which can make them unreadable.

(f) The computer's environment (humidity, temperature, dust) should be properly controlled. This is not so important with microcomputer systems as for mainframes, and Winchester disks are protected from dust. Even so, the computer's environment, and the environment of the files, should not be excessively hot. Temperature changes *can* cause disk failure, even with micros.

(g)   If computer printout is likely to include confidential data, it should be shredded before it is eventually thrown away after use.

4.2   *Maintenance.* All computers are covered by some kind of warranty from the manufacturer when they are bought new. Warranty periods range in length, typically up to one year.

4.3   But what should the computer user do after the warranty period has expired?

(a)   The user can decide to do nothing until the computer has a breakdown or other fault, and then ask a third-party computer repair company to come in and do the repair work. The drawbacks to this approach are that:

(i)   repair companies give priority treatment to contract customers. The waiting time (or 'call-out' time) for a non-contract customer might be very long.

(ii)   One-off repair charges will be very high.

(b)   Instead, the user can arrange a maintenance contract with the manufacturer or a third-party repair company. The cost of these contracts will be quite high (perhaps 10% - 20% of the hardware cost per annum) and cost varies on the agreed call-out time.

(c)   A third option is breakdown insurance, which provides insurance cover against breakdown and certain consequential losses. Insurance provides cover against expense, but the computer user is left with the operational problem of how to get the repair work done within a reasonable time - eg with a short call-out time and the provision of a replacement machine while the repair is being carried out, which is what maintenance contracts can provide.

4.4   *Diagnostics.* Computers are supplied with a diagnostic disk, which can be used to check for certain hardware faults, such as a faulty microchip or a faulty disk drive. These faults can then be detected before any data is corrupted or lost. Instructions on how to carry out a diagnostic check using the diagnostic disk will be included in the user's manual.

4.5   *Telephone support.* Not all the data handling problems of a computer user are attributable to hardware or program faults. Quite often, the computer user comes across a problem that he or she doesn't know how to deal with. A telephone support service might be provided by the software or hardware supplier to help in these circumstances. If the computer user has trouble understanding the documentation, and so doesn't know what to do with a problem, he or she can call a support services 'hotline' for help and advice from an expert. Support systems are commonly run by software companies, but some hardware manufacturers provide a similar service.

Telephone support might also be provided to user departments by an *information centre* within the organisation.

Stand-by hardware facilities

4.6   Hardware duplication will permit a system to function in case of breakdown.

The provision of back-up computers tends to be quite costly, particularly where these systems have no other function. Many organisations will use several smaller computer systems and find that a significant level of protection against system faults can be provided by shifting operations to one of the systems still functioning. Where an organisation has only a single system to rely upon this ready recourse to a backup facility is unavailable. In these instances one response would be to negotiate a maintenance contract which provides for backup facilities. Alternatively, many computer bureaux will also provide access for backup activities though this facility will usually be rather expensive.

5.   BACK-UP AND STANDBY FACILITIES

5.1   A major aspect of system security is to provide the required services continuously without a break or deterioration in performance.

For many applications this will require that some amount of duplication in the system be tolerated or even encouraged. For example, data may be made more secure by using backup files to archive data. It would then be fairly easy to recover from data loss or system fault.

5.2   Administrative controls ought to be introduced to:

(a)   enable file data to be recreated when a file is lost or corrupted; and
(b)   provide stand-by hardware facilities whenever a hardware item breaks down.

Re-creating file data when a file is lost or corrupted

5.3   One of the worst things that could happen in data processing by computer is the loss of all the data on a master file or the loss of a program. Files can be physically lost eg. the librarian might misplace a file, or a file may be stolen, but it is also possible for a file to become corrupted when it is written and so include false data. A file might also be physically damaged and become unreadable.

5.4   An important set of procedural controls is therefore to enable a data or program file to be recreated if the original is lost or corrupted.

5.5   To recreate a master file, it is possible to go back to earlier generations of the master file and transactions files, do the data processing all over again and create a new version of the up-to-date master file.

Grandfather-father-son security concept with tape files

5.6   The reconstruction of *magnetic tape* files is by use of the grandfather, father, son technique of keeping as many generations of historical master files, transaction files and reference files as is considered necessary for the security of both the files and the data contained on them. It is common to keep three generations (grandfather, father and son) of master files, and sufficient transaction files to re-create the father from the grandfather master file. If the 'son' tape out of run number $(x + 1)$ is found to contain corrupted data, a corrected master file can be recreated by going back to the generation 2 master file (the 'father') and the associated transaction file, and carrying out run number $(x + 1)$ again.

Dumping disk files

5.7 Disk files are usually overwritten during updating, and so the grandfather, father, son technique cannot be applied. Instead, a copy of the disk file is periodically 'dumped' on to a backup file (usually a tape streamer or a VCR - ie video cassette recorder tape) for backing up hard disk files, and a floppy disk for back-up copies of floppy disk files and all input transaction data after the dump is kept, thereby allowing for file reconstruction if necessary.

5.8 A typical procedure (say in a microcomputer system) might be:

   (a) update master file (on floppy disk);
   (b) copy master file (at end of day's processing);
   (c) copy master file (at end of week) and move to another location.

The steps (a) and (b) are carried out on a daily basis, while (c) can be weekly (or daily). Transaction data may have to be prepared again, or stored on file for a week (the file being moved to the other location). This should given the capability of reconstructing the files in case of disaster.

5.9 Creating back-up files is now a regular routine with microcomputer systems in many offices. The computer's operating system will have a backup command for creating back-up files, and the computer operator will use this.

'The importance of backing up or making duplicate copies of data files cannot be over-emphasised - one day your computer will go wrong and you may lose all your data. The processes involved in backing up can be very tedious and often occur at the end of a busy day, so once a procedure is set up the supervisor should ensure that it is properly maintained.'

(R Piper: Micro Decision October 1986)

5.10 It might not be necessary to back up every disk which holds transaction data, or even some standing data. For example, word processing data is not necessarily of such importance as to warrant back-up copies. However:

   (a) all program disks should have a back-up copy. Some program disks which are bought from software manufacturers are copy-protected and cannot be backed up, but in these cases, the manufacturer is normally willing to provide a back-up copy as part of the sales package to the customer;

   (b) all master files should be backed up.

5.11 Backing up data on floppy disks can be done on a microcomputer with twin floppy disk drives by inserting the file-to-be-copied into one disk drive and a blank disk into the other, and using a DISKCOPY or COPY command to copy the data on to the blank disk.

5.12 Backing up a hard disk on to floppy disks can be more tedious, because a hard disk holds much more data than a floppy disk. Backing up a hard disk on to a tape is quicker and more convenient, although the user has to go to the expense of buying a tape streamer unit. Backing up from hard disk on to tape cartridges or VCR recorders is now quite common.

5.13 Back-up copies should be stored off-site, especially at weekends, and certainly at least in a different place from the original file.

The file librarian and the data control clerks

5.14 The functions of the *file librarian* and *data control clerks* should strengthen administrative controls in mainframe installations.

(a) The *librarian* has the task of looking after the computer files, and making sure that:

   (i) the files are kept physically secure, protected from damage, theft and unauthorised access;

   (ii) the files don't get lost, and are always traceable;

   (iii) external file labels are maintained and a log is kept of what data is on each physical file;

   (iv) files are not purged until it is safe to remove the data and use the disk or tape for another use;

   (v) the correct version of a file is used for processing;

   (vi) back-up copies of files are made whenever required;

   (vii) files are issued to authorised personnel only.

(b) The *data control clerks* have the task, as their job title suggests, of helping to control the data that is input to and output from processing. The control section might:

   (i) receive batched input documents from a user department. It would then check that the number and identity of the batches received tallies with the batch control document that the user department will have submitted. Lost batches of data would be immediately identified;

   (ii) schedule the input data for processing, and the files and programs needed to do the processing – eg to specify the correct version of the program to be used;

   (iii) to monitor rejected data items (eg exception reports from a data validation program) and where necessary, see to the immediate correction and re-submission of these items;

   (iv) to receive output from the computer, and check that it appears to be correct – eg to make sure that every batch has been processed;

   (v) to distribute the output to the user department, and liaise with it on all problems.

Exercise

You are the manager of a medium-sized accounts department which uses several micros, all linked to the company's minicomputer. You are drawing up a document detailing the security measures which are the responsibility of your department. Under what headings might you consider how best to protect data?

Solution

You might address departmental security by reviewing the following areas.

(a) Personnel.
(b) Organisational controls.
(c) Physical security.
(d) Back-up procedures.
(e) Maintenance.
(f) Helplines/support.
(g) Legal requirements (eg Data Protection Act).
(h) Viruses.

---

6. COST CONTROL

6.1 In an earlier chapter we distinguished between the different types of cost that are incurred in acquiring, developing and operating a computer system. These fell into three headings:

(a) 'one-off' capital costs (eg equipment);
(b) 'one-off' revenue costs (eg changeover);
(c) recurring operating costs (eg salaries).

6.2 Cost control of computer systems involves three issues.

(a) Control over hardware and software purchases by end-user departments (eg microcomputers, spreadsheet packages) to ensure:

(i) company hardware and software standards are maintained;
(ii) the expense is justified.

(b) Control over the costs of the computer department itself.

(c) Ensuring an efficient use of computer time by allocating computer departments costs to users.

6.3 Control over equipment and software purchases by end-user departments can be achieved by including microcomputer purchases in the organisation's normal procedures for authorising capital expenditure.

6.4 Charging out the cost of the computer department can be done

   (a) by allocating total computer department costs to user departments on an arbitrary basis (eg number of terminals);

   (b) by recording the computer time spent by each user department and charging the cost on that basis;

   (c) by charging each service separately so that for example, a programmer's time is charged on an hourly basis;

   (d) by establishing the computer department as a profit centre in its own right;

   (e) by establishing priorities for different applications and allocating computer time accordingly, using perhaps a transfer price mechanism.

6.5 Some costs may be difficult to allocate to user departments (eg indirect costs).

7. SYSTEM DEVELOPMENT CONTROLS

7.1 When a computer system is developed from scratch, either by an in-house DP department or by a software house, there should be controls over the system design, development and testing. Because of the time spent on systems development, the cost of it, and the probable complexity and volume of detail involved, it is essential to lay down high standards of control.

The main objectives of systems development controls are as follows.

   (a) To ensure that new computer systems are developed only if they appear to be beneficial. System justification should be on the grounds of favourable cost-benefit analysis or other performance criteria.

   (b) To ensure that each system under development has clear, specified objectives.

   (c) To control the scheduling of development work.

   (d) To ensure that suitable operational and administrative controls are built into the system design when it is being developed.

   (e) To ensure that users acquire an understanding of the new system.

   (f) To ensure that the system is properly tested, and provides a suitable degree of control and also achieves its objectives.

   (g) To establish a basis for management review of the system.

   (h) To ensure that systems and programs are maintained when the system goes operational.

   (i) To ensure that proper and complete documentation of the system is created and maintained.

Many of these controls will be provided by the methodology adopted.

7.2 Many system development controls have been referred to in earlier chapters. One of the important controls is that senior management on the steering committee or board of directors, and managers in the user department, are given the opportunity at several stages in the development work to satisfy themselves that the project is developing as required. There are several formal reporting stages which may be laid down in the *systems development methodology* adopted.

Controls of costs, progress and system design amendments

7.3 Costs, progress and planning amendments must be reviewed at each phase of the development to ensure tight control.

7.4 *Control of costs* can be achieved in three ways, all of which should be used.

(a) Control over system development costs, using budgets and budgetary control variance reporting. If actual development costs exceed the budget, the manager responsible for the over-spending will be required to take control action, or justify the higher spending to his superiors.

(b) Monitoring changes in the expected future costs and benefits of the system. Costs already incurred in development work to date should be ignored, and the future development costs, expected system running costs and expected benefits should be the factors which determine whether it is worthwhile continuing with the system development.

(c) The post-implementation review of a project should study the actual development costs, system running costs and system benefits, to determine:

   (i) whether the system is currently justifiable, or should be abandoned even at this late stage;

   (ii) whether the original decision to develop the system was a good one, with the benefit of hindsight;

   (iii) by how much actual costs and benefits differed from expectation, the reasons for these differences, and whether there are any lessons to be learned for the future.

7.5 *Control over progress* can be achieved through techniques such as critical path analysis, which was described in an earlier chapter.

7.6 *Control over amendments to the system design*. Once a system development has started, it is all too easy for the systems analysts or user department managers to think of new features to add to the system, or 'improvements' that can be made, with the result that amendments get written into the system as the design work progresses. Some amendments might be desirable; others might not be worthwhile.

Controls should be exercised over amendments, so that if any amendments are proposed which are not included in the system specification, they must be authorised at a suitable managerial level (eg by the steering committee) and the authorisation and details of the amendment should be included in the amendments section of the system specification.

Designing the system: the systems analyst and system controls

7.7 The adequacy of operational controls in the system will depend on the ability of the systems analyst to write suitable controls into the system when he or she is designing it. The systems analyst should build controls into the system, based on the following guidelines:

(a) All data due for processing should in fact be processed. There ought to be both administrative controls and program controls to monitor the completeness of data.

(b) Circumstances which may give rise to the possibility of error should be avoided. Whenever possible, error situations should be designed out of the system.

(c) Errors which do occur should be detected, located and corrected as soon as possible, eg with data validation checks on input data. The sooner the error is located the easier it is to correct, and the longer it remains undetected the more complicated are the subsequent amendment procedures.

(d) Controls must be simple and, whenever possible, should not interrupt the flow of data through the system. The ideal control fits smoothly into the system and becomes an integral part of it.

(e) Controls must not be excessively costly to apply. A reasonable level of control must be set as any attempt to ensure 100% accuracy would be uneconomical.

(f) The controls should be part of a general strategy, over the whole area of data processing activity, to prevent and detect fraud. A systems analyst should consult with the company's auditors when the system is being designed, not after all the work has been done.

Testing

7.8 Program testing, systems testing and the user department's acceptance tests are all important ingredients in development controls, to ensure that the programs are free of bugs, and that the system appears to work and meet its objectives.

Controls over file conversion

7.9 The conversion of master files is one of the big problems of systems implementation and proper procedures and controls must be laid down to ensure that there are no unauthorised conversions and that the correct records are accurately and completely transferred on to the magnetic files. The procedures may include:

(a) full planning of the file conversion, eg staff to be used; records to be converted (possibly via data preparation forms); controls to be set up; date of conversion etc;

(b) a control group may be established to follow up errors which may occur during the conversion;

(c) master files should be printed out after conversion and manually checked back to the original records (or data preparation forms);

(d) accounting records should be reconciled (eg control accounts) to those kept under the old system;

(e)   responsibilities should be divided between the conversion staff (additional staff may have to be brought in to help with the conversion);

(f)   the new master files must be tested using the pre-prepared test data and any changes necessary fully controlled and documented.

System handover: training of users

7.10 The handover of the computer system from the DP software and hardware experts to the computer user's non-technical staff must be done in such a way that the computer users are able to learn as much about their system as they need to know. Training of the user's staff will be necessary, but there should also be full, clear and non-technical documentation of the system - for off-the-shelf packages as well as for tailor-made software - in a *user's manual*.

Problems can occur - eg a program refusing to open a file or a file containing incorrect data, because of an operational error by a poorly-trained user.

Procedures for amending programs: modifications and enhancements after implementation

7.11 Procedures for controlling changes to programs are important because modifications or enhancements to programs that are already operational create opportunities for new errors in the program, or even introducing an element of fraud.

(a)   Program changes must be authorised by the user department, in writing, and at the appropriate management level.

(b)   The extent of the changes required should be assessed by a systems analyst, and the amendment specified in sufficient detail to enable a programmer to make the change.

(c)   The amendment should be written by a programmer, who ought to refer to the existing documentation on the program and the original source program. Having re-written the program, he or she should the test the new version. The amendments should be documented.

(d)   The systems analyst should carry out any further tests that seem necessary before authorising the implementation of the new program version for 'live' processing. The new program authorisation must be documented and sent to the file librarian, who will be responsible for ensuring that in future, the new version of the program is used for processing work. The librarian, remember, looks after the program files.

(e)   The new program version should be monitored carefully when it 'goes live', in case any new errors appear in the program.

8.   THE AUDIT OF COMPUTER SYSTEMS

8.1 Any computer system which processes financial records for a company must be audited. The obvious problem with auditing a computer system is that processing operations cannot be seen, and the results of processing might be stored on a magnetic disk.

Audit trails

8.2 One way of allowing a computer system to be audited is to provide an audit trail. An audit trail is defined by the British Computer Society as 'a record of the file updating that takes place during a specific transaction. It enables a trace to be kept of all operations on files.'

8.3 Whereas an audit package is some external software which can be used to help with computer auditing, an audit trail is inbuilt in to the system itself.

8.4 The original concept of a management or audit trail was to print out data at all stages of processing so that a manager or auditor could follow transactions stage-by-stage through a system to ensure that they had been processed correctly. Modern computer methods have now cut out much of this laborious, time-consuming stage-by-stage working but there should still be some means of identifying individual file records and the input and output documents associated with the processing of any individual transaction.

8.5 A management trail should be provided so that every transaction on a file contains a unique reference back to the original source of the input (eg a sales system transaction record should hold a reference to the customer order, delivery note and invoice). Where master file records are updated several times, or from several sources, the provision of a satisfactory management and audit trail is more difficult but some attempt should nevertheless be made to provide one.

8.6 Common methods of identifying the source of input are:

(a) for transaction records:

   (i)   document serial number;
   (ii) date of transaction;
   (iii) batch number;
   (iv) microfilm number;

(b) for master file records:

   (i) date and run number of last transaction which affected the record;
   (ii) reference to when the master file record was last printed.

8.7 Computer-originated documents may be used to generate new transactions (eg OCR turn-round documents). An audit trail should then enable the new transaction to be referred, if required, back to the computer system/run which created the source record.

Systems checks and controls

8.8 The auditors of a computer system should have confidence in the controls within the system itself, and should not have to rely entirely on audit trails and hard copy historical records. The system controls will include:

(a)   controls over input to ensure that all source documents are correctly completed and are transmitted to the computer department; that all source documents are received by the computer department and are correctly converted into the computer input media; that all the data on the input medium is transmitted accurately to the computer centre and accepted by the computer;

(b)   controls over hardware, including proper maintenance, environmental control and hardware control checks (eg parity checks, overflow checks, validity checks, terminal readiness checks, data transmission checks etc);

(c)   controls over files, to ensure that only the right files are used in processing and are then correctly used in processing (eg maintenance of library logs and internal and external labels; use of write permit rings or file masks; dumping and reconstruction procedures);

(d)   software (program) controls. To ensure that only valid data is processed, all new input will undergo validation tests.

Round the computer vs through the computer audits

8.9   Traditionally, the ways in which an auditor could approach the systems audit of a computer based system fell into the two categories:

(a)   a 'round the computer' approach;
(b)   a 'through the computer' approach.

8.10   Some years ago, it was widely considered that an accountant could discharge his duties as an internal auditor in a company with computer based systems without having any detailed knowledge of computers. The auditor would audit 'round the computer' by ignoring the procedures which take place within the computer programs and concentrating solely on the input and corresponding output. Audit procedures would include checking authorisation, coding and control totals of input and checking the output with source documents and clerical control tests.

8.11   This view is now frowned upon and it is recognised that one of the principal problems facing the internal auditor is that of acquiring an understanding of the workings of the DP department and of the computer itself. It is now customary for auditors to audit *through the computer*. This involves an examination of the detailed processing routines of the computer to determine whether the controls in the system are adequate to ensure complete and correct processing of all data. With the advent of 'embedded audit facilities' we are increasingly seeing the introduction of auditing from 'within the computer'.

8.12   One of the major reasons why the 'round the computer' audit approach is no longer considered adequate is that as the complexity of computer systems has increased there has been a corresponding loss of audit trail. One way the auditor can try to overcome the difficulties of lost audit trails is by employing computer aided audit techniques (CAATs).

Types of CAAT

8.13   Some special computer-aided audit techniques might be used (eg auditing test packs, and computer audit programs to read files, extract defined information and carry out audit work on the controls). There are two principal categories of CAAT, *test data* and *audit software*.

8.14 Audit test data consists of data prepared by the auditor for processing by the computer system. It may be processed during a normal processing run ('live' test data) or during a special run at a point in time outside the normal cycle ('dead' test data).

8.15 The use of test data provides 'compliance comfort' to the auditor in respect of a period of time only if he obtains reasonable assurance that the programs processing his test data were used throughout the period under review. To allow a continuous review of data and the manner in which it is treated by the system, it may be possible to use CAATs referred to as *embedded audit facilities*. An embedded facility consists of program coding or additional data provided by the auditor and incorporated into the computer system itself. Two examples are:

(a) Integrated test facility (ITF); and
(b) Systems control and review file (SCARF).

Audit packages

8.16 Computerised auditing packages are used by auditors to help them with auditing a computer system. They provide two functions:

(a) they generate test data sets which may then be processed by the client's system to evaluate its effectiveness and internal controls, and

(b) they may be used to aid the testing of a client's records as part of the general review of the client's performance and accounting operations.

8.17 Standard software packages are available to help auditors with the audit of a computer system – ie the master files, transaction files and processing routines. Features of these packages include:

(a) reformatting of a master file to allow the auditor *to interrogate the file with his own programs;*

(b) computational checks on interest, discounts, extensions, totals etc;

(c) the verification of file controls;

(d) the verification of individual balances on records;

(e) the extraction of random samples of items for checks;

(f) the facility to print out any data from a master file in any format the auditor requires;

(g) the extraction of records from file which contain a specified field with a value above or below a certain value.

8.18 The organisation's personnel should be isolated from the auditing tests undertaken. Computer crimes are most often committed by the data processing personnel so any intensive review of their work practices or the systems they control will first need to remove them from any position which could alter the normal working of the system. If the system has been subverted the auditor has a duty to catch it in the act if possible.

8.19 Computerised auditing packages which generate rest data sets may be used to check that a system is processing transactions correctly. For example, in the audit package for an accounts system, it would be possible to determine how various test data transactions should show up in the accounts; if some error occurred in processing them, further investigation would be necessary.

8.20 Errors could have two sources: an inadvertent error in the design or implementation of the system, or a purposeful malfunction intended to defraud the organisation. System bugs identified by the auditors should be brought to the attention of the client so that they may be corrected. Fraudulent processing operations will also need to be pursued with a particular view to establishing the extent of the operation and responsibility.

8.21 The use of auditing packages also provides the auditor with a variety of computerised tools which may be used not only for evaluating the computer system and its operations but may also be extended to the auditing of other organisational functions. These programs perform generalised audit tests and may be widely used among a variety of clients.

8.22 Audit packages are being increasingly used by external auditors, and also some internal auditors, and should improve the efficiency of the computer audit.

9. SMALL COMPUTER SYSTEMS

9.1 Control is difficult in small computer systems, largely because:

(a) there are few users, so duties cannot be segregated;

(b) there is unlikely to be any specialist technical expertise easily available;

(c) controls may appear to be too costly in comparison with their potential benefits;

(d) weak self-discipline, (eg to apply backup procedures), particularly with personal computer usage of an 'ad hoc' nature, may mean that the security and integrity of data are jeopardised.

9.2 The ICAEW's Information Technology Statement 5 identifies seven aspects of control, and makes a number of recommendations to remedy deficiencies in each.

(a) *Completeness and accuracy of data.* Controls will include regular checks on standing data, edit checks, maintenance of control totals, review by users of the reasonableness of computer generated results and so forth.

(b) *File storage and backup.* Controls can include backing up files on a daily basis, storing of disks in fireproof cabinets etc.

(c) *Documentation of procedures.* This will assist in the training of new staff, or might allow others to take over if the principal user of an application falls sick or leaves.

(d) *Security of computers, data and files.* Physical security can be maintained by using machine locks, or clear labelling of disks to avoid accidental deletion of important program or data files.

(e) *Maintenance*. A maintenance contract may be a prerequisite for obtaining adequate insurance cover.

(f) *Insurance* cover should include replacement of equipment, costs of any recovery operation, reinstatement of data, and, if possible, loss of profits during the recovery period.

(g) *Contingency plans for alternative processing*, in the event of disasters, should feature written procedures for 'disaster recovery', manual processing during the recovery period, and details of where alternative equipment can be obtained.

10. CONCLUSION

10.1 When a computer system is bought or designed, management must decide what controls for the system are needed. When a system is being written 'in-house' or is being tailor-made for the user by a software house, the user should specify the controls that are wanted. When a software package is being bought off-the-shelf, the user should check to see what controls the package contains, and whether they are good enough.

10.2 The need for controls cannot be emphasised enough, and the choice or design of controls is an important part of the procedures in developing or buying a computer system.

TEST YOUR KNOWLEDGE
The numbers in brackets refer to paragraphs of this chapter

1   What is security? (1.1)

2   List some risks to data. (1.11)

3   What are the security problems related to magnetic storage? (1.12)

4   How would you develop a security policy? (2.5)

5   What type of administrative controls should there be? (2.11)

6   Define audit trail. (8.2)

Now try question 25 at the end of the text

Chapter 20

APPLICATION CONTROLS

This chapter covers the following topics.

1. Controls over data processing
2. Input controls
3. Processing controls
4. Output controls
5. Hardware controls over data and files
6. File access and security issues

---

1. CONTROLS OVER DATA PROCESSING

1.1 Application controls can be built into all three stages of data processing: input, processing and output. These are considered in more detail below. Application controls also function in two other areas where physical security (as discussed in the last chapter) is equally important: protection of data files and restrictions on file access.

1.2 Errors may occur at various stages of data processing.

(a) *Errors in recording data (ie errors in 'data capture')*. Mistakes can be made for example by:

   (i) writing an incorrect figure, such as £1243 instead of £1234 etc; swapping figures around by mistake is referred to as a transposition error;

   (ii) spelling mistakes, such as getting a customer's name wrong;

   (iii) measuring mistakes, such as a timekeeper writing down an incorrect time for a job because he read his watch incorrectly;

   (iv) classifying mistakes, such as a cost accountant recording a direct labour cost as an overhead item, or an expenditure in administration as a production cost etc.

(b) *Errors in transcribing data* or preparing data for further processing;

   (i) transcribing errors occur when data is copied from one form to another. For example, a person might jot down some data on a piece of scrap paper, and then copy it incorrectly on to a formal document later on;

(ii)   data preparation errors are associated with computer data processing, when the original captured data has to be transcribed into a form that the computer can read, ie, into a 'machine-sensible' form such as a magnetic tape or magnetic disk. Errors arise because the original data can be copied wrongly on to the machine-sensible form of data for input to the computer. These errors are sometimes referred to as *data conversion errors*, because they are made by DP staff in the data conversion centre (data preparation centre).

(c)   *Errors in transmitting data.* These involve the loss or corruption of data which is sent to the computer, by post, courier, telecommunications link from a remote terminal etc.

(d)   *Errors during processing.* Errors might occur during data processing, for three broad reasons:

(i)   It becomes apparent during processing, when it would not necessarily have been apparent at the data capture stage, that there is something wrong with the transaction data. An attempt should be made to locate these errors as soon as possible, to prevent the computer from acting on invalid data, and for this reason a *data validation* (or data vet) program is used to 'screen' or vet the input data for errors that can be spotted by computer logic.

(ii)   It becomes apparent during processing that there is something wrong with the master file data, or that it is impossible to match a transaction record properly with a master file record. Examples would be:

(1)   trying to record an invoice sent to customer number 2345, when no such customer account has been opened yet in the sales ledger;

(2)   trying to delete employee number 678 from the payroll, only to find that there is no such employee in the payroll records anyway;

(3)   trying to open a new account for supplier 1234 when there is already a supplier 1234 in the purchase ledger.

In computer processing, these are referred to as 'updating errors' because they come to light when the master file is updated. However, the same sort of errors can occur in manual data processing.

(iii)   There is a programming error - ie a flaw in the logic of the computer program.

1.3   Since errors occur, steps should be taken to identify them and correct them. It is usually preferable to try to identify errors as they occur, rather than to leave dealing with them until later on in processing because processing incorrect data would be time-consuming and wasteful, and it might also result in a knock-on effect whereby other errors are caused by the original error.

1.4   Since errors should be identified as soon as they *do* occur, there should be checks for errors at each stage where errors *can* occur.

2. INPUT CONTROLS

Controls over data capture

2.1 Errors in data capture are difficult to spot once they have been made, because they are often errors on the 'source' document. They can be reduced by double-checking. One person's work might provide a cross-check on the accuracy of another's. For example, errors in recording suppliers' invoices in the purchase day book could be double-checked by getting another person to add up the total amount of invoices received that day, from the invoices themselves. This total could then be checked against the total of invoices for the day recorded in the purchase book. This sort of double-check is called an 'internal check'.

2.2 Another way of dealing with the error problem in data capture is to reduce the likelihood of errors arising in the first place, by including as much pre-printed information on the data recording document as possible, and by giving clear instructions about how data documents should be filled in.

The use of *turnround documents* and OCR, MICR, bar coding, or in some applications, plastic cards with magnetic strips containing some of the input data etc, could be used to reduce the need for manually-prepared input data, and so limit the frequency of data capture errors.

Controls over transcribing data and data conversion

2.3 If input data must be prepared manually, controls can be applied to minimise the number of errors.

(a) Staff who prepare data for input should be well-trained and properly supervised.

(b) Data input documents should be designed in a format to help the person preparing the data to fill them in properly.

(c) When data is input by keyboard, the screen should be formatted so as to help the keyboard operator to input the correct data. User-friendly software packages might provide on-screen prompts and formatted screens for input data, or make good use of icons and the screen cursor.

2.4 If data must be converted from one form to another for input (eg. from a paper document on to disk) double-keying of input to check for copying errors can be done. This checking process is *data verification*, which was described in an earlier chapter.

The staff who prepare the data should be encouraged to look for errors.

(a) If input is done by keyboard, the input data will be shown on the VDU screen, and a visual check on the data can be made.

The input record will often have a key field identification code. For example a sales ledger file will consist of customer records, with each customer having a code number for identification. When a transaction record is keyed in, the customer code would be a part of the input data and the program might search for the customer record on the sales ledger file, and display it on the VDU screen. The input operator can then check visually that the correct customer record is being processed.

(b) If input is done in batches, the program might produce a listing of the input data which can be checked for accuracy. For example, day book listings can be produced for checking from the input data in a sales ledger or purchase ledger system.

Printed listings of input data provide an *audit trail* in computerised accounting systems.

Controls over transmission of data

2.5 When data is input from a terminal, the terminal user should be able to check that the data has been input fully and accurately by:

(a) a visual check of the input data on the user's VDU screen; and

(b) if required, a printed listing of the input. The facility to print out a list of all the accepted data items might be a feature of the system, so that the computer user can check 'manually' that the data has been put on to file correctly.

2.6 When input data is batched and physically despatched to a computer centre for batch processing, batch control checks can be applied to ensure that all the data that has been despatched is safely received at the computer centre. These checks involve:

(a) the user department giving each batch a unique identification number;

(b) the identification numbers of the batches being written on to a batch control document, by the user department supervisor. This document will be sent to the computer centre, with a copy being retained by the user;

(c) the data control clerks in the computer centre checking that the batches that are received tally with the batch numbers on the batch control document.

Validation checks

2.7 Some checks on the validity of input data can be written into the system's programs. These checks can identify those errors in input data:

(a) which can be detected by the logic of a computer program; and
(b) provided, of course, that the check has been written into the program in the first place.

2.8 The main type of checks on the validity of input data are *data validation* checks. These might be performed by a separate data validation program in a batch processing system; alternatively, any program can incorporate validation checks on input data - eg on data keyed in from a terminal into an on-line system.

Data validation program (data vet)

2.9 The data validation program, or a program which incorporates data validation routines, will be the first program in each batch processing application. The program attempts to find errors in the input record or batch, to prevent them being processed any further. Errors may be:

(a) mistakes on the source document, ie errors of data capture;
(b) data preparation errors which somehow 'escape' the verification check.

2.10 The checks which can be made by the data validation program are logical checks which prevent some of the worst types of error from getting through to be processed. The program does not provide a comprehensive error check, however, and some of the errors on the source documents are likely to be undetected. This again emphasises the degree of control that should be placed on source document creation.

2.11 The main types of data validation check are outlined below. You need to know what they are and when each type of check would be suitable. Note that the same type of check can be made on different fields of a record, and that not all types of check need appear in a data validation program. However, a single program might carry out dozens of various validation checks on different records and record fields.

Obviously each application will have validation checks which are relevant to its particular processing requirements. This will include some of the following.

(a) *Range checks*: these are designed to ensure that the data in a certain record field lies within predetermined limits. For example in a wages application, the program may contain instructions to reject any clock card with 'hours worked' outside the range 10-80 hours, and to print out a special report (for checking) for any clock card with hours worked outside the range 35-60.

(b) *Limit checks*: sometimes called credibility or reasonableness checks, are very similar to range checks, but check that data is not *below* a certain value, or *above* a certain value. In the previous example, the check on 'hours worked' might be that the value in the record field should not exceed 80 (or, in other words, is in the range 0-80). With a range check, there is an upper and lower bound, whereas with a limit check, there is either an upper or lower bound, but not both.

(c) *Existence checks*: these are checks on record fields to ensure that the data is valid for that field. For example:

(i) check that the record type is 1, 2 or 3;
(ii) check that the stock code exists by looking up the stock code number of the record against a reference file (in these cases the name of the stock item can be added to the record by copying it from the reference file).

(d) *Format checks* (picture checks): the record is checked to ensure that it has the required data fields and each data field is checked to ensure that the format (and size) of the data in it is correct; eg:

(i) check that the format is all numeric   NNNN   (here, four figures)
(ii) check that the format is all alphabetic   AAAAA (here, five letters)
(iii) check that the format is alphanumeric   ANNN   (here, one letter followed by three figures)

(e) *Consistency checks*: checking that data in one field is consistent with data in another field. For example, in a payroll system, there might be a check that if the employee is a Grade C worker, he or she must belong to Department 5,6 or 9.

(f) *Sequence checks*: checking that records and batches are processed in the correct sequence.

(g) *Completeness checks*:

    (i) a check can be made to ensure that all records have been processed. For example, if a weekly processing run must include one record for each of the 5 working days of the week, a completeness check can ensure that there are 5 input records, one for each day;

    (ii) completeness checks on individual fields would be checks that an item of data has not been omitted from an input record.

(h) *Check digits:* these are numbers (or perhaps letters) added to the end of a code to give it some special mathematical property, and so can be checked by the computer.

(i) *Batch total checks:* in a batch processing system, the number (and/or value, and/or hash totals) of the records processed by the computer from each batch, including rejected records, should reconcile with the control totals in the batch control slip record, which will also have been input as a data record to the program.

2.12 When a validation check identifies an error, there are a number of possible outcomes.

(a) The record concerned will probably be rejected and processed no further with perhaps a message (Error) on screen. *Rejection reports* may be printed out at some stage during processing.

(b) The record concerned may not be rejected, but an *exception report* might still be output or the operator advised in some way on screen. This may happen, for example, where a range or limit check is not satisfied. Just because a record is not within pre-set limits does not automatically mean that it is incorrect. If it is valid, then not processing it would be a waste of time. However, administrative controls must ensure that all exception reports are followed through and checked.

(c) If there is an error revealed by the batch controls, the whole batch must be rejected for checking.

2.13 A data validation program is specified and designed by a systems analyst. The validity checks that are made on input data must therefore be specified, and you must not make the assumption that it is 'obvious' what these checks will be.

The types of checks that can be made on a field of data within a record have been listed, but it will be helpful to look at an example in some detail.

Exercise

The stock file of a department store is updated weekly with data about sales of each stock item during the week. The information contained in the transaction file records includes the following:

(a) Batch header slip records   Example

    (i)   batch number   B37
    (ii)   number of records in batch   30
    (iii)   value of records in batch   63575
    (iv)   hash total of number of items sold   04128

(b) Records:

    (i)   batch number   B37
    (ii)   stock item number   34828
    (iii)   week number   25
    (iv)   number of items sold   0326
    (v)   value of items sold   01633.26
    (vi)   number of items returned   015
    (vii) value of items returned   075.15
    (viii) location of stock in store in the week   A15

Suggest what data validation checks might be carried out on the transaction records.

Solution

(a) Batch header slip record:

    (i)   confirm that the number of records in the batch (which have been input to the data validation program and counted by the program) is the same as the number on the batch header slip record, and that they have the total sales value and hash total value as shown on the batch header slip;

    (ii)   check that the fields in the batch header slip have the correct format, ie:
       - batch number   ANN
       - number of records   NN
       - value of records   NNNNN
       - hash total   NNNNN

       (Note A = alphabetic letter N = number)

(b) Transaction records:

    (i)   batch number. Check the format which should be ANN;

    (ii)   stock item number. It is assumed here that a check digit is the final digit, and so a check digit check should be made to test the validity of the code number. It might also be necessary to carry out a completeness check, to ensure that the code is a five-digit figure (and not, say, just 4 digits) - ie NNNNN.

       If stock codes are within a certain range - eg. 20000 - 60000, a range check can be applied to the code numbers, eg. so that 81116 would be rejected as non-existent.

    (iii)   week number. Range check to test that it is in the range 01-52;

    (iv)   number of items sold. Must be a 4 digit figure. Format check that it is NNNN;

(v)   value of items sold. Must be in the format NNNNN.NN. In practice, the decimal point is likely to be ignored, but it is shown here.

(vi)   number of items returned. Format check NNN;

(vii)   value of items returned. Format check NNN.NN;

(viii)   location. Format check ANN.

Effectiveness of controls over input data

2.14 The effectiveness of controls over input is not always as great as a computer user might like. Five typical checks on input to a purchase ledger system are evaluated in the table below.

Table: effectiveness of input controls
Purchase ledger system

	Control	Effectiveness
1	Input transaction displayed on VDU screen with keyboard input, for a visual check by the input clerk.	Depends on how good the input clerk is is at his or her job. The risk of keying-in errors will be high. Also a possibility of a deliberate keying-in error by a dishonest clerk.
2	Check digit in the supplier account code number.	This reduces the risk of error in the input of the account code number. But it is a check on just one field of data, and so is limited in the number of errors it can find.
3	Batching records with a batch header control slip.	Batching is a time-consuming operation, but it should identify the loss of data, or the failure to input data records.
4	Display of supplier account details on screen when the account code is keyed in.	This should prevent errors where the wrong supplier account is updated. However, the error depends on the input clerk checking the screen and looking at the account details displayed. Experience shows that clerks will often not bother to do this when they have a lot of input records to key in.
5	Double keying-in of all input transactions by different staff.	Should identify most keying-in errors, and also prevent dishonesty or fraud by an input clerk. However, double keying-in takes twice the effort and cost of once-only keying-in.

2.15 With batch processing systems, controls over the completeness and accuracy of input data can be more extensive than with on-line input systems for transaction processing.

Batch processing	*Transaction processing*
1 Can sometimes use turnround documents (OCR, OMR etc)	1 Only verification-type check on input is a visual check of the data on VDU screen, prior to pressing the key to input the data.
2 Data verification on input is possible - ie input data can be checked for keying in errors by keying in a second time	2 Data validation checks will be used in the program
3 Data validation checks will be used in the program	
4 Data validation *control checks* can be applied to data in each batch, as described earlier.	

3. PROCESSING CONTROLS

File controls

3.1 Controls can be applied to ensure that:

(a) the correct data files are used for processing;
(b) data on a file, or entire files, are not lost or corrupted;
(c) if data is lost or corrupted, then it can be re-created;
(d) unauthorised access to data on file is prevented.

In a large computer centre, the administrative responsibility for the physical security of files belongs to the file librarian. With smaller computer systems, such as office microcomputers, responsibility for the correct labelling of disks and their physical security should be assigned to a member of staff.

Software controls over files

3.2 A number of controls can be written into program software. These include:

(a) file identification checks;
(b) checkpoints and recovery provisions;
(c) control totals.

File identification checks

3.3 The computer will check that the correct file has been loaded for processing before it will begin its processing operations. It can do this by checking the 'file header' data written on the file in magnetic form, and comparing this data with data about the file that it has been instructed to process. In other words, if the computer has been instructed to process master file A, it will first of all check that master file A has indeed been loaded for processing, and that it is the correct generation of the file.

3.4 A computer file has 2 labels:

(a) a label recorded in magnetic form, to identify the data on the file, eg file C2100 may identify the data as a stock master file (file 100) in the stock control system (C2);

(b) an external label, with an entirely different numbering system, which is physically written on the file so that it can be identified by humans.

3.5 The file librarian may, for example, arrange that a file with external label 123456 should be used as a master file in the stock control system, created in run number 234. The magnetic data might record the file as C2100 from run 234 with a retention period until run 238. The computer will check that file C2100 from run 234 has been loaded for processing according to specification, and if it has not been loaded, it will report the error and will not process the file.

3.6 Eventually, after run 238 has been completed some time later, the librarian should then be able to decide that the old master file from run 234 can be released and the file 123456 can now be used for other processing (eg as a transactions file in the payroll system).

The magnetic data label of the file will change to identify the new data contained on the file, but the external label will be unchanged as 123456.

Checkpoints and recovery procedures

3.7 A *checkpoint or restart program* is a utility (service program) that intervenes at intervals (checkpoints) during the running of an application program, and dumps the entire contents of the main storage on to a backing file.

Should anything turn out to be 'wrong' with the running of the application program, the checkpoint/restart program can be used to get the application program back to a checkpoint/restart position before the error occurred, and restart the application program with conditions exactly as they were before - eg copying back the contents of the main memory from the dump file.

3.8 Checkpoint/restart procedures are feasible with real-time systems and other on-line systems, and the operating system must decide which message during the course of processing at that time can be completed, and which messages need to be re-transmitted for reprocessing from the terminals.

4. OUTPUT CONTROLS

4.1 There should be controls over output from computer processing.

(a) In a batch processing system, where data is batched and sent off to a computer centre, there should be a check to make sure that the batches that were sent off have been processed and returned.

(b) All input records that have been rejected by data validation checks and master file update checks must be looked at to find out the cause of the error. Corrected data should then be prepared for re-input. Some errors might need immediate correction, such as input records which have been rejected by data validation checks in a payroll program for preparing the monthly salary payments to staff.

(c) Output should be correctly distributed, and a log kept of the distributions that have been made. In a computer centre, this is the responsibility of the data control staff. In an office, someone has to be responsible for dealing with output from the printer - eg management reports.

Output on to magnetic files should be properly labelled and stored, as mentioned earlier.

Control totals

4.2 A control total is 'the sum resulting from the addition of a specified field from each of a group of records, used for checking purposes'.

For example, a control total could be:

(a) the number of records on a file;

(b) the total of the values of a particular field in all the records on a file - eg the total of debts outstanding in all the customer records on a sales ledger file;

(c) the number of records in a batch (batch control total).

4.3 A hash total is a control total that has no meaning, except as a control check; for example, the total of supplier code numbers on a purchase ledger file.

4.4 Control total reconciliation checks are therefore written into programs to ensure that:

(a) no records have been lost;
(b) no records have been duplicated;
(c) input files have been read fully;
(d) all output records have been written to the output files.

5. HARDWARE CONTROLS OVER DATA AND FILES

5.1 In spite of the improved reliability of computer hardware, computer hardware can break down or malfunction, or it might be used incorrectly. Controls can be established to:

(a) identify such errors when they occur, and either prevent them from happening or report them when they do happen;

(b) do something to ensure the continuity of data processing when there is a hardware fault.

5.2 Examples of hardware controls to prevent or report errors are as follows.

(a) *Parity checks.* Parity checks are checks on the transfer of data from one hardware device to another, or from one storage location to another. Each byte of data has a parity bit added to it, set at 0 or 1 so that the number of 1 bits in the byte is an even number (or an odd number, depending on the machine). Whenever data is transferred every byte is automatically checked for even (or odd) parity, so that hardware faults in transmitting data incorrectly in a corrupt form are likely to be identified.

(b) The use of *write permit rings* with magnetic tape files. These are devices (plastic rings) that must be physically attached to a tape reel before its contents can be altered. When tapes are stored in the computer file library, all write permit rings should be removed.

(c) The use of a *file mask* for direct access storage devices. The file mask can be set to prevent either:

(i) all seek instructions (preventing unwanted head movement when a file is being written sequentially); or

(ii) all write instructions. This is similar to a write permit ring on a tape file.

(d) *Device interlocks* which prevent input or output of data, once begun, from being interrupted or terminated. This helps to prevent the corruption of data by either a hardware or an operator error.

(e) *Overflow checks.* These are checks on overflow areas on direct access files.

(f) *Printer timing checks.*

(g) *Terminal readiness checks.*

As the detecting circuits themselves might fail, some checks (eg (f) and (g)) cannot be completely relied on.

5.3 There should be regular maintenance checks on hardware by qualified computer engineers, to prevent hardware faults from happening. Preventative maintenance on computers, just like preventative maintenance on cars with routine service checks, reduces the likelihood of breakdown, and also data transfer faults will be less likely to occur.

6. FILE ACCESS AND SECURITY ISSUES

6.1 There are three aspects to maintaining an organisation's data security. Data, remember, needs to be protected from:

(a) theft;
(b) unauthorised use or modification; and
(c) loss or degradation due to technical or human fault.

6.2 Data may be protected from two of these, theft and unauthorised use through many of the same mechanisms. There is restriction of (a) physical access to the computer hardware and (b) restriction of access from hardware to computer files.

6.3 It is advisable to employ several levels of protection in guarding data, this is based on the recognition that no one method is likely to be completely effective in excluding unauthorised users. The objectives would be to introduce so many obstacles that few people would have either the skills, luck or patience to break through. The primary mechanisms used to exclude unauthorised users emphasise excluding them from access to the system or its data.

6.4 The most effective means for isolating a system and its data is to *physically* exclude everyone not authorised to use the system.

This may be accomplished by locking the terminals and microcomputers away and rigorously controlling keys and who has them; additionally, locks or combinations should be changed from time to time to ensure that the usefulness of duplicates or knowledge of combinations is minimised.

6.5 Data which is critical should be controlled at all times. Records would need to be kept of who accesses the data, when and for what purposes. This level of data control is quite stringent and is generally appropriate for only the most sensitive data. As data decreases in importance the degree of control can be reduced.

The most common level of control over access to files is to simply limit access to specific individuals through a password system.

Access controls

6.6 Access controls are controls designed to prevent, or limit the likelihood, of unauthorised access to data files or programs. Access controls which can be built into a system's software are:

(a) passwords;
(b) personal identification of the user;
(c) encryption and authentication.

Passwords

6.7 Passwords are 'a set of characters which may be allocated to a person, a terminal or a facility which are required to be keyed into the system before further access is permitted.'

(CIMA Computing Terminology)

6.8 Passwords can be applied to data files, program files and to *parts* of a program. The British Computer Society's definition of a password is 'a sequence of characters which must be presented to a computer system before it will allow access to the system or parts of that system (eg a particular file)'

(a) One password (or lockword) may be required to read a file, another to write new data, and a third if both operations are to be permitted.

(b) The terminal user can be restricted to the use of certain files and programs (eg in a banking system, low grades of staff are only allowed to access certain routine programs. Another reported example (Accountancy Age, September 1986) is the computer system of British Alcan, in which the access of site accountants to the computer database is restricted, whereas the head office accountant is allowed greater access and the ability to carry out different processing operations - eg change an accounting policy for the preparation of the group's consolidated accounts.

6.9 The restriction of access to a system with passwords is effective and widely used but the widespread and growing use of microcomputers and distributed systems is making physical isolation virtually impossible.

The wider use of information systems requires that access to the system becomes equally widespread and easy. Requirements for system security must be balanced by the operational requirements for access: a rigidly enforced isolation of the system may significantly reduce the value of the system.

6.10 Virtually all mainframe or distributed processing systems use passwords. In order to access a system the user needs first to enter a string of characters as a 'password'. If the entered password matches one issued to an authorised user the system permits access, otherwise the system shuts down and may record the attempted unauthorised access. Keeping track of these attempts can alert managers to repeated efforts to break into the system, in these cases the culprits might be caught - particularly if there is an apparent pattern to their efforts.

6.11 Many password systems come with standard passwords as part of the system, it is essential for these to be removed if the system is to be at all secure. This is particularly important to guard against external penetration of the security system since such common passwords may become widely known to people in the industry.

6.12 Passwords ought to be effective in keeping out unauthorised users, but they are by no means foolproof. Experience has shown that unauthorised access can be obtained.

(a) By experimenting with possible passwords, an unauthorised person can gain access to a program or file by guessing the correct password. This is not as difficult as it may seem when too many computer users specify 'obvious' passwords for their files or programs.

(b) Someone who is authorised to access a data or program file may tell an unauthorised person what the password is, perhaps through carelessness.

6.13 The main drawback to using password systems is that they rely upon users to use them conscientiously.

Passwords need to be random since the easily-remembered passwords are also highly predictable. Thus, anyone who knows the authorised users well can often guess their passwords. In many cases this is not necessary since users can be extremely sloppy with their security control. Passwords are often left in plain view or 'hidden' beneath keyboards or inside desk drawers where virtually anyone could readily find them. A password system requires both a software system and strong organisational policies if it is to be effective.

Identification of the user: PINs

6.14 In some systems, the user might have a special *personal identification number*, or PIN, which identifies him or her to the system. According to what the user's PIN is, the user will be allowed access to certain data and parts of the system, but forbidden access to other parts.

6.15 An example of authorisation systems with PINs is cash cards for bank or building society cash dispensers. The cash dispenser checks the PIN code on the magnetic strip of the cash card against the code number keyed in by the cardholder, and the two codes must match before the cardholder is allowed to withdraw any cash.

6.16 Other systems can incorporate a PIN system, requiring authorised users to 'log on' by identifying themselves personally before being allowed access to programs or files.

Data transmission (telecommunications) controls: encryption and authentication

6.17 When data is transmitted over a telecommunications link or network, there are three security dangers:

   (a)   a hardware fault;
   (b)   unauthorised access by an eavesdropper;
   (c)   direct intervention by someone who sends false messages down a line, claiming to be someone else – so that the recipient of the message will think that it has come from an authorised source.

6.18 *Encryption* is the only secure way to prevent eavesdropping (since eavesdroppers can get round password controls, by tapping the line or by experimenting with various likely passwords). Encryption involves scrambling the data at one end of the line, transmitting the scrambled data, and unscrambling it at the receiver's end of the line.

6.19 *Authentication* is a technique of making sure that a message has come from an authorised sender. Authentication involves adding an extra field to a record, with the contents of this field derived from the remainder of the record by applying an algorithm that has previously been agreed between the senders and recipients of data.

Hacking

6.20 A hacker is a person who attempts to invade the privacy of a network. Hackers are normally skilled programmers, and have been known to crack system passwords with consummate ease. The *Observer* (19/3/89) reported that hackers can set their machines to try a new word, taken from the electronic version of the Oxford English dictionary, every three seconds until the code is cracked. The fact that billions of bits of information can be transmitted in bulk over the public telephone network has made it hard to trace individual hackers, who can therefore make repeated attempts to invade systems.

6.21 In the past hackers' main interest has been to copy information, but a recent trend has been their desire to corrupt it.

Viruses

6.22 Computer viruses are currently the cause of much concern. A *virus* is a piece of software which infects programs and data and which replicates itself. There are a number of elements of design which may encourage the presence of a virus, including the trojan, the worm, the trapdoor, the logic bomb and the time bomb.

6.23 The features of these are described below.

(a) A *trojan* is a program that while visibly performing one function secretly carries out another. For example, a program could be running a computer game, while simultaneously destroying a data file or another program. A trojan's work is immediate, and obvious. They are easy to avoid as they do not copy themselves onto the target disk.

(b) Whereas a trojan attacks from without, a *worm*, which is a type of virus, attacks from within. A worm is a program that survives by copying and replicating itself inside the computer system it has entered, without necessarily altering that system. When the host program is run, the virus attaches itself to another program, so that if undetected every program in the system will be infected.

(c) A *trap door* is an undocumented entry-point into a computer system. It is not to be found in design specifications but may be put in by software developers to enable them to bypass access controls while working on a new piece of software. Because it is not documented, it may be forgotten and used at a later date.

(d) A *logic bomb* is a piece of code triggered by certain events. A program will behave normally until a certain event occurs, for example disk utilisation reaches a certain percentage. A logic bomb, by responding to set conditions, maximises damage. For example it will be triggered when a disk is nearly full, or when a large number of users are using the system.

(e) A *time bomb* is similar to a logic bomb, except that it is triggered at a certain date. Companies have experienced virus attacks on April Fool's Day and on Friday 13th. These were released by time bombs.

6.24 Viruses can spread via data disk, but have been known to copy themselves over whole networks. 'When transmitted over a network into a clean system, it [the virus] continues to reproduce thus infecting that system. On being triggered by a pre-set date and time it explodes into action'.

(Guardian, 9.2.1989).

6.25 What type of protection can be had against viruses?

(a) Vaccine programs exist which can deal with some of the more widespread varieties, but if the virus lives in the bootstrap program, the virus can work before the vaccine is loaded.

(b) Organisations must guard against the introduction of unauthorised software to their systems. Many viruses and trojans have been spread on pirated versions of computer games.

(c) Organisations as a matter of routine should ensure that any disk received from outside is virus-free before the data on the disk is downloaded.

(d) Any flaws in a widely used program should be rectified as soon as they come to light.

(e) There should be a clear demarcation between *data storage* (on disk) and *program storage*. 'If programs are only allowed to update data-type files and not program-type files then viruses cannot replicate themselves. Operating systems that segregate programs from data and store them in libraries are inherently more resistant to viruses...'

(Management Accounting, July 1989)

(f) In short virus protection controls should become part of the internal control system of an organisation, as is the case with controls to prevent fraud.

6.26 The Computer Misuse Act 1990 makes hacking and the introduction of viruses criminal offences.

6.27 There are three offences identified by the Act.

(a) A person is guilty of an offence under Section 1 if he causes any computer to perform any function with intent to secure access to any program or data held in a computer, the access he intends to secure is unauthorised and he knows that this is the case.

(b) A person is guilty of an offence under Section 2 if he secures unauthorised access with intent to commit an offence.

(c) A person is guilty of an offence under Section 3 if he causes any unauthorised modification of data held by a computer.

6.28 The maximum penalties for persons found guilty of each of these offences are:

(a) for a Section 1 offence a fine of up to £2,000 and/or imprisonment for up to 6 months; and
(b) for a Section 2 or 3 offence imprisonment for up to 5 years and/or an unlimited fine.

7. CONCLUSION

7.1 Application controls are controls within the computer system to ensure that the transactions processed by the system result in information that is accurate, complete and valid.

TEST YOUR KNOWLEDGE
The numbers in brackets refer to paragraphs of this chapter

1 Where might errors occur during data processing? (1.2)

2 List as many data validation checks as you can. (2.11)

3 What are passwords? (6.7)

4 How might you deal with a virus? (6.25)

Now try question 26 at the end of the text

GLOSSARY

This glossary includes terms widely used in the information systems environment. It is not intended to be exhaustive. For definitions of other terms, you should refer to coverage in the main body of the text.

Access Process of retrieving *data* from *files*. May be *direct*, *random*, *sequential*, *indexed sequential* or *serial*.

Acoustic coupler Device which, in conjunction with a telephone handset, allows *data* to be transmitted over the telephone network.

AI Artificial intelligence. Discipline concerned with using computers to perform operations which require intelligence when carried out by humans, eg learning and decision making.

ALU Arithmetic and Logic Unit. That part of the *CPU* that performs functions on *input*.

Analogue computer A computer that operates on continuous physical variables. Used mainly in scientific and industrial applications. (Compare *digital computer*.)

Analogue signal A signal that varies smoothly and continuously in amplitude and time. (Compare *digital signal*.)

Application software Programs written for a specific application within an organisation eg a payroll system.

ASCII American Standard Code for Information Interchange. Standard *character* encoding scheme which can be recognised by different computer systems.

Assembler Program that translates programs written in *assembly language* into *machine code*.

Assembly language Language enabling a program in *machine code* to be readable by humans; symbols are used to represent elements of the machine code.

Asynchronous data transmission Transmission of *data* in a continuous stream, each operation ending with a signal to indicate that it is complete (compare *synchronous data transmission*)

BASIC Beginners All-purpose Symbolic Instruction Code. *High-level* programming language which is used in non-specialist applications.

Batch A group of related items *input* to a computer over a period of time and not requiring immediate processing. Batch processing involves the processing of one or more batches of transactions at a later time.

Baud rate Speed of data transmission. Measured in baud, usually equal to *bits* per second.

Bit BInary digiT. Either of the digits 0 and 1. The bit is the smallest unit of *information* in any computer system. Eight bits form a *byte*.

Byte	An eight-*bit* binary *character*.
C	Programming language developed for use with *Unix*. Combines features of *high-level* and *low-level* languages and is particularly popular with professional programmers.
Cache	Additional *memory* which may be inserted between the *CPU* and the memory proper. Cache memory facilitates access to the main memory.
CAD	Computer Aided Design. Use of computer technology to assist in the design of a product, particularly in engineering and architecture.
CDROM	Compact Disk Read Only Memory.
Character	The smallest working unit of *information* in most computer applications.
COBOL	COmmon Business Oriented Language. *High-level* programming language used in business applications.
COM	Computer Output on Microform. *Output* transferred directly to microfilm or microfiche, usually for archive purposes.
Compiler	Program that translates *high-level* language program (*source code*) into *object code* (normally *machine code*), prior to execution of that program. (Compare *interpreter*.)
CPU	Central Processor Unit. The main operating unit of a computer. It consists of the *ALU*, the *CU* and some *memory*.
CU	Control Unit. That part of the *CPU* that controls the movement of *information* between the *ALU* and the *memory*.
Data	Raw material which is input to a process to produce *information*.
Digital computer	A computer that operates on discrete quantities, usually represented by the use of two separate electrical states. (Compare *analogue computer*.)
Digital signal	A signal whose voltage at any particular time is at one of two discrete levels (eg on/off, true/false). (Compare *analogue signal*.)
Direct access	Access to *storage* such that each item of *data* is read or retrieved in a constant time irrespective of the location in store of the previous item accessed.
DOS	Disk Operating System. Type of *operating system*.
DTP	Desktop Publishing.
Duplex	Simultaneous two-way transmission of data (also referred to as full duplex)

GLOSSARY

EPOS
Electronic Point-Of-Sale. Describes system in which point-of-sale terminals provide *input* to a computer.

EPROM
Erasable Programmable Read-Only Memory. *PROM* which can be reprogrammed by the user.

Field
A group of *characters* which together represent a single *data* item, eg employee name or book value of asset. A group of related fields forms a *record*.

File
A collection of related records. (See also *transaction file*, *master file* and *reference file*)

FORTRAN
FORmula TRANslation. *High-level* programming language used in scientific and mathematical applications.

Fourth generation language
Term used to denote software which performs basic procedural coding, assisting programmers' work

Half-duplex
System of data transmission in either direction but not simultaneously.

High-level language
Problem oriented programming language employing English-like command structure. Examples include *ALGOL*, *BASIC* and *COBOL*.

Hit rate
Proportion of *records* on a *file* that are updated or retrieved during a given process (eg a *batch* run).

Indexed sequential access
Means of *direct access* to *storage* in which address of a *record* is identified by reference to an index of key fields. *Sequential* processing of such records is possible.

Information
Output from a system which has been processed to give it meaning. (Compare *data*.)

Input
The entry of *data* into a computer for processing.

Input device
Unit which accepts *input* for processing by a computer, eg keyboard, bar code reader or *VDU*.

Interface
1. The point at which two pieces of *application software* are linked in a computer system (eg where sales ledger information is read by the nominal ledger and used to update the latter.)

2. The circuitry which connects the *CPU* to its peripherals. (See also *parallel interface* and *serial interface*.)

Interpreter
Software which translates a program in a *high-level language* into *machine code* one line at a time during execution of that program. (Compare *compilor*.)

Kb	Kilobyte. Strictly 1024 (2^{10}) *bytes*, but widely used to denote 1,000 bytes.
Key field	A *field* in a *record* which is used to locate or identify that record, eg customer account codes in a sales ledger *master file*.
LAN	Local Area Network. Network of linked computers in a single geographical location (ie one site or building). (Compare *WAN*.)
Low-level language	Programming language structured to match the operation of a computer, eg *assembly language* or *machine code*. (Compare *high-level language*.)
Master file	Current file showing cumulative position and kept up to date by processing against it all transactions relevant to that file (eg payroll master file or sales ledger master file.)
Machine code	Code made up of binary *characters* forming instructions on which a particular computer operates.
Mb	Megabyte. Strictly 1048576 bytes (2^{20}), but widely used to denote one million bytes.
Memory	*Storage* instantly available to the computer without the need for retrieval. (Also referred to as main memory.)
MICR	Magnetic Ink Character Recognition. The use of characters printed with magnetic ink permitting them to be read directly by an appropriate *input device*
MIS	Management Information System.
Modem	MOdulator-DEModulator. Device used to convert *digital signals* as used by a computer to *analogue signals* for transmission over the telecommunications network, and vice versa.
MS-DOS	An *operating system* (developed by Microsoft) widely used in microcomputers.
Object code	Program in *machine code* capable of being understood and executed by the computer. Produced by translating a program from *source code* using a *compiler*.
OCR	Optical Character Recognition. The use of characters printed in a specific typeface allowing them to be read directly by an appropriate *input device*.
On-line	Device in direct communication with the *CPU*
Operating system	Programs which control the resources of a computer and provide a link between hardware and software.
Output	The results of processing by a computer.
Output device	Unit which presents output in human-sensible form, eg printer or *VDU*.

Parallel interface	A connection between devices by which *data* is transmitted along a number of wires each carrying one *bit* at the same time, for example, eight bits may be transmitted simultaneously as a *byte* along eight separate wires. (Compare *serial interface*.)
Peripheral	Term used to denote any *input, output* or auxiliary *storage* device, ie a unit requiring connection to the *CPU*.
Pixel	(Derived from Picture Element.) The smallest individual element of a graphics image. Contains data representing brightness (and possibly colour).
Prolog	*High-level* programming language widely used in *AI*.
PROM	Programmable Read Only Memory. *ROM* whose contents are added after manufacture, but which is still non-volatile.
RAM	Random Access Memory. *Memory* directly available to the *CPU*, as distinct from backing *storage*.
Random access	Type of *direct access*.
Real-time	System in which processing is almost simultaneous with input, so that the computer provides picture of events as they occur (eg manufacturing process control system or airline booking system).
Record	A collection of *fields*, usually representing a single transaction. A group of related records form a *file*.
Reference file	A *file* which holds reference information and which changes infrequently (eg customer names and addresses).
Resolution	The amount of information that can be shown on a visual display. Measured in lines or pixels.
RISC	Reduced Instruction Set Computer. Computer with a processor designed to execute simple instructions extremely fast.
ROM	Read Only Memory. This *memory's* contents are built in at the time of manufacture. (Also referred to as mask ROM.)
Sequential access	Access to *storage* such that *data* (eg transactions) is presented in the same sequence as the *records* are organised on the storage medium.
Serial access	Access to *storage* such that stored *data* is read in the physical order in which it is organised, until the required item is reached.
Serial interface	A connection between devices by which *data* is transmitted one *bit* at a time along the same wire. (Compare *parallel interface*).
Simplex	Data transmission system which works in one direction only.
Source code	A program in a human-readable form (usually in a *high-level* language).

GLOSSARY

Storage — Internal storage (*memory*) within the *CPU* or backing storage (eg disk or tape).

Synchronous data transmission — Transmission of *data* between two devices which remain synchronised by means of clock pulses. Additional timing *bits* are therefore not required. (Compare *asynchronous data transmission*.)

System software — Another term for operating system software.

Transaction file — File containing *records* which will be used in *batch* processing to update a *master file* (eg weekly payroll run or cheque run).

Turnround document — Document output from a system, subjected to a clerical process and then used as an input document, probably utilising *MICR* or *OCR*. (Eg a payment counterfoil attached to a bill).

Unix — An *operating system* developed for general use with a wide range of mainframes and minicomputers.

Utility — Set of programs used to perform operations on whole files (as opposed to processing). Operations include copying, deleting and re-naming.

VDU — Visual Display Unit.

WAN — Wide Area Network. Network of computers linked over long distances by a telecommunications network. (Compare *LAN*.)

WIMP — Windows, Icons, Mouse, Pull-down menu.

WP — Word Processing.

WYSIWYG — What You See Is What You Get. Describes any screen display which mirrors with reasonable accuracy the eventual printed *output*.

ILLUSTRATIVE QUESTIONS
AND
SUGGESTED SOLUTIONS

ILLUSTRATIVE QUESTIONS

1   CHARACTERISTICS OF INFORMATION (20 marks)

It is generally accepted that effective management is impossible without information.

You are required:

(a) to define information;   (2 marks)

(b) to discuss the characteristics of information that assist the key management functions of planning, control and decision making; and   (8 marks)

(c) to describe how to access whether it is worthwhile producing more information for use in a particular decision.   (10 marks)

2   LEVELS OF INFORMATION (20 marks)

(a) Information distributed within an organisation can be classified as:

    (i)   strategic – used by senior management;
    (ii)   tactical – used by middle management;
    (iii) operational – used by 'front line' managers such as foremen, chargehands etc.

Taking an organisation with which you are familiar, explain the nature of strategic, tactical and operational information giving examples.   (15 marks)

(b) When communicating information to management, name five rules that you would observe so as to ensure that the recipient is likely to be satisfied with the information.

(5 marks)

3   FILES (15 marks)

In relation to magnetic files what is meant by:

(a) serial organisation;   (2 marks)
(b) sequential organisation;   (2 marks)
(c) indexed–sequential organisation;   (2 marks)
(d) random organisation.   (2 marks)

With what forms of backing storage would you associate the above methods of organisation?
(3 marks)

In the case of each method of organisation, how is a particular record located?

(4 marks)

4 DATABASE (20 marks)

Some computer installations, particularly the larger, more sophisticated ones, are using databases in which to store the organisation's data.

You are required:

(a) to define a database; (4 marks)

(b) to list and explain briefly *five* of the advantages claimed for a well-designed database; (10 marks)

(c) to explain briefly *three* of the major problems associated with the implementation and operation of a comprehensive database; (6 marks)

5 HARDWARE (20 marks)

When buying a printer for a small business computer, the purchaser sometimes faces a bewildering range of choices.

(a) Explain the difference between parallel and serial printers and describe how an imbalance between computer and printer can be overcome. (8 marks)

(b) Briefly describe the following types of printer mechanism and explain when they would be the preferred choice:

(i) daisy wheel;
(ii) matrix;
(iii) thermal. (12 marks)

6 DECENTRALISED COMPUTING (20 marks)

Your company's accounting department has a mainframe computer to which the personal department has access. Personnel are proposing to buy their own microcomputer and link it to the mainframe computer.

(a) Explain the additional security measures which may be necessary if the personnel department purchases the microcomputer and access to the computer system is widened? (5 marks)

(b) What benefits may be gained by the personnel department now that they have some decentralised computing power? (5 marks)

(c) If more departments of the company follow the personnel department in purchasing micro-computers what guidelines should the company give to maintain a consistent approach? (5 marks)

(d) What benefits could there be to management from the spreading of computer power throughout the company? (5 marks)

7   AIRLINE SEAT RESERVATION   (20 marks)

The provision of information using a computer involves:

(a)   the input of data;
(b)   the processing input;
(c)   the provision of output.

Taking an airline seat reservation as an example, you are required:

(a)   to illustrate, using a simple diagram, or to briefly describe, the nature of input, processing and output;   (10 marks)

(b)   to name *two* other situations where the data processing requirements are similar to the above;   (2 marks)

(c)   to state the form of backing storage that would be required, and to explain why it is necessary.   (8 marks)

8   OFFICE AUTOMATION   (20 marks)

What features of the modern electronic office facilitate each of the following office tasks?

(a)   Personal information management.   (4 marks)
(b)   Information retrieval.   (4 marks)
(c)   Document preparation.   (4 marks)
(d)   Message distribution.   (4 marks)
(e)   Decision support.   (4 marks)

9   FIXED ASSETS ACCOUNTING SYSTEM   (20 marks)

A company has computerised its fixed assets accounting system (ie accounting for plant and buildings, furniture and fittings, motor cars, etc).

(a)   Name *six* data fields that you would expect to find in the master record for any fixed assets.   (3 marks)

(b)   Briefly describe or list the data inputs that would be required to update periodically the fixed assets master file.   (4 marks)

(c)   Suggest *three* outputs that could be obtained from the system.   (3 marks)

(d)   For any one of the reports given in answer to (c), illustrate its layout.   (10 marks)

10 MANUFACTURING COMPANY DIVISIONS (20 marks)

Computerised management information systems are to be found in both the private and public sector, eg:

(a) central and local government;
(b) nationalised industries;
(c) non-profit making organisations;
(d) business organisations manufacturing goods for profit.

In each case it is usual to break the organisation into manageable divisions so that, for example, a manufacturing company could be divided into the following areas of operation:

(a) production and material control;
(b) marketing and distribution;
(c) personnel and industrial relations;
(d) finance and management accounting.

Taking the suggested divisions given for a small manufacturing company, or alternatively taking an organisation of your own choice, you are required:

(a) to name three reports that could be produced by the management information system for each division of the organisation; (12 marks)

(b) to give *four* brief explanations as to why information is required by management.
(8 marks)

11 SPREADSHEETS (20 marks)

The Managing Director of your company has just attended a seminar on computers and data processing during which he heard a brief reference to 'spreadsheets' and 'spreadsheet packages'. On his return he has asked you, as an accountant attached to the DP department, to explain these terms.

You are required to describe:

(a) spreadsheets and spreadsheet packages; (6 marks)
(b) the typical facilities provided by a spreadsheet package; (10 marks)
(c) an accounting application of such a package. (4 marks)

12 PROJECT MANAGEMENT (20 marks)

Developing and implementing large-scale administrative computer systems requires a formalised and disciplined approach to project management and control.

(a) Outline an approach to project management suitable for controlling the development of such a system. (10 marks)

(b) How can computers be used to help in the administrative support and technical development of a project? (10 marks)

13 DESIGN IN THE SYSTEMS LIFE CYCLE (20 marks)

The logical system design and physical system design are two important stages in the system life cycle. Distinguish between these two design activities by describing the major tasks which need to be accomplished within each.

14 FEASIBILITY REPORT (20 marks)

(a) Outline the main sections of a feasibility report and briefly explain the purpose of the typical contents of each section. (12 marks)

(b) An important part of any feasibility report is a section giving a financial justification for the proposed system. Describe in detail the matters dealt with in this section. (8 marks)

15 BUYING HARDWARE (20 marks)

The two most important decisions in the development of a microcomputer based business system are the selection of suitable software packages and the purchase of an appropriate microcomputer. Produce a list of factors requiring consideration in the *hardware* purchasing decision and outline the main consideration relating to each factor.

16 DP FACILITIES (20 marks)

(a) What are the advantages of installing in-house data processing facilities as an alternative to using a computer bureau? (5 marks)

(b) What are the advantages and disadvantages of facilities management? (5 marks)

(c) Describe the staffing and organisation of a typical information systems department, giving advice suitable for an organisation which plans to use in-house computer facilities for the first time. (5 marks)

(d) What kinds of computer are available to a medium-sized company wishing to install in-house computer facilities? (5 marks)

17 FACT FINDING (20 marks)

An important aspect of system analysis is the 'fact finding' stage of a systems investigation. Depending on the circumstances and the system being studied, several different methods of fact finding may be used.

You are required:

(a) to state *three* methods of fact finding; (6 marks)

(b) to give their advantages and disadvantages and the circumstances in which each might be used. (14 marks)

18 DATAFLOW DIAGRAM (15 marks)

A kitchenware manufacturer distributes and sells its products through a nationwide network of agents. Each agent is sent a bi-monthly product catalogue which he shows to prospective customers. Anyone wishing to order goods informs the agent and pays cash with order. The agent provides a receipt detailing amount and date of payment and itemising the goods ordered. Orders are added to a weekly order form and moneys received paid into a business account.

The order form is sent to the company on a Saturday and the agent also remits a cheque for the full value of orders received, drawn on the business account. He files a copy of the order form in a red binder.

The company delivers goods in the middle of the following week. The agent checks the goods against a delivery note submitted by the company and against his copy order form. He sorts out any discrepancy by telephone. Once this process is completed, he files the delivery note in a blue binder and bins the copy order form.

At the end of each catalogue period the agent is sent a statement detailing all orders made in the previous two months. He checks this statement against the delivery notes in the blue binder and pays the enclosed commission cheque into his personal bank account.

Prepare a dataflow diagram showing the above procedures.

19 COVERDALE (20 marks)

The Coverdale Manufacturing Co has computerised its order acceptance and sales invoicing procedures. Goods are manufactured, placed into stock and sold therefrom according to customer demand.

The files processed by the system are:

(a) transaction;
(b) stock master;
(c) customer master.

You are required:

(a) to define the nature of the records that could be included in the transaction file (eg. customer order record giving details of goods required) for the purpose of master file update and maintenance;   (8 marks)

(b) to state the main fields for the stock and customer master records;   (5 marks)

(c) to name *four* reports that could be produced by the system;   (2 marks)

(d) to explain how an on line interactive system could be of assistance both to the customer and the company, assuming that most of the orders are received over the telephone by an order clerk who has access to a terminal.   (5 marks)

20 DOCUMENT DESIGN (20 marks)

Whatever form of data processing is employed, the design of source documents is of prime importance.

What are the features of good source document design? What safeguards should be taken to ensure success before making changes to existing source documents.

21 DECISION TABLE AND FLOWCHART (20 marks)

(a) A retail store adopts the following policy towards offering credit to customers:

    (i) for orders under £50 in value no credit facility is given;

    (ii) for orders valued £50 up to £499 customers are offered terms over two years. For previous customers the rate of interest is 10% per annum and for new customers it is 15% per annum;

    (iii) for orders valued at £500 and above previous customers are offered terms over two years at a rate of interest of 15% per annum. New customers are referred to the credit manager for a decision.

    Set out this information in the form of a limited entry decision table.   (10 marks)

(b) Draw a flowchart based on the decision table.   (10 marks)

22 FILE CONVERSION (20 marks)

File conversion (of file creation) is always a major practical problem when a new computer-based system is being implemented.

Assume that a new computer-based accounting system is to be implemented and source data are at present held in various types of clerical files in several locations.

You are required to describe:

(a) the objectives of file conversion;   (5 marks)
(b) the typical problems that would be encountered in the situation outlined;   (8 marks)
(c) the way the file conversion process should be planned and controlled.   (7 marks)

23 FILE CREATION AND CHANGEOVER (20 marks)

You have been asked to advise a local firm of solicitors over the operation of their accounting procedures, which are at present done manually.

You are required:

(a) to outline three different options open to the firm assuming that your advice is to computerise the operation of its accounting procedures;   (8 marks)

(b) to explain the problems that will be met in file creation and conversion due to the computerisation of the firms records;   (6 marks)

(c) to explain three different types of systems changeover that can be related to the computerisation of the accounting procedures. (6 marks)

24 SYSTEMS SPECIFICATION (20 marks)

What elements would you expect to find in a system specification for the design of a software system, and what purpose does this play both during development and post implementation?

25 SECURITY (20 marks)

What methods are used in computer installations, including those using remote terminals, to guard against the effects of poor security

26 DATA VALIDATION (20 marks)

What methods are used in computer installations, including those using remote terminals, to validate input data and the processing of that data.

SUGGESTED SOLUTIONS

1 CHARACTERISTICS OF INFORMATION

(a) Information is data processed in such a way as to be of some meaning to its recipient. Data is the raw material which is processed and turned into information. In other words, data is collected and processed into information.

(b) The characteristics of management information that assist planning, control and decision-making are as follows.

  (i) It should have a clear purpose. Without purpose, there is only 'data' not information. The manager should clearly realise what the purpose of the information is.

  (ii) It should be accurate enough for the purpose in hand. There is often no need to produce values to the nearest £1, for example, when dealing in amounts of thousands or millions of pounds. When providing information for planning or decision-making, where uncertainty about the future is an integral factor in the situation, there is no point in providing figures which pretend to have a degree of accuracy that simply would not be possible.

  (iii) Where values are uncertain, some information giving assessments of probability distributions or sensitivity analysis might be particularly useful.

  (iv) Information must be comprehensive but relevant. Managers cannot take reliable decisions without all the necessary relevant information.

  (v) Information must be sent to the proper person - ie the manager who is responsible for the decision in hand. It is valueless if it is sent to a person who lacks the authority to act on it. The level of detail in the information should be suited to the position of the manager in the organisation hierarchy. In general, junior managers need more detail, and senior managers less.

  (vi) Information should be timely. It ought to be available for the time when the planning or control decisions are to be taken (or ought to be taken). At the same time, it should not be provided too frequently. Excess information, in terms of both quantity and frequency, is wasted and time-wasting.

  (vii) Information must be clear to the user. It can be accurate, timely and relevant, but if the user does not understand it (eg accounting reports may contain too much jargon for non-accounting managers) it will not be useable.

  (viii) Where possible, information should be concise. The principle of reporting by exception is particularly useful for control reports, but even planning reports (eg reports to a board of directors with a recommendation) can often benefit from brevity. Lengthy reports take time to read and digest, and might obscure the essential points with much less essential details.

(c) It will be worthwhile producing more information if the marginal benefits expected from using it exceed the marginal costs of providing it. The costs of obtaining extra information or more detailed or more frequent information could be assessed through careful study. The marginal benefits are less easy to establish, although Bayesian theory can be used to estimate the expected value of both perfect and imperfect information.

(i) The benefits will depend on the probability that more information will make it more likely that management will change their decision from what it would otherwise have been if the extra information had not been obtained, and the consequent benefits from the 'change of mind'.

(ii) More information might mean more frequent information rather than more detail. This might be relevant in the case of control decisions.

The benefits from 'feedback' of control information are usually a once-only gain. Once the fault has been identified and put right, there should be no scope for further improvement, and repeated feedback of control information should be of little value until the system gets out of control again. Arguably, continuous monitoring and reporting may be unnecessarily costly; at the very least, the principle of reporting by exception should be used.

The value of information also relates to:

(i) the ability of the receiver to understand it and use it;
(ii) the purpose or decision for which it is intended to help; and
(iii) the quality and availability of other information from different sources.

2 LEVELS OF INFORMATION

(a) The organisation described here is an organisation of retail shops. *Strategic information* is information that will assist management to make strategic planning decisions, most of which will affect the longer term future of the organisation. Strategic planning decisions are those concerned with ensuring that the organisation achieves its objectives which might be expressed, for example, in terms of ROCE or profit and dividend growth.

Examples of strategic information are:

(i) a long term profit forecast;

(ii) a sales forecast for next year and future years;

(iii) capital expenditure requirements over the next few years, potential sources of finance to fund this expenditure;

(iv) the levels of returns and dividends being achieved by rival organisations; the company's share price;

(v) information about companies that might be suitable takeover targets;

(vi) information about consumer spending in retail markets, and trends in retail sales.

Tactical information is information that will help middle management to plan and control the resources of the business for which they are responsible.

Accounting information of a tactical nature includes the budget and monthly performance reports. Ideally, tactical information should include both a target for achievement and actual results for comparison against the target. A store manager within the chain of retail shops would be the recipient of tactical information which might include:

(i) budgeted monthly sales for the store; details of actual monthly sales;

(ii) sales turnover per square foot of display space - budgeted and actual figures;

(iii) budgeted costs of running the store and actual costs, analysed by cost centres (eg departments within the store).

Operational information is information that will help junior managers or front line supervisors to organise and control the tasks for which they are responsible. This is information which is generally more short-term in nature - eg daily, weekly or perhaps monthly in timescale. Examples of operational information are:

(i) the daily sales figures for the section of the retail store for which the supervisor is responsible;

(ii) details of customer complaints about service or goods in the section;

(iii) staffing levels - numbers of staff expected (full time and part time); details of absenteeism, lateness in arriving at work etc;

(iv) the date of expected new deliveries of goods into the section.

(b) Five rules in communicating information to management are as follows.

(i) The information should be as accurate as the recipient would like it to be. The degree of accuracy required will vary according to circumstances, but if the recipient needs accurate figures to the nearest £1, say, he will not be satisfied with broad estimates to the nearest £1,000.

(ii) The information should be comprehensive and complete. The recipient will be dissatisfied with having only a fraction of the information he needs to make well-judged decisions.

(iii) The information should be clear. It is useless to send information that the recipient does not understand, perhaps because too many jargon words are used.

(iv) The information should be sent so that it is received in good time to enable the recipient to use it. Information that is received too late is useless.

(v) The information should all be relevant to the needs of the recipient who will not want to wade through items of irrelevant data searching for the information that is actually required.

3 FILES

(a) Serial organisation means that records are held on file in any order, without an index for accessing individual records directly.

(b) Sequential organisation means that records are held on file in a key field order, but without an index for direct access. Records on file must be accessed sequentially.

(c) Indexed sequential organisation means that records are held on file in a key field order, and with an index for direct access of individual records. Records on indexed sequential files can be accessed either directly or sequentially.

(d) Random organisation means that records are held on file not in any key field order, but there is an index or address-generating algorithm whereby individual records on file can be accessed directly.

The backing storage system associated with each method of organisation and the methods of record location are:

		Backing storage	Access method
(a)	Serial	Magnetic tape (or tape cassette). But also magnetic disk, magnetic drum etc.	Serial
(b)	Sequential	Magnetic tape (or tape cassette). But also magnetic disk, magnetic drum etc.	Serial (sequential)
(c)	Indexed sequential	Magnetic disk Magnetic drum	Indexed sequential or selective sequential
(d)	Random	Magnetic disk Magnetic drum	Random

Selective (or indexed) sequential access and random access are both forms of direct access. The term serial access is here used to describe the access method for serially and sequentially organised files, although the term sequential access can be used for the serial access of sequentially organised files.

4 DATABASE

(a) A database could be defined as a collection of any type of data with a structure that removes the need for the duplication of files and meets the information needs of a large section of an organisation. It is defined in the CIMA's Computing Terminology as:'in its strict sense...a file of data structured in such a way that it may serve a number of applications without its structure being dictated by any one of those applications, the concept being that programs are written around the database rather than files being structured to meet the needs of specific programs'.

(b) Five advantages of a well designed database are as follows.

(i) If duplication of information is removed, then updating information is made easier with fewer errors.

(ii) The amount of file storage space for data is reduced.

(iii) The time taken to access different parts of the same database should be less than accessing separate files.

(iv) The database can be extended to bring in new data in a structure that is well understood by those who need to use it. (A well-designed database should be flexible so that it can be extended without affecting existing applications that already use this database).

(v) Time is saved if data are entered into a system only once.

(c) Three major problems associated with the implementation and operation of a database are as follows.

(i) The start-up costs can be prohibitive if the gains are not well understood or defined.

(ii) The software to maintain and access a database can be complex, and also rigid and expensive. Once locked into a structure imposed by the software, then changing to use another software package is very difficult and expensive.

(iii) All users accessing the data must agree on certain protocols. Its effectiveness is diminished if this control cannot be maintained.

Note. You could have included these alternatives.

(iv) It is difficult to make a database fully comprehensive without incurring system design and development costs that are not justified by the benefits obtained.

(v) There might be security problems, with the danger of unauthorised access to the database file from any of the terminals linked to the system.

5 HARDWARE

(a) There are two main types of interface between a computer and a printer. Inside the computer, all signals travel in parallel (on buses) but signals to a printer might be sent in parallel or serially. A serial interface allows signals to pass serially from the computer to the printer. If the computer outputs in a form different from that expected by the printer then an interface card can be supplied to convert the data to the required form. The most common form of serial interface is RS232 although a newer version of this is RS423. A parallel printer can deal with signals in parallel as they are normally passed around inside the computer. The most common parallel interfaces are IEEE-488 and Centronics.

(b) (i) *Daisy wheel.*

Daisy wheel printers are quite widely used in microcomputer systems. A metal or plastic print wheel is used, which may be changed to alter character styles, and which can normally print 96 different characters. The characters, arranged on the wheel circumference on 'spokes', strike the paper through a carbon ribbon and bold lettering is achieved by a slightly offset second strike. Printing speeds vary from 15-55 characters per second. These speeds are relatively slow but this type of printer is primarily used where print quality is more important than speed.

(ii) *Dot matrix.*

These are the most commonly used printers in microcomputer systems. A set of small pins is arranged in a vertical matrix. The matrix moves along the line of paper to print each character, which is individually shaped by selected pins being pressed onto the paper through an inked ribbon. The main advantages are the greater speed of printing, up to 400 characters per second, and the fact that character styles are under software control, allowing a greater variety of character styles. The disadvantages of dot matrix printers is that print quality is not as high as with character impact printers. Such printers are used where volumes are high and speed is important.

(iii) *Thermal*.

Thermal printers are lightweight printers which use special heat sensitive paper. The printer creates heat that in turn produces printed output on the special paper. Thermal printers are cheap but the paper is expensive. They are particularly useful as portable devices because of their light weight, especially where the quantity of print out is low, thus limiting the cost of the paper.

6   DECENTRALISED COMPUTING

(a)   In the situation proposed (ie whereby personnel department should have their own microcomputer linked to the company's mainframe), additional security measures which may be necessary would be as follows:

(i)   physical security in relation to the possibility of the company's system being accessed via the remote 'terminal' situated in the personnel department. The use of the terminal should be restricted to authorised and properly trained members of staff. A machine with a keyboard lock should be used, with keys being restricted to authorised users;

(ii)   programmed controls designed to ensure that access to the system generally is restricted to authorised users. This could be achieved by requiring individual users to 'log on' by using a unique PIN (personal identification number). The system should perhaps be designed such that 'logging-off' is also required, in order to avoid the possibility of some unauthorised user making use of the system after it has been accessed and then left 'open' by a legitimate user;

(iii)   programmed controls designed to ensure that the personnel department terminal can only be used to access those files which the department would be required to access during the performance of their normal duties. Access to individual files should be restricted by the use of passwords which are notified to authorised users on a 'need to know' basis. In general terms the system should not allow access to any files other than those which one would anticipate being used by personnel department staff;

(iv)   use of the main system program and files should be carefully monitored by means of a terminal log automatically maintained by the mainframe computer. This log should be regularly reviewed by the operations manager in the DP department, with any record of an attempted breach of the security of the system being immediately and thoroughly investigated;

(v)   if it is intended that the personnel department should use the microcomputer in a 'stand-alone' capacity, then normal general and application control considerations would have to be extended to the personnel department in relation to matters such as file reconstruction, file maintenance, fire precautions, stand-by arrangements etc.

(b)   The benefits which might be gained by the personnel department having some decentralised computing power could be seen as follows:

(i)   given the ability to access data on the main files the department would now be able to carry out some local processing, previously done manually, with greater speed and accuracy and with the added benefit of such work being under programmed control;

(ii) in addition to making use of main system programs and files the department could perhaps gain benefit from using the microcomputer in a stand-alone capacity and thus make use of new application packages not currently available through the mainframe system;

(iii) the department may be able to carry out a certain amount of local processing of data before submission to the main system in the traditional way. This could have benefits to all concerned in terms of efficiency and faster output of the required information.

(c) If more departments of the company were to follow the lead of the personnel department then it would be essential for some central guidance to be issued to ensure that a consistent approach was adopted throughout the organisation.

Careful consideration should be given to the particular needs of the individual user department hardware and software requirements but it would be essential to institute a central buying policy in terms of disks, hardware and software to ensure the necessary compatibility, without which future systems changes could be both expensive and perhaps impractical.

Another important factor to be considered would be the need for and benefits of a standard training programme for user department staff.

(d) Amongst the benefits there could be to management from the spreading of computer power throughout the company could be seen the following:

(i) improved staff morale within user departments, with hopefully increased efficiency as a result, as a consequence of user departments perceiving themselves as having a greater 'control over their own destiny';

(ii) an improvement in decision-making processes at all levels of management as a consequence of more up-to-date information being available. This in turn should bring benefits through making the company generally more efficient and therefore more profitable;

(iii) generally an improvement in controls throughout the company as more reliance can be placed on programmed controls with a corresponding reduction in the possibility of errors as a result of human error.

7   AIRLINE SEAT RESERVATION

(a) (i) Input:

(1) from keyboard terminals, airline reservation officials will key in enquiries about the availability of flights, flight details and prices.

(2) from the same keyboard terminals, key in bookings (and cancellations or changes in flight).

(3) the master file must be kept up to date and so either by means of on-line input and file maintenance/updating, or regular batch processing, details will be required to be input of new flights, number of seats, prices etc.

    (ii) Processing:

        (1) answering file enquiries by looking up flights for details of vacant seats and other flight details. Looking for alternative flights perhaps by means of flight cross-referencing on the master file.

        (2) accepting bookings and updating the master file to record the bookings (names of passengers etc).

        (3) updating/maintaining the master file to include details of new flights. Also deleting 'old flight' details from the file when the flight has passed.

        (4) processing to produce management reports.

    (iii) Output:

        (1) on to VDU screen, answers to file enquiries, giving details of flights, prices etc. Also confirmation of bookings.

        (2) output will also include computer-produced flight tickets.

        (3) management reports can be produced, showing details, for example, of the percentage of seats booked on flights and total revenue etc.

        (4) confirmation of details of new flights put on to file (either in printout or on a VDU screen) for checking. It is important that errors should not get on to file and so new inputs must be checked carefully.

(b) The data processing requirements in (a) are real-time processing or interactive processing requirements. Other examples are:

    (i)   stock control systems in retail outlets, where stock records are updated as customers are served at checkout points. When the stock file indicates that shelf space is being emptied of certain items, it will produce output to indicate the need for re-stocking the shelves;

    (ii) the slowly-developing systems of electronic funds transfer at the point of sale, whereby customers can pay for goods or services in a store and automatically have their bank account debited or credit card charged, subject to a satisfactory check by the computer on their bank balance or unused credit.

(c) The backing storage device must be an on-line direct access device, with sufficient storage capacity to hold all the necessary master file details. In large real-time systems, this means having large disk storage devices (fixed disks or exchangeable disks). The master file records would be held in random order, and individual records would be accessed directly by means of an address-generating algorithm within the computer program.

8 OFFICE AUTOMATION

(a) *Personal information management*

Personal information management involves the ability of staff in an organisation to use not just their own, but also each other's electronic diary systems and files.

Joint diary facilities are provided by most network systems, on computers which range in size from mainframes to PCs, although the PCs tend to have more sophisticated solutions available. These diary facilities allow people to enter appointments for themselves and others, and to arrange appointments and meetings which will involve a number of people simultaneously. Since these diary systems depend on their users updating the computer files, they tend to have weak spots when used by people such as travelling salesmen, who might need to make appointments without being able to refer to a central file.

The network systems also provide message storage and retrieval facilities, replacing to a degree the necessity for using paper or other media to send messages.

Many people now use the disks of their PCs to supplement their paper-based files, by using the disks in their computers to store copies of documents rather than relying on manual filing systems.

(b) *Information retrieval*

Information retrieval falls into two main areas. The first is the straightforward concept of being able to access and get back, or retrieve, files which have been stored on disk on the computer system. All computers provide this facility. The second category of information retrieval system uses two main forms of storage: high capacity disks and microfilm. These can be interfaced to single computers or networked systems to allow people to retrieve documents in either image form (for documents which have come into the organisation from outside and have been scanned or microfilmed onto the system) or as text files (for internally generated files). In addition external databases are able to provide information on virtually any subject. The electronic/networked diary facilities referred to above also form part of the overall information retrieval facility.

(c) *Document preparation*

Document preparation covers all the stages from the moment a document is conceived in someone's mind to the point where it is filed or despatched from the premises. In an integrated office this process could involve:

(i) Document origination. Typically this consists of dictation equipment for recording and automatic playback equipment to facilitate typing of the recordings onto word processing equipment. Other methods include the use of 'pen' based PCs for direct capture of handwritten documents, voice recognition hardware and software for interpretation and direct input of either direct or recorded speech and scanners and character recognition software to allow for the automatical bulk capture of documents previously stored on paper.

(ii) Typing of documents onto a system, and enhancing their presentation. Word processing equipment and software can be used for the entry, editing and manipulation of the documents. Alternatively DTP (desk top publishing) systems are used for more professional presentation of the documents.

(iii) Automatic document preparation. Merging facilities allow standard form letters and documents to be generated from master letters and lists of, for instance, names and addresses.

(iv) Output and storage of documents. This involves the use of printers, such as lasers, with the facility to download (send to the printer from the computer) or build in with plug-in cards, standard items such as an organisation's standard fonts, logos etc. An alternative is the use of COM (computer output on microfilm) facilities or computer based document storage and retrieval to automate backup and filing tasks.

(d) *Message distribution*

Messages are usually distributed verbally or on paper. In the medium term this does not look set to change, and the facilities which are currently available to support this include:

(i) EMail, or electronic mail. In organisations where most personnel have access to some form of terminal connected to a central computerised system, EMail, an electronic mail system which stores and transmits messages, can be very useful. EMail facilities normally include the ability to 'broadcast' messages (send them to a number of recipients with a single command).

(ii) Phone systems with built-in broadcast facilities. Many PABX systems now have the ability to broadcast messages to either a selective number of other phones or generally, bypassing the handsets and using loudspeakers built in to the base of the phones.

(iii) Automatic mail distribution in large organisations. Some larger organisations have automated the physical distribution of paper based messages so that they are conveyed on robot-controlled mail delivery systems, and sometimes are printed on a printer which is near the recipient rather than being printed in a central facility.

(iv) FAX machines allow for automatic transmission of messages to a number of recipients, using off-peak phone capacity. Graphics can be transmitted by this means.

(v) Teletex is a potential tool for dissemination of information. This is currently used in some industries to get information from manufacturers to their dealers.

(vi) Radio paging systems also allow for messages to be sent to recipients at locations removed from their base. Current versions of pagers allow for the storage of messages within the pagers, for display at the user's convenience.

(vii) There are also facilities which to a degree bypass the need for messages, including various conferencing systems. These currently fall into three broad groups.

(1) Computer-based conferencing systems. These 'bulletin board' type systems allow for a degree of interactive conferencing as well as providing inexpensive message storage and retrieval facilities which can be accessed from anywhere that a phone system can be used with a computer terminal or PC. Their disadvantage, as with all EMail systems, is that for success they depend on the discipline of the users in regularly accessing the systems to read their messages.

(2) Voice (phone) conferencing. Such facilities are offered, largely as one of the by-products of digital exchanges, in most areas. Listening on a phone makes it difficult to understand what is being said if more than one person speaks on the line at once. As a result the effective use of voice conferencing is limited, and often takes place between two main participants with others listening on loudspeakers but generally not actively joining in the conversation.

(3) Video conferencing. Again such facilities are offered between larger population centres by a number of broadcasting service providers. Due to the nature of the medium (people's unfamiliarity with being filmed, and the artificial environment) their value is limited. In addition the inconvenience of having to travel to a special facility tends to detract from the value of the service.

(e) *Decision support*

The main tools which are available in this area include:

(i) Facilities (such as spreadsheets and the query tools like SQL, Structured Query Language, contained in 4GLs, or 'fourth generation languages') to produce reports on data held within files in the organisation.

(ii) Facilities to produce information in a graphical manner using tools such as the charting options in spreadsheets and specialised charting products.

(iii) EIS, or 'Executive Information Systems' which allow users to interrogate databases and display data summaries, ratios and various other results and information in a variety of 'views' using sophisticated graphics facilities. These facilities are very easy to use and require a minimum of user interaction at the time of viewing or printing the report or graph.

9 FIXED ASSETS ACCOUNTING SYSTEM

(a) (i) Fixed asset name (description)
(ii) Fixed asset category
(iii) Asset number (key field)
(iv) Gross cost
(v) Estimated residual value
(vi) Estimated life
(vii) Location
(viii) Depreciation
(ix) Written down value to date
(x) Method of depreciation.

Ten fields are listed here, but the list is not exhaustive. You only need six for your solution.

(b) (i) Details of installation costs, if added to asset cost as capital expenditure.
(ii) Details of renovation/overhaul costs, if added to asset cost as capital expenditure.
(iii) Details of changes in location.
(iv) Details of disposals (and disposal costs, and sales value, if the update program is also expected to calculate the actual profit or loss on disposal).

(v) Inserting details of newly-purchased fixed assets could be done in an update exercise, although strictly this might be referred to as 'file maintenance' rather than file update.

(c) (i) Statement of current fixed asset values, by fixed asset category and in total.

(ii) Details of profits and losses on disposal of fixed assets. Alternatively, a comparison of asset lives with previously estimated lives, provided that details of disposed-of assets are kept on file for some time after disposal.

(iii) A list of all fixed assets currently in operation and their location (for audit checking purposes).

(iv) A list of all fixed assets according to their location (perhaps cost or budget centre).

(d)
FIXED ASSETS AT COST AND WRITTEN DOWN VALUE
AS AT ....(date)

	At cost £	Accumulated depreciation £	Net book value £
Category:			
Land and buildings			
Plant and machinery			
Motor vehicles			
Fixtures and fittings			
TOTAL			

Note

If required, comparative figures for 12 months previously or any other previous date could be listed too, provided that sufficient data is held on the master file to do this.

10 MANUFACTURING COMPANY DIVISIONS

(a) (*Note*. More than three reports are listed under each heading, to provide a broader solution.)

(i) Production and material control:

(1) Stock analysis report;
(2) Machine utilisation report;
(3) Machine capacity and utilisation budget;
(4) Variance reports (budget reports) on materials usage and labour efficiency.

(ii) Marketing and distribution:

(1) Sales forecasts for each product by region and area;
(2) Actual sales for each product by region and area compared with budget;
(3) Report on distribution costs - eg budgeted and actual costs per ton/mile;
(4) Report on advertising and sales promotion costs.

(iii)   Personnel and industrial relations:

(1)   Reports on labour turnover, absenteeism, time lost through strikes;
(2)   Staff report – numbers and grades of employees and their costs;
(3)   Overtime analysis report;
(4)   Staff review – analysis of the abilities of existing staff and promotion potential, with a view to manpower planning;
(5)   Labour budget or manpower plan.

(iv)   Finance and management accounting:

(1)   Budgeted and actual profitability/contribution statement;
(2)   Breakeven analysis report;
(3)   Aged debtors list and bad debts listing;
(4)   Profit and loss account and balance sheet;
(5)   Value added statement;
(6)   Funds flow statement;
(7)   Cash budget.

(b)   Information is needed by management:

(i)   to assist them in making planning decisions at a strategic, tactical and operational level;

(ii)   to assist them in controlling the efficiency of the use of the resources of the business;

(iii)   to assist them in making decisions that will enable them to be effective in achieving their planning targets;

(iv)   to communicate with each other, subordinates and superiors, so that activities are well co-ordinated;

(v)   alternatively, to evaluate occasional 'one-off' decisions such as a capital expenditure proposal to purchase new equipment or a new building etc.

11   SPREADSHEETS

(a)   A *spreadsheet* is a matrix of rows and columns that holds information in each cell of the matrix. A spreadsheet package is a computer software package that allows the user to insert information into any cell of the matrix, and then to change any of it, to manipulate any row or column of the matrix and to make information within a cell dependent upon other cells in the matrix. Examples of such packages are Lotus 123 and Visicalc.

(b)   The facilities you would expect to find in a typical spreadsheet package are:

(i)   the arithmetical manipulation of rows or columns. For example, to be able to add, subtract, multiply and divide a column (row) by a constant or another column (row). Also the ability to combine a number of these operations in one command. The ability to compare figures in different cells to ascertain which is greater or whether they are equal in value;

(ii)   the logical manipulation of rows or columns of the matrix;

(iii)   the ability to enter titles for rows or columns;

(iv)   the ability to sort both quantitative and character data, and to give simple statistics such as column or row total, average value, square roots etc;

(v)   commands to edit any part of the matrix;

(vi)   commands to scroll through the matrix so that any part may be viewed;

(vii)   the ability to view different sections of the matrix at the same time (the full matrix will be so large that the VDU screen cannot display it all at once, and so the screen can be 'split');

(viii) commands to display information in graphical form;

(ix)   the ability to write information out of the matrix which will be printed or stored for use by another program;

(x)   Perhaps the most important feature of all is that when the user changes one item of data - ie data in one cell - then any other data values in the matrix that are affected by the change will be automatically re-calculated. This facility makes amendments and corrections to data and sensitivity analysis readily feasible.

(c)   An accounting application of a spreadsheet package is cash budgeting. The columns in the spreadsheet would be made to represent time periods, and the rows would analyse cash inflow items, cash outflow items, and opening and closing cash balances. Formulae could be used to express a relationship between items, and the model could be used for sensitivity analysis on matters such as allowing longer credit to customers or higher bad debts etc.

12   PROJECT MANAGEMENT

(a)   The introduction of a new computer system can have a number of effects on the organisation.

(i)   It can be costly in terms of personnel (team of system analysts or programmers if developed in-house, consultancy fees if developed by outsiders).

(ii)   Even if an application package is purchased, this can still be an expensive item.

(iii)   The right hardware must be purchased

(iv)   It is costly in terms of management time and attention. Managers from user departments inevitably get involved in systems development projects. Also different managers can have different ideas as to what is desirable.

(v)   It is disruptive (staff have to take time off work to be trained).

The project is not seen as an organisation's core activity, given it is a finite piece of work, which impinges on the day to day work of the organisation.

SUGGESTED SOLUTIONS

A project involves the management of a number of disparate, yet interdependent activities, within a timetable and a budget set in advance. A particular project is unique, in that by its nature it is not a repetitive activity.

Efficient management of the resources and process of the project is therefore important for the organisation and the achievement of the project's objectives.

A basic approach to project management would be as follows.

(i) *Delegation of overall responsibilities*. A steering committee comprising senior user department personnel, a member of the finance department and various systems professionals is appointed to oversee the project. If the organisation has an Information Director, this individual is likely to have a key role on the steering committee.

(ii) *Appointment of a project manager*. This individual plans manages and executes the project and is responsible for its successful completion. The project manager presents the timetable and budget to the steering committee for their approval and authorisation.

(iii) *Project planning*. The goals of the project identified, and the activities needed to achieve them are outlined. These are then matched to the manpower resources available, so that a project timetable can be outlined and agreed. The timetable will indicate when each activity has to be completed, and in which order. Each stage of the project is then planned in its own right. The stages of the project may be determined by the systems development methodology adopted: SSADM lays down a sequence of six stages, excluding the feasibility study.

(iv) *Controlling the project*. Actual outcomes are compared to the plan and any difficulties dealt with as soon as they become apparent. Regular progress meetings should be held by the project manager with members of the project team to monitor performance. Specified documentation is produced at the end of each stage for review and approval, in accordance with quality control criteria established for projects of this nature.At the end of each stage, progress will be reported to the steering committee. Users should be consulted, as their approval is necessary to demonstrate that the project is meeting its objectives.

(v) *Output of the project*. This must meet any technical criteria of the organisation. This means that all the relevant documentation must be completed to an adequate standard, project files must be cross referenced, and there should be a clear relationship evidenced between the work done in the various successive stages of the project.

In summary, therefore, the project is controlled in two ways. Firstly the technical quality of the output is reviewed. Secondly, the efficiency with which the project tasks are carried out is also subject to management review and control.

(b) Computers can be used in a variety of ways during the course of a project.

(i) Project management software is available which enables project managers to plan the course, and the resource use of the various activities in a project. The computer software might be able to determine the most efficient order in which activities should be performed. A number of alternative solutions can be tested.

Project management software can use PERT or network analysis as the basis for its operation.

(ii) Computers can be used to draw up project documentation. It is possible to acquire computer software packages that construct data flow diagrams, and checks them for accuracy or consistency. Such packages are known as computer aided software engineering (CASE). Software engineering is a discipline which aims to bring mathematical and logical precision into program design. Computer aided software engineering provides computer support for such an approach.

(iii) Fourth generation systems (eg application generators, fourth generation languages) are used the build applications quickly, reducing the time spent on program coding.

(iv) The project team might use prototyping as a technique to evaluate alternative solutions, with the cooperation and assistance of users.

(v) Documents output from the project might be word processed. If large numbers of forms are to be designed a graphics package can assist this task. If manuals are to be printed, use of desk-top publishing software might be an advantage.

13 DESIGN IN THE SYSTEMS LIFE CYCLE

The term system life cycle referred to in the question can be taken to cover all of the many stages in a computerisation project from initial proposal through to operational running and systems maintenance. If the computerisation is to be successful then it is essential that adequate standards and controls are established and maintained throughout all the various stages of systems analysis and design.

As suggested, logical system design and physical system design are two important stages in the overall system life cycle. Logical system design can be seen as that part of the process which determines what it is that the system is supposed to do, whilst physical system design is concerned with determining how the objectives which are the end product of logical systems design are to be achieved. So it can be seen that physical system design will follow on directly from logical system design. In turn, logical systems design will not be started until a full evaluation of the existing system has been carried out and the users have provided an outline of the requirements of the new system.

The major tasks which need to be accomplished during logical system design are as follows.

(a) In consultation with user department staff, management and auditors ensure that agreement has been reached on the requirements of the new system so that the scope of the new system may be formally defined.

(b) Having clearly identified the intended scope of the new system, the next stage will be to detail fully those aspects of the old system which are to be retained, those aspects of the old system which are to be retained but only after amendment and those aspects of the new systems definition which will have to be 'designed from scratch'.

(c) The next stage will be carefully to analyse the data requirements of the new system and to ensure that the necessary data structures to support it have been produced. This process should consider all aspects of data requirements including transactional input, master and reference file contents.

(d) Having considered the necessary data structures for the new system, the next task will be to identify the requirements of the various users in terms of access to that data.

Whilst the above is not a comprehensive list of the tasks involved in the logical system design, it may be seen as sufficient to indicate the nature of the process clearly.

As indicated above, the outputs of the logical system design will form a major part of the input to the process of physical system design. In addition, it will be necessary to ascertain what resources are to be available for the physical system design in terms of personnel, hardware and software resources. Ideally, a number of physical options would be prepared from which management would make the ultimate choice.

Included amongst the major tasks in physical system design would be the following.

(a) Determining the contents and organisation of files required from the data structure and access requirements which have been logically identified.

(b) Once the file contents and organisation have been determined, and bearing in mind the overall objectives of the system so far as end users are concerned, it will be necessary to give detailed consideration to the form, nature and content of all systems inputs and outputs.

(c) A major part of the physical system design exercise will be to identify the most appropriate and cost effective processing method to be adopted. Depending on the nature of the application this could range from centralised batch processing using a central mainframe to having an on-line real-time system involving the use of remote terminals.

One vital control requirement of both stages of the overall systems cycle would of course be to have full standardised documentation of all work done.

14   FEASIBILITY REPORT

(a) The main sections of a feasibility report are as follows.

(i) *Introduction*. Description of the purpose of the report, why it was commissioned and what it proposes to recommend.

(ii) *Terms of reference*. This specifies the limits or constraints on the report, and so identifies the boundaries of the investigation.

(iii) *Method of carrying out the feasibility study*. A brief description of how the study was carried out should be given. If the method seems worthy of a fuller description, this should be given in an appendix to the report.

(iv) *The objectives of the study and the proposed system*. The purpose of the study will be to resolve a problem of organisation or procedural systems, or to introduce a new system to replace an existing one, or to introduce a new system where one does not exist already.

The feasibility report should specify clearly what the study group identifies as the purpose of the system to be proposed, in terms of what the organisation is trying to achieve.

If the report is proposing a new system, it should explain how the new system will integrate with existing systems.

(v) *A description of the alternative systems considered*, and how far each of these would satisfy the objectives. Alternatives which fail to satisfy those objectives should be explained, and then discarded from further consideration in the report.

The preferred system should be identified, and described further in subsequent sections of the report. (If more than one viable option remains, all of them should be explained in some detail. For each of these options considered in further detail items (vi) to (viii) should be included in the report.)

(vi) The effect of introducing the system on current operations, output levels, efficiency, staffing, equipment used, organisation etc.

(vii) *Financial justification*. The costs of the system, and the benefits envisaged.

(viii) A consideration of how successfully the option might achieve the objectives of the organisation, in commissioning a new system.

(ix) A comparison of the options, and an indication of preference.

(x) *A recommendation* as to which option, if any, should be selected and developed into a new system. (A recommendation might be to continue with the existing system, or to defer a change until new system capabilities and more advanced equipment are available on the market.)

(xi) The feasibility study should also have at least two appendices.

    (1) Appendix 1 should describe the existing system, how it operates, what input and output from the system are, speed of processing and what the deficiencies of the system are.

    (2) Appendix 2 should describe the proposed system in similar detail. Although systems design work should not proceed too far, in case the recommendations of the report are turned down, the report should contain adequate information about the type of system, equipment needed, input, output, files, procedures and programs, speed of processing, staffing, changeover procedures from the old to the new system, possible deficiencies in the system, costs, benefits etc. This information can be used to weigh up the report, and subsequently to monitor progress in the development of the actual system (on the assumption that during design work, some of the items envisaged in the feasibility study turn out to be impractical, inefficient or insufficient).

(b) The matters dealt with in the section of the report on financial justification should be:

(i) *Operating costs*. The incremental (or 'relevant') costs of the system should be identified, including:

    (1)   staff costs (clerical, computer operations etc)
    (2)   the cost of stationery and other supplies
    (3)   the cost of external services (eg bureaux)
    (4)   the cost of system maintenance
    (5)   accommodation costs (if incremental to existing costs)
    (6)   any other additional costs.

SUGGESTED SOLUTIONS

   (ii) *Operating costs saved*

      (1) Staff costs
      (2) Stationery and other supplies
      (3) Accommodation
      (4) Other

   (iii) Net increase or reduction in operating costs.

   (iv) Any incremental revenue benefits (eg higher sales volumes) from the proposed system.

   (v) *Development costs*

      (1) Systems design, development and testing
      (2) Staff costs (or bureau costs etc) of file conversion
      (3) Equipment costs
      (4) Installation costs for new equipment
      (5) Staff training costs
      (6) Sale price of any existing equipment or accommodation no longer required.

   (vi) A summary of costs and benefits.

15 BUYING HARDWARE

The factors requiring consideration are as follows.

(a) Suitability. The computer configuration must fit in with the user's requirements (eg direct access facilities, hard-copy output in given quantities).

(b) CPU size. The power of the CPU must be sufficient for current and foreseeable requirements.

(c) Backing storage size and file access speed. Many micros now have a large internal hard disk for backing storage. Hard disks offer more storage capacity and faster file access than floppy disks.

(d) Reliability. There should be a low expected 'break-down rate'. There should be back-up facilities, and in the case of a microcomputer, this *might* mean being able to resort temporarily back to a manual system when the computer breaks down.

(e) Simplicity. Simple systems are probably best for small organisations.

(f) Ease of 'communication' between the hardware and the user. The system (hardware and software) should be able to communicate well with the user. Software is referred to as 'user-friendly' or 'user-unfriendly' but similar considerations apply to hardware (eg not all terminals are of standard screen size; the number and accessibility of terminals might also have a bearing on how well the user is able to put data into the computer or extract information.

(g) Flexibility. The hardware should be able to meet new requirements as they emerge. More powerful CPUs tend to be more flexible.

(h) Security. Keeping out unauthorised users is easier with more powerful systems, although security can be a major problem for any computer system.

(i)   Cost. The cost of the system must be justified by the expected use and benefits to be obtained from it.

(j)   Hardware and operating system standards. When choosing a microcomputer, management should remember that the industry 'standard' for microcomputer hardware has become the Intel processor which is used in the IBM PC and the subsequent IBM AT, and the operating system software standard for stand-alone 16-bit micros is MS-DOS or PC-DOS. O/S2 is emerging as the operating system standard for the 32 bit micro and Unix for network systems.

(k)   Documentation. User documentation should be clear, to help with internal training of staff.

(l)   Maintenance. Will the supplier provide a maintenance service, and if so, what speed of response will the supplier provide to call-outs? (Most microcomputer hardware comes with a one-year warranty, but what about maintenance after the first year?)

(m)   Printer speed. The printer being purchased should be able to print output at the required speed and to the desired quality standard.

16   DP FACILITIES

(a)   Bureaux provide either on-line or batch processing services on their own computer for customers who hire time or facilities from them. Facilities can range from simple provision of a computer, with all the data entry, job control and reporting being done on the customer's premises to a full solution where documents are collected by the bureau, with the documents being captured by the bureau, the data processed and the results in the form of reports, and perhaps terminal enquiry facilities, being made available to the customer.

Some reasons for changing from using a bureau are:

(i)   Company related factors. Factors which might have changed within the company, and therefore impacted on the viability of using a bureau, include the volume of data being processed, the rates being charged by the bureau, the response offered by the bureau and the ability and performance of the bureau in response to requests for new facilities. A further major factor would be any need for personnel in the company to have access to data to be used in spreadsheets, charting or word processing functions.

(ii)   Cost. Costs of bureau facilities can be based on a number of criteria, but normally rise on a periodic basis, particularly as volumes increase, whereas the costs of in-house hardware facilities will fall over time as hardware prices decrease, and if packaged software is used software costs can be contained as well.

(iii)   Control. Using a bureau means that an organisation loses the immediate control that it has over its data processing when the function is performed in-house.

(iv)   Confidentiality. By their nature bureaux pose more of a security risk than an in-house facility. Highly confidential data can require staff being present at the bureau while it is being processed, and even then there is the danger that it could be inadvertently or deliberately copied or lost.

(v)   Lack of response. Since the bureau has to service a number of clients there will be occasions when their priorities and those of the customer differ, and the response which the customer gets from the bureau may fall below that which he wants or needs from a computer system.

(vi)   Lack of flexibility. Bureaux, in common with manufacturers of most products, derive the bulk of their income from selling the same solution to a number of clients. If they need to change the solution for a specific client they may be less happy to do so, but in addition the change will often mean that future changes (enhancements or error corrections) to the un-modified software which the bureau might introduce might not be applied to the modified software, or might be applied at an additional cost or time delay.

(vii) Being locked in to a supplier. The close cooperation between the bureau and the customer will often mean that it is difficult to change suppliers, since the cooperation will often evaporate if the customer decides to withdraw his business from the bureau.

(viii)Problems with moving data. Again, when the time comes to migrate the data from the bureau to another system, it is often the case that problems are presented with regard to the practicality of making the move or with regard to the cost and amount of time and effort involved in the exercise.

(b)   Facilities Management refers to the practice of contracting out all or part of an organisation's computing operation.

The initial reaction to facilities management can be very favourable, and there can be significant benefits in terms of fixing costs, the ability to set costs on a transaction basis, the benefits gained from the IT staff being employed in a more specialist organisation, the ability to use Facilities Management as an interim measure while developing in-house capabilities and the ability to concentrate management attention on core activities (which may not include computing).

However, there are concerns which can be associated with Facilities Management which match quite closely the problems associated with using bureaux: response times, manning levels, control of downtime, crash recovery times, how much management time will be needed to manage the FM facility and whether vital systems can be entrusted to FM are all questions which arise both at the contractual stage and on an ongoing basis.

(c)   Computer staff are expensive. At an early stage in a project it would make sense to buy in packaged solutions to the company's processing needs, and staff the IT department at as low a level as possible until there is a full justification for increasing the complement. Generally staff fall into five broad categories: management, analysts, programmers, operations staff and data preparation and control staff. The analysts' function is to analyse requirements, the design and specify solutions. The programmers' function is to take specifications from the analysts and produce the working programs. An initial functional department capable of writing software would be a single analyst and one or two programmers. Numbers of staff on the operations side would depend on the workload and on what type of machine was installed (mainframe, mini or PC - the larger the machine the higher the staffing requirement, in general).

(d)   The three main categories of computer available are mainframes, mini-computers and micro-based systems. They differ in terms of the following:

(i)   Size and power requirements: the sizes range from mainframes, which are physically the largest machines, requiring special rooms with air-conditioning and conditioned power supplies, through to mini-computers, which should have conditioned power supplies but operate in office environments, to PC based systems, which operate as office-based machines without the need for special supplies (although the file server in network solutions should be connected to uninterruptible power supplies).

(ii) Capacity: although there used to be a significant difference in the capacity of the three types of machines this is no longer so, and networked PC solutions with large file servers can now offer sufficient capacity for many large organisations.

(iii) Costs: there is a significant difference in cost between the most expensive, mainframes and mini-computer systems, and a smaller difference between mini-computers and PC-based systems.

(iv) Response offered to users and speed and power at the users' desks. Both mainframe and mini-computer solutions suffer from the fact that the bulk of the processing is done on a central computer. Networked PCs, on the other hand give each user the full power and speed of their own processor. Although these processors do not normally match the power of the mainframe processor, the power which each user has is much higher than the average power which users have in the mainframe situation, and for applications such as word processing, graphics and spreadsheets there is no real alternative to each user having his own PC.

17 FACT FINDING

(a) Three methods of fact finding are:

(i) interviews;
(ii) questionnaires;
(iii) observation.

Interviews involve face-to-face discussions between the analyst and individuals with knowledge of the system. The analyst asks questions and obtains answers, comments and suggestions.

Questionnaires are written lists of questions. These can be used by a systems analyst in an interview, or given to respondents, who will be asked to write answers in their own time and return the completed questionnaire.

Observation involves the analyst in watching the system in operation as an observer.

(b) The advantages and disadvantages of these three methods are as follows:

(i) *Interviews*. As a fact finding technique, interviewing will to some degree be appropriate in almost all situations. It may be particularly useful where the proposed system will involve a number of related areas in the existing system. This is because it is usually the case that only by talking to all parties involved will the analyst gain a total view and proper understanding of the interaction of the various parts of the system.

Interviewers need background information on those interviewed and many find this valuable later on during implementation. It gives an opportunity to discuss in-depth opinion as well as fact and he may learn of suggestions that are worth looking into further. However, inverviewing is an acquired skill and depends upon the cooperation of those being interviewed. It can be costly in time and effort and the rewards are unpredictable.

(ii) *Questionnaires*. In many ways, the ideal solution to the problem of fact finding will involve a certain amount of direct contact between the analyst and those members of staff concerned with the day to day running of the system. However, it may sometimes be physically impossible, or at least highly impractical, for the analyst to personally talk with all staff members. This may either be because of the sheer numbers of staff involved and/or the decentralised nature of the business organisation. It is in such situations that the use of questionnaires may have to be considered.

Questionnaires can sample a wide range of opinion and collect useful statistics in a short space of time, particularly if those questioned cover a large geographical area. There are potentially many problems with a questionnaire. The response rate may be poor, analysis of a lengthy questionnaire can be costly and design of a good questionnaire is not easy, particularly if consistency of answer is needed to be checked by cross referencing answers.

Where questionnaires are to be distributed for completion by staff members, it is essential that the questions themselves have been designed in such a way that ambiguities are avoided. There is also a danger with questionnaires that staff may give the reply which they feel is expected of them, rather than perhaps what they see as the answer in 'real life'. For these reasons, questionnaires should only be used where the system details which the analyst is enquiring about are comparatively simple.

A questionnaire might be used to survey a new product when the potential customer base numbers many thousands.

(iii) *Observation*. Studying by observation requires a base level of knowledge about a system and should provide experience of the details of the system which is needed if changes are to be introduced. It can be a cheap means of gaining knowledge of a system and has the advantage of showing what actually happens, not what you expect or believe to be happening. On the other hand, direct observation is time consuming and may provoke a reaction in those observed which makes it difficult to allow normal working practice to go ahead as normal. It is for this reason that it would perhaps be necessary to make a number of separate observations, at random intervals, rather than forming an opinion based upon a single visit.

Observation is a useful 'follow-up' procedure, used to gain confirmation that a system outlined 'in theory', perhaps in an interview does actually work 'in practice'.

It might be used for example whenever the flow of documents through a system needs to be assessed for efficiency.

SUGGESTED SOLUTIONS

18 DATAFLOW DIAGRAM

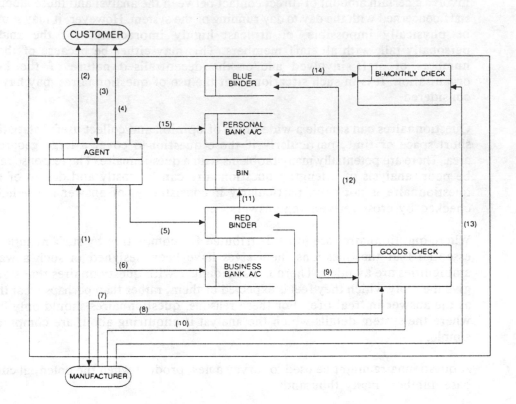

FLOW	DATA	DOCUMENT
(1)	Bi-monthly catalogue to agent	Catalogue
(2)	Bi-monthly catalogue to customers	Catalogue
(3)	Customer orders goods and pays	Order form
(4)	Agent issues receipt for order	Receipt
(5)	Order added to weekly form	Order form
(6)	Money paid into business account	Giro slip
(7)	Cheque and order sent to company	Order form and remittance advice
(8)	Goods forwarded to agent by company	Delivery note
(9)	Agent checks goods	Order form and delivery note
(10)	Phone call to resolve queries	(Telephone)
(11)	Order form binned	Order form
(12)	Delivery note filed in blue binder	Delivery note
(13)	Statement for previous two months and commission cheque to agent	Statement and cheque
(14)	Bi-monthly check of statement by agent	Statement
(15)	Cheque banked by agent	Giro slip

19 COVERDALE

(a) Transaction records for:

    (i)   stock master file update and customer master file update:

        (1)   customer orders, giving details of goods required;
        (2)   details of sales to customers - ie goods delivered;
        (3)   details of sales returns from customers;
        (4)   details of goods manufactured and placed into stock;

        (5)   details of invoices sent out to customers;

        (6)   details of invoices paid;

        (7)   details of credit notes given or refunds.

    (ii)   Stock and customer master file maintenance:

        (1)   details of new stock items;

        (2)   details of changes to standing data on stock records (eg changes in re-order level or re-order quantity);

        (3)   details of obsolete stock items, to be deleted from the file;

        (4)   details of new customer accounts;

        (5)   details of changes to standing data on customer records (eg changes in address,

              or payment terms);

        (6)   details of customers who are bad debt risks and must not be sold goods again;

        (7)   deletions of 'old' customers from the file, eg customers who have gone out of business or who have been taken over.

  (b) Main fields:

    (i)   Stock master file:

        (1)   stock code number (key field)

        (2)   stock description;

        (3)   quantities currently in stock:

              • allocated to customer orders;

              • free balance of items in stock not yet allocated to orders;

        (4)   quantities due from manufacturing: estimated date of delivery;

        (5)   sales price;

        (6)   possibly, manufacturing cost;

        (7)   re-order level

        (8)   re-order quantity;

        (9)   maximum stock level;

       (10)   minimum stock level;

       (11)   cumulative issues to date (dates of issues, quantities);

       (12)   value of issues to date;

       (13)   cumulative receipts into stock to date;

       (14)   value of receipts;

       (15)   stores location of stock item (eg bin number).

    (ii)   Customer master file:

        (1)   customer code number (key field);

        (2)   name;

        (3)   address (delivery address and invoicing address);

        (4)   amount invoiced; and

- paid;
- not yet paid;

(5) invoice details;
(6) amount ordered, not yet delivered;
(7) amount delivered, not yet invoiced;
(8) maximum credit limit;
(9) payment terms;
(10) cumulative sales to date;
(11) bad debt risk indicator;
(12) salesman identification code.

(c) Possible reports:

(i) quantities and value of opening stock, quantities produced, sales and closing stock, item by item and in total;

(ii) monthly customer statements (if these are regarded as 'reports');

(iii) aged debtors list;

(iv) analysis of customers by category (eg old customers, new customers, customers in different regions etc) showing the value of sales to each;

(v) list of stocks currently held (for audit checking purposes);

(vi) report on the value/cost of stocks written off during the period as obsolete.

Only four reports are required. You might prefer other reports of your own choosing.

(d) An on-line interactive system could help the customer because when a customer telephones with an order enquiry, he can obtain immediate information about the availability of stock and, if an item is out of stock, whether more quantities are being manufactured (and expected availability date). He can then order goods and get a confirmation of the order at once. This means that the customer does not run the risk of putting in an order and then being told that the item is out of stock and that he must wait for stock availability for delivery.

The advantage to the company is that the order cycle is speeded up and stock turnover will be quicker. Customer credit details can be checked on-line before the order is confirmed.

20 DOCUMENT DESIGN

The features of good source documents are as follows:

(a) They should contain all the data required (which is not available on file from other sources of input), but not excessive, unnecessary data.

(b) The document should have a clear title (and perhaps a code or identity number).

(c) Where appropriate, unique serial numbers for documents should be used.

(d) Related items should be grouped together on the form.

(e) The items should be arranged in a logical sequence, to suit the needs of the user.

(f) As much data as possible should be pre-printed on the document.

(g) Some consideration should be given to the needs of the person keying in the data (eg the VDU operator) in designing the layout/arrangement of data on the form.

(h) Where appropriate, clear instructions should be given on the form about the input data required.

(i) If possible the documents should be used as a 'turnround' document, to save subsequent input preparation. Turnround documents should be created by printing on to pre-printed computer stationery.

(j) If the document is to be held in a card or document file, its size and thickness should lend themselves to easy handling, filing and retrieval from file.

(k) There should be colour-coding of documents if possible, where there are several different input forms in use.

(l) The documents should have one use as a input document, ie it should not be used more than once to input data to different programs or systems.

Safeguards to be taken before making changes to existing source documents are as follows:

(a) All the information required on the new document should be identified. There may be some data on the current document that is not required, and new data that must be introduced. By specifying exactly what data is required the new document can be designed incorporating the features described above.

(b) The systems analyst should try to establish (from interviews with operational staff) what the good and bad features of the current forms are. The new forms should try to keep the good features of the old forms and remove their bad features.

(c) A new form design should be tested before it becomes operational. Systems testing should indicate whether the new forms work as efficiently and effectively as their designer planned that they should.

(d) Because the contents and user requirements of the new form will be different from those of the old one, the new forms should not be designed in imitation of the old ones. The form designer should be given a free hand to design the form that would seem best to suit the purpose in hand.

(e) Before the changeover occurs, staff must be fully trained in using the new documents. A clear distinction must be kept, in administrative procedures, between the old forms and the new forms.

(f) Staff should be told why the change to the document design is necessary. An explanation of the purpose of the change might help to prevent staff frustration and vexation at the requirements for a new system.

21 DECISION TABLE AND FLOWCHART

(a)

Decision table					
Under £50	Y	N	N	N	N
£50 to £499	N	Y	Y	N	N
£500 or over	N	N	N	Y	Y
Previous customer	-	Y	N	Y	N
No credit	X				
2 years 10%		X			
2 years 15%			X	X	
Refer manager					X

(b)

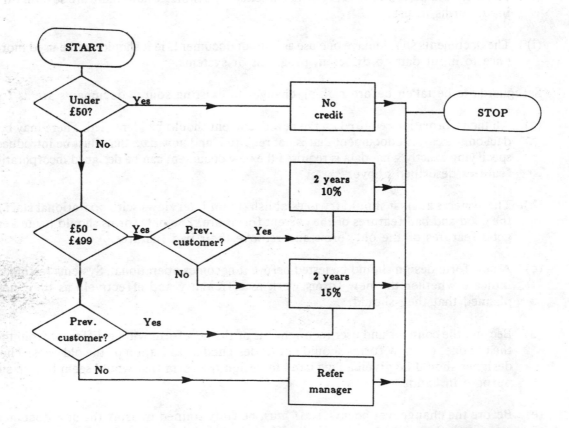

22 FILE CONVERSION

(a) The objectives of file conversion are to produce a file on a specified medium which is capable of being read or written by the computer software involved and which is free from errors. Until master file conversion has taken place, a computer system (eg a sales ledger system or payroll system) cannot become operational.

(b) Some typical problems encountered in file conversion are:

   (i)   Are source documents accurate and complete?

   (ii) Are the source documents up to date?

   (iii) Are the source documents in a form amenable to input into a program?

   (iv) Do different departments in the organisation maintain compatible codes or descriptions for the same information?

   (v)   If different sections have conflicting data then who is correct?

   (vi) What measures can be taken to ensure, as far as possible, that the converted file is free from input errors (eg keying-in errors)?

(c) Planning a file conversion and controlling the work should proceed according to the following guidelines.

   (i)   Set a timetable for conversion, if possible try to do the conversion in a period when the volume of transactions is low.

   (ii) If possible, do a dummy run to see if all the information needed is available, and that the input programs and the data validation routines are all working as planned.

   (iii) Decide upon a date after which no further information is to be held by the old methods, making sure that all subsequent data are held in a form able to be transcribed into the new system until the system is proved.

   (iv) Make sure that all relevant staff have been allocated enough time for training in the new system.

   (v)   As well as running the data validation programs, make continuous appraisal by means of output listings for the scrutiny of senior staff.

   (vi) Try to plan for the quickest possible changeover to the new system, giving the least disruption to users. Make sure all the key staff are available during the exercise and that disruption due to hardware failure has been properly assessed and covered.

   (vii) Authorise whatever overtime is necessary to ensure that file conversion takes place according to the scheduled timetable.

23 FILE CREATION AND CHANGEOVER

(a) When examining the feasibility of computerisation, the normal accounting procedures of the system must be fully understood. Any system for a firm of solicitors must take into account all the problems involved, and the types of clients (both permanent and transient) that are dealt with. Alternative methods of computerisation are open to the firm, three of which are:

    (i) installing an in-house mini- or microcomputer (either purchased or leased) and either designing or (more likely) buying the software. Many small business systems are now available and software firms are producing integrated application programs for various industries, including the legal profession.

    Such packages may require some tailoring to suit the individual organisation and members of staff will have to be trained to use the machine.

    (ii) using a computer bureau to provide the EDP facilities. The range of services offered by computer bureaux is considerable and the appropriate level of involvement has to be determined. It may be feasible for the data to be prepared in-house, but to be processed at the bureau.

    (iii) time-sharing, in which another firm of solicitors or a computer bureau or manufacturer provides computer facilities to the user. The user has a terminal (possibly an 'intelligent' terminal) linked directly by telephone to the computer system which receives and processes (using appropriate programs) data and outputs relevant information.

(b) File creation and file conversion is a major part of any systems development and involves fact-finding, data capture, clerical procedure design, form design and even program specification. Existing records (or parts of them) have to be transcribed onto specially designed forms before they are keyed onto the appropriate computer medium. Once the files have been created extensive checking for accuracy is essential, otherwise considerable problems may arise when the system becomes operational.

There are other problems which have to be dealt with by the systems analyst including the provision of additional staff (where necessary) to prevent bottlenecks, the planning and time-scale of the operation, the establishment of cut-off dates and cut-off controls and deciding whether files should be converted all at once, or file by file.

(c) Once the new system has been fully and satisfactorily tested the changeover can be made. This may be by:

    (i) *direct changeover*, in which the old system is completely replaced by the new system in one move. This may be unavoidable where the two systems are substantially different, where the new system is a real-time system, or where extra staff to oversee parallel running are unobtainable. While this method is comparatively cheap it is risky (system or program corrections are difficult while the system has to remain operational) and the systems analyst must have complete confidence in the new system;

    (ii) *parallel running*, whereby the old and new systems are run in parallel for a period of time, both processing current data and enabling cross checking to be made. This method provides a degree of safety should there be problems with the new system, but there is a delay in the actual implementation of the new system, and a need for more staff to cope with both systems running parallel;

(iii) *pilot operation*, which is cheaper and easier to control than parallel running, and provides a greater degree of safety than does a direct changeover. Either the new system operates on data already processed by the old system, or a complete logical part of the whole file is chosen and run as a unit on the new system. If that is shown to be working well the remaining parts are then transferred.

24   SYSTEMS SPECIFICATION

The elements that should be found in a system specification are listed in the paragraphs in the chapter on system documentation (chapter 18) which describe the systems specification.

The purpose of a system specification:

(a) *during development* is to communicate with the user, programmers, operators and other systems analysts:

(i) the user can confirm that the design meets the requirements for the new system;

(ii) the user can prepare operating manuals for the system;

(iii) programmers need the system specification to write the programs;

(iv) the costs and benefits of the system are set out, for senior management to approve;

(v) computer operating instructions are set out, from which an operator's manual will be prepared;

(vi) changeover arrangements for implementing the new system are set out;

(vii) when a team of analysts works on a system, the systems specification provides documentation which helps the analysts to co-ordinate their work properly.

(b) *post implementation*

(i) the systems specification should provide a record of changes made to the system (error corrections and improvements) which can be referred to. This will keep the user and operators informed of changes, and will provide programmers with the information they need to amend programs. The authorisations for changes to the system can be recorded to provide a management control over system changes;

(ii) when a change is made to a system, the systems specification provides an important source of information for the analyst who is responsible for making the change.

Management controls should be established to ensure that a systems specification is kept up-to-date as the system is amended.

25   SECURITY

Security is usually defined as meaning that the computer facilities are available at all required times, that data is processed completely and accurately and that access to the data in computer systems is restricted to authorised people.

SUGGESTED SOLUTIONS

The different forms of control which should be instituted to safeguard against computer security risks may be considered under three main headings:

(a) *Physical security*

    (i)   Strict control of access to the computer area, using such devices as magnetic keys, alarm systems, etc.

    (ii)   Effective precautions against fire or other natural disruption including alarm systems, automatic extinguishing systems and regular inspections.

    (iii)   Established and well practised emergency procedures in the event of fire etc and alternative power supply.

    (iv)   Location of the computer so that it is difficult for unauthorised personnel to have access, with the minimum of entrances and exits.

    (v)   Possibility of remote storage of security copies of data.

    (vi)   Location of the computer room so that it is, if possible, situated away from known hazards such as:

        (1) flooding
        (2) fire/explosion risks in adjoining premises
        (3) magnetic fields generated by machine motors

(b) *Software security*

    (i)   Effective control over the preservation of information contained on files by ensuring that before a file is to be overwritten a check is made on the file label.

    (ii)   Prevention of unauthorised access by the use of devices such as passwords.

(c) *Systems security*

    (i)   Strict control and verification of all input data, with control totals prepared outside the computer department and with all tabulations balanced to them.

    (ii)   All input should pass through a 'vet' program as the first stage in being entered on to the computer files. This program should clearly indicate all items accepted and rejected, the latter to be investigated by the user department.

    (iii)   Adequate controls should be in force to ensure that amendments to programs are properly authorised, checked out and validated before use.

    (iv)   There should be adequate recovery, restart and standby procedures in the event of power failure, machine breakdowns, etc which can be facilitated by a 'log' of all work performed and by frequent dumping of files.

    (v)   Controls should be instituted to ensure that computer output is properly distributed, especially confidential print-outs, payments etc.

(vi)   Proper control over storage and issue of magnetic media with manual records being kept of physical maintenance performed (cleaning, changing filters on disk packs etc). Such records also frequently record current status of the media and the detail of the file(s) currently stored upon it.

26   DATA VALIDATION

The required methods of validating input data and the processing of that data are as follows.

(a)   Authorisation and scrutiny of input and output by responsible officials.

(b)   When data is converted to a machine sensible form (eg punched cards, magnetic tape, direct input via terminal, etc) there should be adequate verification of input to ensure it is correct.

(c)   Validation of input and processing:

(i)   on input, checks to ensure:

(1)   correct file being processed
(2)   character check
(3)   check digits to confirm account numbers etc
(4)   format checks for completeness
(5)   reasonableness of data

Control totals and items outside accepted parameters should be printed and followed up by a responsible official. In case of terminals, it is possible to have VDU display checks on input or 'hard copy' of input

(ii)   on processing procedures:

(1)   ensure master file record exists
(2)   ensure correct file being processed
(3)   overall master file control by value and number of records
(4)   run to run controls
(5)   computer log of interruptions to programs
(6)   batch control procedures/controls
(7)   on-line systems 'daily' totals followed up
(8)   on-line systems 'matching' tests
(9)   sequence checks.

3-D graphics, 149

Acceptance testing, 301
Access, 31
Access controls, 368
Accounting package, 127
Acoustic coupler, 83
Address locations (in memory), 49
Administrative controls, 338ff
Algorithm, 276
Amending programs, 350
Analogue signals, 83
Animated graphics, 149
Application controls, 356ff
Application software, 125
Application-specific systems, 125
Applications backlog, 182, 214
Applications generator, 273
Arithmetic and logic unit (ALU), 48
Artificial intelligence (AI), 18
ASCII, 49
Assembler, 270
Assembly language, 270
Assignment briefs, 199
Asynchronous transmission, 82
Attributes, 39
Audit packages, 353
Audit trail, 351, 359
Automated teller machines (ATM), 120

Back-up facilities, 106
BACSTEL, 115
Bar coding, 61
BASIC, 270
Batch processing, 98
Batch total checks, 361
Baud rate, 81
Bit, 48
Bit parallel transmission, 81
Bit serial transmission, 81
Block codes, 260
Bootstrap program, 75
Bubblejet printer, 67
Business applications (software), 125
Buy or lease decision, 205
Byte, 48, 50

C (programming language), 270
Cache (memory), 50
CD-ROM, 73
Cell (spreadsheet), 155
Central processing unit (CPU), 47

Centralised processing, 78
CHAPS, 115
Character, 24
Check digits, 260
Checkpoints, 365
COBOL, 270
Code design, 258
Codes, 27, 258
Coding system, 258
Communications, 80
Competitive advantage, 20
Compiler, 270
Completeness checks, 361
Computer
 - acquisition, 202ff
 - aided audit techniques (CAATs), 352
 - aided design (CAD), 150
 - aided software engineering (CASE), 289f
 - bureaux, 214
 - configuration, 85
 - manufacturers, 219
 - output on microform (COM), 67
 - systems efficiency audits, 310
Computer-to-computer links, 85
Concentrator, 83
Consistency checks, 360
Cost/benefit analysis, 202
Consultancy firms, 219
Control environment, 330ff
Control information, 8
Control totals, 366
Control unit, 48
Controls, 262, 331
Conversational mode, 261
Cost control, 348
Costs of a proposed system, 202
Critical path analysis (CPA), 177
Cursor, 261
Cursor control keys, 57

Data, 3
 - capture, 358
 - control clerks, 345
 - controls, 331
 - conversion, 358
 - description language (DDL), 165
 - dictionary, 43
 - flow diagram (DFD), 234
 - independence, 36
 - link, 80
 - manipulation language (DML), 165
 - modelling, 233
 - preparation control, 253
 - preparation errors, 357

- processing, 3, 356
- processing standards, 322
- processing system, 15
- redundancy, 33
- switching, 81
- transmission, 81, 370
- validation, 359
- verification, 58, 358
Database, 37
Database management system (DBMS), 37
Debugging, 271
Decentralised processing, 78
Decision
 - support system (DSS), 16
 - table, 281
 - tree, 284
Demand processing, 98
Design, 249ff
Desktop publishing, 152
Device interlocks, 367
Diagnostic systems, 18
Dialogue design, 261, 266
Digital computer, 48
Digital signal, 83
Direct access (files), 32
Direct changeover, 305
Direct input devices, 59
Discounted cash flow (DCF), 205
Disk operating system (DOS), 75
Distributed data processing, 80
Division of responsibilities, 338
Document
 - creation, 145
 - description form, 228
 - design, 254
 - image processing (DIP), 116
Documentation, 299, 320, 327
Documentation Standards, 327
DP Standards, 322
DP Standards manual, 324
Dumb terminals, 86
Dumping disk files, 344
Duplex, 82

Electronic
 - data interchange (EDI), 114
 - funds transfer (EFT), 115
 - funds transfer at point of sale
   (EFTPOS), 121
 - mail (e-mail), 112
 - office, 109ff
 - point of sale (EPOS), 63
Embedded audit facilities, 353
Encoding, 59

Encryption, 370
End-user computing, 181
Entity modelling, 39
EPROM, 50
Errors in data capture, 356
Ethernet, 89
Exception reports, 101
Exchangeable disk packs, 70
Executive Information Systems (EIS), 17
Existence checks, 360
Expert systems, 18
Extension boards, 50

Faceted codes, 260
Facsimile, 112
Fact finding, 225
Feasibility study, 197ff
Fields, 23
File
 - access, 31, 71
 - controls, 364
 - conversion, 301, 349
 - design, 267
 - enquiry, 29
 - identification checks, 364
 - librarian, 345
 - maintenance, 29
 - mask, 367
 - organisation, 30, 71
 - update, 28
Files, 23
Finance systems, 125ff
Flat file database, 163
Floppy disk, 70
Form filling, 262
Format checks, 360
Formatted screens, 262
FORTRAN, 270
Fourth generation
 - languages, 273
 - systems, 221
Frequency division multiplexing, 83
Full duplex transmission, 82
Function keys, 57

Gantt charts, 179
General purpose systems, 125
Grandfather-father-son security concept, 343
Graphic user interfaces (GUI), 265
Graphics, 148
 - card, 50, 149
 - software, 148

Hacking, 370
Half duplex transmission, 82
Hardware
- controls, 366
- maintenance, 312
Hierarchical
- codes, 260
- data structures, 40
High level language, 270
Hit rate, 268
Human factors, 184

Icons, 263
Indexed sequential access, 32
Information, 3
- centre, 182
- processing, 4
Input design, 252
Input devices, 56ff
Inputs, 55, 309
Intermeter, 270
Instruction set, 47
Insurance, 295
Integrated
- circuit (IC) store, 49
- system, 33, 127
- systems digital network (ISDN), 84
- test facility (ITF), 353
Interactive computing, 86, 104
Internal store (memory), 48
Interpreter, 270
Interviews, 225
Inverted files, 163
Investment, 203f

Jackson structured programming, 193

Key fields, 25
Key-to-disk, 57
Keyboard, 57, 261
Kilobyte, 50

Laptop computers, 53
Leasing, 205
Librarian, 345
Limit checks, 360
Line graphics, 149
LISP, 19
Local area network (LAN), 80, 88
Low level language, 270

Machine code, 269
Magnetic
- disk, 70
- ink character recognition (MICR), 60
- stripe card, 62
- tape cartridge, 72
Main store (memory), 48
Mainframe computer, 52
Maintenance, 310
Management information systems (MIS), 15
Manufacturers and suppliers, 208
Mark sensing, 60
Marketing systems, 140f
Master files, 24
Megabyte, 50
Memory, 47
- expansion, 50
Menu selection, 262
Methodology, 192, 348
Microcomputer, 53
Minicomputer, 52
Modem, 83
Modules, 127
MS-DOS, 93
Multi-user system, 80, 92
Multiple file databases, 164
Multiplexor, 83
Multiprogramming, 51
Multitasking, 51

Near letter quality (NLQ), 66
Networks, 41, 92
Network analysis, 177
Network data structure, 41
Networked micros, 88
Non-programmed decisions, 9
Normalisation, 42

Object code, 270
Observation, 228
Office automation, 109ff
On-line, 99
On-line input, 100
Open systems interconnection (OSI), 84
Operating information, 8
Operating
- software manuals, 328
- system, 75, 187
Operational information, 7
Optical
- character recognition (OCR), 60
- mark reading (OMR), 60
- storage, 73

Output, 65
- controls, 365
- design, 250
Output devices, 66ff

Parallel running, 305
Parity checks, 367
Passwords, 368
Payroll systems, 135
Performance
- criteria, 206
- reviews, 307
- standards, 325
Peripheral, 47
Permanent files, 25
Personal identification number (PIN), 370
Personnel systems, 141
Phased implementation, 306
Physical security, 341
Pilot operation, 306
Pilot tests, 305
Pixel, 57
Planning information, 8
Point of sale (POS), 63
Pointer-based system, 41
Post-implementation review, 307
Presentation graphics, 149
Printers, 66
Problem definition, 199
Problems/requirements list, 200
Production systems, 139
Program
- development, 269
- flowcharts, 286
- maintenance, 312
- specifications, 320
Programmed decisions, 9
Project teams, 174ff
Prolog, 19
PROM, 50
Protocols, 84
Prototyping, 274
Public Services Network (PSN), 81
Purchases system, 132

Query language, 166
Questionnaires, 226

Random
- access, 32
- access memory (RAM), 50
- file organisation, 31

Range checks, 360
Re-creating file data, 343
Read only memory (ROM), 49
Real-time processing, 105
Reconciliation checks, 366
Records, 23
Recovery procedures, 365
Reduced Instruction Set Computer (RISC), 47
Redundancy, 42
Reference files, 24
Relational
- data structure, 41
- database, 165
- model, 41
Relationships (databases), 39
Remote job entry (RJE), 86, 100
Resolution (monitors), 57
Restart program, 365
Restricted data running, 306
Retrieval of data, 4
Retrospective parallel running, 306
Risk analysis, 335
Risks to data, 333

Sales ledger, 128
Scanners, 64
Scenario analysis, 335
Screen design, 261
Scrolling, 58
Security, 330ff
Selection of personnel, 338
Sensitivity analysis, 161
Sequence
- checks, 360
- codes, 259
Sequential
- access (files), 31
- file organisation, 30
Serial access (files), 31
Seven-layer reference model (OSI), 84
Significant digit codes, 260
Simplex transmission, 82
Smart cards, 63
Software
- controls, 364
- houses, 218
- support, 209
Source code, 270
Spreadsheet, 154
SSADM, 193
Staff training, 296ff
Stand-alone computers, 92
Stand-by hardware facilities, 342
Standards, 314ff

Steering committees, 174
Stock control systems, 134
Storage, 4, 69
Store-and-forward (messaging), 81
Structured
  - narratives, 287
  - programming, 279
SWIFT, 115
Synchronous transmission, 82
System
  - design, 233
  - development controls, 347
  - flowcharts, 240, 241
  - justification, 201
  - maintenance, 310
  - software, 75
  - testing, 300
  - trials, 300
Systems
  - analysis, 232, 326, 349
  - changeover, 305
  - control and review file (SCARF), 353
  - development life cycle, 190
  - documentation, 314ff
  - evaluation, 307
  - installation, 292ff
  - investigation, 223ff
  - specification, 314

Tactical information, 7
Tape streamer, 72, 344
Telecom Gold, 112
Teletex, 111
Teletext, 113
Telex, 111
Temporary files, 25
Test data, 301
Testing, 271, 349
Time division multiplexing, 83
Timesharing, 220
Timing of information, 9
Training, 209, 298, 350
Transaction processing, 14
Transaction file, 24
Transcribing errors, 356
Turnkey systems, 202, 219
Turnround document, 358

Unix, 93
Unordered (or serial) file organisation, 30
User
  - department, 315
  - documentation, 299, 320
  - manual, 320
  - staff issues, 296
Utility, 76

Value Added Network Services (VANS), 115
Validation, 59
Variable length field, 25
Verification, 59
Viewdata, 113
  - electronic mail, 113
Virtual circuit, 81
Viruses, 371
Visual display unit (VDU), 57

Walkthroughs, 300
'What if?' questions, 161
Wide area network (WAN), 80, 91
WIMP, 262
Winchester disks, 70
Windows, 263
WYSIWYG, 153
Word processing, 144
Wrap-around, 58
Write permit rings, 367

FURTHER READING

For further question practice on Analysis and Design of Information Systems, BPP publish a companion Practice and Revision Kit. This contains a bank of 95 questions, mostly drawn from past examinations, plus a full test paper. Fully worked suggested solutions are provided for all questions, including the test paper. The current (1992) edition is priced at £7.95; a new edition will be published in March 1993.

You may also wish to test your grasp of the subject by tackling short questions in multiple choice format. BPP publish the Password series of books, each of which incorporates a large collection of multiple choice questions with solutions, comments and marking guides. The Password title relevant to Paper 11 is called *Information Technology*. This is priced at £6.95 and contains about 350 questions.

To order your Practice and Revision Kit and Password books, ring our credit card hotline on 081-740 6808. Alternatively, send this page to our Freepost address or fax it to us on 081-740 1184.

To: BPP Publishing Ltd, FREEPOST, London W12 8BR   **Tel: 081-740 6808**
                                                         Fax: 081-740 1184

Forenames (Mr / Ms): _____

Surname: _____

Address: _____

_____

Post code: _____

Please send me the following books: *Quantity*   *Price*   *Total*
AAT Analysis and Design of Information Systems Kit   ....   £7.95   ....
Password *Information Technology*   ....   £6.95   ....

Please include postage:
UK: £1.50 for first plus £0.50 for each extra book   ....
Overseas: £3.00 for first plus £1.50 for each extra book   ....

I enclose a cheque for £_____ or charge to Access/Visa

Card number ☐☐☐☐☐☐☐☐☐☐☐☐☐☐☐☐☐

Expiry date _____ Signature _____

On the reverse of this page there is a Review Form, which you can send in to us (at the Freepost address above) with comments and suggestions on the Text you have just finished. Your feedback really does make a difference: it helps us to make the next edition that bit better.

Name: _____

How have you used this Text?

Home study (book only) ☐   With 'correspondence' package ☐

On a course: college_____ ☐   Other _____

How did you obtain this Text?

From us by mail order ☐   From us by phone ☐

From a bookshop ☐   From your college ☐

Where did you hear about BPP Texts?

At bookshop ☐   Recommended by lecturer ☐

Recommended by friend ☐   Mailshot from BPP ☐

Advertisement in _____ ☐   Other _____

Have you used the companion Kit for this subject?   Yes/No

Your comments and suggestions would be appreciated on the following areas.

Syllabus coverage

Illustrative questions

Errors (please specify, and refer to a page number)

Presentation

Other